CRITIQUE
OF ACCOUNTING

CRITIQUE
OF ACCOUNTING

Examination of the Foundations and Normative Structure of an Applied Discipline

RICHARD MATTESSICH

QUORUM BOOKS
WESTPORT, CONNECTICUT • LONDON

Library of Congress Cataloging-in-Publication Data

Mattessich, Richard.
    Critique of accounting : examination of the foundations and
normative structure of an applied discipline / Richard
Mattessich.
        p.   cm.
    Includes bibliographical references and index.
    ISBN 0–89930–863–5 (alk. paper)
        1. Accounting.   I. Title.
HF5625.M368   1995
657—dc20   95–3776

British Library Cataloguing in Publication Data is available.

Library of Congress Catalog Card Number: 95–3776
ISBN: 0–89930–863–5

First published in 1995

Quorum Books, 88 Post Road West, Westport, CT 06881
An imprint of Greenwood Publishing Group, Inc.

Printed in the United States of America

The paper used in this book complies with the
Permanent Paper Standard issued by the National
Information Standards Organization (Z39.48—1984).

10 9 8 7 6 5 4 3 2 1

Copyright Acknowledgments

The author and publisher gratefully acknowledge the following for permission to reprint passages, articles, figures, and tables previously published (R. M. is short for Richard Mattessich as author):

Translation from Dieter Schneider. 1981. *Geschichte betriebswirtschaftlicher Theorie.* Munich: © Oldenbourg Verlag GmbH, pp. 137, 140, 141, 142.

Table 1, Dimensions of Multi-Person Information Economic Models of Accounting, from Gerald A. Feltham. 1984. Financial accounting research: Contributions of information economics and agency theory. In *Modern accounting research: History, survey and guide*, ed. Richard Mattessich, 183–184. Vancouver, B.C.: © Canadian Certified General Accountants Research Foundation

Tables 2, 3, and 4 from W. F. Chua. 1986. Radical developments in accounting thought. *The Accounting Review* 61(4): 611, 615, 622. © *The Accounting Review* and American Accounting Association, with permission of the Executive Director.

Musée de Louvre (©) for reproducing Figures 2.1, 2.2, 2.3, and 2.4 of the present Chapter 2, with permission of the Conservateur Général du Département des Antiquités Orientales.

J. Thomas Frecka, ed. 1989. *The state of accounting research as we enter the 1990's* (one quotation from the paper by Abdel-khalik and three quotations from the paper by Dopuch). Urbana: University of Illinois at Urbana–Champaign, Department of Accountancy, pp. 45–46, 175.

Denise Schmandt-Besserat. 1992a. *Before writing.* Vol. 1, *From counting to cuneiform.* "Introduction" by W. Hallow, x–xi, and quotations from Schmandt-Besserat, pp. 9, 170, 189, 191, 235 (note 55). Austin: © University of Texas Press, with permission of publisher.

R. M. 1972. Methodological preconditions and problems of a general theory of accounting. *The Accounting Review* 47(July): 469–487. © *The Accounting Review* and American Accounting Association, with permission of the Executive Director.

R. M. 1981a. Major concepts and problems of inflation accounting: Part I. *CGA Magazine* 15(May): 10–15. © Richard Mattessich, with permission of the Research Director of the CGA-Canada Research Foundation.

R. M. 1981b. Major concepts and problems of inflation accounting: Part II. *CGA Magazine* 15(June–July): 20–27. © Richard Mattessich, with permisssion of the Research Director of the CGA-Canada Research Foundation.

R. M. 1986. Fritz Schmidt (1882–1950) and his pioneering work of current value accounting in comparison to Edwards and Bell's theory. *Contemporary Accounting Research* 2(Spring): 157–178. © Canadian Academic Accounting Association and *Contemporary Accounting Research*, with permission of editor.

R. M. 1987b. Prehistoric accounting and the problem of representation: On recent archeological evidence of the Middle East from 8000 B.C. to 3000 B.C. *The Accounting Historians Journal* 14(2): 71–91. © *The Accounting Historians Journal*, with permission of editor.

R. M. 1989. Accounting and the input–output principle in the prehistoric and ancient world. *Abacus* 25(2): 74–84. Oxford: © Blackwell, with permission of editor.

R. M. 1990. Epistemological aspects of accounting. *Keiri Kenkyu* 34 (Autumn): 3–30. © *Keiri Kenkyu*, with permission of editor.

R. M. 1991a. A passage from Editor's commentary: A decade of growth, sophistication, and impending crisis. In *Accounting research in the 1980s and its future relevance*, ed. Richard Mattessich, 10–14. Vancouver, B.C.: © CGA-Canada Research Foundation, with permission of the Research Director of the CGA-Canada Research Foundation.

R. M. 1991b. Counting, accounting, and the input–output principle: Recent archeological evidence revising our view on the evolution of early record keeping. In *The costing heritage—Studies in honor of S. Paul Garner*, ed. O. Finley Graves, 25–49. Harrisonburg, Va.: © The Academy of Accounting Historians, with permission of editor.

R. M. 1991d. Social reality and the measurement of its phenomena. In *Advances in Accounting*, vol. 9, ed. Bill N. Schwartz, 3–17. Greenwich, Conn.: © JAI Press, with permission of publisher.

R. M. 1991e. Social versus physical reality in accounting, and the measurement of its phenomena. In *Contemporary issues in accounting research*, ed. Bhabatosh Banerjee, 1–30. Calcutta: © The Indian Accounting Association, with permission of editor.

R. M. 1992. On the history of normative accounting theory: Paradigm lost, paradigm regained? *Accounting, Business and Financial History* 2(2): 181–198. London: © Routledge, with permission of the publisher.

R. M. 1993a. On the nature of information and knowledge and the interpretation in the economic sciences. *Library Trends* 41(Spring): 567–593. © *Library Trends*, with permission of editor.

R. M. 1993b. Paradigms, research traditions and theory nets of accounting. In *Philosophical perspectives on accounting—Essays in honour of Edward Stamp*, ed. M. J. Mumford and K. V. Peasnell, 177–220. London: © Routledge, with permission of publisher and the book editors.

R. M. 1994a. Accounting as a cultural force: Past, present and future. *The European Accounting Review* 3(2): 354–374. © European Accounting Association, with permission of editor and publisher (London: Routledge).

R. M. 1994b. Archeology of accounting and Schmandt-Besserat's contribution. *Accounting, Business and Financial History* 4(1): 5–28. London: © Routledge, with permission of publisher.

R. M. 1994c. The number concept in business and "concern economics." In *Leonardo Fibonacci—Il tempo, le opere, l'eredità scientifica* (a publication of Fondazione IBM Italia), ed. Marcello Morelli and Marco Tangheroni, 109–135. Pisa: Pacini Editore.

R. M. 1995. Conditional–normative accounting methodology: Incorporating value judgments and means–end relations of an applied science. *Accounting, Organizations and Society* 20(4): 259–284. Oxford: © Elsevier Science, Pergamon Imprint (The Boulevard, Langford Lane, UK), with permission of publisher.

Short passages, quoted from various authors (J. E. Boritz, L. A. Daley, J. Denman, J. A. Milburn, and W. R. Scott) in Ernst & Young Foundation, ed. 1994. *Measurement research in financial accounting.* Toronto: © Ernst & Young Foundation, with permission of the Foundation.

To Hermi

Contents

Figures and Tables

FIGURES

TABLES

Preface

This book is partly based on previous publications of mine but goes beyond an anthology.[1] Here I have tried to integrate my views and research into a mosaic that conveys a picture richer and more coherent than a glance at individual fragments can afford. Most of the publications incorporated have been changed, brought up to date, merged with, and supplemented by, new material. No chapter is a mere replication of a single previous article, and the connection between the various topics is better visible than by reading those papers in isolation—though individual *chapters* should make sense, even without the prerequisite of preceding ones. Even though basic tenets of the views expressed here go back a considerable time (see, for example, Mattessich 1964a, 1972), these notions have evolved and matured, and in its present form may have more immediate relevance. As for individual chapters, I have tried to avoid overlapping passages, except where specific ideas required reinforcement or illumination from different angles. Chapter 1 begins with outlining the purpose and philosophy of this book; it continues with a discussion of the alleged "crisis" in accounting and concludes by offering a *concise overview* of the problems to be explored in subsequent chapters. The results of these explorations are summarized in Chapter 12.

This may be the appropriate place to add a candid word about "modesty." If it appears that this quality might not have been put into my cradle, I can only vindicate the frequent reference to my own publications as the result of a struggle of ideas. This book tries to show that more traditional questions still have a place in accounting and, even more so, are capable of generating ideas relevant for the present as well as the future. It may be time to reconsider the question of what needs to be discarded and what needs to be preserved.

Furthermore, when one searches for an adequate methodology (instead of a theory), one can no longer brush value judgments aside. These judgments and biases can only be justified through long-standing soul searching and careful analysis. For more than half a century, I have watched academic accounting grow into a fascinating discipline with innumerable facets and many achievements. Nevertheless, I wonder about the priorities involved; and I cannot help feeling that such essential problems as valuation, income measurement, and other aspects are basically still unresolved. This view seems to be shared even by some illustrious scholars of the leading edge, such as Beaver and Demski (1994) (for details, see Chapter 11). How can such long-standing inadequacies of our discipline be explained? My analysis indicates that the attempt to make a pure or positive discipline out of accounting led to two related but unfortunate consequences: first, an inadequate methodology, and second, the acceptance of economic foundations too narrow to embrace aspects and objectives vital for understanding the practice of accounting.

The applied sciences with their goal-orientation and means–end relations require a different methodology than the pure sciences. Does academic accounting belong to the applied sciences? If so, there is little indication in the current literature. As for leading researchers, I doubt whether many of them would answer this question in the affirmative. It is at this point where my struggle and reaction begin. If this leaves little room for false modesty, I may assure the reader that my humility is fully restored when I compare the scientific contributions of accounting—as impressive as its "input" may have been during the last few decades—with the actual results in the natural sciences or such applied sciences as medicine and engineering. Yet, compared with other applied disciplines, such as the legal profession, accounting has made great strides and must be recognized as a significant cultural force. I have tried to illustrate this in Chapter 2.

Finishing the manuscript of a book, one is bound to wonder how well one has succeeded in conveying its key ideas and the logic behind them. Although the thoughts expressed here are basically simple, they point at a target different from the one presently pursued by most accounting academics. Since my aim is *greater accountability through better information about ends and means*, this book *surveys* the terrain for building a more *direct* link (a kind of "Panama Canal") between the high waters of empirical research and the deep sea of norms, with its many strata of goals and objectives. If this can someday be achieved, the roundabout way of positive accounting theory—through the stormy "Cape Horn," where value judgments are thrown overboard—could be avoided. Nor does one need to embark on a journey without truth criteria and testing procedures—the nebulous and hazardous "Northwest Passage"—which the more radical members of the British critical–interpretive school might suggest (see Chapter 10). Creating a direct link requires the firm resolve of the accounting community and cooperation on all sides; it is an arduous task that can be achieved neither overnight nor by a single person. Thus, this book is a trumpet call to battle rather than a hymn of victory; it should incite academics to clarify the hierarchy of objectives and the variety of means that achieve them.

In closing this Preface, I take the opportunity to thank the many persons who, in one way or another, supported this publication or offered help, advice, and expert opinion. First, I want to express my gratitude to various publishers and editors who gave permission to draw freely on the series of publications of mine (for a list of the publishers and original sources, see the Copyright Acknowledgments and unnumbered notes at the end of most chapters) and other material. Second, I should like to express my thanks to Professors George Gorelik, Yoshiaki Koguchi (to whom I am indebted for another reason as well [see Koguchi 1992–1993]), and Dan B. Thornton, for reading the original manuscript and for valuable advice, as well as Jerry (G. A.) Feltham for important counsel on Chapter 8 and Table 8.1. Needless to say, it is I who bears responsibility for any errors. Furthermore, I am most grateful to my research assistants, particularly Marielle Bergeron, but also Michael Chiasson and Kevin Au, as well as to the secretary of our Accounting Division, Mrs. Corinne Baker. I also want to thank my wife, Hermi Mattessich, not only for proofreading, helping with the production of indexes, and the bibliography but also for sustaining me unflinchingly in the trials and tribulations which the writing of a book brings about.

Further thanks go to the Social Sciences and Humanities Research Council of Canada (which gave financial support to this project, as it gave to most of my other research) and to the Faculty of Commerce and Business Administration of the University of British Columbia (which offered office and research facilities despite my emeritation in 1988). Last, but not least, I should like to thank Quorum Books and its acquisition editor, Mrs. Marcy Weiner (who approached me in October 1992 to write such a treatise), as well as the editorial staff and advisors of the associated company, Greenwood Publications, Inc., whose invaluable help insured the successful completion of this work.

NOTE

1. Most of the papers forming the basis of this book are from the 1980s and 1990s. An exception is "Methodological Preconditions and Problems of a General Theory of Accounting," *The Accounting Review* 47(July 1972): 469–487, which received the AICPA/AAA "Award for Notable Contribution to the Accounting Literature." The other award-winning papers taken into consideration here are "Counting, Accounting, and the Input–Output Principle: Recent Archeological Evidence Revising Our View on the Evolution of Early Record Keeping" (reprinted in *The Costing Heritage—Studies in Honor of S. Paul Garner*, ed. O. Finley Graves, 25–49. [Harrisonburg, Va.: Academy of Accounting Historians, 1992]), which garnered the 1988 Best Paper Award of the Canadian Academic Accounting Association (CAAA Annual Meeting), and "Social Reality and the Measurement of Its Phenomena," in *Advances in Accounting*, vol. 9, ed. Bill N. Schwartz, 3–17 (Greenwich, Conn.: JAI Press, 1991), which received (together with other recent contributions) in 1991 the "Haim Falk Award for Significant Contribution to Accounting Thought" of the CAAA. The papers on which the individual chapters are based are indicated in the unnumbered notes at the end of each chapter.

CHAPTER 1

Introduction

WHAT IS A CRITIQUE?

This is an unconventional look at accounting, steeped in historical, methodological, and moral aspects. Eliminating those considerations from our discipline would be no different than separating the roots from a plant. The ultimate objectives of the book are the professional and theoretical foundations as well as the normative structure of accounting. The term *critique* is not to be identified with "criticism" but is here understood in the Kantian sense of critically examining the extent to which a discipline can represent the pertinent reality. Just as the eighteenth century critiques tried to synthesize rationalism and empiricism, so does this book aim at a synthesis of the two major opposing camps of present-day academic accounting: the "critical–interpretive view" of Great Britain and the "positive accounting theory" of America. Although some criticism of present-day accounting shall be aired, the focus is on investigating the methodology and reasoning process appropriate for our discipline. Accounting is dominated by normative aspects; yet this is acknowledged only in a roundabout way by current accounting theory. It may be time to pay heed to the role of moral issues and value judgments in general, but this requires a careful analysis of the relations that connect those objectives to the means by which they are achieved. The foundations of our discipline are hardly sufficiently consolidated to reject a critical look from an angle unencumbered by the social and academic mores of the last two decades. The attempt of academics to cast accounting in the image of a pure science may need to be modified and extended to accommodate explicit value judgments and the means–end relations so indispensable for an applied science.

PROBLEMS AND EXPECTATIONS

The expectations of the next century are likely to be very different from those of the decades gone by. Confidence into material progress is waning, while the awareness of previously unimaginable environmental and ecological problems—as well as those of a demographic, economic, and moral nature—is mounting. One need not march into the new age under the banner of gloom; pessimism paralyzes and has little place in this book. Blind optimism will not do either. As Kenneth Clark in his unforgettable book and television series so wisely remarked: "Civilisation requires a modicum of material prosperity. . . . But, far more, it requires confidence—confidence in the society in which one lives, belief in its philosophy, belief in its laws, and confidence in one's own mental powers" (Clark 1969, 4). As long as we can trust that this confidence and those beliefs can be restored, there is hope for long-term recovery.

Historians might label the past decades as the "Age of Unaccountability." It slowly began after the assassination of President John F. Kennedy; it reached its peak in the 1980s and, hopefully, may have run its course by the end of this century. Though it has been an exciting age (evil usually fascinates more than goodness), it has been a period in which too many people have lost sight of the fundamental notion that every right carries a responsibility. This loss seems to pervade the entire spectrum of society, from individuals and families to school and workplace up the hierarchy to big business and governments. Indeed, the staggering fiscal debts are only the most glaring manifestation of a society that seems to accept debt and ownership claims as something *not quite real*—even some academics seem to share this belief (see Chapter 3).

Where do accountants, the paragons of responsibility, fit into this picture? Even they did not quite escape the trend. Some merrily joined the unaccountability game, while others made their protests heard. However, those voices were drowned by political rhetoric, while the public wrung their hands in helpless desperation. To master the considerable problems facing us, a clear vision is required and the heroic resolve to master them. This holds for accounting no less than for economics and politics.

Though our discipline plays merely a small part in this world drama, it is a crucial one. The beginning and end of accounting is *accountability*. The importance of our discipline, so often disparaged by lay persons and even by experts, lies in its function as a cybernetic mechanism (a feedback that controls and regulates) that preserves confidence in the trustees of public and private resources and financial markets no less than in the entire economic system. No dynamic system can endure without a control mechanism. Whenever this cybernetics breaks down, the entire system is in jeopardy.

Portentous signs indicate that not only the political but also the economic and financial feedbacks are too often failing. To blame individual greed, dishonesty, and the like is too simplistic an answer. Those vices, as old as humankind, can hardly be eradicated; but they must not be allowed to get out of hand and become the hallmark of the system. When they are rampant, when they overwhelm every facet of social life, when a philosophy of false idols begins to take over, then one may suspect the existence of a fundamental systemic failure. This is not a criticism of the free market system but rather of those who are destroying it. Even capitalism may exist in forms capable of keeping destructive forces at bay.[1]

If our concern is the ethical and general normative education of accountants, the *myopic* attitude of society at large cannot be overlooked. This includes thoughtless consumer habits no less than the shortsighted strategies of politicians, business leaders, economists, and, often enough, even scientists. In accounting, this manifests itself in a wide spectrum of attitudes, ranging from the problem of "auditor's independence" and the public accountants' concern for the benefit of management, rather than that of shareholders and the public at large, to the academic acceptance of economic theories concerned with short-term rather than long-term consequences.

As for the flaws of our educational system, only those bearing directly on accounting will be relevant here. How can accountability be achieved without a clear vision of the goals and value judgments involved in the accounting process and without awareness of efficient means to attain those goals? This aspect, together with the need for *analyzing* those means–end relations, seems to constitute a particularly difficult hurdle for most academic accountants. After all, neither are they trained to think in terms of those relations, nor are they familiar with the pertinent methodology. To draw attention to this flaw is one of the major objectives of this book. If society has the will to embark on a process of genuine reform, accounting cannot be excluded. I do not merely think of industry and public accounting firms; revision is equally necessary on the theoretical level, though this may take time and require a series of successive steps.

ACCOUNTING IN CRISIS

It is occasionally asserted that accounting will be, or already is, in a state of crisis. One example is Belkaoui's (1989) book, *The Coming Crisis in Accounting*, dealing mainly, though not exclusively, with the crisis in accounting practice. This concern has been expressed more recently in the Introduction to the proceedings of a workshop of the Ernst & Young Foundation with the following words:

> There is a deep concern that financial accounting and reporting is losing relevance in a world characterized by increasingly complex financial transactions and management practices. A parallel and equally important concern is that accounting research lacks relevance to the problems that standard setters and practitioners must deal with. Critics argue that little, if any, accounting research published in the last two decades is relevant to the problems that business and standard setters face. (Ernst & Young Foundation 1994, 1)

This study, containing over a dozen papers (beyond the Introduction), is seriously concerned with the present crisis in financial accounting and presents many suggestions for improving the situation. Even such issues as the overextension of positive accounting theory and neglect of normative issues, the need for a "synthesis" and for taking the "pluming side" of accounting into consideration (e.g., my reference to Milburn 1994 in Chapter 11) are raised. All those ideas are taken from the last twenty-five years (i.e., the time since the empirical and information–economic revolution); and it is surprising that no steps are recommended to remedy the most fundamental flaw, namely, the lack of well-formulated means—end relations in accounting. An enduring solution to this problem will need to include the supplementation of positive hypotheses (cause–effect relations) with instrumental or pragmatic hypotheses (means–end relations)—something I suggested more than thirty years ago, together with some concrete steps (separating basic assumptions from specific hypotheses with the help of placeholder assumptions, and the like). The fact that this issue is still not clearly seen by the majority of accountants is ample justification for the present analysis.

Another study, concentrating on the academic aspects of this crisis, is "A Statement of Academic Accounting," written by six prominent accounting researchers (Joel Demski, Nicholas Dopuch, Baruch Lev, Joshua Ronen, Jerry Searfoss, and Shyam Sunder [see Demski et al. 1991]), which, though not published, was publicly distributed. In the following, I present the gist of this latter "criticism" (a good deal with which I agree, despite some reservations) and take the liberty of adding my own reactions to it. These authors speak of a "market failure" and the "lack of a self-correcting mechanism," thus of a "serious crisis" in accounting. The symptoms (S) of this crisis are characterized in five points concisely paraphrased in the following section.

Symptoms of the Crisis

1S. Accounting research has *failed to lead* practice; instead, research lags behind.

Comment: The authors suggest that during the past twenty years, hardly any academic innovation (with the exception of audit sampling and human information processing) has had an impact on accounting practice. I wonder why those authors are treating the considerable impact of research in auditing and spreadsheet simulation (including its incredibly successful application in everyday accounting practice) as "exceptions" instead of highlighting those achievements. After all, that kind of research originated in academic accounting and not in practice. Admittedly, this was thirty to forty years ago, but the broad success of those applications occurred during the last two decades. Does this not prove that academia was leading by two decades or more?

2S. In contrast to research in other scientific disciplines, accounting seems to lack a mechanism of regenerative force and thus does not have periodic cycles of innovations.

Comment: This, too, may be questioned to some extent. If those authors consider the last two decades a trough in accounting theory, what do they have to say about the 1950s and 1960s? As pointed out earlier, these were the decades when such pioneering works as statistical sampling for auditing appeared (compare Vance 1950, Neter 1952, Vance and Neter 1956, Cyert and Trueblood 1957, as well as Cyert and Davidson 1962). It was also the period that brought forth research preparing the ground for the present computerization of spreadsheets and financial simulation for accounting purposes (compare Mattessich 1961; 1964a, Chap. 9; 1964b; Bonini 1963; and Sprowls 1962).

3S. The research and teaching efforts during the last two or three decades did not bring accountants closer to any solution of its fundamental problems (such as optimal choice of accounting standards and institutions).

Comment: This and the next items are, indeed, difficult to refute. All the more urgent becomes the call for a synthesis; and I agree wholeheartedly with Thornton, who suggests to "marry rigorous methods with the institutional richness that is unique to real-world accounting, employing a rigorous methodology of our own" (Thornton 1994, 79).

4S. In contrast to other disciplines, there seems to be hardly any demand for academic researchers or their product by industry or the profession (with the possible exception in auditing).

Comment: Indeed, I believe that this is a phenomenon rarely found among members of professional schools. It indicates something most disquieting—a growing gap between an ever-more sophisticated cadre of academics and the bulk of practitioners who take less and less interest in new accounting research, partly because it is beyond them, partly because they fail to see its relevance to their own work. However, it is also true that "accounting is much more difficult than other professional disciplines such as finance, medicine, architecture. Extremely complex issues of social choice are involved. Tradeoffs between the demands of different clienteles have, to date, largely been made at a policy level, not at a research level" (Scott 1994, 65).

5S. Accounting is considered to be a mere service area; and during the recent decade or so, the "MBA student majoring in accounting has become an endangered species."

Comment: Even the relatively high pay of accounting researchers (perhaps because of a distorted demand-and-supply pattern) is being questioned.

Possible Reasons

In the attempt to explain the crisis, those authors presented the following six reasons (R), to which I have added a seventh as well as further qualifications.

1R. Accounting researchers are claimed to feel insecure in their discipline; they are believed to lack the courage as well as the monetary incentive necessary to challenge traditional paradigms. The history of science, however, offers plenty of evidence that the "reward" is not the major impetus for truly creative scholarship. Furthermore, one might heed Kuhn's (1962) widely acclaimed study, according to which a distinction between "revolutionary" and "ordinary" research must be made. Taking such a distinction into consideration, I believe that the true innovators in any scientific field are relatively few and are, in general, fiercely resisted by the scientific establishment, not only at the beginning but often for a considerable time afterward. The last few decades have undoubtedly produced original accounting thoughts as well as courageous pioneers. However, practitioners and even academics are reluctant to listen to innovative voices. Too often one loses sight of the global and long-term picture; and if immediately applicable solutions are not readily supplied, the interest fades quickly. Furthermore, many academics fail to realize the fundamental difference between a pure and an applied field; and modeling accounting in the image of the pure or positive sciences need not be the choice appropriate for long-term solutions.

2R. The authors also speak of "a weakness of entry-level PhDs in accounting and institutional knowledge" that cannot be sustained without penalty in our discipline. If this refers to the insufficient practical experience of some young and not-so-young academics, one must add that the majority of academic accountants on this continent have *professional* degrees. Some of the more "high-powered" accounting researchers may have received their basic training in economics, mathematics, or other areas and thus might lack a genuine feel for accounting as an applied discipline.

3R. They suggest insufficient correlation between research funding as well as remuneration, on the one hand, and the results and relevancy of this research (except in the area of auditing) on the other. Although this explanation has substance, it must be added that the application of several areas of highly important accounting research was obstructed by practice, often for "political" reasons. Fundamental or "disinterested" research is crucial even for an applied discipline, and revolutionary innovation could arise from such research as it does in other sciences. In an applied discipline, this requires the full cooperation of practice. Regrettably, it is precisely in this quarter where the major resistance arises—in part, because of insufficient appreciation (in spite of occasional lip service), and in part, because vested interests feel threatened by some potential accounting innovations. Hence, it appears, for example, that the Financial Accounting Standards Board (FASB) paid little attention to the opinions of such scholars as Sterling, who were temporarily invited to the staff of this institution.

The promising start of "legislating" supplementary current value accounting and price-level adjustments in several countries during the late 1970s and early 1980s is another case in point. If these efforts were ultimately doomed, it was partly because corporate management resisted it; partly because of the political trend toward less regulation; and partly because of lack of enthusiasm on the side of many public accounting firms (in spite of exceptions, such as Arthur Andersen & Co., which has a long-standing record for promoting price-level adjustments). Further reasons were the ebbing of inflationary trends and the misconception that current-value accounting is useful only during inflationary times—not least because of insufficient training on the part of financial analysts and other readers of financial statements (but this can hardly be attributed to insufficient research by academics).[2]

Another example is the conceptual framework project of the FASB. Although the results of this project still stand, academics and even practitioners consider them with skepticism (compare Archer 1993). The project was developed without any attention to rigorous logic and scientific methodology. These two projects—a conceptual framework (which could have been based on scientific foundations) and the "legislation" for supplementary price-level adjustments of financial statements (in the United Kingdom, the United States, Canada, and other countries)—would hardly have been launched without the extensive research that preceded it in academia. Both of these projects were poorly handled in practice. Had at least one of these projects been a practical success, there would be much less reason for our six authors to complain about the failure of academic accounting during recent decades.

Yet more illustrations can be offered (e.g., the efforts by Briloff [1972, 1981, 1986, 1990] and Gaa [1986, 1988a, 1988b, 1994] or those by the British "critical–interpretive school" [see Chapter 9], including Hopwood [e.g., 1988] and Tinker [1985]) to improve business ethics in industry and the public accounting profession. Should these efforts be considered academic failures because vested interests were too strong to prevent their materialization? An affirmative answer would be almost as bad as saying that the rejection of Galileo's findings by the Inquisition invalidated his research. To what extent has academia failed business, and how much has business failed academia?

Academic research must be evaluated on the basis of its intellectual and potential social values rather than on the whims and timing of actual application, particularly when the latter was prevented by "political" forces. One of the two major differences between accounting and other applied sciences is this: In our discipline there is considerable resistance to innovations when the latter are likely to benefit the public at the cost of the vested interests that dominate industry as well as the profession.[3]

Let me take this opportunity to point out another major difference between accounting and the rest of the applied sciences. Accounting (similar to the pure sciences and in contrast to other applied disciplines) tries to *represent* segments of reality; yet in accounting, this always is a *pragmatic* representation (depending on the cost–benefit criterion as well as other factors, such as the need for "conservative valuation," and the like) and not a representation in the positive or purely scientific sense.

4R. They point at the trend of wresting from accounting specific research areas (security analysis, valuation of financial instruments, and the like) and assigning it to finance. The authors seem to attribute this to too narrow a curriculum definition as well as a lack of "entrepreneurship" in accounting. However, it is quite natural that a scientific discipline is budding from time to time, bringing forth new and more or less independent areas. Not too long ago, most of finance was the domain of accounting, just as science was once the domain of philosophy. Indeed, I expect this trend of diversification to continue, but it will threaten academic accounting only if we fail in two endeavors: (1) to produce potentially relevant research (not necessarily useful to the narrow realm of vested interests) and (2) to convince legislators, practitioners, and the public at large of the social importance and long-term benefit of serious accounting research. If we have not succeeded in this public relations endeavor, the term *market failure* and the call for entrepreneurship may well be justified.

5R. They see a tendency of senior faculty to evaluate the performance of their juniors on too narrow a basis, discouraging original or innovative research. I admit the existence of such a trend but believe that it is much broader and not limited to the relation between senior and junior faculty. In recent years, a tendency of intolerance has arisen between competing camps that pursue different methodologies. Some representatives of the leading camp seem to believe in the absolute truth of their own methodology (compare Watts and Zimmerman 1990). This testifies less to arrogance than to an inordinately narrow vision of our field. Such circumstances precipitated a complaint heard repeatedly: that today the "ruling elite" of accounting researchers (e.g., those controlling and influencing the leading journals) is less accessible to ideas beyond their own vision than ever before. Could this be a contributing factor to the crisis?

6R. According to these authors, financial accounting, in contrast to the area of finance, does not serve so much (or respond to) the free market (and its forces) but mainly serves institutions exercising regulatory functions. This is construed as a disincentive for practitioners to demand accounting research. I agree that during the last two decades financial accounting and auditing was overemphasized at the cost of other areas (managerial and government accounting, and the like—not to mention macro-accounting, which was almost entirely left to economists except in Japan, where economic faculties have their own accounting departments). This may well have had a detrimental effect on accounting, its research direction, as well as the demand for pertinent research.

7R. For me, the present crisis of accounting has three major components. The first one is *a legislative and social crisis,* in which management is greatly favored over shareholders and the public at large (related to the "problem of corporate governance"). This concerns the long-standing "problem of auditor independence," and no expert has exposed this more clearly and forcefully than Briloff (e.g., 1981, 1986, 1990). It also concerns those who believe that the task of accounting is no longer to promote accountability but mainly to facilitate decision making. This seems to be reflected in the accelerating trend of public accounting firms to shift from the high-risk (and sometimes unrewarding) task of auditing to the more profitable task of management consulting. (For these and other aspects of the organizational climate in public accounting firms, see Belkaoui 1989). If this tendency continues, who will be responsible for monitoring accountability? Many experts seem to forget that the major inefficiencies of our economies are caused not so much by productivity issues than by excessive debt loads which, in turn, are the direct result of corporate and, in particular, government failures in accountability.

The second is a *moral or spiritual crisis*. It has its root in the decline of business ethics during recent decades as well as the lack or scarcity of theoretical work to provide a comprehensive framework for guidance beyond the lip service professional standards pay to this issue. For a long time, the major publication in this area was the work by Mautz and Scharaff (1961), and only recently have such authors as Gaa (1988a, 1988b, 1994) and Ponemon and Gabhard (1993) begun to go beyond this original effort.

The third is predominantly an *academic crisis;* it has been dealt with by the six experts referred to earlier. This discussion must be complemented. First to be mentioned is the overemphasis of the valuation and decision function at the expense of the stewardship function. Not only is accountability the oldest objective, dominating our discipline for some 10,000 years (see Chapter 3); it also is the function that will endure long after others have been taken over by disciplines such as finance, operations research (OR), and management information systems (MIS). Perhaps accounting academics have overextended their subject matter and are now surprised to find themselves in a dilemma. This suspicion seems to be confirmed by a panel of the 78th Annual Meeting of the American Accounting Association (1993) at which—under the chairmanship of Robert Ashton—Rick Antle, John Dickhaut, Yuji Ijiri, and Katherine Schipper pleaded for more attention to the stewardship role of accounting.

A related aspect of this third crisis is to be found in the ever-widening gap between the highly sophisticated theoretical issues explored in academia and the relative disregard that these explorations encounter in practice. This is not a criticism of theoretical accounting research in general, but it is directed against the attempt to convert a basically applied discipline into a *positive* science.

Of course, the ultimate dilemma of academic accounting is shared by all the social and, in particular, applied sciences. In these areas, reality turns out to be so complex that even the most sophisticated mathematical and statistical models prove to be woefully inadequate. This does not mean that I am opposed to model building or that we should no longer concern ourselves with such models; on the contrary, I am full of admiration for those meticulous scholars, among which I find the best of my own colleagues. It means that we cannot grasp reality with one jaw only; we need both of them—the scientific–rational one as well as the philosophical–intuitive. Bertrand Russell called one of those jaws the "simpleminded" approach; the other he called the "muddle-headed" one. The first, manifest in the rigorous models of agency theory, affords a firm but very limited and unrealistic basis that grows too slowly to master everyday problems. The second, so sorely lacking in our discipline, grants an overall picture. It gives direction and prevents us from getting lost in the forest of innumerable details and intricate subtleties. I firmly believe in this *two-pronged methodology;* but since academic accountants have recently overindulged in the first approach, I do not hesitate to cultivate in this book the second one.

Science cannot dispense with speculation, and I do not merely think of the philosophers from Democritus to Aristarchus (who anticipated crucial parts of the atomic theory and modern astronomy almost 2,500 years ago) but also of the innumerable scientists from Darwin and Kekulé to Mendel and Einstein who envisioned their theories before having had all the supporting evidence at their disposal. The path to knowledge cannot be found without visions and an overall picture. It is no coincidence that such philosophers as Whitehead and Wittgenstein, who began in the simpleminded camp, switched in their mature age to the muddle-headed one. One should not believe that "simpleminded" scholars can make it on their own; they cannot close the circuit alone, it is but a short circuit.

Returning to our six authors of the unofficial 1991 report, they also presented an "Agenda for Action," in which the identification of relevant issues and research questions was submitted. They recommended several short-term as well as long-term steps toward overcoming the present crisis (such as conferences, panels, developing proposals, and the like). The roots of this crisis, however, go fairly deep and may not be extracted by such painless means. In this book too, some actions are recommended; but they require the recognition of accounting as an applied science. Perhaps this is the pivot on which a resolution to the present crisis hinges.

OUTLINE OF THE BOOK AND SOME BASIC QUESTIONS

Chapter 2 explores the earliest beginnings of our discipline as well as subsequent periods. Starting from recent revolutionary archaeological insights, it goes back some 10,000 years and explores the beginning of "token accounting." It also tries to answer the intriguing question whether the more sophisticated token accounting after 3250 B.C. may have already been a kind of double-entry record-keeping system. The chapter examines the strong archeological evidence that accounting was a precondition as well as an impetus for the invention of writing and abstract counting. Certainly, two decades ago, no one would have suspected this humble discipline to be the very fountainhead for most of our culture. Apart from this, did accounting not have from the very beginning important *practical* purposes such as monitoring stewardship and presenting legal evidence? It seems that such normative orientation has been maintained for thousands of years and still deserves due recognition. Has not this *purpose orientation* in the service of control and accountability (a topic that pervades this book to the very end) endured for thousands of years? Hence, the chapter casts a further glance at the cultural and ethical mission of our discipline into later periods, until the twentieth century, which saw accounting emerge as a full-fledged academic discipline with exciting analytical as well as empirical research.

Chapter 3 examines whether income and owners' equity are mere concepts, as it has been claimed by some accountants, or whether they represent empirical phenomena. If our aim is understanding *reality* and our means is *conceptual representation,* then confusing the dichotomy between "the empirical versus the conceptual" with that between "the physical and the social" deserves attention. No less serious is the doubt as to the reality status of major accounting variables; this, too, indicates unresolved foundational problems. A clear picture of what is real versus what represents this reality is a prerequisite of any serious empirical research. For this reason, fundamental issues about the physical as well as social reality of accounting are analyzed here and, hopefully, clarified. This requires some agreement about the nature of reality and its various layers. Such an agreement is extracted from everyday business life and the way we deal with such phenomena as income, debts, property claims, and similar issues. The chapter tries to show which types of accounting variables are nothing but concepts and which are backed by real things and facts.

Chapter 4 begins by looking at major changes of accountancy since its academization more than 100 years ago. The main focus is on the "adolescent years" (since the 1950s) and the forces behind those changes. Subsequently, the chapter examines such foundational issues as the principles of input–output and symmetry and probes the question whether, or to what extent, these concepts can be related to the physicist's notion of conservation. The chapter also discusses terminological and conceptual difficulties (e.g., defined vs. undefined, interpreted vs. uninterpreted concepts) as well as the adaptation of scientific methods (e.g., analytical and empirical approaches, measurement theory, behavioral research) to accounting.

Chapter 5 examines past endeavors to explore the foundations of accounting by postulational and axiomatic means. In presenting some updated illustrations, the emphasis lies in demonstrating the need for distinguishing between basic assumptions and purpose-oriented hypotheses. The latter lend flexibility to the theory and make an interpretation possible that relates means to ends, an idea indispensable for the conditional–normative methodology explored in this book. These efforts are linked to the less rigorous conceptual framework of the FASB, which may be considered a preliminary compromise resulting from the preceding postulational and axiomatic research. A short section advances some thoughts for dealing with the thorny problem of testing systems and theories. During the 1970s and 1980s, accounting formalization shifted its emphasis from the axiomatic to the information-economics approach; this is taken into consideration by offering a concise survey of various aspects of information economics and its influence on academic accounting. An appendix sketches a novel proof of the "double-classification theorem," which might be of interest to those who believe that accounting duality has a deeper meaning than mere arithmetical control and the mechanical balancing of accounts.

The ultimate objective of Chapter 6 is to illustrate the notion of "instrumental hypothesis" *(formalized means–end relation)* because different capital maintenance models lend themselves particularly well to this task. That requires familiarity with valuation models and various price-level adjustment methods. Such models and methods have been much neglected in recent years, and the younger generation of accounting academics seems to be only superficially acquainted with them. Therefore, I have chosen a concise, *algebraic* way (with additional numerical illustrations) of explaining different holding gains (monetary vs. nonmonetary, real vs. fictitious, realized vs. unrealized, and so on) and other fundamental concepts. This offers the opportunity of juxtaposing six famous valuation models, and allows the discussion of different capital maintenance concepts.

Furthermore, I have tried to explain the notion of an instrumental hypothesis by means of the real financial capital maintenance concept. Last, an attempt is made to illustrate the fundamental difference between hypotheses of positive accounting theory, on the one hand, and instrumental hypotheses, on the other.

Chapter 7 pivots on the new notion of "theory," which emerged relatively recently in what is called the Post-Kuhnian era. Leading philosophers of science no longer see a theory as a single axiomatic framework or similar structure but as a net of several such *interrelated* structures. Although there may still exist some minor competition between those "subtheories" (which usually develop as a result of "normal science"), the dialectical debate (i.e., the real competition in the Kuhnian sense) arises between competing theory nets (also called theories, research traditions, research programs, and the like), which are the true harbingers of Kuhn's "revolutionary science." The significance of these methodological and epistemological insights for accounting arise from the following question: Can such a twofold development—formation of various theory nets and research traditions, on the one hand, and competition between entire research traditions, on the other—be discerned in our discipline? Chapter 8 tries to answer this question.

Chapter 8 offers an overview of recent trends in accounting research and shows that it is possible to distinguish different research traditions in our field. The chapter discusses the stewardship-allocation program and its three phases (plain periodization, descriptive agency approach, and agency-information approach), the investment–valuation program with its three phases (present and current value approach, the risk-sharing approach, and the capital market approach), and the purpose-oriented program. Since the 1950s, there has been some competition between the first two programs (both of which constitute well-established traditions). The originally dominating stewardship-allocation program was, at least in theoretical quarters, pushed aside during the 1960s and 1970s by the investment–valuation program. This, in turn, was rivaled in the 1980s by the agency approach which enabled a "rebudding" (in Lakatos' sense) of the stewardship-allocation tradition. The third or purpose-oriented theory net is still in a more or less programmatic stage, and its methodology is to be further analyzed in subsequent chapters.

Chapter 9 discusses the historical aspects of as well as needs for empirical research in accounting that is wide and broad-minded enough to encompass not only positive but also instrumental hypotheses (which connect means to ends). The chapter argues that positive accounting theory is foremost a methodology and hardly covers empirical accounting research in general. It examines the criticism and the limitations of positive accounting theory and also raises the question to what extent the opposition between positive accounting theory in America and the more critical and ethical direction in Europe might not be rooted in a different cultural–philosophical climate of the two continents.

Chapter 10 distinguishes ethical–normative, pragmatic–normative, and conditional–normative accounting theories. It examines the historical roots of normative accounting by first discussing the early German ethical–normative theories of Schär and Nicklisch and shortly touches upon the pragmatic–normative approach in the Anglo-American literature after World War II. It then examines the behavioral–organizational direction, which includes a more traditional empirical branch as well as the British critical–interpretive school with its moderate "organizational–interpretive perspective" and its Marxist "critical–radical perspective." The chapter then shows the need for a methodology that not only clarifies different accounting objectives but also reveals the means for attaining those ends. This might lead to a full-fledged conditional–normative accounting theory (see discussion of Chapter 11 in the next paragraph) that encourages explicit disclosure of value judgments and puts specific purpose-oriented models at the disposal of the users of accounting information.

Chapter 11 contains the major message of this book, which follows as a consequence of the investigations in this and preceding chapters. It tries to find answers to the following questions: What is the significance of means–end relations for accounting? What alternatives do accountants have in dealing with value judgments? What are the arguments in favor of regarding academic accounting as an applied science? In which way can accounting models, "tailor made" or "customized" for individual needs (based on the conditional–normative methodology), be considered objective? Why is there a need for more attention to the great variety of accounting objectives and their hierarchy? What is the current status of the conditional–normative methodology (CoNAM)? How and to what extent does accounting practice represent reality, and can the gap between this pragmatic representation and the positive representation be explained? What are the future requirements for a successive as well as a successful implementation of CoNAM, and which hurdles must still be overcome?

Chapter 12 summarizes and concludes the findings of this research and casts a glance into the future.

NOTES

1. Lodge (1991, 15–16) and Thurow (1993, 32–38), for example, distinguish between two different types of capitalism: the unfettered, *individualistic* (British–American) form versus the *communitarian* (German and Japanese) variants. The danger of economic instability, monopolism, excessive income inequalities, and failure to exploit governmental aid and cooperation is claimed to be higher under the individualistic form of capitalism.

2. It should be pointed out that the practical application of the vast amount of accounting research for price-level adjustments (ongoing since the first decade of this century) may have been defeated by a single academic study. The latter was sponsored by the FASB and authored by Beaver and Landsman (1983). For details, see Chapter 6.

3. Other applied disciplines also have their share of resistance to innovation, but their reactionary forces endure only for a limited time. A glaring historical case is the discovery of the cause of puerperal fever by the Hungarian obstetrician Ignaz P. Semmelweis (1818–1865), who, for years, was haunted by the medical establishment. Today, no one would question his signal achievement in saving the lives of millions of child-bearing mothers by the simple recommendation that physicians performing autopsies must thoroughly disinfect their hands before aiding in the birth process.

CHAPTER 2

The Historic and Cultural Mission of Accounting

THE EVOLUTIONARY KEY

The key to a better understanding of accounting, its essence and mission, may well lie in the evolution of our discipline. Until recently, the origin of accounting or commercial record keeping was shrouded in mystery. New and exciting archeological research has revealed that this origin goes back to prehistoric times (i.e., the time before the invention of writing) and is to be found from about 8000 B.C. onward in form of clay tokens of different shapes (each *shape* representing a type of commodity account). These tokens—each of which stood for one unit of a specific commodity—were stored in containers and transferred in and out of them, depending on the transactions to be recorded.

Originally these containers seem to have been perishable and, in contrast to the clay tokens themselves, did not survive the ravages of time. From about 3250 B.C. onward, hollow clay balls (now called "envelopes") were used to store the accounting tokens. Many of these envelopes survived and were found on numerous archeological sites of the Middle East. Since their recent unearthing, astonishing facts about early record keeping were disclosed. The most revolutionary of these insights are the following three: (1) that accounting existed thousands of years before writing and abstract counting; (2) that accounting became the impetus through which writing (as well as counting in the abstract sense) was created; and (3) that a kind of double-entry recording, let us call it a "prototype," existed already some 5,000 years ago.

Thus, the first cultural mission of accounting was to be midwife to two of the greatest and most important inventions in the history of humanity: the creation of writing and counting in the abstract sense (in which this term is now understood). Another mission preceded this one—the task to make people accountable for their commercial transactions: to record their obligations or debts and ownership rights, to store and classify their resources, and to exercise proper stewardship. Such insights may remind us that *accountability* has been the major function of accounting for some 10,000 years, while other functions, such as aiding investment decisions, are of more recent origin. This accountability function might be the most enduring one our discipline possesses.

ARCHEOLOGY OF PREHISTORIC ACCOUNTING

Archeology is the "scientific study of material remains of human cultures to derive knowledge about prehistoric times" (*The Concise Columbia Encyclopedia* 1983, 40), though occasionally the term is used in an extended, perhaps metaphorical, sense. Foucault (1972), for example, speaks of "the archaeology of knowledge"; and Hopwood (1987), following this example, refers to "the archaeology of accounting systems" when discussing *different layers* of accounting thought and practice during the past century or so; while Power (1992, 37) uses the term *prehistory* in a metaphorical way.

Here, however, *archeology* and *prehistory* are not used in this extended fashion but in the sense of *digging out* as well as interpreting prehistoric and ancient objects in the literal sense. Is it meaningful to speak of an "archaeology of accounting" in the genuine, prehistoric sense? Is there such a kind of archeology? The word prehistoric commonly refers to "the time before the invention of writing;"[1] and this chapter shows that an archeology of accounting, in this sense, does exist—though it is in its infancy. A major pioneer of this subarea is Professor Denise Schmandt-Besserat (of the University of Texas at Austin); but her achievement touches many disciplines and is by no means confined to accounting. As an archeologist (originally specializing in prehistoric clay objects), she hardly started out with the intention to contribute to accounting.[2]

Clay is such a versatile material that even man himself is claimed to exist of it. This may be religion or mythology, but the fact that accounting has its origin in clay has a more scientific basis. The reader might readily think of the thousands of tablets from ancient Sumer and Babylonia, bearing early accounting records in form of cuneiform writing; yet here I am not so much referring to those tablets—which belong to history rather than prehistory—than talking about their precursors: clay tokens (small objects) of diverse shapes and hollow clay envelopes containing those tokens, sealed strings with perforated tokens (see Figures 2.1 to 2.5), as well as tablets *impressed* with tokens.

From an accountant's point of view, the surprising achievement of Schmandt-Besserat is the insight that record keeping for commodities (including labor and metals) and related accountability purposes *preceded* writing as well as abstract counting. Even more startling is her claim that this kind of accounting was the precondition and impetus to the invention of writing as well as abstract counting. This would make prehistoric accounting a foundation stone of culture. Such news is a potential booster to accounting. Indeed, it is of such enormous magnitude that it may take time before its consequences are fully realized. To appreciate the archeology of accounting, as well as the contribution of Schmandt-Besserat, we must probe deeper.

The emergence of agriculture in the neolithic age (emergence of agriculture and domestic animals)—and later the foundation of early cities in the Fertile Crescent (reaching from ancient Persia and Mesopotamia to the border of Egypt)—necessitated a quantitative system of recording various commodities. The existence of those commodities in a certain location, their transfer, their ownership, as well as possible debt or ownership claims connected to such commodities or their transfer, had to be identified and recorded by prehistoric people. At a time when neither counting (in the abstract sense) nor writing existed, which form could such an early accountability system have possibly taken? The answer to this lies less in a detective story than in the ingenious stroke of a most astute observer. The reason I hesitate to regard it a detective story is this: Schmandt-Besserat was originally not searching for but rather stumbled on *the origin of accounting*. Its discovery came as a fortuitous afterthought.

MYSTERIOUS CLAY TOKENS AND THE
ORIGIN OF WRITING

The focus of Schmandt-Besserat's research as well as her book (1992a, 1992b) is primarily the origin of writing and abstract counting, it is secondary only to that of accounting. In the introduction of her book, she presents various myths advanced since ancient times and designed to explain the origin of writing, generally regarded as a kind of instantaneous invention (be it by either gods or mortals). Although this notion of a relatively sudden event was kept alive until recently, William Warburton (1738) introduced in the eighteenth century the first *evolutionary theory* of writing. Meanwhile, archeologists working in the Near East found on many sites small clay artifacts (hitherto unexplained and of various shapes). Schmandt-Besserat now calls them "tokens" or, occasionally, "counters" (see Figures 2.1 and 2.4) and has illustrated them abundantly in her book. Whether in Israel, Syria, Iraq, Turkey or Iran, those artifacts were present all over the Near East in layers dating from 8000 to 3000 B.C. and even later. This ubiquity and wide dispersion pointed to either the religious–cultural or the economic importance of those tokens.

Apart from individual clay tokens, which often were loosely distributed in prehistoric sites, archeologists discovered hollow clay balls containing such tokens. The oldest of these receptacles (called envelopes by Schmandt-Besserat) date back to about 3250 B.C. They all bear seals impressed on the surface (see Figure 2.2), a widespread custom of the Sumerians for identifying debtors or other persons.

Figure 2.1
Plain Clay Tokens

Figure 2.2
Clay Envelope (Showing Seal on Surface) with Five Clay Spheres

From about 3200 B.C. onward, the container surface not only bears a seal but also is imprinted with every token contained in the envelope (see Figure 2.3). Obviously, the need to identify the contents from outside (i.e., without breaking the seal and envelope) was soon realized and taken care of; and this imprinting of the tokens on the surface of the envelope was a decisive step toward the invention of writing.

In visiting many museums as well as archeological sites, Schmandt-Besserat puzzled over these tokens and containers. She soon distinguished between two major types (and many subtypes) of tokens: (1) the so-called *plain tokens* (spheres, disks, cylinders, triangles, rectangles, cones, ovoids, and tetrahedrons), which can be traced as far back as 8000 B.C. (used mainly in the countryside), and

Figure 2.3
Clay Envelope (Showing Traces of Seal as well as Impressions of Hardened Tokens)
with Tokens

(2) the later *complex tokens* (variously incised or punctated and often perforated, also of a greater variety of forms [see Figure 2.4]). *Added* shapes (vessel forms, parabolas, bent coils, and the like) are used mainly in cities and temple precincts. These small, ubiquitous objects (approximately 1 to 4 cm in size) were carefully hand molded of clay and hardened by burning at a relatively low temperature. At some sites, only small numbers of these tokens were preserved; but at other sites (e.g., at Jarmo, Iraq, dated 6500 B.C.), some 1,500 specimens were unearthed. What was their precise function? Although most archeologists working in the

Figure 2.4
Complex Clay Tokens

Fertile Crescent encountered those tokens, none had a satisfactory explanation of their former use. Some deemed them to be amulets or even game figures; others compared them to suppositories.

However, a crucial paper by Oppenheim (1959) discusses a curious, oblong, hollow clay ball (called in the following quote from Schmandt-Besserat a "hollow tablet" because its outer surface bore *cuneiform* writing). But this belonged to the second millennium B.C. and not to the prehistoric period; it was found in the late 1920s in Nuzi (north of Babylon) and contained forty-nine tokens. Strangely enough, it was accompanied by a regular cuneiform tablet "bearing the account of the same transaction, in the family archive of the sheep owner Puhisenni, son of Musapu" (Schmandt-Bersserat 1992a, 8).[3] This tablet listed seven different kinds of sheep and goats (twenty-one ewes that lamb, six female lambs, eight rams, four male lambs, six she-goats that kid, one he-goat, three female kids). It bore the seal of Ziqarru, the shepherd who seems to have received those small cattle from the owner.

When opening the hollow tablet, the excavators found it to hold forty-nine counters which, as stipulated in the text, corresponded to the number of animals listed [note 59 omitted: Starr 1939, 316]. This hollow tablet constitutes the Rosetta stone of the token system. The counters (Akkadian *abnu,* pl. *abnati,* translated "stone" by Oppenheim), the list of animals, and the explanatory cuneiform text leave no possible doubt that at Nuzi counters were used for bookkeeping. Although no other example of a cuneiform tablet holding counters has ever been encountered at Nuzi, or for that matter in Mesopotamia or the Near East, Oppenheim made a case that *abnati* were commonly used in the bureaucracy. He suggested that each animal of a flock was represented by a stone held in an office in a container. The tokens were transferred to various receptacles to keep track of change of shepherds or pasture, when animals were shorn and so on. He based his argument on short cuneiform notes found in archives that referred to *abnati* "deposited," "transferred," and "removed." (Schmandt-Besserat 1992a, 9)

Schmandt-Besserat points out that in 1959 nobody knew the shapes of those stones or tokens, for the latter were meanwhile lost and the original excavation report did not describe their shapes. What was the rationale for the duplication of the cuneiform tablet by a receptacle containing tokens? A plausible explanation for this duplicate recording is this: The clay container was probably destined for the shepherd (one might say, the steward or "debtor"), while the tablet constituted the owner's (or "creditor's") receipt. Why did they use a token envelope when the latter was already out of fashion for about a 1,000 years or so? Illiterate folks (like the shepherds of 2000 B.C.) could easily grasp token accounting, whereas cuneiform writing might have been legible only to more sophisticated people.[4] Tokens are tangible and relatively easy to understand, and this may have been the reason for their survival as an *auxiliary* accounting device in the historic period.

Amiet (1966), the teacher of Schmandt-Besserat, made the leap from Oppenheim's second-millennium stones to the counters or tokens of the fourth millennium B.C. of Susa, interpreting them as "calculi" and representing commodities. Now the geometric shapes of the counters were revealed, and their prehistoric nature was manifest. Amiet even made the suggestion that those calculi might be an antecedent of writing. The task to fill the gaps and gain the insights necessary for a complete picture fell upon Schmandt-Besserat. By connecting the loosely dispersed tokens (between about 8000 to 3500 B.C.) with the tokens in clay envelopes (ca. 3500 to 3000 B.C. and beyond), she recognized that the tokens were the basis of a widely used accounting system that lasted for some 5,000 years (compared to *double-entry bookkeeping,* which seems to have existed for only 600 to 700 years). Particularly striking is Schmandt-Besserat's presentation of such tokens from Uruk. She was able to match those tokens to the commodities to be represented, as shown in Table 2.1.

Starting from these and similar clues, she correlated the shapes of many tokens with the imprinted or incised signs on later clay tablets, thereby offering a kind of token dictionary (compare Schmandt-Besserat 1992a, 143–149, and Mattessich 1994b, 10–12, Figure 1). Such a "dictionary" has perhaps even more the character of a Rosetta Stone for prehistoric accounting than the paper by Oppenheim (1959), the key significance of which remains, of course, undisputed—at least insofar as it correlated *known symbols with unknown ones.*

Table 2.1
Forms of Tokens Used in Prehistoric Record Keeping

Tokens (Accounts)	Commodities
3 incised ovoids	= 3 jars of oil
1 cylinder	= 1 animal (sheep or goat)
9 tetrahedrons	= 9 units of services
3 shapes of trussed ducks	= 3 trussed ducks
5 ovoids	= 5 (still unidentified)
4 parabolas	= 4 (still unidentified)
1 triangle	= 1 small measure of grain?
26 spheres	= 26 bariga (larger measures of grain)

Adapted from Schmandt-Besserat 1983, 120.
Note: In prehistoric times the shape of each token fulfilled the function of what we call a "commodity account" (in the generic sense), while a "personal account" was represented by a clay envelope (identified by the debtor's seal, impressed on the surface of the envelope).

Schmandt-Besserat's insight to juxtapose the imprinted (or later incised) images of early historic times (the meaning of which was by this time already known) to the token shapes, the meaning of which was then still unknown to archeologists, was the crucial step. For example, the sign of a "circled cross" incised on tablets was revealed to correspond to the token of a "disk with incised cross." Those relatively primitive two-dimensional signs could, in turn, be directly linked to cuneiform writings. For example, the crossed disk or, alternatively, the encircled cross stands for sheep; similarly, an ovoid with circular incision stands for a jar of oil; a disc with four parallel lines stands for wool; and so on. Meanwhile, many more shapes have been interpreted. Thus, Schmandt-Besserat claimed that token accounting was the forerunner and impetus to writing as well as counting in the abstract sense. Finally, she collected (in almost two decades of meticulous work) an overwhelming amount of archeological evidence to support her hypothesis. Her extensive research is best summarized in Schmandt-Besserat (1992a, 1992b). For an overview of both the various stages in the evolution of token accounting from 8000 B.C. to 3000 B.C. and the major steps in the archeology of accounting, see Tables 2.2 and 2.3, respectively.

THE ADVENT OF ABSTRACT COUNTING

The notion that *counting* evolved in several phases seems to have been more readily accepted than have the different stages in the evolution of writing. Archeologists (e.g., Schmandt-Besserat 1992a, 184–187) characterize three evolutionary phases of counting: (1) one-to-one correspondence (mainly through tallies, pebbles, and the like), (2) concrete counting (mainly with tokens), and (3) abstract counting (with numerals).

Counting by One-to-One Correspondence

This involves the one-to-one matching between a sign (e.g., a notch on a bone, a pebble, a seashell) and a commodity, such as a goat, a measure of grain, or a coconut, repeating the sign for every additional unit of this commodity. Animal bones and antlers marked with notches excavated at paleolithic and mesolithic sites fall into this category.[5] This one-to-one correspondence seems to be the first of the two universal principles of primitive counting (observable even in preschool children); the other principle arises from the fact that many primitive tribes distinguish only between *one*, *two*, and *many* when counting, thus having only a three-number notion. Schmandt-Besserat (1992a, 185) mentions the Weddas of Ceylon (Sri Lanka), who, until the past century or so, applied this method. In counting coconuts, for example, they piled up a heap of small sticks, adding one stick for every coconut counted. The total of coconuts then corresponded to the total of sticks.

Concrete Counting

This concerns the enumeration through concrete tokens (or even body parts and similar objects) and specific number words. Vestiges of the latter are found in

Table 2.2
Stages in the Evolution of Accounting and Symbolic Representation in the Prehistoric Middle East

---

I. 8000 B.C.: **Plain clay tokens of various shapes** (spheres, disks, cylinders, triangles, rectangles, cones, ovoids, and tetrahedrons, each standing for a unit of a specific commodity) account for the stocks and flows of agricultural goods and services--coinciding with agricultural revolution.

II. 4400 B.C.: **Complex tokens with incised lines or punctation** (and occasionally perforated) appear in the old as well as some new shapes (parabolas, vessel forms, trussed duck forms, bent coils, and the like). This coincided with the first monumental architecture and the rise of temple governments and indicated a need for greater accounting accuracy.

III. 3250 B.C.: Emergence of **sealed aggregation devices,** such as hollow clay envelopes, to safeguard accounting tokens (usually representing agricultural products that were common "currencies") and sealed string systems for safeguarding perforated accounting tokens (usually representing manufactured goods and *labor units*). Both devices were impressed with personal or institutional seals and often used simultaneously to give evidence for inventories and debt claims as well as the equities behind them. This indicates increasing legalism and bureaucratism.

IV. 3200 B.C.: **Surfaces of clay envelopes are impressed with each token** to be enclosed (or each token shape combined with a number symbol) to reveal from outside the assets and equity represented by the token content. This constitutes a kind of double-entry system. Actual tokens inside represent assets; token impressions on the surface are counter-entries representing the corresponding equity. See Figure 2.3

V. 3100-3000 B.C.: First pictographs incised in soft stones (very rare in contrast to the abundance of clay tokens and early pictographs in clay). Emergence of **archaic cuneiform writing, using many symbols identical or similar to negative token impressions.** This stage is also the beginning of abstract counting and writing. Continuing use of both token accounting systems.

Note: The term *prehistoric* is perhaps not a particularly fortunate choice, since it too has temporal, hence historic, dimensions.

many languages where *different things are counted by different sets of number words.* A striking example is Japanese; but as Schmandt-Besserat points out, even in English, one still uses such expressions as "a couple," "a brace," and "a pair," all indicating the number two but not necessarily interchangeably (e.g., one cannot speak of "a brace of shoes," but one can say "a brace of pheasants"). It is noteworthy that those enumerations do not go very far and usually end with a word

Table 2.3
Major Steps and Publications Towards an Archeology of Accounting

1964	A. Falkenstein (1964) emphasized that cuneiform writing was (originally) created for the exclusive purpose of recording economic transactions.
1959-1966	Publication of **Leo Oppenheim's** crucial paper (1959) on **counters and a cuneiform envelope** with accompanying cuneiform tablet from the second millennum B.C., revealing this envelope as a kind of IOU, containing tokens. **Pierre Amiet** (1966), following Oppenheim's lead, interpreted **clay counters in envelopes** of the prehistoric period (i.e., before B.C.) as **representing commodities**. Maurice Lambert (1966) identified impressed signs on envelopes as token impressions.
1969-1993	Research and publications of **Denise Schmandt-Besserat** (e.g. 1978, 1979, 1992a, 1992b), collected and interpreted clay artifacts and evidence of the use of tokens, envelopes, and imprinted and incised tablets for purposes of commercial record keeping; **correlated the tokens with imprints and signs on archaic tablets;** identified the meaning of dispersed tokens from 8000 B.C. (and later) with the meaning of tokens in envelopes of the fourth millennium, and **inferred the meaning of token shapes from cuneiform tablets.** Further research on "Ancient Bookkeeping" by Nissen et al. (1993).
1987-1994	Interpretation of Schmandt-Besserat's research from the accounting point of view by **Richard Mattessich** (1987b, 1991b, 1994b): **token shapes fulfilling the function of commodity accounts** (in the generic sense), envelopes as receivable/payable accounts not only containing the details of loans but also representing separately (as imprints) the total equity of commodities loaned or stored in specific places or allocated to specific flocks, and the like. Inferred the **double-entry character of prehistoric token accounting** from both, the transfer of tokens (representing physical inputs and outputs), and the impression of tokens on the outside of envelopes (representing social relations). See also Table 2.2

for "many" (e.g., triangle, square, . . . , polygon) and are not used for counting but merely for classifying numerically. Hence, the main characteristic of concrete counting is the identification of a set of words or tokens with a set of specific things.

Schmandt-Besserat believes that the notion of *cardinality* was introduced already at this stage of concrete counting:

The hypothesis that from the beginning of the token system groups of counters were no longer the mere repetition of one unit ("and one more") but expressed a cardinal number is based on my argument that certain tokens stood for sets (x = n). I posit, for example, that tetrahedrons, which occur in two distinct subtypes "small" and "large" . . . , represented two different units of the same commodity. (Schmandt-Besserat 1992a, 189)

Abstract Counting

Only abstract counting liberates the number symbol from a specific set of things, creating *numerals* general enough for counting anything and creating the abstract notions of "oneness," "twoness," "threeness," and so on. Schmandt-Besserat suggests that, in contrast to concrete counting (which may have limited counting to a score of objects or so), abstract counting knows no limits and is the beginning of arithmetic and higher mathematics. For laypersons, so familiar with our abstract numerical system, it is occasionally difficult to understand the difference between the various phases of counting; but as Bertrand Russell mentioned, it "required many ages to discover that a brace of pheasants and a couple of days were both instances of the number 2" (Russell [1919] 1960, 3). Schmandt-Besserat (1992a, 192–193) points out that the accountants of Uruk IV-a (refers to the excavation level) can be credited with creating numerals and, by doing so, revolutionizing accounting and data manipulation. In fact, the accountants of the Uruk IV-a period devised two types of signs: *numerals* (symbols encoding abstract numbers) and *pictographs* (expressing commodities). Each type of sign was traced in a different technique. Pictographs were *incised*, whereas numerals were *impressed*, clearly standing out from the text. In fact, the impressed signs that came to represent numerals never lost their primary meaning. Instead, they had either an abstract or a concrete value, according to the context. For example a wedge preceding a pictograph was read "1"; but alone, it stood for a measure of grain. This must have been confusing to Sumerian accountants, who eventually eliminated the ambiguity by introducing a pictograph in the shape of an ear of grain.

Schmandt-Besserat's hypothesis (for its first outline, see Schmandt-Besserat 1977, 1978, 1979) has not remained unchallenged. It was attacked by Lieberman (1980), who contested that the meanings attributed by Schmandt-Besserat to tokens are the same as those of impressed, incised, and cuneiform tablets. Lieberman also believed that the idea that tokens represented commodities is mere speculation.[7] Further reservations were advanced by Brandes (1980), Schendge (1983), and others. Professor Hallo points out in the Foreword to Schmandt-Besserat (1992a) that, in her continuing research and gradual refinements, she "confronted all of these challenges. She has identified envelopes, notably from Susa and Habuba Kabira, impressed with non-numerical tokens, indeed with the very tokens enclosed inside." (Hallo 1992, x). He also adds,

Not trained as an Assyriologist in her own right, she [Schmandt-Besserat] has wisely sought the collaboration of specialists in cuneiform writing and the Sumerian language, including Margaret Green, a former member of the Berlin team dealing with the archaic texts from Uruk. These texts may be said to stand midway between the tokens of the neolithic period and the fully evolved cuneiform script of the Early Dynastic and subsequent periods in Mesopotamia. The case for linking the tokens via the archaic Uruk texts to the clearly intelligible logograms of the third and second millennia is today substantially stronger than when the first tentative suggestions were advanced in the 1970's. In a special issue of *Visible Language*, devoted to "aspects of cuneiform writing" in 1981, this point was already recognized by Green and Marvin Powell. Powell's defense of the theses (its *ad hominem* arguments apart) is particularly important for its numerical aspects, given his long involvement with the evolution of cuneiform numeration systems in the historic period. . . . But what about the rest of the hypothesis? Here its latest refinement as first elaborated in the pages of this book is crucial. In effect, we are offered a credible hypothesis that provides a possible, even plausible evolutionary model, not only for the emergence of literacy but of "numeracy." (Hallo 1992, x–xi)

DOUBLE-ENTRY IN PREHISTORIC TIMES

Before offering my own inferences from an accountant's point of view, let me first *summarize* Schmandt-Besserat's hypothesis: The clay tokens (of different shapes, with increasing variety as time progressed, and used abundantly between 8000 and 3000 B.C.) represented various commodities. Before 3250 B.C. the tokens were presumably kept in perishable containers; but after this date, they were preserved in clay envelopes, each representing a commodity aggregate owed by one person to another or, more often, owed to a temple precinct (as most of these envelopes were found in ancient temple sites). However, simultaneously with the envelopes there existed an alternative system, using the same tokens but perforated, stringed, and held together by a sealed blob of clay (see Figure 2.5). In conformity with such confirmed practice, the debtor was identified by the seal (the latter wrapped around the envelope or impressed on the blob connecting the ends of the strings). Obviously, the advantage of the alternative accounting device lay in the instantaneous visibility of the debt and the individual assets of which it consisted.

By 3200 B.C. the envelope (as an IOU) was also improved for the sake of quicker content identification. By this time, the surface of the clay ball revealed not only the debtor but also the contents. This was achieved by impressing each token on the outside of the envelope before putting it into the receptacle (see Figure 2.3), enabling a quick identification of the entire debt (i.e., the equity owed) without opening, hence breaking, the envelope. Consequently, the sum total of the various tokens in a particular envelope or on a string stood for that part of the entity that a creditor lent to a debtor.

As the shapes of various kinds of tokens were fairly well standardized across the Fertile Crescent, I established (Mattessich 1987b, 77)[7] that each *shape* then had the same function nowadays fulfilled by the commodity *account* of a specific type. As I am not sure whether this point has been presented clearly enough or fully grasped, I take this opportunity to further elaborate it. Although Schmandt-Besserat refers on several occasions to the envelopes, stringed bullae, and tablets as "accounts," she never refers to the shape of the tokens as fulfilling the function of accounts.[8] Yet these shapes do represent *asset accounts in the generic sense.*[9]

While generally the envelopes and the like represent debt (or ownership) equities, that is, a *social reality*, the token shapes are commodity accounts, thus repre-

Figure 2.5
Sketched Reconstruction of String Aggregate (Showing Clay Seal on Top and Five Ovoid Tokens on String) Designed by Ellen Simmons

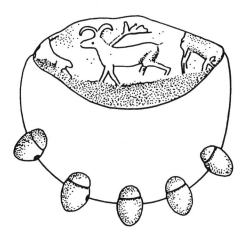

senting a *physical reality*.[10] It seems that laypersons (including archeologists) find it easier to associate an account with a debt or ownership claim than with a commodity. Pure commodity transactions (e.g., the exchange of sheep for a goat) are relatively few in internal accounting systems, compared to those involving equities (e.g., the transfer of a sheep from one shepherd to another, when each shepherd is regarded as a steward or kind of debtor).

In a later passage (Mattessich 1987b, 79–81), I deduced that the ancient Sumerians practiced a kind of double-entry record keeping some 5,000 years ago. This means, first of all, that those ancient people of the Middle East had record-keeping systems, the logical structure of which was basically the same as that of modern double entry. This structure manifests itself *empirically* in such economic events as sales and purchases, investment and debt transactions, production, and other transfer processes. At the same time, this same structure can *conceptually* be represented not only in form of journal and double entries but also in form of matrixes, algebraic equations, flow diagrams or networks, and vectors.[11] One might reply that the transfer of ordinary goods, from one person to another, already possessed this logical structure, usually called the *input–output* or *duality principle*. This is perfectly correct, but the ingenious stroke was to transfer this idea or principle from actual commodities by a one-to-one correspondence to a conceptual system of representation. Once this crucial fact of the "input–output" or, better said, "duality" principle has been established, the question whether the ancient Sumerians or any other tribe used (more than 5,000 years ago) a double-entry system is actually of secondary importance. However, a good case can be made that even double entry, in the literal sense, emerged as early as 3200 B.C.

From this time stem the earliest clay envelopes that bear on their surface the impressions of the tokens contained inside. Putting those tokens into an envelope undoubtedly meant the recording of quantities of various assets, or what we to-day would call "making debit entries." Apart from this, there were two further needs: (1) to reveal from outside the hidden *contents of the envelope* and (2) to reveal at a glance the entire *equity* represented by the envelope—as far as such an aggregation is possible without a common denominator. By sheer coincidence, both of these functions could be fulfilled by a single act, namely, by impressing the hardened tokens into the surface of the softer clay envelope. If this interpretation is correct, then those "mirror impressions" can be regarded as genuine *counter-entries* (in this case, credit entries) on the equity side of such an accounting system (compare Mattessich 1987b, 80–81).

Double entry before 3000 B.C.? This must appear outrageous to many accountants and laypersons alike. Of course, it was *not* "double-entry *bookkeeping*," as neither writing nor books were in existence at that time. Nevertheless, commercial transactions were rendered in a dual fashion, and I should like to reinforce my argument in the following way:

1. The rich evidence accumulated up to this point leaves little doubt that commodity transactions were conceptually represented by the transfer of clay tokens. The paper by Oppenheim (1959), in particular, shows that tokens were used to reflect the *physical input and output of assets*. See, for example, the quote from Schmandt-Besserat (1992a, 9) in the third section. There it was suggested that the transfer of small cattle from one pasture to another was represented by the transfer of the pertinent token from one envelope to another.

The conclusion is inevitable: The *input* of, let us say, the token for a sheep into an envelope (representing, for example, a pen or a pasture A) corresponds to a credit of the "Sheep account"—here, the *shape* of the token characterizes the account in the generic sense—and the charging or debit of "Pasture A account." While the eventual *output* of this token from the same envelope would mean a credit to account A, and the *input* of this token into another envelope (e.g., for pasture B) would be equivalent to a debit to "Pasture B account."

No one can deny that this is "double-entry recording" of the transfer of *physical objects* (real sheep) from one location to another, at least in the sense that it fulfills the requirements of all three constituents of this expression: "double," "entry," and "recording." Of course, it is *not* a "double-entry bookkeeping system" in the modern sense, where an arithmetical control checks whether the *monetary* values were equally entered on both sides.[12]

To take such a *monetary* check as the criterion for deciding whether something is a system of "double-entry recording" would not only be a grave misinterpretation of this expression but would also mean to get stuck on the surface. The *essential* characteristics of a system of "double-entry recording," in my view, are structural as well as empirical. They are: (1) the *simultaneous recording of the two aspects of inputs and outputs* in different places (equivalent but not necessarily identical to "accounts") of the system; (2) the function of accountability together with the availability of an *empirical control* (by taking inventory and comparing it with the recording) as well as a *nonmonetary tautological control* (number and shapes of tokens in the envelope must exactly correspond to imprints on the surface). These two control features are more essential than the arithmetical check mentioned above. Another essential characteristic is (3) the manifestation and *interconnection of three different dualities* (that of physical transfers, relevant for this item 1; and those of owning and owing things, discussed in the next item).

2. As for the recording of *social relations*, strong evidence indicates that the clay envelopes represented debt or property claims[13] and that (from about 3250 B.C. onward) the totality of each claim was represented through token impressions on the envelope's surface. Indeed, the *token impressions* (1) constitute a "converse" and more abstract image of the tokens;[14] (2) are *no longer separable* (i.e., individually movable) from each other, in contrast to the transferability of individual tokens; and (3) *reveal* at a glance the *entire claim*.

This leads to the conclusion that the clay impressions constitute *the total equity* (in the *inclusive* sense)[15] of the individual items owed by one person to another. This corresponds to Mattessich (1987b, 81), that is, taking a token impression on an envelope to be a credit to an equity account and the input of the token (into the same envelope) as the corresponding debit to an asset account. This obviously is seen *from the viewpoint of the debtor*, despite the fact that in most cases the owner (creditor) stored the envelope as a kind of receipt.

Occasionally, as the case quoted from Schmandt-Besserat (1992a, 9) shows (see the third section), the accompanying cuneiform tablet (instead of the original envelope) was the "owner's receipt." The input of a token (representing a sheep) into an envelope (now representing, for example, person X) is equivalent to our debiting "Account Receivable X" and crediting the "Sheep account." Again, this is a double-entry system; yet in contrast to item 1, it is not for transferring physical objects but for recording social relations like debt and ownership claims.

3. In one respect, the double entry of token systems is superior to present-day double-entry bookkeeping. An "impression" on an envelope immediately reveals itself as equivalent to a "credit entry" of an equity account, while the output (removal) of a token from an envelope also reveals itself as a "credit" but to a commodity or similar asset account. In modern accounting, however, those two types of credit entries are not so easily distinguished, as anyone can vouch who ever taught accounting to beginners. Without the benefit of an immediate distinction, as available in token accounting, students are easily confused between those two types of credits because one constitutes an *augmentation* (of an equity), while the othern constitutes a *diminution* (of a commodity or other asset).

Another "superiority" of token accounting appears to be the absence of valuation problems that plague modern accountants. Token accounting only concealed this problem; it did not solve it. What seems to be a disadvantage of the modern system is more than compensated by its greater flexibility, which the common denominator (numeraire) of *monetary* evaluation affords (bringing with it the fringe benefit of monetary control, mentioned in item 1). However, prehistoric record keeping possessed a kind of *nonmonetary valuation*: Complex tokens, for example, achieved greater accuracy in discriminating between various types of cloths (and presumably *values*) by different numbers of lines incised on the token disks.

4. Items 1 to 3 become still more plausible when considering that the ultimate significance of double-entry record keeping lies not so much in entering the same thing twice; rather, it lies in the exposition of the *dual nature* of every commodity transaction as well as of every debt–creditor and asset–ownership relation. This hints at the fact that double entry is not merely based on the single input–output relation of a commodity transfer. Its basis is the combination of three very different relations which all have, fortuitously, two dominating aspects. These aspects are fairly different in each relation, as revealed by the following three items:

1. The physical transfer of goods and services connects an *input location* to an *output location*.
2. A debt claim connects a *debtor* to a *creditor*.
3. An ownership claim connects a *resource* (asset) to an *owner*.

I might possibly agree with Chatfield that "recording each transaction twice is a necessary but not sufficient condition of double-entry" or with his assertion that "the essence of double-entry is . . . category integration" (Chatfield 1974; 35). For me, "double-classification" means the ingenious interconnection of the above three different dualities rather than the "integration of real and nominal accounts" (which Chatfield attributes to a somewhat misinterpreted passage by Littleton and Zimmerman [1962, 74]). In principle, even modern double-entry bookkeeping systems can function without separate nominal accounts (including the income or profit and loss account). Nominal accounts are merely a subcategory of the owner's equity account, which, if necessary, can assume the function of any nominal account. Furthermore, many early *double-entry* Renaissance bookkeeping systems might not qualify as such if the "integration of nominal accounts" (beyond the absorption of all nominal accounts in owners' equity) were accepted as the decisive criterion for characterizing a well-functioning double-entry system. This suggests that there is little use in drawing arbitrary criteria; it is more important to recognize that the development of double entry went through several phases, each possessing somewhat different features.

A careful study of the more sophisticated version of prehistoric "token/envelope accounting" reveals that the dual use of each token (first impressing it on the surface of the clay envelope and then putting it into the latter) reflected the different dual aspects of the relations listed earlier in this chapter. Thereby, the actual tokens represented a *physical reality* (commodities), while the totality of all those counter-impressions (on a specific envelope) represented the corresponding debt equity, hence a *social reality*. (For a discussion of reality issues, see Chapter 3.) The legalistic distinction between debt–credit relation versus ownership relation was still blurred 5,000 years ago. Money did not yet exist, and the

debt had to be expressed in terms of commodities. Even when repayment occurred merely in *equivalent* goods, one might speak of either an ownership or a
debt–credit relation in such a nonmonetary economy.

5. All this does not imply that the Sumerians were conscious of every one of
those considerations, nor do I claim that this was the beginning of a continuous
effort leading to double-entry bookkeeping. On the contrary, it was nothing but a
prototype; and it was "progress" that prevented the continuation and further development of this double-entry aspect. The Sumerians soon discovered that the
recording goal (as well as the economic and legalistic functions) could be
achieved in a simpler way than by first producing tokens and hollow clay balls
(which required impressing the former onto the latter, then closing and sealing the
envelope and ultimately breaking it open). Using a flat clay tablet (instead of a
hollow ball) and impressing the tokens on it (or incising the tablet with a similar
shape) required only a single entry but was obviously more efficient.

By 3000 B.C., even greater efficiency was achieved through substituting cuneiform strokes for the token imprints on the clay tablets. Thus, these early efficiency
drives had a casualty, namely, double-entry recording. The latter fell by the way-
side at the second stage of impressing tokens onto flat tablets. Here, tokens were
still needed, but they lost the function of representing assets; tokens became mere
tools for making impressions on the tablets—only the impressions were left to
represent real events. Without this innovation, those stumbling beginnings of recording all the dual aspects of commercial transactions might have easily been
further developed. Perhaps humankind could have attained double-entry bookkeeping and its controlling function thousands of years earlier.

The crucial conclusions of items 1 and 2 involve nothing but deductive inferences from Schmandt-Besserat's research. They are based neither on induction
nor on mere interpretation. In other words, if her findings are correct, my inferences hold by necessity. To disagree with these findings, one would have to refute Schmandt-Besserat's (1992a, 1992b) overwhelming evidence by even
stronger counter-evidence. For a concise summary of the features of prehistoric
token accounting, see Table 2.4.

THE HIERARCHY OF ARCHAIC ACCOUNTS AND
THE DIFFUSION OF ACCOUNTING

We have previously established that every "asset account" seems to have been
characterized by a specific token shape. These accounts were not limited to purely
tangible assets. Occasionally, they included a claim to services (the tetrahedron
token seems to have represented a day of labor [see Schmandt-Besserat 1980,
375]). Beyond this lower echelon of accounts, one or two higher echelons must
be distinguished.

The second level of accounts is represented by the receptacles (i.e., clay envelopes) as well as string aggregates. Similar to the income statement, these would

Table 2.4
Summary of Double-Entry Features of Prehistoric Token Accounting

---

PHYSICAL REALITY (Transfer of Assets)

> **Output** of tokens from envelope A: equivalent to a **credit** in account A.
> **Input** of tokens into envelope B: equivalent to a **debit** in account B.
> **Token shape** indicates type of **asset account** (e.g., "Sheep," "Cloth," "Wheat") **Number of tokens** indicates how many **units** (of sheep, cloth, bread, wheat, etc.)

SOCIAL REALITY (Ownership and Debt Claims)

> **Impressing token shapes** on the outside of envelope: equivalent to a **Credit** in an equity account, recording the existence of a debt or ownership relation on the asset (indicated by the token inserted; see next line).
> **Inserting tokens** in envelope: equivalent to a **debit** in an asset account (corresponding to token shape)

CONTROL FEATURES

> **Empirical control:** taking of inventory (e.g., counting of assets, such as sheep in pasture A) and comparing with content of sheep tokens in envelope (e.g., envelope A). If the two do not perfectly correspond in numbers and shapes, an empirical discrepancy is established (i.e., either some asset item or items are missing or some token or tokens got lost or were erroneously added, etc.).
> **Tautological control:** counting tokens in envelope A and comparing with impressions on the surface of envelope A. If the two do not perfectly correspond in numbers and shapes, an analytical recording error has occurred (i.e., either the scribe forgot to impress some tokens on the surface or impressed too many, or he forgot to insert a token already impressed, etc.). If all has been entered properly, the impressions and insertions will match for the same tautological reason that gives rise to the equality of all debits and credits in the trial balance, etc., of a *monetary* double-entry accounting system.

---

undoubtedly have been accounts of a higher echelon, since they usually contained tokens of different shapes and thus summarized the content of several accounts (but unlike the income statement, they summarize "real," not "nominal" accounts).

The third level of accounts can be found in the accumulation of all clay envelopes and string aggregates within one temple precinct or other entity. If all those receptacles were kept in one room, then this room would, in a way, have been equivalent to our modern balance sheet (e.g., each receptacle representing an "accounts receivable account" and the totality representing the entire "owner's equity" of that institution).

What about income measurement? Those archaic accounting systems do not offer any direct evidence, neither for the notion of income nor for any attempt of its measurement. However, it may well be possible that whenever a genuine debt relation (instead of a stewardship relation) was entered and the pertinent token receptacle was created, a token was added by means of which the pertinent aggregate did not constitute the original debt but the final debt (i.e., augmented by an interest or income item represented by this added token)—similar to later accounting practices during the 16th and 17th centuries, when debts were invariably recorded at their discharge value. If interest was charged at all, this scenario is more likely than the alternative of establishing the interest at the time of repayment without having any agreement and record in advance.

In Babylonian and Assyrian times accounting and accountants (scribes) flourished and promoted trade and commerce, banking, and shipping, as well as bureaucracy. Thousands of preserved cuneiform tablets represent accounting records of real estate transactions and rental income, wage and interest payments, receipts and disbursements, expense accounts, tax collections, and the like. In Egypt, the widespread use of papyrus greatly facilitated the production of less cumbersome accounting records. These, in turn, sustained strong and highly centralized governments without which the cultural sophistication of ancient Egypt might not have been possible.

ACCOUNTING IN ANCIENT GREECE, ROME, AND THE FAR EAST

As crucial as the impact of early accounting has been, it must not keep us from noting those subsequent events that continued to confirm this discipline as a truly cultural force. Ancient Greece was enriched by the invention of money and coinage (in seventh-century Lydia). This made possible a common denominator that greatly facilitated public as well as private accounting. The most elaborate accounting records passed on to us from this time are the so-called Zenon-papyri of the third century B.C. (for details, see Chatfield 1974, 9–12). Ancient Roman government and bank accounting (growing out of household accounting) developed a series of distinct features, but some historians (compare de Ste. Croix 1956, 33) do not regard these developments as important improvements over the accounting developed in Greece.

Except for the morphological similarities between prehistoric token accounting and the cuneiform record keeping on clay tablets, there seems to be little direct evidence for a continuous development of early accounting. To establish a link between the accounting systems of ancient Mesopotamia and those of subsequent civilizations, in particular, of ancient Greece and Rome, one must search for further evidence. In other areas, such as writing, religious myth, technology, astronomy, and astrology, there does exist evidence for cross-cultural influence if not continuity. On the basis of such indirect and extended limits, one might conjecture that the previously discussed accounting systems of the Fertile Crescent must have had some impact on accounting systems of later periods. For example, Filios points out that "a detailed examination of the primary sources in particular, provides significant evidence about the existence of the duality principle in the bookkeeping of banks, temples and states' treasuries in ancient as well as in Byzantine Greece" (Filios 1984, 171).

Whether this later duality notion evolved out of the input–output principle, as conceived in prehistoric times, is a more precarious question. The advent of token accounting may constitute a refutation of Filios' further claim that

systematic accounting is shown to be in particular the product of Greek thought which laid the foundation of accounting science. . . . In this paper the main thesis to be supported is that the double-entry system of bookkeeping is a Greek invention and in the early years of Ancient Greece it had been applied in the presentation of transactions of the time. The Venetians had inherited from the Byzantines not only their commercial growth, but also their commercial methods. (Filios 1984, 171–172)

By no means do I claim that double-entry bookkeeping of the Renaissance is the direct descendant of the double-entry token accounting of the Sumerians. However, the more fundamental duality principle, conceived by prehistoric man, may be regarded as the spiritual ancestor of the logical structure encountered in accounting systems of modern times.

Whether the type of double-entry bookkeeping known to us from the civic stewards of Genoa, from Cotrugli ([1573] 1990; for details, see Yamey 1994), and from Pacioli (1494) or other historical records, is derived from ancient Grecian or Roman times is another controversial issue. According to Filios, many historians have supported the view that the bankers of ancient Greece originated a systematized way of accounting:

This is understood to be the advent of double-entry accounting or at least of an accounting system which is based on the duality principle—the core of contemporary accounting. Thus debts were offset by capital transfers from one account into another. Several tens of historians have strongly supported this view like Guillard, Goldschmidt, Huvelin, Hasebroek, Eisler, Galhoun, and first of all Kraus already from the beginning of [the] eighteenth century. (Filios 1984, 178)

The qualification in the first sentence of this quotation is crucial because, as we have seen, token accounting was already based on such a duality principle thousands of years before the banking system of ancient Greece evolved in the temples of Delphi, Olympia, Delos, Ephesos, and Corinth. Filios admits that "we should distinguish, first of all, between the duality *concept* and double-entry technique" (1984, 188). The duality concept of the ancient Greeks may very well have been derived from that of the Middle East and handed on to the Romans and later to the Italians. We have no hard and fast evidence that the double-entry bookkeeping technique peculiar to Renaissance Italy was derived from ancient Greece or any other predecessor.

Something similar holds for Lall Nigam's claim, asserting that the Bahi-Khata double-entry system of India preceded and inspired Venetian Renaissance book-keeping: "The Bahi-Khata is a double-entry bookkeeping system that predates the 'Italian' method by many centuries. Its existence in India prior to the Greek and Roman empires suggests that Indian traders took it with them to Italy. . . . it is difficult to pin down the precise period of the advent Bahi-Khata. . . . the traditional Indian way of studying and teaching . . . [was] by mere word of mouth." (Lall Nigam 1986, 148–150). Since bookkeeping itself was done in writing, and since many old historical documents are available (from the time of the Vedas to the Gupta and Mogul periods as well as beyond), some accounting records would surely have survived to substantiate at least part of Lall Nigam's claim. Without offering a single piece of firm historical evidence, this claim cannot be taken as expressing a legitimate historical fact; it must wait for further research and reliable documentation. Nobes (1987, 183) even rejects Lall Nigam's claim as being based on "inexpert hearsay."

However, there exists an important aspect in which Indian mathematics did, indeed, essentially contribute to accounting. This is the use of *negative numbers* for characterizing debts and positive numbers for assets—something which Leonardo da Pisa (1202), also called Fibonacci, seems to have absorbed from the Arabians and brought, together with the "Arabic" (or more correctly "Indian") numerals, to Italy. This usage of identifying debts with negative numbers occurred in India as early as the seventh century A.D.[16] Here is another instance illustrating the cultural impact of accounting on mathematics. To fully understand this particular case, one has to be aware that even during the Renaissance, most mathematicians still regarded negative numbers as "absurd," or "impossible," "fictions."[17] Indian mathematicians, on the other hand, did not let a narrow logical view interfere with their intuition that negative numbers are meaningful. In the presumed search for a real manifestation of negative numbers, the Indian mathematicians noticed—almost a millennium before the Europeans did—that debts (which are undoubtedly a social reality) are a kind of negative assets (e.g., negative "accounts receivable"). In this way, accounting and legalistic notions such as assets, debts, and the like facilitated the acceptance of negative numbers in mathematics. What a difference this made for mathematics. At the same time, such usage is a crucial contribution to accounting itself; but it can hardly be identified with the invention of double-entry bookkeeping. It shows the intricate and enduring association of mathematics with accounting. Furthermore, Bhattacharyya (1988) presented exciting evidence that the ancient treatise of *Arthaśāstra* (ca. 300 B.C.) by Kautilya operated with some "modern" concepts of accounting, costing, and auditing, using not only various types of expenditure and revenue items but also a variety of income notions, distinguishing between income and our "holding gains" (possibly foreshadowing the difference between such notions as real vs. fictitious and realized vs. unrealized holding gains—see Chapter 6) already some 2,300 years ago.

Accounting in China, in particular, governmental accounting, reached its peak during the Shang (1600–1100 B.C.)[18] and Chou (1121–255 B.C.) dynasties. As Chatfield (1974, 8–9) points out, this was hardly exceeded in sophistication before the introduction of double-entry bookkeeping. There existed monthly and annual reports, a powerful and independent Comptroller General who supervised annual budgets, and audits that were based on random samples. Chatfield even mentions that the great Confucius himself is supposed to have been a government record keeper. What better and more ethical ancestors could present-day accountants wish for?

Of special interest is the fact that in the tenth century A.D., or even earlier, Chinese scholars conceived what I should like to call the "*extended* input–output principle," expressed by the balancing equation:

Jinguang ("old trust" or beginning balance) + *Xinshou* (new receipts)
= *Kaicu* (disbursements) + *Shizai* ("real existence" or ending balance)

According to Guo (1982, 352–354) and Lin (1992, 107–108), the books of the *Jingtu* Temple (A.D. 925) contain this equation of four variables (or, literally translated, the "four-pillars balancing") already more than 1,000 years ago; although this, too, may be a step toward double-entry bookkeeping, it does not imply the latter.

There also exists evidence in China (compare Guo 1982 and Lin 1992) that during the late Tang and early Sung dynasties (A.D. 960–1279) a transition from single-entry to double-entry accounting took place. During the Ming dynasty (A.D. 1363–1644) "The *Sanjiao Zhang* method was a mixture of double-entry and single-entry" (Lin 1992, 110); and the *Longmen Zhang* method of the late Ming period was a primitive double-entry system, claimed to have originated with Chinese bankers. This system was superseded by the *Shijiao Zhang*, a more sophisticated double-entry method, which remained in existence until the mid-nineteenth century (compare Lin 1992, 111–119).

LATER CULTURAL ASPECTS OF ACCOUNTING

During the Middle Ages, for example, the government accounting reforms of Charlemagne and his instructions (the *Capitulare de Vilis*) are famous. They helped to strengthen his empire no less than did his military and diplomatic actions. Furthermore, manorial accounting and government tax rolls, tally sticks, and the proffer system (semi-annual and annual meetings of stewards, auditors, and so on), although relatively simple and predominantly based on oral communication, played an important role in keeping feudal estates functioning and in preventing entire realms from falling apart. In the thirteenth century, the need for manorial stewards and auditors became so pressing that Oxford University began to include "manorial accounting" in its curriculum (compare Chatfield 1974, 28).

Since the first published treaties on double-entry bookkeeping occurred in a mathematical text (in Pacioli's [1494] *Summa de arithmetica, geometria, proportioni et proportionalita*),[19] accounting remained intimately connected with commerce and mathematics as well as their achievements. Innumerable book-keeping texts in Italy, Holland, England, Germany, and many other countries followed Pacioli's book.

This cultural significance of our discipline is also intricately interwoven with the Industrial Revolution and is confirmed in the literature. Goethe, for example, in his educational fiction *Wilhelm Meister*, refers to double-entry bookkeeping as one of the finest discoveries of the human intellect; and Werner Sombart says that "double-entry is born of the same spirit as the system of Galileo and Newton.... With the same means as these it orders the phenomenon into an elegant system" (Sombart 1902, 119, translated). On the other hand, Oswald Spengler (who deemed Pacioli to be the creator of the double-entry system) considers, in reference to the monetary and economic thinking of Western society, the invention of bookkeeping as the decisive event. Spengler (1928, 490) even ranks its inventor as equal to Columbus and Copernicus. Two of the most eminent ninetenth-century mathematicians did not find it beneath their dignity to write on bookkeeping: August de Morgan (1846, 180–189) used a matrix framework for presenting accounting[20] in the fifth edition of his *Elements of Arithmetic*; and the co-founder of matrix algebra, Arthur Cayley (1894), continued by making a similar effort in his book *The Principles of Book-Keeping by Double Entry*. On a purely geometrical basis, this matrix notion of accounting was later exploited by Léon Gomberg (1927).

Throughout these ages, from its early beginning in about 8000 B.C. until the start of the twentieth century, the predominant goal of accounting was *accountability* (i.e., the monitoring of stewardship) and such associated objectives as *profit determination* and *cost control*. New goals then began to compete with the traditional one. Among these, the most important seemed to be the supplying of information to "decision makers" for *investment* purposes (i.e., measuring rentability). This mainly occurred during the "academization" of our discipline, which may be considered the ultimate cultural contribution of accounting (see Chapter 4). The benefit of this academic activity to accounting practice (and society at large) may still be controversial, but its intellectual effort during the twentieth century can hardly be denied. Where there is honest intellectual work, long-term consequences usually follow. The rest of this book discusses some of this work as well as potential contributions that loom on the horizon.

NOTES

This chapter draws upon my plenary address at the 17th Annual Congress of the European Accounting Association in Venice, April 1994, "Accounting as a Cultural Force: Past, Present and Future" (Mattessich 1994a) and my invited presentation on occasion of the 650th anniversary of the University of Pisa, "The Number Concept in Business and 'Concern Economics'" (Mattessich 1994c), as well as on such papers as "Prehistoric Accounting and the Problem of Representation: On Recent Archeological Evidence of the Middle East from 8000 B.C. to 3000 B.C." in *The Accounting Historians Journal* (Mattessich 1987b), and "Counting, Accounting, and the Input–Output Principle: Recent Archeological Evidence Revising Our View on the Evolution of Early Record Keeping," in *The Costing Heritage—Studies in Honor of S. Paul Garner*, ed. O. Finley Graves (Mattessich 1991b).

1. The term *prehistoric* is perhaps not a particularly fortunate choice, since it, too, has a temporal—hence historic—dimension.

2. Schmandt-Besserat (1992a) discusses many aspects of her discovery as well as its implications for linguistics and communication, mathematics, anthropology, sociology, and economics. Strangely enough, she mentions neither the implications for modern accounting nor those for philosophy (particularly epistemology). My own interpretations and deductions concern mainly those relevant to accounting (compare Mattessich 1987b, 1989, 1991b, 1994b) but to some extent also the philosophic *problems of conceptual representation*, of which token accounting was one of the first manifestations (compare Mattessich 1988). For details about "archaic bookkeeping" of a subsequent (early historic) period, see Nissen et al. (1993).

3. In contrast to the genuine double-entry features of token accounting (discussed in the penultimate section of this chapter), I would *not* regard this particular duplication as a double-entry within a specific entity.

4. See Schmandt-Besserat, citing Starr (1939): "It is likely that the tablet was meant for Puhisenni's archive and the envelope was intended for Ziqarru, who was probably illiterate" (Schmandt-Besserat 1992a, 235, note 55).

5. One of the earliest paleolithic evidences is the famous "wolf bone," approximately 18 cm long, containing fifty-five notches and found in Moravia in 1937 by Karl Absalom. This is "clear evidence that the tallying principle for numbers goes back at least thirty thousand years" (Flegg 1983, 42).

6. Schmandt-Besserat (1992a) proves Lieberman (1980), who is not an archeologist, factually wrong. Schmandt-Besserat's volume fully documents that plain and complex tokens are both enclosed in envelopes and are therefore part of the same system of accounting. Pictographs follow tokens by 200 years; they do not precede them.

7. In the accounting literature the first mention of Schmandt-Besserat's early archeological research on clay tokens seems to have been by Most, for example, endnote 1 of this second edition (Most 1982, 52) refers to Schmandt-Besserat (1978, 1979). Walgenbach, Dittrich and Hanson (1980, 6) reprinted in their textbook a page from the August 1, 1977, issue of *Time* magazine dealing with Schmandt-Besserat's research. Next, Swanson (1984) published a short paper drawing accounting historians' attention to her research. Its first interpretations and consequences from an accountant's point of view seem to have been that of Mattessich (1987b), followed by Mattessich (1989, 1991b, 1994b).

8. The passage of Schmandt-Besserat that comes closest to hinting at (but not mentioning) "commodity accounts" is the following: "Accounting, on the other hand, involves keeping track of entries and withdrawals of commodities" (Schmandt-Besserat 1992a, 170).

9. The term *account* can be used in the *generic sense* when we speak, for example, of cash accounts in general; or it can be used in the *specific sense* when referring to the cash account of a particular firm or other entity.

10. The exception is the case (also mentioned by Schmandt-Besserat 1992a, 9) in which the envelope, bulla, or tablet does not represent a person but a location such as a specific pasture, shed, or stable. In such cases, the envelopes and the like could be taken

to represent a physical reality, unless the primary purpose is to record a debt claim toward the person responsible for the assets at this location. It is questionable whether, at this time, the legal difference between a debt and the obligation to return *custodial* goods was clearly conceived (compare penultimate section of this chapter).

11. For decades I have tried to show that the crucial event in accounting is not double entry—which is a mere technique—but the *logical structure* behind it (compare Mattessich 1957, 1964a, 1987b). A set–theoretical analysis of this flow or input–output structure in terms of ownership and debt relations is found in Appendix A of Mattessich (1964a, 448–465). In that book, I have demonstrated that this structure need not manifest itself in a twofold entry but may be represented in form of a single-matrix entry or a net-work relation between two points, or a vector, or an algebraic equation, or the like. Now we have evidence that this logical structure was conceived some 10,000 years ago by transferring accounting tokens from one container into another and was further manifested (about 5,000 years ago) also by means of impressing the tokens on the surface of clay envelopes (credit entry) and inserting the same token into this envelope (debit entry).

12. However, the basic idea of such a *tautological control*, though in the nonmonetary sense, is maintained even in a double-entry token system when recording property or debt claims. This is best demonstrated by imagining an ancient scribe who ultimately checks whether all the tokens put into a clay envelope were actually impressed on its outer sur-face. Finding a discrepancy, he knows an error has occurred.

13. Schmandt-Besserat (1992a) confirms this in several places (e.g., pp. 8, 108, 109) by speaking of "accounts" in connection with clay envelopes, stringed bullae, or tablets.

14. Schmandt-Besserat admits that "when tokens were replaced by their images im-pressed on the surface of an envelope or tablet, the resulting signs were already 'more abstract' than the previous clay counters" (Schmandt-Besserat 1992a, 191).

15. I am using the term equity in the *inclusive* sense here, as does Kohler's dictionary (Cooper and Ijiri 1983, 196). The latter defines "equity," first of all, as "any right or claim to assets." That means that an equity is either a property right or a debt claim. By 3200 B.C. or so, and even a long time before, people and institutions held property rights as well as debt claims against other persons or institutions.

16. "The Hindus added to the logical woes of mathematicians by introducing negative numbers to represent debts. In such uses positive numbers represented assets. The first known use was by Brahmagupta about A.D. 628, who merely stated rules for the four op-erations with negative numbers" (Kline 1980, 110).

17. Kline, for example, states that "most mathematicians of the 16th and 17th century did not accept them [negative numerals] as numbers, or if they did, would not accept them as roots of equations" (Kline 1980, 114–115). Though Descartes (1596–1650) accepted them to some extent, as did Leibniz (1646–1760), even if only for formal reasons and without much logical foundation.

18. "China's ancient record keeping techniques reached a stage that could match the developments in other ancient civilizations in the world. Particularly significant was the development of the Ancient World's most sophisticated governmental accounting system during the Shang Dynasty (1600–1000 B.C.)" (Lin 1992, 104–105).

19. An earlier book (*Della mercatura e del mercante perfetto*), also partly dealing with double-entry bookkeeping, was written in 1458 by Benedetto Cotruglio (called "Ragueo" that is, of Ragusa, the present Dubrovnik) but was not published before 1573 (compare Peragallo 1938, 54–55, and Yamey 1994, 43–50).

20. The term *matrix framework* is here understood as a rectangular array of figures. The previous remark must not be misunderstood. It does *not* mean that De Morgan (1846) presented a *matrix algebraic* formulation of accounting as found by later authors—such as Leontief (1951), Mattessich (1957, 1964a), and so on—who, like De Morgan, used the rows as credit sides and the columns as debit sides, while others (e.g., Kohler 1952, Ijiri 1965b) used the rows for debits and the columns for credits.

CHAPTER 3

Social Reality and the
Measurement of Its Phenomena

No moment passes without reality staring into our face; and yet, most accountants of the 1980s were reluctant to ponder issues of reality and its representation. A good deal of present-day accounting research is concerned with ever-increasingly complex statistical techniques, mathematical models, and their surface structures but only marginally with foundational issues. Just as observations are naught without good theories, so are theories naught without sound philosophical foundations.

However, even during this past phase of "accounting positivism,"[1] a few academics have found it worth their while to concern themselves with problems of reality. On the metaphysical level, there is the paper by Tomkins and Groves (1983), which led to a series of responses by Abdel-khalik and Ajinkya (1983), Morgan (1983b), and Willmot (1983). The more recent concern about accounting reality is less of speculative–metaphysical than of methodological, semantical, epistemological, and partly ontological nature. It is dictated by the pressing empirical need to clarify which variables are *purely* conceptual and which have a reality behind them, and what kind of reality. Only empirical variables will be either directly or indirectly *observable* and, hopefully, also measurable. Indirect observability, in turn, leads to the question about what some accountants call "proxies" or "surrogates" and "surrogate relations" (compare Ijiri 1967, 3–13, 27, 121) or what is known in modern science as "indicators" and "indicator hypotheses," respectively (see Bunge 1983a, 1983b, 1985b). Indeed, the concern for observability and its lack or difficulty pervades the contemporary empirical accounting literature, and this may open the door to a new respectability for reality issues in accounting. For example, Patell (1979) has been much concerned with the distinction between *observable* and *unobservable* variables in accounting, and

Dyckman and Morse repeatedly emphasized how difficult it is to find the appropriate observational variables for certain theories of accounting and finance:

Testing strong-form market efficiency is difficult because the existence of private information in the market cannot be directly *observed*. . . . Unfortunately, the market portfolio is not easy to *observe*, which makes the *testing* of CAPM [capital–asset pricing model] difficult if not impossible. . . .The problem in *testing* for market efficiency under this definition [relating market efficiency to the proximity of expected prices to existing prices] is in not being able to *observe* when information is received by all investors. . . . Accounting researchers, unfortunately, cannot directly *observe* individual investor use of information. . . . Once again, however, individual investor welfare cannot be *observed*. (Dyckman and Morse 1986, 7, 81, 83, 89, italics added)

Thus, for the sake of sound empirical research, a clarification of the reality problem and the elimination of inconsistencies have assumed some urgency (for further aspects of the reality issue, see penultimate section of Chapter 11). However, because many accountants pay little attention to the difference between concepts and phenomena, it seems opportune to state at the beginning three simple prerequisites crucial for understanding this chapter:

1. A clear distinction between empirical phenomena and the concepts by means of which accountants represent them.
2. An awareness that some concepts are empirically empty and the need for a keen eye to distinguish those that are not backed by phenomena from those that are.
3. An admission that empirical reality is not confined to physical phenomena but engulfs a hierarchy that includes social, psychological, and other phenomena as well.

IS INCOME A MERE CONCEPT, OR DOES IT HAVE EMPIRICAL REALITY?

The question of whether income, owners' equity, and so forth have empirical reality is crucial for accounting. Indeed, Heath has taken up this question, but emphatically denies any empirical reality to income, stockholders' equity, and other basic accounting notions: "income does not exist in the real world any more than a family with 1.6 children exists in the real world. . . . stockholders' equity is simply a name" (Heath 1987, 2, 4). Heath presents this view in the course of his criticism about the frequent confusion between concepts and reality, and the lack of reality behind those concepts by referring to what Synge (1970) calls the "Pygmalion Syndrome." Heath also offers a series of what he believes to be illustrations of such "confusion" from the area of accounting. A year later, Thornton took issue with some aspects of Heath's publication, asserting that "much of what Heath sees as confusion is metaphor. . . . People confuse concepts with real things and events if they take metaphors literally. . . the cure would be not to confiscate the maps, but to show them how to read the maps more effectively" (Thornton 1988, 1).

Thornton thereby justifies a good deal of usage, well rooted in accounting terminology, to which Heath originally objected. Thus, Thornton assumes a much more conciliatory attitude; and his metaphor of a map in relation to the real landscape seems to indicate that he, too, regards owners' equity and income as being real. However, there is another side to this issue. The core problem of Heath's position is not merely his blind spot toward the important function of metaphors but a much graver one: Heath, in some of his accounting illustrations, believes himself to deal with the dichotomy of concepts versus reality, while he actually is dealing with that of social reality versus physical reality. This confusion must be clarified before one can deal with the complementary measurement problem raised by Sterling: "With rare exceptions accounting numerals do not represent phenomena, *any* phenomena. . . . there are no phenomena that correspond to most of the numerals that appear on financial statements" (Sterling 1988, 4–5).

I shall first demonstrate that the notions of income and owners' equity are not empirically empty concepts and that they and their values, as well as those of assets and debts, have corresponding referents in social reality. These values are observable or documentable and, at least in principle, also measurable (valuation and measurement issues are discussed in the last three sections of this chapter).

SOCIAL REALITY AND EMERGENT PROPERTIES

I agree with Heath and Sterling on two issues: first, that a clear distinction between the real and the conceptual is important; second, that unjustified "reification" does occur in science and philosophy.[2] Although Heath is concerned about the confusion between the real and the conceptual, his (perhaps subconscious) neglect of social reality suggests a physicalist or reductionist attitude. Regrettably, his paper offers no firm criteria for distinguishing the real from the conceptual. General agreement and our five senses are not even in physics reliable reality criteria. Did humankind not take the sun's apparent rotation around the earth as real for millennia? In past centuries (particularly in the nineteenth), did most scholars not deny the reality of atomic (and subatomic) particles?[3] Nowadays, scientists accept even quarks as real though the latter seem to be permanently trapped within the hadrons (protons, neutrons, mesons, and so on) and are (or, at least, were) not expected to be seen. Thus, science has already abandoned the narrow reality criteria of the past century.

I believe that the notion of "emergent property" (illustrated in the next paragraph), highly relevant to such social and legalistic issues as debt and property claims, offers a more plausible criterion for defining different reality levels.[4] The implication that everything can be reduced to physical phenomena must be challenged. Hofstadter, for example, rejects reductionism because it "sees all the world as reducible to the laws of physics, with no room for so-called 'emergent' properties" (Hofstadter 1981, 144). In fact, it is the notion of emergent or holistic properties (see Mattessich 1978a, 29, 31, 54, 233, 320) that is the key for avoiding confusion. These so-called *emergent properties*, although usually taken for granted, lead to a better understanding of total reality. Through their formation, an immense hierarchy of different empirical realities (which make up total reality) is brought about.

This may be best illustrated through what I call the "onion model of reality," which may facilitate a better understanding not only of our notion of reality but also of the nature of conceptual and linguistic representation. We are all aware that such atoms as hydrogen and oxygen or sodium and chloride can combine (in specific proportions) to generate substances like water and table salt respectively. Those newly emerging entities possess properties totally different from their constituents (e.g., the boiling points of hydrogen and oxygen are 20° K and 90° K respectively, while that of water is 373° K).

First of all, one should distinguish between *ultimate reality* (which is not our concern—it is the subject of metaphysics rather than accounting) and the *realities of higher order* (physical–chemical, biological, psychological, and social reality levels).

1. *Physical–chemical reality*: consisting of electrons; quarks; and so on; and, on higher sublevels, atoms; molecules; amino acids; proteins; and so on. Each of these "entities" already possesses emergent properties. For example, although the mass of a hydrogen atom may be equal or approximately equal to the cumulative mass of its electron and proton, most of the other properties of such an atom are very different from those of an individual electron and an individual proton (e.g., as observed in a plasma).

2. *Biological reality*: characterized by the criteria of life and its emergent properties, as empirically evidenced in modern botany and zoology. It would be a serious mistake to confuse the acceptance of emergent biological properties with either *vitalism* or with von Bertalanffy's (1968) *general systems theory*. My opposition to both has been emphasized in Mattessich (1978a, 276–286). The notion of emergent properties—though not always under the same name—can be found in the "scientific realist" philosophy of Bunge (1979, 29–30, 249–251), the "critical realism" of Hartmann (e.g., 1940), and the "hypothetical realism" of Campbell (1966a, 1966b) and Lorenz (1977).

3. *Psychic reality*: characterized by mental and quasi-mental phenomena, such as having preferences, intentions, pleasure, or pain. To ask whether pain is real, for example, seems to invite trouble and controversy. Under the "onion model," this controversy is resolved by regarding pain as real on the psychic level and possibly on subsequent levels but not on the physical level (because the notion of pain is meaningless in physics). Its reality on the biological level depends on the area of overlap between the biological and psychic level (i.e., some life forms possess only very primitive neural reaction mechanisms and protoforms of pain). The most common and, perhaps, gravest error is to confuse the distinction between *the conceptual* and *the real* with that between *the mental* and *the physical*. Such "mental" events as feeling pain, having preferences, and the like are not merely conceptual but possess biological–psychic reality beyond neuronal or mere chemoelectric currents. The conceptual, on the other hand, is inevitably reserved for the *representation* of physical, social, and other realities. Indeed, specific areas of the brain are activated when we "conceptualize" and entirely different ones when we feel pain or form preferences. Thus, the conceptual

representation of reality is only part of our total mental activity and must not be confused with such empirical phenomena as feeling pain or having preferences.

4. *Social reality*: wherever groups of animals or humans generate social properties, which on the higher sublevels become moral, economic, legalistic, and similar properties. The economic and legal relations of ownership claims and debt claims are as empirically real on this level as is an atom on the physical level, or pain and preference from the psychic level onward.[5]

These higher realities *envelop* ultimate reality, like the layers of an onion, so we may justifiably speak of an *onion model of reality*.[6] In accounting, the level of social reality obviously plays a crucial role because almost everything there pivots on ownership and debt relations, their derivatives, and evaluations. The notion that specific emergent properties are real and that reality consists of different levels implicitly underlies all sciences. It assumes particular importance in the social disciplines. Indeed, to regard such emergent properties as consciousness, social bonds, ownership claims, value, and so forth as not being something empirical would reduce all the social sciences, including accounting and business administration, to *formal* sciences (i.e., disciplines without empirical but merely conceptual content, as are logic and mathematics). As this contradicts the premise of any social science, it is unlikely that Heath as well as Sterling would consider themselves to be "physicalists" or "reductionists." Their pronouncements, here quoted, may well be nothing but a consequence of the general neglect of reality research in accounting.

The philosophical attitude assumed in this book is not so much that of naive realism but, rather, corresponds to the "critical realism" of Hartmann (1940), closely related to the "hypothetical realism" of Campbell (1966a, 1966b) and so much enriched by the renowned ethologist and Nobel laureate Konrad Lorenz (1977). This attitude recognizes that our awareness of reality is based on the interdependence of the objective and the subjective, in which the former constantly adjusts the latter step by step. Of course, we see reality through glasses tinted by the utilitarian trend of the evolutionary process. This does not imply that what we "see" is unrelated to such a reality. Kant's notion of *a priori* knowledge (whether analytical or synthetical) must be adapted to such new insights. Although it is *prior* to an individual's experience, it is *acquired by experience* in the evolutionary process of the species and its precursors. Lorenz regards the idealist as concentrating only on the mirror (i.e., the mind) without admitting the reality beyond it, while the naive realist is seen as focusing on the outside but neglecting the mirror as part of reality: "Thus, both are inhibited from seeing that there is an obverse to every mirror. But the obverse does not reflect, and to this extent the mirror is in the same category as the objects that it reflects" (Lorenz 1977; 19). Is not the biological mechanism that enables us to reflect reality just as real as that which is being reflected? The affirmative answer to this question leads to Figure 11.1, where the accountant's conceptual representation is deliberately shown as part of this reality. Thus, conceptual representation—so far juxtaposed to reality—is part of one of its layers, namely, the mental or psychic layer.

DEBT CLAIMS, OWNERSHIP CLAIMS, AND
INCOME AS SOCIAL REALITIES

For simplicity's sake, I shall here deal with not more than two levels: that of "physical reality," which some people have subconsciously in mind when talking about "real phenomena," and "social reality," which is every bit as real as is physical reality. Specific debt and ownership claims (on both sides of the balance sheet) have been among the most important verifiable social realities for more than 5,000 years (see Chapter 2). Without them there would hardly be a need for lawyers and accountants. Try to convince the banker who granted you the mortgage on your home that his debt claim is not real, and he will soon convince you of the contrary by supplying the necessary empirical evidence. Or alternatively, how would you react if someone asserted that the *ownership claim* to your property is not real? Thus, there seems to be reason enough to recommend the acceptance of a reality notion in conformity with everyday life and language.

If an ownership claim is real, then income, as a specific kind of change in this claim (including its value), and as a social and usually legal entitlement, is just as real. Let me offer a down-to-earth illustration: the apple tree in your own or your neighbor's garden, for example, may yield annually a crop of fruit. The *income* from this tree is, contrary to common belief, *not* the crop of apples (not even in the absence of expenses) but, rather, *the property claim on this annual crop*. The apples are merely the momentary physical manifestation of this income. To call the apples the income would be, at best, one of those *metaphorical* expressions to which Thornton (1988) refers. Although an ownership claim is virtually meaningless without an asset behind it, to identify the two is an error all too often made. *The physical reality of those apples is quite independent of the ownership.* Whether those apples belong to you, to your neighbor, or to somebody else, they remain the same apples. Of course, in the business world, this problem is more complicated than in the apple yard. First, there are valuation issues; second, the change of a firm's stockholders' equity does not manifest itself in a single type of tangible commodities but in a variety of assets together with liabilities. Thus, the concrete manifestation of income (i.e., the object of ownership, in contrast to the ownership relation between a person and an owner) no longer needs to be a specific asset (e.g., some apples) but may be any value-equivalent asset. Even then, undistributed earnings are an incremental ownership claim, and the distribution of earnings (whatever concrete manifestation it may assume) is the physical consequence of this social reality. Although in such a situation the nature of income remains the same, the determination (measurement) of this income usually requires monetary or similar evaluation.[7] This leads to our second issue, Sterling's (1988) problem, to be addressed in the following sections.

Heath's problem (of denying the reality of a "stockholder's equity," which undoubtedly is one kind of ownership claim) seems to be triggered partly by equating an asset or equity with the asset's value or the equity's value, respectively, but even more so by the custom to use the same word for the concept as well as the reality behind it (i.e., the referent). That Heath (1987) would fall prey to this confusion is surprising because he refers to Synge (1970), who, on his part, quite successfully disentangles those very issues. Only in relatively rare cases are we used to assigning a designation to a concept different from the name of its referent. This is done in philosophy where usually not only two but *three* different levels of scientific discourse are distinguished (see Figure 3.1).[8] It is crucial to realize that the term *stockholders' equity* refers to both a concept—namely, the idea or image in your mind—but also to the actual ownership claim, which is the real thing. Thus, we are actually dealing with three levels or meanings (the conceptual, the linguistic, and the reality beyond the first two levels), which are best illustrated—in the case of *income*, for example—by the following three sentences:

1. Income as a pure concept: "*Income* is one of the basic notions of accounting."

2. Income as a name (term): "*Income* has six letters."

3. Income as a social reality: "The growing *income* of the Dow Chemical Co. in 1987 was reflected partly in an increasing dividend, partly in an increase of its common stock price."

Figure 3.1
Relations between Three Levels of Scientific Discourse: Conceptual, Linguistic, and (the Rest of) Reality

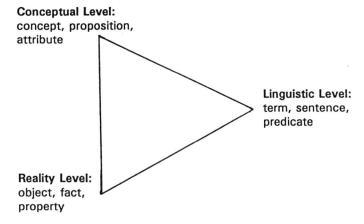

Conceptual Level:
concept, proposition, attribute

Linguistic Level:
term, sentence, predicate

Reality Level:
object, fact, property

Explanation: a *proposition* (on the conceptual level may correspond to a *sentence* (on the linguistic level) and a *fact* or *potential fact* (on the reality level). Similar correspondences hold for other expressions (*concepts, terms, objects*; or *attributes, predicates, properties*). By employing different terms at each level, one can avoid the potential for confusion of everyday speech.

It is important, first, to keep these three meanings clearly apart, in particular, when using one and the same word for the corresponding elements; and second, to realize which concepts and names have a counterpart in reality and which do not. Such purely mathematical and logical concepts as *prime number* as well as the sentential connectives *and, or, not,* for example, have no empirical referents (although they help to describe structures inherent in empirical objects or events). As for Heath's (1987, 2) example of "a family with 1.6 children," it obviously has no empirical referent, since to have 1.6 children (in the normal sense of this phrase) is a biological impossibility. This cannot be compared (as Heath tries to do) with a firm having an income or increase in ownership claim (e.g., obligations toward its shareholders) of, let us say, one million dollars. This additional claim (if it is genuine) is a social reality representable by accounting concepts.

A special case, for example, is the astronomical concept called *Ursa Major,* popularly known as the stellar constellation of the Big Dipper. This is a mere concept, though it is "connected" with the reality of several stars, because as a *constellation* it is a pure fiction of the mind or *pseudo-real notion.* This example may be of particular interest to accountants because in our discipline, such *pure* concepts, in spite of some realities looming in the background, do occur: Ideas such as *working capital* or *price–earnings ratio,* for example, seem to be such pseudo-real notions because, as in the case of the Big Dipper, a reality (e.g., various assets and liabilities, income, values, and so on) is connected to them—although those concepts themselves are fictions—and are neither rooted in social life in the same fundamental way as are *ownership, income,* and *value,* nor can they be traced to such basic biological realities as *possessive and territorial instincts, periodic food intake,* and the *preference* for one type of food or environment over another.[9] By now, it will be clear that a specific *income* and *stockholders' equity* does not belong to the set of empirically empty concepts, though being concepts, the social reality of an ownership claim (backed either by convention, law, or brute force) stands behind both of them.[10]

Furthermore, the reader may be tempted to identify the distinction between concepts versus real objects (things, events, properties, and the like) with the neopositivists' distinction between theoretical versus observational variables. Although the comparison of those two dichotomies offers many similarities, an identification is inadvisable. Not only does this positivistic dichotomy fail to stand up to scrutiny, it even seems to have been one of the major reasons why neopositivism (as an epistemic system) crumbled (compare Suppe 1974, 62–118 and Bunge 1974a, 160–166). In recent years, attempts have been made to replace the positivistic observational–theoretical dichotomy by more appropriate schemes, for example, by Sneed (1971) who introduced a context-dependent (instead of the neopositivists' *absolute*) dichotomy—namely, that between theoretical versus nontheoretical variables—and Mattessich's (1990) proposal of an equally context-dependent *double dichotomy* of (1) theoretical versus nontheoretical variables on the conceptual side, and (2) nonobservational versus observational objects on the reality side (for details, see Figure 7.1).

DO ACCOUNTANTS MEASURE REAL PHENOMENA?

The ultimate problem in this controversy is not merely the identification of the reality behind ownership or income but the complementary issue of evaluating both of them as well as their corresponding assets. It is "complementary" because here another reality question arises: In determining accounting values (e.g., cost value or exchange values), do we measure real phenomena? Although this question is partly answered by showing that there is a physical reality behind tangible assets and a social reality behind debts, owners' equity, and income, one also must demonstrate that the *value* of those realities has reality status (though not necessarily an independent one). Furthermore, it requires clarification of the notions of measure and measurement in the social sciences, particularly in accounting. At this stage, we begin to approach the problems raised by Sterling (1988), and it might be appropriate to remind the reader of his major argument as well as his methodology.

Sterling (1988) started with some behavioral tests (questionnaires) he submitted to twenty-eight third-year accounting students and thirty-two third-year physics students "to discover whether physicists differ from accountants in regard to their ability to recognize the correspondence of numerals to phenomena." (See Sterling 1989, 82–93, for different aspects of the same empirical study.) He then claims that "it is fairly easy to demonstrate that there are no phenomena that correspond to most of the numerals that appear on financial statements" (Sterling 1988, 5). It is worth noting that he also emphasizes the difference between numerals (concepts) and the reality to be represented by them. Sterling also admits that rubber yardsticks are no less employed in the natural sciences as in economics and accounting. This hints at the fact that changes in the cost or price of material because of other economic fluctuations parallels the changes in volume of material (e.g., mineral oil) brought about by temperature fluctuations. He offers a concrete inventory example (with fluctuating stocks and temperatures) in which the dollar value of an oil tank is compared to its volume in barrels (but also introducing its weight in tons), determining the cost and the volume of oil shipped under such different flow assumptions as FIFO (first in, first out), LIFO (last in, first out), and average. Such pragmatic assumptions are typical for an applied science such as accounting and cannot have an equivalent in a pure science like physics. However, they do have a correspondence in engineering (an applied science based on physics) where, for example, safety factors are assumed on the basis of more or less arbitrary conventions and "common" experience.

Sterling supports his claims by the answers to his questionnaire, primarily by the divergence of the answers he received from the physics students, compared to those from the accounting students. Though this approach is quite original, it does not offer sufficient support to Sterling's claims. Without going into the details of Sterling's example, his questionnaire measures mainly how knowledgeable those two student groups were, in particular, as to their knowledge in thermodynamics rather than a fundamentally different approach to thinking. Although

Sterling pointed out to them that volumes vary with temperatures, a physics student will make the connection much easier that the volume of so many tons of oil purchased on a cold January day has probably somewhat expanded by March so that, at this time, the storage tank will yield a few more barrels of oil than previously; and on a hot June day, the same weight of oil might (because of further expansion) yield an even larger number of barrels. It is no wonder that the majority of the physics students gave the right answer (particularly to one of the questions) than did the "thermodynamically innocent" accountants. Moreover, Sterling leaves no doubt about the ultimate purpose of his paper:

Although the initial purpose is to discover whether physicists differ from accountants in regard to their ability to recognize the correspondence of numerals to phenomena, the ultimate purpose is to try to explain that accounting numerals are *neither* true nor false because there are no phenomena to examine to determine whether there is or is not a correspondence. (Sterling 1988, 5)

The task of this investigation is not to point out any (if there is any) technical weakness of Sterling's approach but its inappropriateness to what he considers the "ultimate purpose" of his paper in the above-cited quotation. It seems to be secondary whether students, or even some accomplished accountants, fail to realize the referents behind present-day accounting figures. For us, the crucial questions behind Sterling's challenge are the following:

1. *Do empirical phenomena or referents to accounting concepts exist and, if so, what is their reality status?* This has been answered in the preceding sections not only for tangible assets but also for owner's equity, income, and related notions as well as their values.

2. *To what extent is it possible to measure the value of those empirical referents, and which cost-efficient alternatives are available for such measurement?* In spite of the vast accounting and economic literature on valuation, Sterling's objections indicate that some basic issues of accounting measurement are still obscure and must be illuminated. I shall attempt to clarify this point in the remaining parts of this chapter.

Such questions cannot be answered by student's questionnaires, however ingeniously or flawlessly they might be designed. Only when we grasp the "substance" or reality behind our accounting numerals can we fully appreciate what accounting measures can do for us and what they cannot do. Others, such as Brown (1988) and Griffiths (1986), seem to confirm this: "Griffiths suggests that an understanding of the substance behind the accounting numbers can lead to a more meaningful deciphering of management maneuverings. I concur completely" (Brown 1988, 539). The title of Arthur Andersen's (1970) collection of *personal* papers, *Behind the Figures*, is even more suggestive in reminding us of the reality behind the representation.

Everything real can be recognized only through its properties. An important question is, are values the properties of tangible assets as well as debt and ownership claims, or of something else? Values are derived from individual preferences, which are not so much properties of things as of specific situations (composed of persons, things, and a set of circumstances). Exchange values (i.e., past and present market values), as used in accounting, are the result of a bargaining process in which two factors become the ultimate constituents: (1) *subjective preferences*, which constitute boundary conditions, and (2) the *bargaining positions* of at least two persons (endowments of wealth, elasticities of demand and supply functions, and the like). In other words, out of such a specific economic situation emerges a new property or phenomenon, shortly called "exchange value." This value is a concept behind which stands a social reality as soon as one transgresses from the psychic level of preferences (a psychic reality) into the economic arena of money and potential exchange.

From all this follows that, quite independently of whether something is a physical asset or social claim, the *exchange values* of both have "merely" social but not physical reality status. Without breaking through the misconception that intangible items must be empirically empty concepts, we are bound to have difficulty in accepting the determination of accounting and economic values as an estimation or measurement of real properties. I suspect that the subconscious, or even unconscious, focus on physical reality—or the reduction to it—is the ultimate reason for Heath's view and that of other accountants. In Sterling's case, it may be because of his concentration on the positive traits of a pure science and the mere lip service to the normative traits of accounting as an applied discipline.

For a satisfactory conceptualization and measurement of value in the economic sciences, it may be almost as complex as that of time in the physical sciences. Let us not forget the tortuous path the conceptualization and measurement of time has taken: From Saint Augustine, who asked, "What then is time? Provided that no one asks me, I know. If I want to explain it to an inquirer, I do not know. . . . But who can measure the past which does not now exist or the future which does not yet exist, unless perhaps someone dares to assert that he can measure what has no existence? At the moment when time is passing, it can be perceived and measured. But when it has past and is not present, it cannot be" (Saint Augustine 1991, 230, 233), to Einstein's insight (that time alone, that is, without its space coordinates, cannot be measured in any absolute way), it took more than one and a half millennia. Similarly, with continuing research, further insights into the phenomenon of value can be expected.

THE COST–BENEFIT CRITERION
OF ACCOUNTING VALUATION

Another aspect related to a "physicalist" undercurrent is the expectation that measurement in the social sciences should be direct (i.e., not derived from secondary measures by calculations) or should approach the rigor of measurement and testing encountered in the natural sciences.

The difference, in brief, is that accountants are trained to calculate whereas physicists are trained to observe. Calculations are the end product of accounting whereas in physics

calculations are an intermediate product, the numerical output of which must be compared
to observations. Accountants often refer to methods of calculations as "conventions" and
they "test" them by examining documents and recalculating: they seldom concern themselves with whether the calculated numerals represent anything or not. Physicists refer to
methods of calculation as hypotheses and they "test" them by comparing the calculated
numerals to direct observations: they almost always concern themselves with whether the
numerals represent something and are disdainful of numerals that do not represent anything. (Sterling 1988, 8–9)

   While I agree with the first sentence of this quotation, I disagree with the spirit
of the rest. All too many measures in the physical sciences are indirect and thus
rely not only on observations but on subsequent calculations which then constitute the end product. Even if accounting students are not being trained to observe,
the practitioners nevertheless base their figures ultimately on observations and
inferences from them (e.g., inventory taking, random tests). Most balance sheet
items can be observed either directly, if physical reality is involved (i.e., the quantity of inventory, machinery, buildings, and so on), or indirectly, if social reality
is involved (e.g., debt and ownership contracts as well as exchange values). The
crucial point is that in accounting most social realities are observable only by
looking at documents, either the original ones (contracts, original market quotations, and the like) or derived ones (copies, secondary documents, price quotations in newspapers, and the like). The very nature of these items is *contractual*
or based on other manifestations of preferences and similar social phenomena.
Because aggregations and allocations of values are further necessities of accounting, indirect measurement via calculations often puts great distance between an
accounting figure and the document or "observation" it is based on. This distance
is hardly greater than that between the measurement result of subnuclear properties and the observations of the pertinent particles on a photograph or television
screen from a bubble chamber or, to mention an example from astronomy, the
measurement result of our distance from a specific quasar (quasi-stellar radio source)
and its observations through a radio telescope, spectral red shifts, and so on.[11]

   Among the social sciences, psychology is particularly prominent in dealing
with measurement problems; Buros (1978), for example, lists more than 1,000
pertinent tests or measurement procedures. Stevens (1946) regards measurement
"as the assignment of numerals to objects or events according to rules"; this notion too arose in psychology and has become prominent in all social sciences including accounting (compare Mattessich 1964a, 57–74). Some experts reject such
a definition for accounting valuation. This is merely a semantical issue, and I
would have no objection to talking about value "determination" or "assignment"
instead of value "measurement."

   Besides, most of accounting "measurement" is not for scientific but for practical business needs. Here the expected long-run benefit must exceed the corresponding cost. This *cost–benefit criterion*, as applied not *in* accounting but *to*
accounting, is crucial for a deeper understanding of traditional accounting valuation. I very much sympathize with Sterling's dissatisfaction of the acquisition cost

method from a scientific point of view; but in an applied discipline such as accounting, it is ultimately the user, or the users' consensus, that decides which method is considered to be cost-effective—even at the risk that it may not be cost-efficient at a scientific level. This is not to suggest that academics should stop constructing better accounting and valuation models; it is merely to remind them that the decision of whether to use those models must be determined by a consensus of the major users of these tools. If this consensus is rigged in favor of a certain social group, an academic solution cannot be imposed, but a political solution must be sought. The duty of the scholar is *to prepare the best possible models for various purposes and information needs, to put them at the disposal of the practitioners, and to educate the latter as to their relevance.* Whether practice will accept academic advice and use those models is a pragmatic and often political matter. Sterling is quite explicit that his objection refers not only to the acquisition cost method but also to what he conceives to be the lack of empirical referents for accounting valuation in general:

Evidently because of my reputation for endorsing current values, many take the assertion "accounting numerals have no empirical referents" to refer exclusively to the historical cost versus current value debate, and then they assess the assertion on the basis of their convictions about that debate rather than assessing it on the basis of evidence and argument about the existence of and need for empirical referents. (Sterling 1988, 5)

CONCLUSION

The failure to distinguish clearly between physical versus social reality and, even more so, between concepts versus social reality is by no means limited to Heath and possibly Sterling. There is evidence that accountants in general seem to be confused about the proper distinctions between those dichotomies. Skinner, for example, calls "'income' an artificial construct—a mere matter of definition. Moreover, there is no single definition. The word means different things to different people" (1982, 126). This certainly sounds plausible; but if Skinner means by "an artificial construct" a concept that has no reality behind it, he is mistaken. First of all, every concept—even a non-empty one—is manmade, hence artificial. More important, the fact that there are many definitions of income—none of them absolute—is a problem of representation, interpretation, classification, and measurement, but not one of reality. Capital, as a claim on assets, changes constantly in most firms, even without consideration of dividends and new investments. If such a claim on assets is a social reality, so is its change in which way we ever may represent, partition, or evaluate it. Whether we use the noninclusive or the all-inclusive income definition, we do nothing but partition this reality in different ways, maybe according to different needs. This manipulation is the prerogative of every representation, be it scientific or for everyday use.

Another particularly striking example is the notion of *capital lease.* Textbooks state that "for accounting purposes this type of lease is viewed as a *sale* of the leased property by the lessor and a *purchase* of it by the lessee" (Welsch et al.

1987, 521). Even a dictionary concurs that "the lessor treats the lease as a sale of the asset in return for a series of future revenue payments" (Cooper and Ijiri 1983, 85). This makes it appear that the value of a *physical reality* (e.g., a photocopier) is recorded on the asset side of the lessee's balance sheet, while actually (e.g., from a legal point of view) it is the value of a *social reality* (e.g., the property claim on the *long-term lease* on this photocopier, but financed by debt capital), which is capitalized. Welsch, Short, and Chesley show their uneasiness about this by stating that "such practice provides a classic illustration of a victory of 'substance' over 'form' because a lease is a lease in form, not a purchase" (Welsch et al. 1987, 541). The very fact that they speak of substance versus form suggests that they mean physical reality versus conceptual representation (instead of social reality, as it would be proper to say).

Some readers may ask, "So what? Is all this not pedantry? Does it make any difference whether we call something social reality instead of regarding it a pure concept?" My reply is that the *end* of any science is the cognition of *reality* and its *means* is the *conceptual representation* and approximation of those very structures. If we are unable, or worse, if we do not care to distinguish one from the other, our endeavors become an empty pretense. Why is representation so important? It is the most important source of information and knowledge. Representation, in particular the conceptual kind, informs us about the nature and structure of segments of reality (for further details, see Chapters 5, 7, and 11, especially Figures 7.1 and 11.1).

I have little quarrel with Heath's complaint about some terminological uses or abuses mentioned in his paper. Most of them are taken care of by Thornton's (1988) response and are more or less legitimate metaphors. We should not identify metaphor with theory. A metaphor exploits structural similarities (as Thornton correctly points out), but one of the most creative functions of a metaphor is to play on structural *differences* and *ambiguities* (e.g., in literature and the arts). In a scientific theory, however, the emphasis must be on attaining the clearest and broadest structural description of the real object or event (as far as possible under given circumstances). Because this is much more difficult to attain through words—many of which are loaded with metaphors—than with mathematics, the preference of science for the latter finds a quite natural explanation.

There is another important function that technological metaphors have fulfilled for centuries in science and to which Jonathan Miller (1982, 187–208) referred in his renowned book and television series. There he discusses, for example, the persuasive analogy between the heart and a pump—an analogy which William Harvey (1578–1657) induced to his crucial discovery of blood circulation. In our time, the *information analogues* encountered in biology, neurology, linguistics, computer science, and so on, are examples of this stimulating function of metaphors—indeed, even the "reality model" in this chapter was initiated in this way as the term *onion model* vividly suggests.

In some of Heath's examples, the roundabout way via metaphors may not even be necessary. Heath, for example, says, "When a corporation pays a dividend, it distributes cash (or other assets), not earnings or income. . . . Unfortunately, however, reification of stockholders' equity and the accounts within that section of the balance sheet is common in accounting textbooks" (Heath 1987, 4). It *is* common because behind all those items of this section stand real things; and these are not tangible assets but social realities like income, equities, and values. An ownership claim certainly can be "distributed" among persons. Shares of stocks are a striking example of such a "distribution" in the true sense of the word. Some experts of finance regard the paying of dividends as "equivalent" to purchasing stocks from shareholders; seeing it this way, the dividends' cash (on the asset side) may correspond to the distribution of income (on the equity side). Instead of saying "income is distributed in form of cash," it may be more accurate to say "income (as an additional ownership claim) is *settled* in the form of cash." The metaphoric relation between "distributed" (as an equity) and "settled" (through its corresponding asset), however, is minimal; and many accountants might not bother about it.

All this illustrates that the papers by Heath (1987) as well as Sterling (1988, 1989) fulfilled important functions. They made some accountants, such as Thornton (1988), ponder the significance of metaphors in our literature, and others to search for the reality behind such pivotal accounting concepts as income, owners' equity, and so forth. Heath, somewhat desperately, closes his essay with the following words: "I wish I had some sort of elixir I could prescribe that would stamp out the Pygmalion Syndrome, but in spite of all the research now going on in accounting, I see nothing of that type even in the distant future, much less on the horizon" (Heath 1987, 8). Is such pessimism justified? First, no "elixir" is necessary because metaphors, emergent properties, and the onion model of reality are much better remedies. Without those notions, a good deal of reality may slip through our fingers unnoticed. Thus, the onion model is not merely an alternative to the physicalist trend but offers a much better fit to the reality of human language and actions. In this view of reality, in contrast to that of previously mentioned interpretations, *the words do not belie the deeds.* Human beings in their everyday dealings do not behave as though only physical objects were ultimately real. The daily actions of owning things and claims—of entering into lending and debt relations, of having preferences, expressing values, and acting upon them in such socioeconomic contexts as markets—requires the recognition that such events, relations, and properties are real. Therefore, social realities do exist; and for those who still have doubts, I can only paraphrase Shakespeare that "there are more things *real* in heaven and earth, Horatio, than are dreamt of in your philosophy," with "Horatio" becoming a free variable or, more fittingly expressed, a concept behind which there is the physical as well as social reality of more than one person.

NOTES

This chapter is primarily composed from the following two papers: "Social Reality and the Measurement of Its Phenomena" (Mattessich 1991d) and "Social versus Physical Reality in Accounting, and the Measurement of Its Phenomena" (Mattessich 1991e), as well as some new material.

1. Although "accounting positivism" is a somewhat broader notion than "positive accounting theory," the acclaimed dissociation of this theory from positivism (see Watts and Zimmerman 1986, 8) holds only partly. A major tenet of positivism, the exclusion of normative premises from theories, still seems to manifest itself in Watts's and Zimmerman's theory.

2. One is reminded of Plato's (1963, 747–748, 1589–1590) view that concrete objects, such as a particular apple or a specific triangle, are mere shadows of the only true reality which is found in the abstract and generalized *ideas* of apple, triangle, and so on. Thus, Plato not only reified concepts, but simultaneously relegated concrete objects to the realm of pseudo reality—a criticism already raised by Aristotle in his theory of form. Today, few empirical scientists would be prepared to defend the radical Platonic point of view, which contradicts the Aristotelian as well as the modern *realist* belief in the existence of a reality independent of, but representable through, concepts.

3. "Physicists have a strong positivist streak which is manifested by their never introducing any concept into physics unless it can be empirically verified in a direct way. Ernst Mach, an influential physicist at the turn of the century, never accepted atoms because he never saw one. Eventually physicists devised direct tests for the existence of atoms which previously were just convenient fictions for describing the behavior of gases" (Pagels 1983, 203).

In another book, Pagels describes how Eddington (the renowned astrophysicist) suggested to Rutherford (the no-less-renowned experimentalist) that atoms and electrons might be *mere concepts*. Upon this, "Rutherford leaped up from the table as if the woman he loved had been insulted. Taking Eddington to task, he said that atoms were not just concepts; he met them every day in the laboratory and they were his friends" (Pagels 1986, 211). In a similar vein, I would say that income and owners' equity are important friends of mine because, without them, I would have no ownership claim on the money I withdraw from the bank for our daily needs and would need to borrow this money until I am bankrupt.

As for physics, the invention of the *scanning tunnelling microscope* (early 1980s) enabled researchers to "see" atoms, and there can no longer be a dispute whether they are real.

4. For further details on "emergent properties" (also called "holistic properties") see Mattessich (1978a, 29, 31, 54, 233, 320). Furthermore, one should be aware that "empirical confirmation" refers to more than our five senses; it includes mental experiences as well (after all, the term *empirical* comes from "experience"; see Bunge [1983a, 74–75] who distinguishes between *empirical* knowledge and *factual* knowledge, contrary to their usual combination under one heading).

5. "In factual science something can be inferred to exist if it holds certain connections (not just relations) to something else whose existence has already been established or at least assumed" (Bunge 1977, 160).

The *connection* between a person and a property in case of a property claim (or between two persons, in case of a debt claim) is much more than a mathematical–logical relation. It is based on sociobiological facts rooted in territorial and possessive instincts, which in most human societies are sanctioned by legal or quasi-legal institutions.

6. The most prominent philosopher expounding the notion that reality consists of different layers is Nicolai Hartmann (1940). The Nobel laureate Konrad Lorenz also embraces Hartmann's theory and rightly asserts that

Hartmann's philosophy has been rejected as being a "pseudo-metaphysical construct", but this is completely wrong. It is not built on deductive speculation but on empirical evidence, and takes full account of the multifarious phenomena in the world without breaking it into a mass of heterogenous parts. (Lorenz 1977, 38)

Nowhere did I encounter the conception of theses layers as enveloping one after the other, yet I believe it is just the idea of onion-like layers that conveys this evolutionary sequence (in which every higher layer is all-around dependent on preceding ones) more completely than any other.

7. Hicks's (1946) renowned notion of income (for his definition, see Chapter 6) not only brings out this need for valuation but also the "well-offness" aspect that implies the social entitlement (e.g., the ownership claim) on this income.

8. Elsewhere I pointed out that "the Stoics were the first to express clearly the difference and relation between three fundamental notions of (1) the *sign* (sound, written symbol, etc.), (2) the *conceptual idea* ("lekton," meaning) communicated by sign, and (3) the actual *object* or *event* behind the concept" (Mattessich 1978a, 90). Even a physicist like Synge, who coined the term *Pygmalion Syndrome*, admits this: "You might argue that understanding concepts is merely a matter of understanding what words mean. But that, I think, would be putting the cart before the horse, for the concept lies deeper than the word (or words) you use to refer to it" (Synge 1970, 13).

9. Another example of such a fictitious or quasi-real notion seems to be the following entry 1 (or "accounting transaction") of entity E_1:

	Debit	Credit
1. Receivables (of entity E_1)	$1,000	
Inventory (of entity E_1)		$1,000

Although this entry appears to represent the "conversion" of something physical (inventory) into some social reality (accounts receivable), a closer analysis reveals that such a conversion is only imaginary and actually impossible. The entry is rather derived from the following two exchanges or *real* economic transactions (entries 2 and 3, a physical and a social one) between two different entities, E_1 and E_2 (though the entries of the latter are not shown in item 1):

	Debit	Credit
2. Inventory of entity E_2	$1,000	
Inventory of entity E_1		$1,000
3. Receivables of entity E_1	$1,000	
Payables of entity E_2		$1,000

In other words, the accounting transaction (entry 1) is merely a *shorthand* for combining in one entity two *real* economic transactions concerning two entities (compare the proof offered in Appendix to Chapter 5). Not all accounting transactions are fictitious. Some have empirical referents and are simultaneously economic transactions (in the above sense), for example, the following entry 4:

	Debit	Credit
4. Work in process (of entity E_1)	$2,000	
Raw material (of entity E_1)		$2,000

This not only is a legitimate accounting event but also represents a *real* (economic) transfer of raw material from the storeroom into the working process.

10. Thus, Heath (1987), who invokes Synge, is refuted by his own role model: "I have invented the name *Pygmalion syndrome* for that disease of the mind which blurs the distinction between R-world (reality) and M-worlds (model worlds or conceptual representation)" (Synge 1970, 8).

Thus, it seems that Heath himself fell prey to the Pygmalion Syndrome or, more precisely, to a *reverse* Pygmalion Syndrome; because, in contrast to the legendary Greek sculptor Pygmalion—who fell in love with his own art work and thus may have confused a *physical representation* with the real girl he tried to represent—Heath mistook the social reality of stockholders' equity for an empty *conceptual representation*. The purpose of this paper is by no means to discredit such reputed scholars as Heath and Sterling (who, meanwhile, may well have changed their views on this particular matter). On the contrary, it is to show that the neglect of reality issues (and other methodological and philosophic foundational research) during the past decades has left some of the most basic accounting issues in darkness.

11. For example, when P. A. Millikan, in 1919, measured the mass of the hydrogen atom for the first time, he could do it only in an indirect way involving a series of calculations. Something similar holds for the measurement of even smaller entities, and it is no coincidence if Davies points out that "the weight of a nucleus is in the region of 10^{-25} kg, which is an inconveniently small quantity" (Davies 1979, 91). Thus, the weight and mass of such a nucleus are measured *indirectly* by way of its electric charge (in electron volts [Ev]) and the end product results from calculations.

Finally, the distance measurement (or estimation) of galaxies and quasars (occasionally more than 10 billion light years away) can be done only indirectly (via Doppler's principle and the chemistry of spectral red shifts, Hubble's law, and many calculations).

CHAPTER 4

Foundational and Conceptual Issues

THE ACADEMIZATION OF ACCOUNTING

The academization of accounting began more than 100 years ago. Léautey and Guilbault's (1885) book, Schär's *Versuch einer wissenschaftlichen Behandlung der Buchhaltung* (1890) and the monumental three-volume *La Ragioneria* by Fabio Besta (1891), as well as Dicksee (1892) in the area of auditing, are the best-known examples of those early explorations. These efforts gained acceleration in the first half of the twentieth century and produced many renowned works. The best known among them are those by Sprague (1907), Gomberg (1908, 1927), Hatfield (1909), Schmalenbach (1919a), Schmidt ([1921] 1953), Paton (1922), Dumarchey (1925), Rieger (1928), Zappa (1927, 1937), Canning (1929), and Paton and Littleton (1940), to name only a few of them in temporal order. This first phase was partly concerned with ethical questions. The main focus, however, was on definitional and classificational problems that pivoted on problems of valuation, allocation, and the question whether the balance sheet or the income statement has priority. Although the methodology was predominantly descriptive–pragmatic, some analytical aspects (e.g., in Schmidt's research) began to emerge.[1]

The truly "revolutionary" efforts of making an analytical and empirically testable science out of accounting began in the late 1950s and flourished in the 1960s. It was during this time that four major contributions were made:

1. Systematic application of modern *analytical methods* to accounting.
2. Application of computers and *computer simulation* to accounting.

3. The analysis and controversy around price-level adjustment and *valuation* issues. This continued Schmidt's ([1921] 1953) work but ultimately led to the *conditional–normative* question whether different information objectives may not need different valuation and other accounting models.

4. The application of *hypothesis testing* and related statistical–financial techniques and *empirical methods,* including applications of behavioral–empirical and organizational–sociological research to accounting.

Thus, in the second half of the twentieth century, academic accounting has experienced a fundamental transformation: A relatively loose and informal approach has been replaced by more rigorous analytical as well as empirical methods. A change in spirit and the application of techniques as well as new insights borrowed from other disciplines were the main forces behind this trend that began in the late 1950s. It aimed at clarification, purification, and sophistication but has still to exhaust its potential. The major thrust of this transformation may concisely be characterized by the following five items:

1. Formulation and utilization of well-defined terms and empirically meaningful concepts versus employment of vaguely described expressions and nonoperational notions.

2. Adaption of general scientific tools and methods from mathematics and statistics, finance and economics, computer science, the behavioral sciences, and even philosophy to accounting and auditing problems.

3. Occasional orientation toward specific accounting and management information models for specific objectives versus dogmatic acceptance of a single overall purpose.

4. Introduction of statistical and other empirical testing procedures to evaluate the acceptability, relevance, reliability, accuracy, efficiency, timeliness, or general usefulness of theories, models, or hypotheses of accounting.

5. Sporadic, though rarely successful, attempts to integrate specific accounting areas into a coherent entity (e.g., the FASB's creation of a conceptual framework as well as its supplementary accounting for price-level adjustment) versus collecting loosely connected conventions, dogmas, rules, and isolated particularized models.

From time to time, the need arises to look at past research activity from the bird's perspective with the aim of an overall picture. Such surveys are offered in a series of theory texts (Belkaoui 1985, Henderson and Peirson 1983, Hendriksen 1982, Hendriksen and van Breda 1991, Kam 1990, Most 1982, Wolk et al. 1992) as well as several anthologies (e.g., Devine 1985; Frecka 1989b; Mattessich 1984, 1991a). The following discussion sketches in a few strokes major trends that dominated academic accounting after World War II. Many of those endeavors followed fashions, some of which found only temporary response or continued to persist in certain specific niches despite occasional setbacks (e.g, the axiomatic approach). Others dominated accounting for longer periods before receding into the background, yet often without losing their future importance (e.g., current-value accounting). Most of those efforts are still experimental, and few brought

forth definitive solutions. The literature cited in this chapter is often limited to the
pioneering efforts in each particular area as manifested during the second half of
the twentieth century. This transition period I regard as the adolescence of accounting. It is marked by experimentation, restlessness, a bent for extremes, and
what seems to be a continuing state of crisis. It also connects the childhood years
of our discipline (i.e., the first half of the twentieth century) with the adult period
still to be expected.

Such remarks are not intended to diminish regard for the contributions of accountancy before World War II or the period after it. There can be little doubt that
the first half of the twentieth century created the very basis of most subsequent
accounting developments. Despite the more "scientific approach" in the second
half, many problems remained unresolved. The existence and persistence of value
judgments in our discipline, for example, raise serious questions still to be addressed. It is for this reason that I will repeatedly return to the need for a conditional–normative approach, which takes care of value judgments and connects
them to the appropriate means.

It would be extravagant to regard academic accounting as a pure or cognitive
science, but neither medicine nor meteorology nor engineering are pure sciences.
They are not concerned with finding scientific laws but with applying them and
with serving specific practical purposes in a fairly pragmatic fashion. These disciplines are generally addressed as applied sciences. They operate with such scientific concepts as hypotheses, models, theories, systems, and diagnoses and
endeavor to test them systematically; yet they can serve practical goals. In accounting also, such tests should be directed at least as much toward practical as
theoretical ends. Applied sciences cannot be concerned with the disclosure of
"truth" without taking "usefulness" into consideration.[2] OR and MIS seem to be
more readily accepting the label of applied sciences and, in this regard, might well
serve as models for accounting. The ultimate purpose of accounting is to provide
managerial and related information systems that are satisfactory (or quasi-optimal)
for specific needs. That this should be done by finding means–end relations (i.e.,
developing an *instrumental theory*) and their testing procedures hardly appears
to be an unreasonable quest.

DUALITY PRINCIPLES AND THE
PRINCIPLE OF CONSERVATION

Physical versus Social Duality

To illustrate the conceptual clarification required, let me begin with one of the
most fundamental notions of accounting—the duality aspect (see also Chapter 5
and its Appendix). This concept, which has fascinated scholars and lay persons
for centuries, is here re-examined with the help of insights gained from prehistoric token accounting. As hinted at in Chapter 2, accounting duality is not the result but the cause of double entry. This duality can be reflected in a single matrix

entry just as well as by a vector, a flow diagram, an equation, and some other means. Such insight has stirred the minds of accountants from time to time, particularly in the 1960s, but is pretty much taken for granted today. Occasionally, one has the impression that the duality aspect of accounting is again identified with double entry and thus regarded by some academics as a mere technicality, irrelevant to accounting in general. As some might suppose, such a view is not brought about by the proposal for triple-entry bookkeeping (Ijiri 1982, 1989), which was born of the same analytical spirit as double entry and which is an ingenious extension of the latter. To regard the duality aspect as something of secondary importance, or even as an irrelevancy, is brought about by recent attempts of rejuvenating accountancy from the outside (i.e., imposing aspects of economics, finance, the behavioral and computer sciences, and so on) rather than from the inside, as Ijiri (e.g., 1989) and others have done. What is the meaning of the *duality principles* for accounting? Their significance is summarized in the following four items:

1. There exist three different kinds of accounting dualities that must be clearly distinguished (as already hinted at in Chapter 2). The first arises out of a physical transfer, that is *the output of a commodity from one place, and its input to another*. This duality is manifested not only in an economic transaction (as an empirical event) but also in its conceptual representation, be it in the token transfer from one clay envelope to another in ancient Mesopotamia or in a twentieth-century computerized spreadsheet entry, connecting the debit and credit sides of two asset accounts.

The second type of duality arises from the fact that an asset "belongs" to a person and thus corresponds with some owner's equity (or part of it). The third kind has its root in the debt relation between two persons (natural or juridical). While the first type (involving the mere transfer of goods) possesses undoubtedly a manifestation in physical reality in the broadest sense (i.e., goods and services are physical, and so is their transfer), this does not hold for the second and third type. Both of these belong to the reality of *social* relations. Although persons (and the objects they own, owe, or claim as creditors) have physical manifestation, debt and ownership relations are not physical but social; however, this does not diminish their reality status. These social relations are *empirical transactions* and, like the commodity transfers, are representable by accounting transactions, which belong to the conceptual domain (see Chapter 3). Since debt and ownership claims both belong to social reality, one may combine them in a single principle (the "principle of symmetry"), provided one does not lose sight of the social and legal differences between debt versus ownership. While a debt is a financial–legal relation between two persons, an ownership is a legal or quasi-legal relation between a person and an object.

2. In accounting there is a systematic *integration of those three dualities*, reflecting structures manifested in physical as well as social reality. The fact that persons can own assets (economic resources) as well as owe debts to other persons

(i.e., have social relations with each other and have claims on assets) obviously means that there exists a connection between physical and social manifestations. The reflection of those empirical connections is a fundamental function of accounting. To execute such a conceptual representation requires a further leap of abstraction. While each of those three types of relations connects two entities (firms), the pertinent accounting transactions are reflected within a single entity. This *leap* is discussed in the next item.

3. *Investing and lending activities* usually result in the transfer of some commodity or purchasing power between entities. Obviously, the duality is no less present in the intraentity transactions (i.e., those between two independent firms) as it is in any interentity transaction (i.e., one within a single firm). After all, any borrowing is ultimately matched by some lending, and any investing (hopefully) by some ownership. Thus, the representation of intraentity transactions in the accounting system of one of those firms occurs through "substituting " an interentity transaction by an intraentity accounting transaction. That is to say, the debt and owner's equity accounts (together with other accounts) are *internalizing* what otherwise would be an *external* duality (i.e., a transaction from one entity to another). This peculiar relationship is illustrated in Figure 4.1. It reveals both the internal (or intraentity) as well as the external (or interentity) flows or transactions.

The combined matrix in Figure 4.1 represents the following inter- and intraentity transactions of two entities (E_1 and E_2) doing business with each other. The matrix shows the credits in the rows and the debits in the columns:[3]

1. Investment of owner's equity by entity E_2 in entity E_1 by handing over some machinery.
2. Entity E_1 receives raw material from E_2 on a credit basis.
3. Entity E_1 supplies some finished goods to E_2 in cancellation of some of its debts against E_2.

The intraentity transactions are recorded for each of those two entities and bear the pertinent sequence numbers in a circle. Since the entities are considered to be independent of each other, each event must be recorded twice—even in a two-dimensional matrix (once for entity E_1, the second time for entity E_2). The matrix also reveals in the *empty circles* the, yet unrecorded, physical flows (of machinery, raw materials, and finished goods from one entity to another, that is, the interentity transactions).

However, if the two entities were to be consolidated and become, for example, two departments of the same firm, only those transactions with empty circles, instead of the corresponding ones with numerals would be recorded. This shows that there are *physical* events behind the interentity transactions, even if some of the latter transactions are purely conceptual (e.g., showing "abstract transfers" between such different "objects" as machinery and owner's equity). Another consequence of such an assumed "merger" is this: The transactions marked by a ⊗ (a second kind of what were originally interentity transactions) would be required to cancel

Figure 4.1
Accounting Matrix for Two Entities with Interentity and Intraentity Flows

	Entity E₁					Entity E₂					
	RM	FG	Ma	R/P	OE	RM	FG	Ma	R/P	Invst.	OE
Entity E₁ Raw Materials	○										
Finished Goods				③			○				
Machinery			○								
Rec./Payables	②								⊗		
Owner's Equity			①							⊗	
Entity E₂ Raw Materials											
Finished Goods											
Machinery							③		②		
Rec./Payables				⊗							
Investments										①	
Owner's Equity											

Note: The rows are Credit sides; the columns are Debit sides.

out the claims or obligations between the two departments (formerly two separate entities).[4] To show how inter- and intraentity transactions are linked with each other, one may connect them (in Figure 4.1) with horizontal and vertical dashed lines.

Hopefully, this analysis has clarified those connections and shed some light on our previous assertion that the various dualities, although by no means identical, are closely tied to each other (some experts may even consider them as different aspects of a basically physical duality). Above all, the economic transactions involving debt or investment relations, though themselves social events, are linked to physical inputs and outputs (as shown in the case of consolidations and mergers).

4. There exists some analogy (perhaps even a direct connection) between the duality principles of accounting and the conservation principles of physics. The next subsection deals with this point so crucial for a deeper understanding of our discipline.

Input–Output, Symmetry, and Conservation

An examination of the foundations of accounting raises the question whether the *duality principles*—which, according to the following analysis, consist of the input–output principle and the symmetry principle[5]—might fulfill a similar function in accounting as do the principles of conservation in physics.[6] In prehistoric accounting, for instance, the transfer of commodities was represented *directly* (i.e., without involving monetary valuation), reflecting a conservation of physical substance. In other words, the transfer of a token from one location to another conveyed that in the act of transferring a commodity from one person (or institution) to another, certain qualities of that commodity were preserved. This dual representation resembles that of chemistry where each atom appears on each side of the equation, reflecting a chemical reaction but also a preservation of substance.

Accounting is not merely concerned with physical transfers but also with the change of wealth over time. Just as the conservation laws of the physical sciences[7] are giving account of what happened to the input of energy and matter, momentum, spin, and so on, in terms of the corresponding output; so accounting tries to give account in terms of commodity utilization and financing.[8] Even if some commodities get consumed, lost, or dissipated during a certain transformation, it is that "giving account" of the total input in terms of the total output (or vice versa) that is crucial for every principle of conservation.

For some accountants and economists, it may be a flagrant contradiction to consider something "consumed" or even "lost" as something "conserved" (compare, for example, Adam Smith's *narrow* income definition from which mere "services" were excluded because they are instantly consumed [Studenski 1958, 18–20]). Asserting such a contradiction would be like insisting that the second law of thermodynamics (entropy law, that is, the increase of dissipated energy in the universe) contradicts the first law of thermodynamics (conservation of energy). The fact that some energy is wasted (i.e., no longer available to do work because it is dissipated as "useless" heat) does not negate the constancy of energy in the universe (even if this energy is a *constant* zero, as modern physics asserts).

When the accounting process is extended to valuation, it still is possible to cope with this problem. One might talk about *value accountability* of inputs in terms of outputs, provided "wasted (dissipated) value" is included under value conservation no less than "wasted (dissipated) energy" is included under energy conservation. Again, the criterion for "conservation" is not whether the pertinent item is useful or useless, but whether it has been accounted for. Whoever is confused by the expression conservation may substitute for it the term *symmetry*—even physicists nowadays speak of *principles of symmetry* when referring to the laws of conservation.

But is there not a fundamental difference between the immutable empirical symmetry laws of physics and accounting symmetry which, to many experts, appears to be nothing but a tautology? Indeed, there may be a category difference between the two; yet symmetries break in physics as well as in accounting. As regards energy conservation, a recent conjecture asserts that *the total energy in the cosmos is zero*. Stephen Hawking, the most reputed expert in this field, points out that matter in this universe is regarded as positive energy because the gravitational field that causes all pieces of matter to attract each other is a kind of negative energy: "Two pieces that are close to each other have less energy than the same two pieces a long way apart, because you have to expend energy to separate them against the gravitational force that is pulling them together" (Hawking 1988, 129). He furthermore indicates that this negative energy has been demonstrated to be exactly equal in amount to the total positive energy of the universe.[9]

This leads to the conclusion that the ultimate explanation of existence is found in a kind of gigantic quantum (or vacuum) fluctuation that split into positive energy (radiation, matter) and negative energy (gravitational), creating the balance or symmetry between the two. Apart from suggesting that physics could be regarded as a kind of cosmic accounting system,[10] it raises questions about the corresponding analogies in business and economic accounting. Consider a proprietor's investment in a new firm. Does it not also create a symmetry between assets invested (debit) and owner's equity (credit)? Would the liquidation of his or her business not equally break the symmetry in the accounts of the firm?

The structural analogy between physics and accounting can be carried even further:[11] Not only is *energy* being analyzed in terms of its *manifestation* (as matter, radiation, potential or kinetic energy) as well as in terms of its *force* (electromagnetic, gravitational, strong, and weak force); *capital* also is being analyzed in terms of its manifestation (as assets such as cash and receivables, inventory, fixed assets) as well as in terms of its force (claims such as payables, loans, preferred stocks, common stocks, earned surplus). Of course, the crucial question arises: Is not the symmetry behind accounting a tautology (based on legalistic or other definitions of asset and ownership), while energy symmetry is an empirical phenomenon? The answer to this question may be more complex than one might expect. First, there exists a well-known "acid test" to make sure that a proposition is empirical and not tautological: If the proposition is, in principle, open to factual refutation, it cannot be a tautology. After some preparation, we shall apply this test and examine another more subtle point.

The notion of *property claim* is not created by definition. Behind the purely legalistic term *ownership right* lies an ingrained behavior pattern, deeply rooted in social reality. Communist countries, for example, tried to redefine property rights (at least as far as those of major means of production are concerned); but in the end it did not work in the USSR, and even China had to make major revisions (the propelling idea of property just proved to be overwhelming). Furthermore, it must be remembered that accounting symmetry (in its monetary–quantitative formulation) is closely related to the law of demand and supply. The latter assures that only those goods that are scarce as well as useful are assets (economic resources as distinct from free goods), and thus have a market value; furthermore, this law provides a basis for valuing those assets and the claim on them.

We are now ready to formulate the duality principles of accounting. First, the input–output *principle*: The transfer of a *concrete* economic good (i.e., nonmonetary asset) from one "location" (e.g., accountability center) to another preserves some relevant attribute (substance, quantity, volume, value, and the like) in regard of which the output from one location corresponds to the input in the other. Second, the symmetry principle: On any asset (scarce economic resource) there is a claim (either ownership or debt claim), the value of which is equal to (but not identical with) the asset value (even if the magnitude of the value is the same—an equity value is obviously something fundamentally different from an asset value). This symmetry principle is closely related to another important notion, which we may call the principle of change (or gain and loss): If there is an ownership claim on an asset, and if its relevant attribute does change, then this change is also reflected in the corresponding ownership claim. The repeated application of this principle of change makes it possible to determine gain or loss on the basis of some attribute change in ownership claim.

Should all this seem trivial, the reader may be reminded that most fundamental propositions sound no less trivial. Consider, for instance, Newton's third law that every action is associated with a corresponding reaction.[12] Should it turn out that the duality principles are not tautologies, the previously mentioned acid test could confirm this. Let me begin with the second principle: Imagine a highly ethical society living in such abundance that all commodities are "free goods" (as water still is in some places). In such a situation, there would be neither markets nor assets with claims on them. Although this is unrealistic, it is empirically not impossible; and this is all that is required by the acid test. Compare, for example, the accounting symmetry principle with a conventional tautology (like "either something is red, or it is not red"), and the difference becomes obvious. This tautology cannot be empirically refuted (even if the color red were non-existent, the proposition would still be true). The input–output principle, too, seems to be, in principle, open to refutation. Is it not imaginable that a loss or diminution of the essential quality might occur in the process of the transaction? This obviously would be such a potential refutation. Is this not in conflict with our analysis of "accountability" at the beginning of this chapter?

I think the resolution of the tautology problem requires a consideration that so far has been neglected. The basic idea behind it can be made plausible by comparing the following two propositions: (1) "The President of the United States is the Commander-in-Chief of its armed forces;" (2) "The Constitution of the United States stipulates that the President is Commander-in-Chief of its armed forces." Although these sentences are similar in content, the first is a tautology (because it is true by constitutional definition), while the second conveys an empirical proposition (a change in the constitution—abandoning the personal union of President and Commander-in-Chief—is not an impossibility; a *coup d'état* with sudden constitutional change is a potential refutation).

The same holds for accounting; here, too, the "level" on which the proposition is regarded determines whether it is tautological or empirical. The basic level of double entry is obviously analytical, but behind it stand physical as well as social (i.e., empirical) forces. Just as Proposition 1 (in the tautology above) is incorporated in the empirical Proposition 2, so the incorporation of the double-entry tautology into the empirical context of accounting can change the picture. It should also be noted that the conjecture of "constant zero (positive–negative) energy" of physics, at a first glance, looks very much like a tautology; and yet it is based on empirical principles.

Even if the input–output principle and the "two-pronged" symmetry principle were considered to be social laws, I still would hesitate to call them "scientific laws of accounting" because the physical transfer of resources as well as the facts of ownership rights and debt claims all have their origin in the evolution of society at large. They have legal, economic, and other social implications and exist independently of accounting; the latter merely *represents* some of the many facets of those facts. These are challenging problems and future scholars will surely have to say more about them.

TERMINOLOGICAL AND CONCEPTUAL DIFFICULTIES

Defined versus Undefined Terms

Traditional accounting, as most other academic disciplines, partly borrows concepts from neighboring disciplines and partly creates its own conceptual apparatus; yet accounting theoreticians rarely show an effort of indicating clearly which of their terms are primitive (or borrowed from outside) and which are derived from these primitives by means of nominal definitions within the accounting theory proper. This vagueness is one reason the boundaries of traditional accounting theory and its subareas are blurred and why accounting itself is usually described instead of defined. For example, the well-known "definition" of accounting, offered ages ago by the Committee on Terminology of the American Institute of Certified Public Accountants (AICPA 1961, 9), was neither a nominal nor an analytical nor an operational definition; it did not set sharp boundaries to the term *accounting*, nor did it prescribe operational rules by means of which one can test whether something is an accounting system. Indeed, the "definition" would have fitted other areas of business administration almost equally well. Although the neglect to distinguish between primitive (undefined) and defined terms may have led to confusion, the failure to discern between interpreted and uninterpreted concepts and calculi probably had even more serious consequences.

Interpreted versus Uninterpreted Concepts

Whereas a *definition* is a relationship between terms or between a term and its constituents, an *interpretation* is a relationship between a phenomenon (usually a fact) and the term representing it. General concepts require specific and, in many cases, empirical interpretations.[13] In accounting, unfortunately, the distinction between interpreted and uninterpreted concepts is even more neglected than that between defined and undefined terms. Concepts like *income, wealth,* and *value,* for example, are treated as though they were well interpreted concepts; but, at best, an interpretation is merely implied. In the case of scholarly controversies, the two opponents often imply different interpretations, often without realizing it.

In this regard, the example of the probability concept offers a valid analogue from which accountants can learn much. For a considerable time, hot controversies were fought over the question whether probability is an objective–empirical, an objective–formal, or a subjective–empirical concept. This controversy was resolved after Kolmogoroff (1933) created the general and thus uninterpreted probability concept stipulated by the axioms of the probability calculus. Then different rules of interpretations were devised in such a way that under one set of rules, the relative frequency concept (an objective–empirical one) emerged, under another set the degree of confirmation (an objective–formal concept), and under a third a subjective–empirical probability concept. Later even more interpretations were forthcoming (see Bunge 1967a, 428). Would it not be possible, in a similar fashion, to devise certain conditions or common traits for the concepts of income, wealth, value, and other accounting notions to create general uninterpreted concepts and then rules of interpretations for specific needs? In this way, much clarity could be brought into our discipline and many a futile controversy would be avoided.

Systematic attempts to create a series of clearly defined but uninterpreted concepts of the major accounting notions are a relatively recent phenomenon (e.g., Feltham and Ohlson's [1994] paper and its "clean surplus" notion), and so are alternative interpretations (for specific or standardized needs) of those concepts. In an informal, vague, and incomplete manner, such interpretations have been customary in traditional accounting for a long time. One might argue that the acquisition cost basis, the market value basis, and the present value basis are nothing but "interpretations" of a general uninterpreted value concept; but the essence of the methodological achievement of distinguishing between uninterpreted and interpreted concepts and theories lies in the specification of the conditions characterizing every uninterpreted concept. The rules of interpretation are rarely, if ever, spelled out in accounting. Apart from that, the practice of distinguishing various species of one and the same super-concept is merely a first step on the way to a more important methodological prerequisite. Occasionally academic accountants did concern themselves with such problems or closely related ones. Bedford, for example, recommended using an operational income concept: "The fact is that there is a need for one overall general concept of income in our society. The formulation of the set of operations to be used in developing such a general concept of income is by far the most difficult aspect of such a process of theory formation" (Bedford 1965, 8–9).

Apart from distinguishing between business income and "income as a generalized means to gratify a variety of human needs," which Bedford (1965, 11) deems beyond the concern of accounting, he regarded business income as an interpreted instead of uninterpreted concept.

Devine (1985, 3: 1), too, recommended in his essay, "Principles, Theories, Systems—Again," that principles should be operationally defined and regarded as guidelines. The explicit mentioning of "semantical rules" (i.e., rules of interpretation) in the accounting literature was made by Sterling (1970a, 444–457) as well as in the "Report of the Committee on Accounting Theory Construction and Verification" (American Accounting Association 1971b, 51–79). But the actual significance of the rules of interpretations for creating subconcepts and subtheories from the general concept or theory, respectively, was not emphasized in these writings.

To attain better conceptualization in accounting and related systems, comprehensive and systematic taxonomic research is indispensable. Such research will need to formulate both the conditions of each of the uninterpreted accounting concepts as well as the rules of interpretations of all the specific and standardized subconcepts. Such classificational research is tedious and hardly glamorous; hence it is not surprising that the "Linnaeus" of accounting has not yet appeared. But if biology was in a position to classify more than two million species of plants and animals within a complex taxonomic system of kingdoms, phyla, classes (with subclasses), orders (with suborders and sections), families, genera, and species, then it should be possible for accounting to produce a classificational structure of a few dozens or hundreds of concepts, subconcepts, sub-subconcepts (including a hierarchy of objectives). The hurdle is the apparent subjectivity of many accounting concepts.

ADAPTATION OF SCIENTIFIC METHODS

Mathematical and Economic Contributions

The greatest progress during this transition period stemmed from adapting ideas from economics and the behavioral sciences, mathematical methods, and statistical–empirical techniques, as well as computer technology to accounting.

Most prominent among these are (1) present value and investment calculations, as developed in modern finance (capital–asset pricing and portfolio theory, and so on, including probabilistic versions of the present value approach); (2) adaptation of information economics and agency theory; (3) application of matrix algebra, linear programming, and other OR techniques, as well as game and decision theory; (4) simulation techniques, computer applications, electronic data processing, and artificial intelligence (e.g., computerized spreadsheets and experiments with expert programs); and (5) empirical studies reinforced by the rigorous application of hypotheses testing and other statistical methods.

Present value and investment calculations are no novelty in accounting. Their applications must be credited to traditional accounting but were ultimately derived from economics. It is Irving Fisher's (1906) merit to have interpreted capital theory by means of accounting concepts. The fundamental significance of this Fisherian interpretation lies in a new and much broader vision of our discipline, which (a couple of decades later) was further developed by Canning (1929) and, in a somewhat different fashion (current market values instead of present values), by Fritz Schmidt ([1921] 1953). This trend and concern with valuation was the first and perhaps most important step toward a more general theory of accounting. It was a radical innovation though, and some accountants still have difficulty in accepting anything beyond historical costs. Nevertheless, further steps were undertaken by Moonitz and Staehling (1950–1952), Moonitz (1993), and others (Albach, Bell, Bierman, Chambers, E. O. Edwards, Hansen, Honko, Jordan, Mattessich, MacNeal, Sprouse, Sterling, and so on) to elaborate the application of the present value or the market value approach to accounting. Both Corbin (1962) and Philips (1963) spoke more than three decades ago of a "revolution" in our discipline; but this referred mainly to the economic valuation facet, without entering into other revolutionary aspects then visible on the horizon. Meanwhile, the term *revolution* has recurred in accounting, most notably in Beaver's (1981) well-known book. Last, the most recent extension of the present value approach to accounting by Ohlson (e.g., 1987, 1990), Feltham and Ohlson (1993, 1994), and others must be mentioned.

Another insight, revived and exploited after Word War II, concerns the matrix notion as a convenient means for representing the duality aspects of accounting (see Mattessich 1957, 1964a, 1964b). A matrix reveals the double-classificational structure of accounting in a more mathematical and generally understandable fashion than does the language of traditional bookkeeping. Matrix algebra also lends itself to the solution of many allocation problems and related issues of micro- and macro-accounting. To regard this matrix mode as a new "paradigm" for accounting, as Cushing (1989, 33–34) suggests, may be exaggeration; but its many applications, from national income accounting and Leontief's input–output analysis to budget simulation and computer spreadsheets, cannot be denied. Through such best-selling spreadsheet computer programs as Visi-Calc, Super-Calc, and Lotus 1-2-3, the matrix approach combined with the simulation aspect (as first presented in Mattessich [1961, 1964b]) may, in hindsight, have been the most successful contribution of modern accounting theory to actual practice. A further advantage of the matrix mode grows out of its mathematical generality and association with any kind of input–output structure. Originally, some accountants hoped that this might lead to an applicable general theory. But these hopes have not (at least not yet) been fulfilled.

Apart from those methodological aspects which have been treated extensively elsewhere (Mattessich 1964a), the more algebraic aspects of matrix accounting have inspired a series of contributions on the application of input–output models to accounting. Starting from the insight that Leontief's input–output analysis need not be restricted to the macro-economy (see Mattessich 1957), several authors tried to apply matrix algebra, its OR aspects, and related areas (including linear programming) to accounting (e.g., Churchill 1964; Williams and Griffin 1964; Ijiri et al. 1963; Ijiri 1965b, 1968; Manes 1965; Farag 1967; Gambling 1968; Livingstone 1968, 1969; Feltham 1970; Butterworth and Sigloch 1971; Kaplan and Thompson 1971). Linear programming, simulation, and computer applications are all related to this research area. They, too, constitute a comprehensive body of mathematical studies that greatly contributed to more rigorous analytical thinking in accounting. Both linear programming and the matrix calculus are part of linear algebra. Although the matrix application of accounting is strongly oriented toward allocation procedures, it also may be geared to planning and budgeting, like linear programming and systems simulation.

Another feature of the "transition period" was a strong orientation of accounting toward budgeting and monthly, quarterly, or yearly forecasts of earnings. Apart from government accounting—which for hundreds of years (particularly in Europe) has basically been a kind of budgeting process—it was McKinsey (1922) who laid the foundation for systematic and comprehensive business budgeting (see also Edey 1959). For decades, this area has never been more than a side issue of secondary importance. This original neglect of business budgeting deprived traditional accounting of one of its most important tasks—comparing the targets of production, marketing, and profit with the figures actually achieved.

Mueller, for example, confirmed that in traditional accounting (in contrast to modern accounting) "the information was not designed for planning purposes or necessarily for measuring performance against organizational objectives" (Mueller 1971, 291). Applications of linear programming (e.g., Charnes et al. 1963) and system simulation, however, indicated that the control function as well as the exploration of alternative factor combinations—by means of flexible budgets, spreadsheet computer programs, and the measurement of divisional performance (see Solomons's [1965] important contribution)—had become dominant issues of modern accounting. It was also claimed that budgeting and similar projections of accounting correspond to predictions in the pure sciences. Greenball correctly pointed out that "it is incorrect to speak of the predictive ability of an accounting method or an accounting number" (1971, 6). Yet this does not mean that *conditional scenarios* of accounting systems are useless.

Statistical applications and information economics are other areas that greatly enhanced the rigor and quality of accounting research. This spans a broad spectrum of which several subareas might be mentioned: first, the application of statistical sampling and hypothesis testing (especially in auditing and control charting; see Vance 1950, Vance and Neter 1956, Trueblood and Cooper 1955, Cyert and Trueblood 1957); second, the econometric study of cost behavior (e.g., Dean 1951; Johnston 1960); third, decision theory, information economics, and the evaluation of information (e.g., Lev 1969; Feltham and Demski 1970; Demski and Feltham 1976); and fourth, all other statistical accounting applications difficult to classify otherwise.

Statistical sampling and control charting are subareas of most immediate practical usefulness, while the econometric determination of cost curves and the like were occasionally neglected in accounting. The third subarea—the evaluation of accounting information—touched the very core of our discipline and has had, particularly in combination with agency theory, a considerable impact on modern accounting (see also Chapters 5 and 9).

Measurement Theory

The application of basic concepts of modern measurement theory (not to be confused with the "measure theory" of mathematics) to accounting has contributed to conceptual clarification of several accounting issues. Accounting describes past events and projects potential scenarios. Whether one regards it as a kind of measurement activity depends on one's viewpoint. For those who identify measurement with the quantitative description of objects and events, *including expectations* (as in Mattessich 1964a, Ijiri 1967, Mock 1976, and other publications), accounting is measurement, while others (e.g., Chambers 1965) oppose this view. The conceptualization of measurement theory goes back to von Helmholz (1895) and Norman R. Campbell (1928) but assumes special significance in the social sciences with the contributions of Stevens (1946) and other social scientists or mathematicians.

Stevens's scales and related aspects were first applied to accounting in Mattessich (1959), and further concepts of modern measurement theory were introduced to this discipline in subsequent years. Some authors, like Bierman (1963), recognized the significance of these new measurement concepts at an early stage; but, in contrast to the mathematical developments mentioned previously, accountants, in general, only slowly absorbed those ideas. Among the sixteen papers on accounting measurement presented at the 1965 Seminar on Basic Research in Accounting Measurement (compare Jaedicke et al. 1966), only one (Devine 1966) referred to S. S. Stevens. A more widespread and profounder familiarity with the special conditions of "measurement" in accounting could certainly have avoided many misunderstandings (compare the controversy between Chambers [1971a, 1971b] and Mattessich [1970b, 1971a, 1971b]), but further light was shed on measurement issues by the American Accounting Association (1971a, 1971b) and Mock (1976).

Apart from such technical features, four items must be taken into consideration: (1) economic information research has indicated that "the very presence of a measurement system can result in changes in the behavior of actors in an economic setting" (Daley 1994, 45); (2) objectives and professional judgment play an important role in the highly contextual phenomenon of accounting measurement (compare Gibbins 1994, 54); (3) the need for re-evaluating recent research, based on the "increasing evidence that investors may not be as rational and security markets may not be as efficient as previously believed. This threatens the foundation upon which most financial accounting research over the last 25 years has been based, and has led to calls for a 'return to fundamentals' . . . , in which research attention would shift to the measurement of value in financial statements" (Scott 1994, 62); and (4) as Denman states quite correctly, "Leading accounting academics have largely abandoned accounting measurement issues when, whether we like it or not, the 'bottom line' is still considered by users of financial information to be of overriding importance and the measurement of the fair values of assets and liabilities is becoming increasingly important" (Denman 1994, 85).

Accounting, conceived as a scientific discipline, cannot rely on formal propositions alone. On the contrary, apart from normative premises, the substance of accounting ultimately rests on empirical propositions. Since most of the latter are of behavioral nature, it falls to behavioral accounting to formulate specific empirical premises that ultimately should fit into a more general framework. This area will be concisely discussed in Chapter 10.

As for the possibility of reducing accounting (through behavioral and similar studies) to more elementary foundations, it is hardly acute. Whether such a reduction and integration would be desirable, it would require a better understanding of the pertinent "laws" of those more basic disciplines and, above all, of the long causal chains involved in the reduction process. As long as such understanding eludes us, accountants must do what the chemists did before the periodic table could be explained in terms of subatomic particles. They must construct self-contained theories on the basis of what they know. Then slowly, step by step (with the progress of their own discipline as well as that of the more basic disciplines in which accounting is embedded), one might be able to extend such a theory by reducing it to explanations in more basic terms. This hardly can be done by accountants devising their own sociological, psychological, or economic postulates on a wholesale basis. Rather, one must draw on the foundations of those basic disciplines as worked out by their own experts. Only then may accountants borrow them and try to add their own modest contributions to these parental disciplines.

So far, the adaptation of the scientific approach to accounting has mainly been based on analytical as well as statistical–empirical methods, despite the awareness that "accountants must determine which accounting and management information systems should be accepted for a specific situation and which are not applicable.

These central questions concerning the theory and practice of accounting ultimately belong to the science of knowledge. . . . Management scientists and systems analysts during the last decade have gained two important insights: (1) that epistemological research is indispensable for probing the fundamental problems of the management sciences, and (2) that model building and especially the construction of systems may impart new vistas to epistemology" (American Accounting Association 1971d, 40). In their fascination with mathematical and statistical techniques, accountants seem to have neglected important philosophic aspects. Occasionally, however, some warning voices are still heard; for example, Gaffikin (1987, 1988), Subotnik (1988), Mouck (1989), and others who do not believe that positive accounting theory is the only legitimate research approach to our discipline.

NOTES

This chapter consists of a major revision of my paper, "Methodological Preconditions and Problems of a General Theory of Accounting" (Mattessich 1972), as well as the last section of "Accounting and the Input–Output Principle in the Prehistoric and Ancient World" (Mattessich 1989). The beginning of the chapter is based on parts of my plenary presentation at the 17th Congress of the European Accounting Association in Venice (Mattessich 1994a).

1. For profiles of notable accountants of this period (as well as other periods) see the following: for the English literature, Gaffikin and Aitken (1982); for those limited to the Berkeley School, Moonitz (1986); and for literature on a more international basis, Edwards (1994), Guo and Yang (In preparation), Chatfield and Vangermeersch (In press).

2. "As we shall see in some detail, applied research has the advantage of being able to formulate criteria of its own efficiency in terms of the objectives for which the problem is being investigated. Because of its lack of specific objectives, pure research cannot formulate such criteria as explicitly" (Ackoff 1962, 24). "In science, whether pure or applied, a theory is both the culmination of a research cycle and a guide to further research. In applied science theories are, in addition, the basis of systems of rules prescribing the course of optimal practical action" (Bunge 1967b, 121).

3. This accounting convention (in contrast to the later "Gomberg 1927 convention" that was adapted by Kohler [1952] and Ijiri [1965b] who use the rows as debits and the columns as credits) was first adopted by De Morgan (1846) and, in the twentieth century, by Leontief (1951) as well as Mattessich (1957).

4. In contrast to having separate raw material inventory and machinery accounts for each department, *no separate* receivables and payables accounts are assumed to be kept for each department (they are not legal entities, and as such cannot owe or own).

5. I regard the "input–output principle of accounting" (in the narrow sense) as referring only to the corresponding inputs and outputs of physical goods or services in a specific transaction, while the "symmetry principle of accounting" (also in the narrow sense) as referring to the fact that every asset has a corresponding equity (either debt equity or owner's equity) aspect. The "duality principle(s) of accounting" (which could be regarded as synonymous to the input–output principle or symmetry principle in the broad sense) may then comprise both the principles of input–output as well as the symmetry, and thus refers to the debit and credit entries of physical as well as social realities in transactions.

6. Compare Mattessich (1980, 233; 1984, 408), Thornton (1985, 137), and Swanson (1987, 82, 90, 91), who even speaks of a "matter–energy flow" in accounting.

7. Apart from the law of conservation of matter and energy, quantum theory knows conservation principles with regard to electric charge, linear momentum, spin (angular momentum), iso-spin, baryon charge, muon charge, strangeness, combined parity (space reflection) plus charge reflection plus time reversal, and so on. For further details, see Parker (1983, 38, 175–176, 891–892, 1135–1141, 1213–1215).

8. Physicists freely admit that their conservation or symmetry laws imply *accountability* (even helpful in discovering subatomic particles) which, for example, is greatly facilitated by such notions as "work" (force × distance): "Work is merely a bookkeeping device to keep track of transfer of energy from one thing to another" (Olenick et al. 1985, 249).

9. This postulation of a total-zero energy in the cosmos is confirmed by Tryon: "But there is also another form of energy important to cosmology that acts, in some sense, in opposition to this mass–energy. Namely gravitational potential energy" (Tryon 1973, 396–397). Bartusiak continues to say that "one could think of this as the supply of energy needed to push the galaxies infinitely far apart; hence it is traditionally regarded as *a negative energy on the ledger books of the universe*" (Bartusiak 1986, 256, italics added).

10. For other analogies between accounting and information, on one side, and physics, on the other, see Ijiri (1989, 84–86), and Mattessich (1991a, 34; 1993a, 568–570).

11. Despite all those analogies, there exists at least one major instance in which a "balance sheet equation of physics" leaves an unexplained residual: the alleged matter–antimatter asymmetry (much matter but very little antimatter) of the universe. There have been several attempts to explain this imbalance. One of them assumed that most of the original matter and antimatter eliminated each other such that our universe is but a tiny and accidental residual of a giant conflagration. Expressed in accounting language, this would mean that God or Nature is a *sloppy* bookkeeper; but this hypothesis seems to have been abandoned in favor of some other symmetry break in the early universe.

12. Both the accounting symmetry principle as well as Newton's third law can be *directionally* quantified. For example, "Every asset value is associated with an equal but *inverse* equity value," on one side, and "Every action is associated with an equal reaction of *inverse* direction," on the other.

13. There also exists a semantics (which is concerned with interpretation) that relates concepts of lower generality to concepts of higher generality (instead of empirical phenomena to concepts). This kind of semantics is usually called "model theory" and encountered in mathematics.

CHAPTER 5

Formalization and Information

ENDEAVORS TOWARD A GENERAL
THEORY OF ACCOUNTING

Many scientific disciplines aspire not only to form theories but also to formalize them; therefore, the premises and consequences of those theories are revealed. Formalization lends a theory a higher degree of logical precision, reflects the theory structure more clearly than does a mere verbal presentation, and often attains some pedagogic objectives. To create an accounting theory of practical use, one must go beyond a purely *analytical* approach and give it *empirical* content as well a *normative* direction. From the late 1950s onward modern analytical methods have been applied to accounting; and in the late 1960s empirical–statistical procedures began to join them. As for normative directions, a series of attempts have been made, ranging from the early ethical–normative group of Germany before World War II (see Chapter 10) and the pragmatic–normative camp of the 1960s to the more recent British critical–interpretive school and other critical publications (e.g., Briloff 1972, 1981) and the social-contract studies by Gaa (1988b, 1994).

The first attempt to formulate postulates of accounting was made by Paton (1922). Although this effort was not immediately appreciated, postulational and axiomatic attempts were taken up again in the 1950s, pursued more intensively in the 1960s, and are still occasionally encountered—though more on the fringe than in the center of accounting research. Most of the recent analytical work concentrates not so much on axiomatization as on model building in agency-contract theory, information economics, security valuation theory, and other problems.

The Postulational and Axiomatic Approach

Although the expressions "postulation" and "axiomatization" are often used synonymously, it might be useful to make a distinction between them in the following fashion:

Postulation: the formulation of basic premises and possibly consequences of the theory in a natural language (like English) without demonstrating rigorously the conclusions that follow from those premises.

Axiomatization: the mathematical or partly mathematical formulation of basic premises (axioms); the deduction of conclusions (theorems) through more rigorous logical or mathematical means. Eventually this leads to interpretation, which enables the formulation of more *specific* models.

Modern logic supplies a variety of formal languages (propositional logic, set theory, predicate logic of first order and of higher orders) with different shades of precision and rigor. A survey of this subarea is encumbered not only by the many alternative approaches but also by mathematical complexity and a number of concepts often unfamiliar to accountants. The following sketch tries to avoid those complications and guides the reader to the specialized literature. While the first contact of higher mathematics with accounting belongs to the nineteenth century (e.g., De Morgan 1846; Cayley 1894), the first book that comes close to a postulational approach (i.e., without mathematical or other formal means) is William W. Paton's classic *Accounting Theory* (1922). At the end of his book (in Chapter 20), the reader finds what its author considers to be "all the important postulates of accounting." Thus, Paton was the first to search for the premises on which accounting rests and deserves highest recognition, even though only *some* of these notions might nowadays be considered fundamental enough to be taken as postulates.

The next steps toward accounting postulation were undertaken by Chambers (1955, 1966), Moonitz (1961), and a Study Group of the University of Illinois (1964). Furthermore, Sprouse and Moonitz (1962) tried to relate accounting principles to the Moonitz postulates. This attempt, however, was criticized by Spacek, who states that "there is very little attempt to demonstrate how these principles flow from or are based on the postulates set forth in the previous study" (Spacek 1962, 77–79). This flaw is characteristic of most "postulational" (though not of the "axiomatic") studies. The wealth of related publications of the late 1950s and the 1960s has been collected in Zeff's (1982) anthology.

The studies by Moonitz (1961) and Sprouse and Moonitz (1962) were commissioned by the AICPA in the expectation of some practical relevance. Indeed, the "Conceptual Framework" publications of the FASB (1974, 1976a, 1976b, 1978) may be regarded as the major practical consequence of all the earlier postulational and axiomatization attempts. (For a comparison of accounting standards in Canada, the United Kingdom, and the United States, see Gorelik 1994.) The FASB's expensive effort of creating a conceptual framework was criticized from many quarters, for example, Dopuch and Sunder (1980), Archer (1993), Haller (1991). The latter complains about the FASB's conceptual framework: "In places where the curious reader would expect normative statements, one is offered either awkward definitions or descriptions of conventional accounting practices" (Haller 1991, 220, translated).

Whether the *limited* success of this conceptual framework has its ultimate roots in the avoidance of rigorous means of deduction—which it shares with the Sprouse and Moonitz (1962) study—is questionable. Nevertheless, had the earlier warning of Spacek (1962) and his call for a deductive approach been heeded, the FASB's conceptual framework project could have become an enduring and intellectually satisfying foundation of accounting.

A program for a more general and rigorous approach to micro- and macro-accounting was suggested in Mattessich (1956). This was followed by the first attempt to axiomatize business accounting and its later elaboration (Mattessich 1957, 1964a). Stimulated by these endeavors, a host of similar efforts (including some of the postulational attempts mentioned earlier) precipitated in the accounting literature. For example, Rosenblatt (1960) presented an axiomatization of what he refers to as the "Paciolo System"; in a doctoral dissertation, Winborne (1962) applied set theory to accounting principles, and Ijiri's (1965a) axiomatization paper, followed by his well-known book (Ijiri 1967), began his defense of the *historical* cost method.

After a respite of several years, interest in accounting axiomatization arose again, first in Germany by Kosiol (1970), Mattessich (1970a—a German, revised version of the 1964a axiomatization), and Schweitzer (1970). Then an exchange of ideas between Saito (1972, 1973) and Mattessich (1973) led to some technical improvements of Mattessich's system in a Japanese journal. Later, the dissertation by Orbach (1978) presented an axiomatization of accounting, and so did an Italian book by Galassi (1978) as well as a paper by Tippett (1978).[1] Meanwhile, several of Ijiri's (e.g., 1975, 51–74; 1989, 104–106) publications appeared, containing further axiomatic and postulational contributions (the latter contains three postulates—reconciliation, conservation, and attribution of momentum—for his theory of triple-entry and momentum accounting).

In the 1980s, another series of contributions to accounting axiomatization appeared: Carlson and Lamb (1981), who not only used first-order predicate logic (instead of set theory) but also took particular care in defining and using a formal language; Deguchi and Nakano (1986); Avilà, Bravo, and Scarano (1988); de Pree (1989); and Willett (1985, 1987, 1988), who, in a comprehensive dissertation and a subsequent two-part survey article, emphasized the distinction between measurement (for decision-making) versus disclosure (for stewardship) of accounting information. Furthermore, a dissertation by Nehmer (1988) addressed accounting information systems as an algebraic system, as well as a system of first-order formulas (Nehmer's dissertation uses "model theory" and presents a comparison with "organizational communication theory").

In the 1990s an attempt was made by Balzer and Mattessich (1991) to apply the "axiomatization methods of structuralism" (for the latter, see Chapter 7) to accounting. The most recent pertinent work (Herde 1992) not only evaluates and analyzes the previously mentioned axiomatic systems of Carlson and Lamb (1981), Willett (1987, 1988), and Balzer and Mattessich (1991)[2] but "transforms" each of those attempts into a logic of higher order (i.e., formalizing not only the *object language,* in which one talks about the *scientific* objects, but also the *meta-language,* in which one talks about the *logical* objects and the pertinent "object language" itself). This is the ultimate stage in purifying the thought process of accounting as far as analytical foundations are concerned. Such a common meta-linguistic basis enables a better comparison between those three axiomatic approaches.

To illustrate how an axiomatic basis can be used for a conditional–normative approach (see Chapter 11), the next section presents some basic assumptions as well as theorems. It also demonstrates the distinction between *ordinary* "basic assumptions" (A-1 to A-11) and "placeholder assumptions" (A-12 to A-21). The latter provide flexibility and enable the incorporation of specific purpose-oriented or instrumental hypotheses that are the linchpins for a normative–conditional approach (for illustrations of instrumental hypotheses, see Chapter 6).

Is a General Theory of Accounting Feasible?

Accounting research during the "adolescent period" spread in many directions. The present state of accounting research resembles a jigsaw puzzle, where some areas grow slowly into meaningful configurations but without yielding the entire picture. Indeed, the individual fragments seem to spread outward and not toward a common center. The centrifugal force at work is manifested in the great variety and constant proliferation of accounting topics. Above all, if the fugitive pieces of our discipline cannot be held together, there is danger that accounting as an academic discipline might either disintegrate or be partly absorbed by neighboring fields.

Promoted by a greater interest in axiomatization, the effort to integrate accounting was stronger during the 1960s and 1970s than it is today.[3] The FASB's attempt to create a conceptual framework could have provided an excellent focus for integration; but apart from lacking a formalized approach, the exclusion of managerial as well as macro-accounting and other subareas limited this undertaking to financial accounting. In related fields, such as MIS and management science, the need for integration is also perceived and becomes particularly pressing in times of opulent growth, specialization, and the designing of expert systems.[4]

Where no general theory is available there are no means to integrate the specific theories that might need to be devised anew, again and again, every time a specific system is employed in a particular situation. Under such circumstances, generalization—the quintessence of the scientific approach—is impeded; and all other endeavors, such as better conceptualization and interpretation or rigorous employment of scientific methodology, lose a great deal of their ultimate power. This problem of integration concerns every academic accountant, as the lack of an overall framework affects most research areas and makes it difficult to fit them into a coherent whole.

An early proposal to integrate *all* areas of micro- as well as macro-accounting was launched in Mattessich (1957) and its elaboration coincided with the axiomatic literature mentioned earlier. The difficulty of integrating various accounting areas lies in formulating the connections between the relatively simple basic assumptions and the great number of mathematical as well as verbal models encountered in our discipline. Obviously, it is much easier to develop specific accounting theories that are only loosely connected with each other; but this led to a steady decrease of interest in a general accounting theory. Thus, the fate of a comprehensive general theory rests with future generations. Will they consider such research to be worthwhile; or will they, perhaps, deem the effort too great in comparison to the expected reward? Watts and Zimmerman, in referring to normative theories, brush off the possibility of a general theory of accounting with the remark that "the diversity of positions prevents general agreement on a theory of accounting. . . . Not only are the researchers unable to agree on the objectives of financial statements, but they also disagree over the methods of deriving the prescriptions from the objectives" (1979, 273, 274).[5] This is precisely why an underlying and unifying framework of general assumptions, leading to specific hypotheses (capable of properly connecting ends to means), is called for.

Whatever happens, the question will persist whether a unified or general theory of accounting is possible in principle and, if so, to what degree and in which way a formalized integration of various subareas of accounting would be feasible. Answering those questions will require much experimenting. My own answers are found in the attempt to combine uniformity *with variety* by offering a framework consisting of two kinds of premises: (1) basic assumptions, and (2) specific purpose-oriented hypotheses.[6] The basic assumptions manifest the general characteristics of all accounting systems, some of which provide placeholders for the specific assumptions. The latter enable adaptation to a variety of particular purposes through the choice of exchangeable alternatives, as outlined later.

Interpretation through Specification of Objectives

The basic maxim underlying this study is the fact that a clear knowledge of one's goal is required to determine efficient means for achieving such a goal. This social truth is so general that it reaches beyond the framework of accounting as here considered. The major goals of accounting proper are, on one side, the monitoring of custodial, financial, and managerial accountability; on the other side, the supplying of further information to facilitate various decisions (primarily of investment and resource allocation [see Chapter 8]). The means to attain these goals

82   CRITIQUE OF ACCOUNTING

become *objectives*; the foremost among these is the pragmatic *conceptual representation* of a segment of social reality on the basis of cost–benefit and similar considerations (in contrast to the positive conceptual representation of the pure sciences [see Figure 11.1]). Further objectives and subobjectives are found in the establishment of various hypotheses of valuation, classification, realization, and so on, depending on different specific ends (needs) to be stipulated by the consumer of such information or in anticipation of such stipulation. Illustration of specific ends are offered in Chapter 6, where, for example, the need for different ways to maintain capital is discussed.

Such considerations lead to a hierarchy of objectives, the first formal manifestation of which may be found in a distinction between basic assumptions and specific hypotheses (see Mattessich 1964a, 1972). Whereas the *basic assumptions* ought to constitute a common frame of accounting systems in general, the *specific hypotheses* would give interpretation to the overall theory. The need for "interpretation" in accounting is mentioned in Chapter 4.[7] In Mattessich (1964a), I used budgeting systems in the attempt to offer illustrations for pragmatic (i.e., instrumental) hypotheses. In Chapter 6, I shall continue my endeavor to clarify the essence of those kinds of hypotheses. To disregard the empirical nature of the specific hypotheses (and thus of the entire theory) would create a misunderstanding of the basic thrust of my original endeavor as well as the present search for a conditional–normative methodology following from it. Despite this, some colleagues seemed to have misunderstood those endeavors and believe that "the mathematical formulations of the accounting processes by Mattessich [footnote omitted] are examples of theoretical expositions which rely for their validation on the truth criteria of mathematics" (Williams and Griffin 1969, 163).

As hinted at previously, the first prerequisite for a conditional–normative theory is the specification of various information objectives—a need that has been sporadically emerging in accounting. The early distinction between financial and cost accounting, and the later distinction between tax accounting, financial accounting, auditing, and so on, were the first modest steps toward purpose-oriented accounting and a corresponding taxonomic structure. Further evidence lies in the weary controversies about the correct accounting method as to valuation basis, realization criterion, depreciation and allocation methods, classification schemes, and so forth. This issue is blurred because rarely is the question asked, "Which instrumental hypotheses (means–end relations) are appropriate for a relative narrowly defined purpose, and which for another?" Too often, accountants behave as though there existed only one overall purpose of accounting. Thus, for decades, the inquiry was directed toward the one and only correct set of rules—something bound to lead to futile discussions and misunderstandings. However, the root of the problem seems to lie much deeper, namely, in the difficulty of formulating specific, well-defined purposes that can be matched to specific sets of hypotheses.

Some experts deem this to be a hopeless task and hold on to the ill-defined uni- or multipurpose accounting system of the past, while others seek refuge in a positive approach that banishes norms altogether from the theoretical framework of accounting.[8] Those who plead for an objective-oriented approach believe that such impediments constitute a challenge rather than a deterrent. Many accountants, however, are uncommitted, perhaps not recognizing the crucial issue involved. If optimism is justified, it is because we are not alone in the dilemma of identifying objectives and determining the optimal model for a specific purpose. We share this challenge with management scientists, systems experts, and applied scientists in general. Their search for a solution might even lead to a cooperative effort between academic accountants and other applied scientists.

The most promising approach to this problem still seems to be the acceptance of a limited number of typical standard purposes (tax accounting, commercial–legalistic accounting, short-run planning and control, long-run planning, investment decision making, decision making in current operations including personnel policy, and so on) from which a larger number of subpurposes may be derived. Since different concepts and subconcepts are required for different purposes and subpurposes, respectively, the need for a comprehensive taxonomic system of accounting is closely tied to the hierarchy of objectives.

The great variety of interacting accounting concepts and situations complicates this task. Take the example of "three" different depreciation methods which lead to different interpretations of the income and capital concepts. Heaping on this, three different valuation methods would lead to nine different interpretations of income and of capital. Since there are more than three depreciation and more than three valuation methods, and since there are many more factors (e.g., issues of allocation, classification, data input, duration, realization, relevance, and the like, beyond depreciation and valuation methods), the concepts of income, capital, and so on, will be affected. Thus, the problem gets easily out of hand, and a huge maze of subconcepts and interpretations could arise.

Such complexities do not come into being through the resolve of building a hierarchy of concepts. They lie in the very marrow of our discipline. Hence, the task is not so much to invent concepts but to better define and impose an order upon them. The problem of specifying objectives goes beyond that of a conceptual hierarchy; it depends, above all, on the ability to test whether an intended purpose has been fulfilled by a specific system.

ILLUSTRATING ACCOUNTING AXIOMS AND THEOREMS

The main purpose of this section is to illustrate the difference between the ordinary basic assumptions and those that hold a place for specific purpose-oriented hypotheses of a double-classificational accounting system. This distinction is crucial for understanding the link between my previous work (e.g., Mattessich 1964a) and the conditional–normative approach presented in this book (particularly in Chapter 11). To illustrate this, it is sufficient to list the basic axioms and a few theorems without going into the entire axiomatic framework with all the definitions, proofs, interpretations, and so on (though the Appendix to this chapter will show how a proof to the first theorem may be constructed).[9]

The following basic assumptions (A-1 to A-11) all refer to some empirical phenomena used in the conceptual representation of accounting, while the remaining ten assumptions (A-12 to A-21) are placeholders for the specific objective-oriented hypotheses that depend on the managerial goal and the information objective (to be specified in assumption A-12). These placeholders make an axiomatic system flexible; create room for interpretation; and in combination with the pertinent specific or instrumental hypotheses, enable the transition from a positive basis to a conditional–normative accounting system.

A-1. *Attribute*: There is some (i.e., at least one) changeable attribute (value, quantity, quality, and so on) belonging to an economic object; the magnitude of such attribute is representable within a number system.

A-2. *Time measure*: There is a sequence of relatively small time intervals (e.g., dates) that can be ordered, added (to longer time periods), measured, differentiated, and so on, by means of a number system.

A-3. *Economic objects*: There is some economic object (asset, debt, ownership claim, and so on), the changeable attributes (e.g., values, quantities, and so on) of which are representable by an accounting system.

A-4. *Economic subjects*: There is some economic subject which owns, or owes, or controls economic objects, or has preferences and is setting objectives for the accounting system.

A-5. *Economic entity*: There is some economic entity (with such attributes as income, assets, debts and owners' equity, and the like) represented by a specific accounting system. Such entity consists of economic subjects and economic objects and can enter into contracts.

A-6. *Structure*: There is some empirical structure (e.g., a hierarchy of economic subjects, objects, attributes, and so on) reflecting essential facts about the pertinent entity.

A-7. *Input–output principle*: Every transfer of a concrete economic good (nonmonetary asset) from one "location" (e.g., accountability center) to another, *preserves* some essential property (substance, quantity, value, and so on) in regard of which the output from one location corresponds essentially to the input in the other location.

A-8. *Symmetry principle*: On any asset (scarce economic resource), there is a claim (of either ownership or debt), the value of which is *equal to* but not identical with the "asset value" (the latter is something different than an "equity value," usually designated by an opposite or negative sign).

A-9. *Economic transactions*: There is some empirical event (either a transfer of a commodity within *one or more* entities or the creation or redemption of a debt or ownership claim, including pertinent changes in attributes) that changes the composition or structure of an entity. Such an event is representable within a single entity by an "accounting transaction" (e.g., a debit to one account and credit to another account [see theorem T-1 later in this section]).

A-10. *Linear aggregation*: For every account (a_i; $i = 1, \ldots, n$) at any time (after some time period [p^s] has elapsed) and the values (v, with various sub- and superscripts), an addition operation (B, called "balancing") is carried out such that a value can be assigned at any time to the account:

$$B(a_i, p^s) = v_i^s = \sum_{s=1}^{r} \sum_{j=1}^{n} (v_{ji}^r - v_{ij}^r);$$

$$j = 1, \ldots, n \text{ (n being the number of accounts)}.$$

A-11. *Additivity of attributes of the same kind*: There is some attribute (of an economic object) that is additive; that is, in an aggregate of "similar" economic objects, the numeric values of the pertinent attribute can be added (linearly) to the numeric value of the attribute of the same kind of other objects.

A-12. *Purpose orientation*: There is some specific purpose and information objective to be attained by a particular accounting system. *Comment:* This purpose determines the set of specific hypotheses for which the further placeholder axioms are provided. Hence, an *instrumental hypothesis* consists partly of the specification of this purpose and partly of specifications called for by subsequent axioms (A-13 to A-21), which then lead to the means to be sought (compare Chapter 6).

A-13. *Valuation*: There is some specific hypothesis, that (in correspondence with A-3) assigns a value to the objects of a particular accounting transaction.

A-14. *Redemption of debts*: There is some specific hypothesis (e.g., legal conventions) regulating the redemption of debts (e.g., repayment at nominal value in spite of price-level changes).

A-15. *Realization*: There is some specific hypothesis determining whether an accounting transaction either
   a. changes the current income (and, therefore, owners' equity) of the entity
   b. changes the value of owners' equity without changing the current income
   c. does not change owners' equity during the current period.

A-16. *Classification*: There is some hypothesis determining the chart of accounts that reflects the structure and hierarchy of the accounting system.

A-17. *Data input*: There is some hypothesis determining the data input.

A-18. *Duration*: There is some hypothesis determining duration of the accounting period (and conjecturing the continuation or noncontinuation of the entity).

A-19. *Relevance* (materiality): There is some hypothesis determining when an economic event requires an accounting transaction.

A-20. *Distribution*: There is some hypothesis determining the distribution of value flows to subunits of the entity.

A-21. *Consolidation*: There is some hypothesis determining the conditions under which two or more accounting systems can be merged (i.e., to be united to a more comprehensive accounting system).

The set–theoretical representation and proofs of the subsequent theorems are similar to those presented in Mattessich (1970a, 106–112) with the exception of the proof for T-1. This latter statement was previously formulated as an axiom (e.g., assumption 5 in Mattessich 1964a, 35; item 17 in *idem*, 454; and, with greater clarity, as assumption 8 in Mattessich 1970a, 35) but is now presented as a consequence of more basic propositions. Theorem T-1 is based on fundamental social–empirical facts, and its proof is sketched in the Appendix of this chapter.

T-1. *Double-classification theorem*: If there is some accounting transaction (T), it attributes a value (v or v^r_{ij}) to a three-dimensional vector. This vector consists of an account to be credited (a_i), an account to be debited (a_j), and a time point (t^r):

$$T(a_i, a_j, t^r) = v^r_{ij} \quad i, j = 1, \ldots, n \ (n = \text{number of accounts})$$

T-2. *Trial balance equality theorem*: In a trial balance, the total of all debit balances (positive) is equal to the *negative* total of all credit balances.

T-3. *The two statements theorem*: If there are two accounting statements comprising together all accounts with nonzero balances contained in the chart of accounts (at the end of period p^s), then the balance of the first accounting statement is equal to the *negative* of the balance of the second statement.

T-4. *Combination theorem*: Two accounting transactions (F_1 and F_2, for "flows"), occurring simultaneously and belonging to the same entity, can together be substituted by a third accounting transaction (F_3), provided the value going to the credit account(s) of the original transaction is identical with the value going to the debit account(s) of the original transaction.

T-5. *Substitution theorem*: A pair of requited (interentity) transactions can be substituted by two intraentity transactions each of which belongs to one of the two entities involved.

T-6. *Consolidation theorem*: Two or more trial balances ($B^s_1, \ldots, B^s_m$) of distinct entities ($e_1, \ldots, e_m$ at the end of period p^s) can be consolidated in a single trial balance (B^s_n) of an "aggregate entity" (e_n) if so desired.

IN SEARCH OF PRINCIPLES OF TESTING

Systematic testing procedures are a crucial element in any scientific approach. The pure sciences test the truth of hypotheses and theories by means of verification, confirmation, or refutation. The applied sciences test the efficiency, relevance, reliability, or other properties of a normative theory or a system (like a machine) by a variety of means. Mechanical devices, such as automobiles, are tested in many ways and with respect to many properties. Some or all of these properties (price, relative gasoline consumption and other economic aspects, horse power, acceleration speed, sturdiness, and other safety features), or their combinations, are compared from model to model or against a standard pattern determined by the intended usage. Only then can the appropriate choice for a specific purpose be made. Most readers are familiar with this kind of "testing" from reading consumer reports and buying various contraptions. Although accounting models or information systems are more than mechanical devices, there can be little doubt that they, too, are part of the realm of applied science and thus are subject to similar principles of testing. Obviously, this testing can span a wide spectrum of rigor, from informal estimation of certain properties to highly sophisticated measures; but the more complex an information system is or the more demanding its users are, the more difficult the testing procedures are likely to be.

Testing a General Theory of Accounting

Whenever a general framework for accounting—with basic assumptions, supplemented by sets of specific instrumental hypotheses (as outlined previously)—is seriously considered, the following maxims for testing such a system are required:

1. The testing (be it verification, confirmation, or the like) of a general theory of accounting must be tied to the specific hypotheses governing the specific system.
2. A particular accounting system is tested by trying to determine systematically whether it is "satisfactory under the circumstances," that is, for a well-specified purpose.
3. A general theory of accounting may be created in a *recursive* but noncircular way: Starting from the basis of an operational definition of accounting, one would draw, on the basis of experience and existing information needs, sharp but preliminary boundaries of what constitutes an accounting system. Then, all systems obeying the conditions of the operational definitions ought to be tested. If some of those specific accounting systems do not fulfill the specified purpose to the degree desired, it must be determined why this is so. If the failure is because of some auxiliary propositions, then these hypotheses must be exchanged or amended, changing, first, only the structure of the *specific* part of the accounting system. If, however, the failure is because of some basic assumption, the latter must be exchanged or amended; thus, the structure of both the general theory and the specific parts will change. In this way also, the general theory is confirmed or refuted every time a specific system is put to test. For this reason, refutation of a general theory is conceivable, and circularity can be avoided.[10]
4. The methodology thus described is independent of the boundaries of the general theory. By choosing a narrower or broader set of basic assumptions (forming the boundary), accountants may agree to concern themselves with double-entry or triple-entry models only, or with MIS of even wider scope.
5. The formulation of hypotheses for specific accounting objectives (means–end relations) through behavioral and other empirical research might be one of the major tasks faced by future accountants. For now, there are no satisfactory answers to such questions as the following: (a) How purpose oriented are users of accounting information (and how much are they aware of it), and which kind of information would they desire or need for which objective? (b) What is the effect of different interpretations of value, income, and realization on users of accounting; and above all, which interpretation matches which information purpose? (c) What is the effect of different allocation and classification schemes, and different degrees of aggregation, different periodization (interim reports) on users of accounting, and above all, which scheme matches which purpose?
6. The cathartic task of this transition period would lie in converting rules of thumb into well-grounded, objective-oriented hypotheses.[11] Such a process of conversion is not based on the fallacious notion that action is the test of theory but on the insight that, in the long-run, action can be improved by searching for and implementing reliable means–end relations.

In the 1960s and the beginning of the 1970s, high hopes still existed that academic search for a general theory of accounting would continue and eventually be successful. These hopes were abandoned, or at least postponed, because of a combination of various circumstances, among which two factors were decisive: (1) the advent of positive accounting theory (trying to banish normative premises) and its strong influence on young accounting researchers; and (2) the failure of professional accounting bodies and the FASB to employ rigorous analytical means in developing a conceptual framework of accounting. Such a trend did not involve abandoning all analytical methods in accounting research; it merely caused a shift in direction from axiomatization toward information economics and related areas. The next section sketches this development in a few rough strokes.

ECONOMICS OF INFORMATION

The two major pioneers of information economics are Jacob Marschak (e.g., 1954, 1964, 1974—including Marschak and Miyasawa 1968, and Marschak and Radner 1972), and George Stigler (1961, 1962). The latter received the 1982 Nobel Memorial Prize for his seminal work in the "economic theory of information" (together with his theory of public regulation).[12] In the wake of these pioneers and their publications followed a host of other authors who greatly elaborated each of these fields or branched out into new related ones. Analytical accountants, too, were greatly influenced by these developments and made conspicuous contributions by designing information models adapted to accounting situations (e.g., Feltham et al. 1988; Feltham and Demski 1970; and Demski and Feltham 1972, 1976, 1978, who received not only the AICPA/AAA Literature Award in 1971 but the even more prestigious AAA Award for Seminal Contribution to Accounting Literature in 1994). But those models rely on simplifying assumptions and are hardly designed for immediate use in actual practice, yet the subsequent fusion of information economics with agency theory offers some hope for a more practice-oriented approach. Noreen (1988) and Chi (1989) even tried to relate agency theory to ethics.

Another early paper on this subject by Mock (1971, winner of the AAA Manuscript Contest) supplemented the research by Demski and Feltham. Among other things, it drew attention to the fact that the concept of information value used in information economics is only one among several concepts or interpretations. Mock distinguished between various types of information (economic value of information, model value of information, and feedback value of information). This classification was later extended by Butterworth and Falk (1986), who put particular stress on the distinction between contracting information and decision-making information.

Information Economics as an Extension of Decision Theory

Information economics analyzes the economic consequences of, as well as the demand for, alternative information systems. As Feltham points out:

> The development of models of *rational choice under uncertainty* by such pioneers as von Neumann and Morgenstern (1944) can be viewed as the starting point of information economics. They demonstrated that if an individual's choice behavior satisfies a few rather basic "consistency" axioms, then this behavior can be represented as the maximization of his expected utility for the consequences of the actions available to him. (Feltham 1984, 181–182)

Thus, information economics is an extension of statistical decision theory,[13] which usually begins with a finite number of *strategies* or possible actions to be chosen by the decision maker (e.g., alternative crops to be planted), and a number of alternative *states of the world* (e.g., different weather situations) the occurrence of which are beyond the control of the decision maker. To each of these combinations (of crops and weather alternatives), an estimated payoff value (e.g., a dollar profit) is assigned. If each state of nature has a known (or estimated) probability of occurrence (determined, for example, by long-term weather forecasts), one can calculate not only the expected payoff (i.e., average value) of each combination but also of each strategy, covering all alternative states of weather. Last, among these alternatives, the *strategy with the highest expected payoff is chosen.*

Information economics, the most important theorem proven by Blackwell (1951, 1953),[14] introduces explicitly to this basic statistical decision model the notion of information. It asks how can each strategy (e.g., of crop planting) be improved by an information system (e.g., subscribing to a long-term weather forecasting information service), provided the probabilities of a successful forecast of each state can be estimated (e.g., from the track record of this service). Again, the expected value of each strategy, now in light of the weather forecast, can be calculated and compared with the expected value from the previously mentioned decision model (i.e., without benefit of a long-term weather forecasting service). The difference in the expected payoff of each strategy is supposed to indicate its gross benefit of using the information system (i.e., subscribing to the forecasting service). The net benefit of each strategy results from deducting the information cost (i.e., subscription fee). Most important, with the use of such an information system, the optimal strategy need no longer be the same as the one recommended by the simple decision model. Furthermore, similar analyses can be employed for competing information systems in order to choose the optimal system among them by determining not only the value of information but also that of each of those systems. Thus, decision making in the longrun could be improved by using information that (1) costs less than its value, and (2) is cheaper than supplied by another available information system.

Information and Team Theory

Marschak's (1954) seminal paper explored the finding of what is nowadays addressed as the optimal or quasi-optimal "information structure" within a firm.[15] In other words, which information and communication scheme between individual entities or persons (e.g., departments or their heads as a "team") is most desirable for attaining the goal of the entire enterprise? Or who (in a firm or other entity) must know what, and who must report or communicate to whom? This analysis was later greatly elaborated in Marschak and Radner (1972). By its very nature, this research focused on internal relationships between persons of supposedly common interest. It stimulated much interest in circles of game and decision theory, organization theory, and academic accounting. For the pertinent accounting literature, refer to Chapter 7.

Information and the Market

External relationships were neglected by this kind of information research, and it is in the area of market information where another seminal paper, that by Stigler (1961), filled a crucial gap. He was led, as admitted in his memoirs (see Stigler 1988, 79–80), to the problem of information by the obvious fact that when shopping around long enough, one can often find a lower price for a (homogenous) commodity than originally encountered. This is contrary to the teachings of traditional economics of perfect competition. He also noticed that it costs time and often money to search for a better price and stipulated that the major obstacle to a complete search in finding the best price are the information costs. The latter are a type of "transaction costs" which were, at about the same time, exposed by Coase (1960), another Nobel laureate, as crucial in impeding the workings of perfect competition according to standard economic theory.

Phlips (1988, 26–27) points at the limitations of Stigler's work, which later stimulated others to overhaul some aspects either partially or even fully. Phlips claims that in reality consumers are usually aware which shops are expensive and which are cheap but are less aware about the distribution of prices, which is opposite to the assumption of Stigler, who also fails to offer an analysis of price distribution. Furthermore, Stigler assumes that the number of price searches (and other search rules) is determined beforehand, while it would be more realistic to keep the number of searches open ended and take a certain learning process into consideration. Thus, Stigler's search rule is not optimal, while a sequential rule (i.e., after each price quotation the buyer decides whether to continue the search) is claimed to be optimal.

Some publications by another Nobel laureate, Arrow (e.g., 1973, 1979, 1984), show his long-standing interest in information economics. In a way, it was Arrow who created the preconditions that tie information economics to the rest of modern neoclassical theory. Other economists as well as accounting academics contributed to this area, in particular to the special problem of public information. Hirschleifer (1971) provided the original analysis of public information (under pure market conditions and other stringent assumptions); and accountants such as Hakansson et al. (1982), Kunkel (1982), and Ohlson (1988) extended this analysis (the latter two papers included production conditions). Ohlson (1988) also examined the social or welfare value of public information, attempting to answer under what conditions public information had value. If the consumer has all the competing prices at his or her disposal, one speaks of *complete* information. This is rarely the case in actual practice, and such a situation is analytically less interesting than cases of *incomplete* information. This explains why, in recent times, experts prefer to speak of the "economics of incomplete information."

A large amount of research has accumulated in this area, well surveyed by Phlips (1988), Laffont (1989), and others. It ranges from an examination of information sequences (e.g., predecision versus postdecision information) to different types of auctions, price dispersions and predatory pricing, signals and "signaling theory," credit rationing, antitrust implications, different kinds of economic equilibria, contingent markets and constraining contract clauses, competition among agents, and even to cheating and misinformation.

One of the most influential ideas in this area is the notion of *informational asymmetry* (i.e., one party possessing better relevant information than the other) so characteristic for most situations of market uncertainty. This notion is best illustrated by Akerlof's (1970) widely known paper, "The Market for 'Lemons,'" which uses the second-hand car market to analyze and demonstrate the informational advantage the dealer has over the prospective buyer (the dealer is more likely to know about the accidents and repairs of a specific second-hand car than is the buyer). Because the information asymmetry cannot be resolved without cost, only a fraction of potential trades occurs, at a lower equilibrium price.

Information asymmetry is a widespread phenomenon wherever contracts are being entered into, be it in hiring a manager or other employee (where the person to be hired knows much better his or her qualifications as well as shortcomings than the prospective employer does), in a medical insurance contract (where the person to be insured is often much better aware of his or her ailments than the insurer), or many other contractual arrangements. Its major conclusion confirms the insight that the optimal policy of the seller is to abstain from revealing some information (e.g., the product's quality) if the latter cannot be readily verified. If such verification is possible, it is economically optimal for the seller to grant a warranty to the buyer, which, in turn, induces the production of better qualities. Information asymmetry is closely related to two other important notions: moral hazard and adverse selection (see also Chapter 8).

The problem of *moral hazard* arises out of the agent's or the principal's temptation to act in one's own interest, even if the contractual interest of the other party is thereby short-changed. As the principal can usually not fully monitor the agent's activity—and since agency-information theory assumes that each party maximizes its own utility—the agent's optimal action may not be optimal for the principal (unless special contractual arrangements, as recommended by this theory, are being made).

The problem of *adverse selection* is a possible consequence of asymmetric information between principal and agent (often, but not always, in favor of the agent). For example, the agent or manager may have an *information advantage* over the principal because of the former's better or more specialized training and experience. If, therefore, one party withholds some information that otherwise would lead the other party to choose a contract or action less favorable to the first but more favorable to the second party, then this adverse selection impedes a first-best solution.

Another basic insight of information economics, particularly relevant to the analysis of this book, is expressed by Daley:

One of the most pervasive results of early analytical research on information is that there are very few situations in which a single summary measurement can convey all of the underlying information of use to a decision maker about an object. Researchers refer to this situation as not being able to provide a "sufficient statistic" for a distribution where sufficiency implies that once a decision maker has a single summary measure, all of the characteristics of the distribution are described. (Daley 1994, 40)

Despite much insight provided by information economics, one must realize that the notion of information is by no means limited to economics. The information revolution of the twentieth century has affected all sciences, from physics to biology and the social sciences, from medicine to genetic engineering and computer technology. Just like energy, information is a fundamental organizing force. Without it, cybernetic feedbacks cannot function, organisms perish, organizations break down, and accounting systems become meaningless (for further details, see Mattessich 1993a, 567–576).

APPENDIX

Sketch for a Proof of Theorem T-1 (Double-Classification Theorem)

Comment: This refers to the penultimate section. For the sake of better understanding the theorem is here repeated and its proof formulated, predominantly verbally. A purely mathematical formulation could be rendered with greater precision, but it is hoped that the gist of this proof is conveyed with sufficient clarity in spite of its surprising length. The comprehensiveness of this proof is a result of the insight that double classification is a consequence, not of one but of *three different* dualities (see Chapter 3). These dualities interact in a fashion that makes possible a conceptual representation of economic transactions between several entities by means of accounting transactions of a single entity. This is the greatly misunderstood ingenuity of "double entry" (or, more generally, "double classification") not the fact that every entry must be recorded in the debit as well as in the credit.

T-1. *Double-classification theorem*: If there is some accounting transaction (T), it attributes a value (v or v^r_{ij}) to a three-dimensional vector. This vector consists of an account to be credited (a_i), an account to be debited (a_j), and a time point (t^r):

$$T(a_i, a_j, t^r) = v^r_{ij} \quad i, j = 1, \ldots, n \ (n = \text{number of accounts})$$

Proof/Step 1: Suppose an accounting transaction (T) is to represent the transfer of a *tangible* economic object (e.g., a commodity [see A-3]) with attribute v (e.g., a dollar value [see A-1]) from "output location" (i) to "input location" (j) at time *(T)* [see A-2] within entity (e) [see A-5]). Suppose further that accounts a_i and a_j (of entity e at time t^r) represent the output (credit) and input (debit) locations of a commodity, respectively. If, according to A-7, the attribute (v [e.g., value]) can be assumed to be preserved in such a transfer, then the representation through an accounting transaction (T) consists of three components (a_i, a_j, and t^r) to which the value v is to be assigned. Furthermore, if it is assumed that the first component of a three-dimensional vector stands for the account to be credited, the second for the account to be debited, and the third for the transaction time, then such an accounting transaction can be considered as an operation

$$T(a_i, a_j, t^r) = v$$

on a three-dimensional vector to which a value v is assigned. For better distinction (from different values in other transactions), v can be written as v_{ij}^r; hence, $T(a_i, a_j, t^r) = v_{ij}^r$ (*quod erat demonstrandum* [QED] for the conceptual representation of the transfer of a tangible economic object).

Step 2: Suppose that the event to be represented is not the transfer of a commodity from one location to another within the entity (e) but the creation of a claim (ownership or debt) on entity e at t^r, whereby the economic object to be invested or loaned has the attribute v (e.g., value). Suppose also that account a_i (of entity e) represents the investor or the lender (credit) and that account a_j (also of entity e) represents the economic object (debit), respectively. If, according to A-8, there is a symmetry in the attribute (e.g., value) of the object invested or loaned, on one side, and the ownership or debt claim, on the other side, then the representation of such an event through an accounting transaction (T) also consists of the three components (a_i, a_j, and t^r) to which the value v (or v_{ij}^r) is to be assigned. Furthermore, if the first component of the three-dimensional vector stands for the account to be credited, the second for the account to be debited, and the third for the transaction time, such an accounting transaction can be considered as an operation

$$T(a_i, a_j, t^r) = v$$

on a three-dimensional vector to which a value v (or v_{ij}^r) is assigned; Hence, $T(a_i, a_j, t^r) = v_{ij}^r$ (QED for the conceptual representation of creating of an ownership or a debt claim).

Step 3: If the event is not the creation but the *redemption* of a claim (ownership or debt), the argument and result are the same, except that account a_i would stand for the economic object (e.g., asset to be credited), and account a_j for the claim (to be debited); hence, $T(a_i, a_j, t^r) = v_{ij}^r$ (QED for the conceptual representation of redeeming an ownership or a debt claim).

Step 4: Suppose the event concerns a transaction in which entity e "exchanges" a *tangible asset* (represented either in account a_j or a_i) for an asset constituting a claim (represented either in account a_i or a_j)[16] at time t^r (e.g., credit "commodities" and debit "receivables" or vice versa). Then there exists a claim (usually an ownership claim) against the newly acquired asset (according to A-8). To the extent the exchange creates an incremental value in the new claim (e.g., a profit, as an increment in the ownership claim), it is taken care of in Step 2; to the extent that such an exchange does not create a new claim, the same value (v or $v_{ij}{}^r$) is assigned to both accounts at time t^r, hence, $T(a_i, a_j, t^r) = v_{ij}{}^r$ (QED for the exchange of a tangible asset against an asset constituting a claim).

Step 5: Suppose the event concerns an accounting transaction in which *one claim is exchanged against another claim* (e.g., a debt is converted into an ownership claim or vice versa). To the extent that such an exchange creates a new claim (e.g., a profit, as an increment in the ownership claim), it is taken care of in step 2; to the extent that such an exchange does not create a new claim, the same value (v or $v_{ij}{}^r$) is assigned to both accounts at t^r, hence, $T(a_i, a_j, t^r) = v_{ij}{}^r$ (QED for the exchange of two claims).

Step 6: Considering that the results of steps 1 to 5 (exhausting the basic category of accounting transactions [see A-9]) are identical, any accounting transaction (T) can be represented as an operation to a three-dimensional vector to which a value (v or $v_{ij}{}^r$) is assigned. Hence, at any time^r, to debit any account a_j and credit any other account a_i with the same value ($v_{ij}{}^r$ [double-classification]) is a vector operation

$$T(a_i, a_j, t^r) = v_{ij}{}^r \text{ (QED)}$$

NOTES

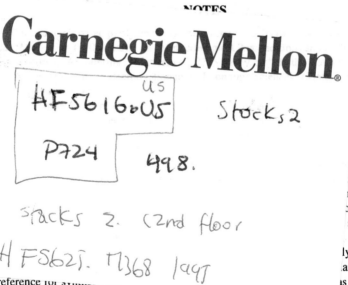

ytical Meth-
ns of a Gen-
Information
1993a), and

ound in Lee
ge CANDID,
:e and admin-

ause he based
:ation.
n the need for
onceptual, and
specifically in

lysis of minute
.arger frames of
is been focused
work in various

reference for syn......
more and more on overall-systems as frames of referen...
areas" (Johnson et al. 1964, 368).

5. To complain *flippantly* about the different methods, results, and so on, of the "normative" researchers of the 1960s has become a pastime among some "younger" academics. With reference to the axiomatic approach, for example, Dopuch states, "although each work seemed to take off from the same set of basic postulates, each was still able to arrive at a different destination" (Dopuch 1989, 42). Frecka, recapitulating this very passage of Dopuch adds a further unjustified twist by saying, "While many works [of the "axiomatic method"] started with the same basic postulates, each arrived at a different conclusion" (Frecka 1989a, 10 [note that "destination" has become "conclusion"]). Anyone familiar with the various postulational and axiomatic attempts of accountants must realize that the fact that the different conclusions (e.g., historical costs versus current entry value versus current exit value) are contained in the very premises which those authors made. Indeed, it would be a logical impossibility to reach different conclusions from the same premises (unless one wants to accuse those accountants of being ignorant of proper deductive procedures).

6. This approach seems to be confirmed as methodologically sound by Bunge (1967a, 402–403). See also American Accounting Association (1971d, 43–44).

7. The interpretation of a calculus or uninterpreted theory may be achieved by either a separate set of rules of interpretations or by incorporating these rules as premises. In the latter case, Carnap (1942) speaks of *meaning postulates*.

8. *Norm* usually means a standard or a rule. In this book, I use it in the first sense, above all, as a standard derived from one's value judgments, goals, or objectives pursued. As for the second sense, the term *means–end relation* (and its formalistic manifestation in "instrumental hypothesis") corresponds here to the notion of *rule*.

9. Similar, but more comprehensive, formalization attempts can be found in Mattessich (1964a, 16–45 and 446–465; 1970a, 27–112) and Balzer and Mattessich (1991).

10. Circularity, for example, would be involved in the following situation: (a) The general theory and analytical definition stipulate the basic assumptions (conditions); (b) the basic assumptions determine the specific systems; and (c) the general theory is verified by testing whether the specific systems fulfill the conditions stipulated in the analytical definition. The reader will have noticed that my suggestion for verification of the general theory is radically different from this circular one because the former depends on the fulfillment of well-defined purposes by the interpreted systems, whereas the latter merely hinges on the observance of definitional conditions.

11. "A rule is *grounded* if and only if it is based on a set of law formulas capable of accounting for its effectiveness. The rule that commands taking off the hat when greeting a lady is groundless in the sense that it is based on no scientific law but is conventionally adopted. On the other hand, the rule that commands greasing cars periodically is based on the law that lubricators decrease the wearing of parts by friction: this is neither a convention nor a rule of thumb like those of cooking or politicking: it is a well-grounded rule. We shall elucidate later on the concept of basing a rule on a law" (Bunge 1967b, 132–133).

12. Another pioneer, Fritz Machlup (e.g., 1962, 1980, 1982, 1984), laid the groundwork and elaborated what has become to be known as the "economics of the production and distribution of knowledge" (not pursued here because of its more limited impact on accounting; see also Machlup and Mansfield 1983). For a more general view of information and its nature, see Gorelik (1975) and Mattessich (1993a, namely, pp. 567–574).

13. This is confirmed by Arrow (1984), who points out in his Preface that "statistical method was an example for the acquisition of information" but warns that it is difficult to formulate a general theory of information because different kinds of information so far

have "no common unit." This book also contains an excellent (though dated) survey article (Arrow 1973) that is based on a presentation to businessmen, thus relatively easy to comprehend, offering insight into many aspects and implications of information economics.

14. Blackwell regards one information system as more informative than another. Precisely speaking, it should be "at least as informative" as another if it is never less valuable (if there exists no other single-person decision situation in which it is less valuable). Compare Feltham (1984, 182).

15. Phlips distinguishes the following three elements contained in the information structure: "the set of possible states of the world, the set of possible signals, and the probability that a signal is observed given that a state prevails" (Phlips 1988, 2).

16. A *claim asset* is any asset that represents a social claim (e.g., accounts receivable, bonds, or equity investments) of the entity against another person or entity.

CHAPTER 6

Valuation Models, Capital Maintenance, and Instrumental Hypotheses

The ultimate objective of this chapter is to examine and demonstrate how instrumental hypotheses (formalized means–end relations) can be formulated. One of the best ways to illustrate the need for, as well as the structure and components of, such hypotheses is by means of different capital maintenance requirements and the various valuation and price-level adjustment models based on them. This requires some familiarity with current value and other inflation-adjustment issues that have been somewhat neglected during the last decade or so. Even if such issues may not presently be considered relevant in some countries, they are highly acute in others. In Mexico and other Latin American countries, regulations for inflation accounting play an important function; and a truly international accounting cooperation and comparison will require greater competence in inflation issues. For these reasons, I shall first take the opportunity to recapitulate some details of an area which, despite its present neglect, will continue to be important for any accounting system aiming to separate operating from nonoperating gains. Such separation and the related call for all-inclusive income statements (the "clean surplus principle") has recently become particularly prominent in fundamental research on valuation theory by Ohlson (1990) and Feltham and Ohlson (1993, 1994), even though their notion of operating versus financing activity may deviate from the distinction between operating profit versus holding gains found in current value accounting.

Inflation accounting contains a number of subtle concepts that do not seem to be well understood by many accountants. Indeed, there exists a panoply of concepts expressing different holding gains (or losses) and their combinations, as well as income notions based on them. Such gains arise from "holding" nonmonetary or monetary (financial) assets and liabilities in times of inflation, deflation, or due to price changes of specific assets. Apart from being either *monetary* or *nonmonetary* or partly one, partly the other (*mixed* $_{M\&N}$), these holding gains may simultaneously be *real* or *fictitious* or partly one, partly the other (*mixed* $_{R\&F}$) and, in addition, may be *realized* or *unrealized* or partly one, partly the other (*mixed* $_{r\&u}$). Historical (acquisition) cost accounting not only ignores many of those holding gains but conceals some of them in the profit from ordinary operations. The more of these details an accounting system reveals, the more informative it is expected to be, ceteris paribus. Thus, an explicit determination and separation of various holding gains from operating profits should reveal details about the operation and management of an enterprise, though authors like Prakash and Sunder (1979) seem to object to such a separation. Apart from the cost–benefit question (see Thornton 1986), this information is useless if accountants, financial analysts, and other users of financial statements are insufficiently trained and cannot properly interpret this kind of information. Indeed, this may be the primary reason why Beaver and Landsman (1983), in studying the reaction of statement users, came to the surprising conclusion that financial statements based merely on historical costs are at least as informative, or even more so, than those using current values or any other kind of price-level adjustment.[1]

For these reasons, I shall first try to explain the most important concepts of holding gains and the basic valuation models by means of schematic presentations (using a general price index [p] and a limited number of specific price indexes [r]) with concise algebraic formulas as well as concrete illustrations. In contrast to most previous discussions, based on numerical illustrations alone, the algebraic formulation in this chapter is more general, may enable a better comprehension, and may be helpful in the future computerization of inflation accounting, even though some simplifying assumptions had to be made (e.g., charges and revenues of interest are hidden in "depreciations and other expenses," and dividend and tax payments are here neglected).

Subsequently, I shall clarify the relation between price-level adjustment models and different capital maintenance requirements and point out the need for an empirical determination of the situations under which different capital maintenance bases are relevant. This demonstrates the need for instrumental hypotheses and their illustration in specific situations.

NOMINAL AND REAL CURRENT VALUE MODELS AND THEIR HOLDING GAINS

Table 6.1a shows in account form the beginning balance sheet (BS) at time t_0 (forming the starting point for all subsequent ending balance sheets at time t_1). Since monetary assets (M_0 or M_1) and nonmonetary assets (N_0 or N_1) behave differently

Table 6.1
Nominal CVA Model, without Operating Activity

Table 6.1a
BS at t_0 (Beginning Balance Sheet)

Monetary Assets	M_0	L_0	Liabilities.
Nonmonetary Assets	N_0	OE_0	Owners' Equity.
	$M_0 + N_0$	$L_0 + OE_0$	

Table 6.1b
BS at t_1 (nominal CVA, no operations)

$M_1 = M_0$	$L_1 = L_0$	
$N_1 = N_0 \cdot (1 + r)$	$OE_1 = \begin{cases} {}_NM_0 + N_0 \\ \quad + N_0 \cdot r \end{cases}$	Owners' Equity at t_0. Fictitious and Real Holding Gains.
$M_0 + N_0 \cdot (1 + r)$	$L_1 + OE_1 =$ $M_0 + N_0 \cdot (1 + r)$	

| ${}_NM_0 = M_0 - L_0$ $OE_0 = {}_NM_0 + N_0$ | Netmonetary assets (or liabilities, if $L_0 > M_0$, then M_0 becomes negative). |

Table 6.1c
BS at t_1 (real CVA, no operations)

$M_1 = M_0$	$L_1 = L_0$	
$N_1 = N_0 \cdot (1 + r)$	$OE_1 = \begin{cases} {}_NM_0 + N_0 \\ + ({}_NM_0 + N_0) \cdot p \\ - {}_NM_0 \cdot p \\ \\ + N_0 \cdot (r - p) \end{cases}$	Owners' Equity at t_0. Inflationary Adjustment to OE. Monetary Holding Gain (or Loss if $M_0 > L_0$). Real Nonmonetary Holding Gain (or Loss if $r < p$).
$M_0 + N_0 \cdot (1 + r)$	$L_1 + OE_1 =$ $M_0 + N_0 \cdot (1 + r)$	

under inflation and specific price changes, the asset side of the balance sheet shows such classification, while the equity side uses the customary division of liabilities (L_0 or L_1) and owners' equity (OE_0 or OE_1). Occasionally, it will be advantageous to represent the original owners' equity by its equivalent net worth ($_N M_0 + N_0$), whereby $_N M_0$ represents the *net* monetary assets or liabilities ($_N M_0 = M_0 - L_0$; whenever liabilities exceed monetary assets, $_N M_0$ will be negative).

I begin by making the following three assumptions: (1) a system of CVA (current-value accounting) is to be employed; (2) there exists, for the time being, only a current-value index $1 + r$ (applying to N_0 and indicating changes of a *specific* price, regardless of whether general price-level changes [represented by p] did or did not occur); and (3) *no* other transactions (than the specific price changes of nonmonetary assets) have occurred. Thus, we obtain the ending balance sheet at t_1 as shown in Table 6.1b.

Since the nominal values of monetary assets and liabilities are not affected by r (the percentage increase in the price of commodity N), it follows that $M_1 = M_0$, and $L_1 = L_0$, (provided there was no business operation, as stipulated by the third assumption). Then the value of the nonmonetary assets will increase by the mixed nonmonetary holding gain ($N_0 \cdot r$); hence,

$$N_1 = N_0 \cdot (1 + r) \text{ and } OE_1 = OE_0 + N_0 \cdot r = (_N M_0 + N_0) + (N_0 \cdot r)$$

Thus, both sides of the balance sheet are augmented by $N_0 \cdot r$; on the Dr side under "nonmonetary assets" and on the Cr side under "owners' equity." However, it is important to realize why $N_0 \cdot r$ is addressed as a *mixed* holding gain. At this stage, we do not know whether the specific price change of the nonmonetary assets contains some general (i.e., inflationary) price-level change p. Therefore, there exist the following three possibilities:

1. $N_0 \cdot r$ consists partly of a fictitious nonmonetary holding gain $N_0 \cdot p$ because of inflation and partly of a real nonmonetary holding gain $N_0 \cdot (r - p)$, provided $r \neq p$. (The term *gain* refers here also to losses, hence to positive as well as negative magnitudes.)
2. $N_0 \cdot r$ is identical to the real holding gain, provided $r \neq 0$ and $p = 0$.
3. $N_0 \cdot r$ is identical to the fictitious holding gain (merely because of inflation), provided $r = p$.

It will be obvious that any "real gain" from holding nonmonetary assets cannot be made through mere inflation or deflation; a real holding gain from nonmonetary assets requires that the specific (perceptual) price change (r) exceeds the inflation rate (p) (or vice versa in the case of a real holding loss) during an inflationary period. Thus, the *nominal* CVA version (i.e., without special consideration for inflation or GPL changes), as depicted in Table 6.1b, yields a distorted picture whenever $p \neq 0$ because it makes the reader of financial statements believe that $N_0 \cdot r$ augments the original owners' equity (N_0) by a real holding gain. This, however, may be partly or fully a fictitious gain.

One might argue that the available measures of general inflation are inaccurate and constitute only rough approximations; thus, they could be neglected. This argument not only confuses a mere measurement problem with a problem of substance and principle but also promotes, from the very outset, distorted figures within owners' equity in the balance sheet and an incorrect income statement. The previously mentioned weakness of this nominal CVA model is overcome by the real CVA model (Table 6.1c), which takes specific as well as general price-level changes into consideration.

In Table 6.1c, the asset side, as well as both balance sheet totals, are precisely the same as in Table 6.1b. The difference consists merely in a more informative subdivision of $N_0 \cdot r$ of the owners' equity section. First, we endeavor to reveal that, in times of inflation (or deflation), a monetary holding gain (or loss) emerges because of an excess of liabilities over monetary assets (or vice versa).[2] Further, we now reveal a real (instead of only a fictitious) nonmonetary holding gain $N_0 \cdot (r - p)$. Last, an inflationary adjustment (IA_{OE}) to owners' equity $(_NM_0 + N_0) \cdot p$ is required since all the new subdivisions must amount to

$$N_0 \cdot r = -_NM_0 \cdot p + N_0 \cdot (r - p) + (_NM_0 + N_0) \cdot p$$

This inflation adjustment $(N_0 \cdot p + _NM_0 \cdot p)$ actually consists of the fictitious gain $(N_0 \cdot p)$ and the monetary holding gain $(-_NM_0 \cdot p)$. The minus sign in front of the latter might be confusing, but it is because of the fact that only a negative "net monetary asset" can generate, in times of inflation, a "positive" monetary holding gain. Previously, income statements were not required, since we originally assumed that no operating transactions have occurred. As this assumption is now being abandoned, we find in Table 6.2 the BS and income statement (i.e., its profit adjustment) for the nominal CVA model (corresponding to Table 6.1b but under operating conditions), and Table 6.3 presents the BS and income statement for the real CVA model.

REALIZED VERSUS UNREALIZED HOLDING GAINS

The major differences between Tables 6.1c and 6.3a are as follows: first, the nonmonetary year-end assets can (in such a schematic presentation) no longer be stated in terms of original asset values, $N_1 = N_0 \cdot (1 + r)$, but must be expressed in terms of a weighted average (N_w) reflected on the asset as well as equity side of the BS (alternatively, one could weight the coefficient r). Furthermore, the CVA-adjusted (current) operating profit π_{co} (here assumed to be undistributed) appears as a separate component of the owners' equity section as well as the ultimate total of the income statement. The latter begins with the unadjusted (historical cost) operating profit π_{ho} but incorporates specific price-level adjustments for (weighted) cost of sales (i.e., cost of goods sold), $CS_w \cdot r$, and for (weighted) depreciation and similar expenses, $DE_w \cdot r$.

Table 6.2
Nominal CVA Model, with Operating Activity

Table 6.2a
BS at t_1 (nominal CVA)

M_1	L_1		
$N_w \cdot (1 + r)$	$OE_1 =$	$\begin{cases} {}_NM_0 + N_0 \\ \quad + N_w \cdot r \\ \\ \quad + \pi_{co} \end{cases}$	Owners' Equity at t_0. Fictitious and Real Non-monetary Holding Gains. Oper. Profit (CVA adjusted).
$M_1 + N_w \cdot (1 + r)$	$L_1 + OE_1$		

Table 6.2b
Income Statement (nominal CVA) or Profit Adjustment
(for period between t_0 and t_1)

π_{ho}	Historical Cost Operating Profit (unadjusted).
$- CS_w \cdot r$	Adjustment for Specific Price Changes of Cost of Sales.
$- DE_w \cdot r$	Adjustment for Specific Price Changes of Depreciation and Other Expenses (w = weighted).
π_{co}	(Current) Operating Profit, Adjusted for Specific Price Changes.

So far, we have distinguished between monetary and nonmonetary holding gains (depending on the source of assets or liabilities held) as well as between real and fictitious holding gains (depending on the cause—excess of specific over inflationary price changes versus mere general inflationary price-level changes). Now we need a third distinction, that between realized versus unrealized holding gains (in conformity with the well-known realization principle, according to which the value increase of a still unsold asset is considered to be unrealized). The two income-adjustment items, $CS_w \cdot r$ and $DE_w \cdot r$, are actually realized nonmonetary holding gains (but since referring to operating activity, they are called "realized cost savings" by Edwards and Bell [1961]), hidden in the historical cost operating income. Under a current value scheme, they are eliminated (see $-CS_w \cdot p$ and $-DE_w \cdot p$ in Table 6.2b) in order to show the CVA income π_{co} (called "current operating profit" by Edwards and Bell), which then is free of any such "hidden" holding gains.[3]

The Financial Accounting Standards Board's (1979) solution of the United States (Statement of Financial Accounting Standards No. 33 [SFAS 33], in force from about 1979 to 1984) adopted a version of the real CVA model that is roughly

Table 6.3
Real CVA Model, with Operating Activity

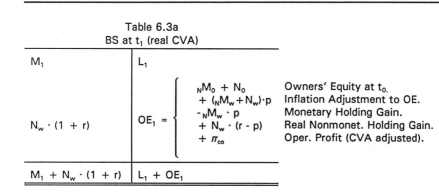

Table 6.3a
BS at t_1 (real CVA)

M_1	L_1		
$N_w \cdot (1 + r)$	$OE_1 =$	$\begin{cases} {}_NM_0 + N_0 \\ + ({}_NM_w + N_w) \cdot p \\ - {}_NM_w \cdot p \\ + N_w \cdot (r - p) \\ + \pi_{co} \end{cases}$	Owners' Equity at t_0. Inflation Adjustment to OE. Monetary Holding Gain. Real Nonmonet. Holding Gain. Oper. Profit (CVA adjusted).
$M_1 + N_w \cdot (1 + r)$	$L_1 + OE_1$		

Table 6.3b

Income Statement (real CVA) or Profit Adjustment
(for period between t_0 and t_1)

π_{ho}	Historical Cost (operating) Profit (unadjusted).
$- CS_w \cdot p$	General Price Level Adjustment for Cost of Sales.
$- DE_w \cdot p$	General Price Level Adjustment for Depreciation and Other Expenses (w = weighted).
π_{po}	Operating Profit, Adjusted for General Price Level Changes.
$-CS_w \cdot (r-p)$	Current minus General Price Level Adjustment of Cost of Sales.
$-DE_w \cdot (r-p)$	Current minus General Price Level Adjustment of Depreciation, etc. (w = weighted).
π_{co}	(Current) Operating Profit, Adjusted for Specific Price Changes.

represented by such items as $-{}_NM_w \cdot p$ and $N_w \cdot (r - p)$ of Table 6.3a, while Table 6.3b, corresponding to Table 6.1c, now reveals the CVA profit resulting from operating activity (the subdivision of the owners' equity section, OE, is similar to Table 6.1c, except that an operating profit appears and nonmonetary as well as net monetary assets are now expressed in terms of *weighted* averages).

SFAS 33 recommended a reconciliation and construction of owners' equity for real CVA balance sheet presentation but made only the real CVA income statement obligatory as supplementation to traditional financial statements. However, it also required that the income statement be extended by the "gain from decline in purchasing power of net amounts owed" (i.e., the monetary holding gain, $-{}_NM_w \cdot p$) as well as revealing the "excess of increase in specific prices over increase in the general price-level" (i.e., the real nonmonetary holding gain $N_w \cdot (r - p)$). These are the crucial items of the owners' equity section from which (together with traditional statements) a real CVA balance sheet is relatively easy to construct.

NUMERICAL ILLUSTRATION

The following specific illustration would have been put into an Appendix, were it not for the fact that the resulting figures are used in the section, Concepts of Capital Maintenance (and its Tables 6.6a to 6.6d). However, readers not interested in all the details of this illustration might be satisfied with glancing through Table 6.4 (a to g). To make the transition from algebraic presentations to illustrations with dollar figures (of the *nominal* and *real* CVA model, as well as the calculation of various holding gains), I have chosen a simplified example with two specific price changes—$r_1 = 0.25$ for inventory (on the FIFO basis), and $r_2 = 0.18$ for machinery—as well as a general inflation rate $p = 0.10$. Table 6.4a shows the beginning balance sheet and its data. Furthermore, I will make the following assumptions:

Mid-year events: Sales revenues (cash) $SR = 160,000$, the cost of sales (i.e., cost of goods sold) are $CS_h = 80,000$ (at historical cost), and $CS_c = CS_h \cdot (1 + r_1/2) = 80,000 \cdot 1.125 = 90,000$ (at current mid-year cost). Inventory purchases (cash) $_1P_c = 90,000$ (at current mid-year cost).

Year-end recognition of events: Annual depreciation rate of machinery (i.e., of $_2N_0$) $d_2 = 0.10$; liquidation of an old machine, the undepreciated historical cost value of which (included in $_2N_0$) was $_2N_h = 30,000$ for cash $_2N_c = {_2N_h} \cdot (1 - d_2) \cdot (1 + r_2) = 30,000 \cdot 0.90 \cdot 1.18 = 31,860$.

Assuming there are no further events (and no other expenses than cost of sales and depreciation), the various holding gains could be calculated in the following way (provided the CVA income figures and pertinent adjustments are based on average dollars of the pertinent year; however, the balance sheet items are all in current year-end prices, except for income items and adjustments to OE, which are in average dollars):

1. Monetary Holding Gain *(MHG):*

$$M_w = M_0 + \frac{SR - CS_c}{2} = 60,000 + \frac{160,000 - 90,000}{2} = \qquad 95,000$$

(*Weighted average* monetary assets here neglect cash from sale of the old machine, since this sale takes place at the end of the accounting period.)

$L_w = 180,000$ (no change during the period or year).

$$_NM_w = M_w - L_w = 95,000 - 180,000 = \qquad\qquad -85,000$$

$$MHG = -{_N}M_w \cdot p = -(-85,000 \cdot 0.10) = \qquad\qquad\qquad \underline{+8,500}$$

Table 6.4
Numerical Illustration of Nominal and Real CVA Models

Table 6.4a
Balance Sheet (in dollars) at t_0

Monetary Assets M_0	60,000	Liabilities	L_0	180,000
Nonmonetary Assets:				
Inventory $_1N_0$	100,000			
Machinery $_2N_0$	300,000	Owners' Equity:	OE_0	120,000
				300,000

Table 6.4b
BS at t_1 (nominal CVA)

M_1	161,860	L_1	180,000
$_1N_1$	126,250	OE_0	120,000
$_2N_1$	116,820	$N_w \cdot r_w$	51,450
		π_{co}	53,480
	404,930		404,930

Table 6.4d
BS at t_1 (real CVA)

M_1	161,860	L_1	180,000
$_1N_1$	126,250	OE_0	120,000
$_2N_1$	116,820	IA_{OE}	16,000
		MHG	8,500
		NHG	26,950
		π_{co}	53,480
	404,930		404,930

Table 6.4c
Income Statement
(nominal CVA)
t_0 to t_1

SR	160,000
- CS_h	-80,000
- DE_h	-14,000
π_{ho}	66,000
- $CS_w \cdot r_1$	-10,000
- $DE_w \cdot r_2$	-2,520
π_{co}	53,480

Table 6.4e
Income Statement
(real CVA)
t_0 to t_1

SR	160,000
- CS_h	-80,000
- DE_h	-14,000
π_{ho}	66,000
- $CS_w \cdot p$	-4,000
- $DE_w \cdot p$	-1,400
π_{po}	60,600
- $CS_w (r_1 - p)$	-6,000
- $DE_w (r_2 - p)$	-1,120
π_{co}	53,480

Table 6.4f
Merchandise Inventory at t_1
(LIFO)

$_1N_0$	100,000	CS_c	90,000
$_1P_c$	90,000		
$_1N_0 \cdot r_1$	25,000		
$_1N_1'$	125,000		

Table 6.4g
Merchandise Inventory at t_1
(FIFO)

$_1N_0$	100,000	CS_c	90,000
$_1P_c$	90,000		
$_1N_0 \cdot r_1/2$	12,500		
$(_1N_0 - CS_h) \cdot r_1/2$	2,500		
$_1P_c \cdot r_1/2$	11,250		
$_1N_1$	126,250		

2. Real Nonmonetary Holding Gains (NHG_R):

$_1N_w \cdot (r_1 - p) = (_1N_0 + (_1N_0 - CS_h) + _1P_C) \cdot (r_1 - p)/2 =$

$(100{,}000 + (100{,}000 - 80{,}000) + 90{,}000) \cdot (0.25 - 0.10)/2 =$

$210{,}000 \cdot 0.075 =$ 15,750

$_2N_w \cdot (r_2 - p) = _2N_0 \cdot (r_2 - p) = 140{,}000 \cdot (0.18 - 0.10) =$ 11,200

$NHG_R =$ <u>26,950</u>

Comment: Under the FIFO method, $_1N_w = (_1N_0 + (_1N_0 - CS_h) + _1P_C)/2$, since the weighted average inventory value (for the period $t_1 - t_0$) consists of half of the beginning inventory (for the first half period) plus half of the ending inventory (for the second half period); furthermore, $_2N_w = _2N_0$, since depreciation and sale of the old machine both took place at year's end. Of course, a good deal of NHG is unrealized, and the (real) *realized* portion NHG_{Rr} consists of the following three components:

a. the portion realized through CS_c (cost of goods sold at *current* values):

$CS_h \cdot \dfrac{r_1 - p}{2} = CS_w \cdot (r_1 - p) = 80{,}000 \cdot 0.075 =$ 6,000

b. the portion realized through depreciation:

$DE_h \cdot (r_2 - p) = (_2N_0 \cdot d_2) \cdot (r_2 - p) = DE_w \cdot (r_2 - p)$

$= (140{,}000 \cdot 0.10) \cdot 0.08 =$ 1,120

c. the portion realized through sale of the old machine (the first set of subscripts before the symbol, $_{MS}$, stands for Machinery Sold, while the second set, $_{Rr}$, stands for Real and realized)

$_{MS}NHG_{Rr} = N_h \cdot (1 - d_2) \cdot (r_2 - p) =$

$30{,}000 \cdot 0.90 \cdot 0.08 =$ <u>2,160</u>

$NHG_{Rr} =$ <u>9,280</u>

Hence, the *unrealized* part is

$NHG_{Ru} = NHG - NHG_{Rr} = 26{,}950 - 9{,}280 =$ <u>17,670</u>

3. Fictitious Nonmonetary Holding Gains *(NHG_F):*

$$_1N_w \cdot p = \frac{_1N_0 + (_1N_0 - CS_h) + _1P_c}{2} \cdot p = \frac{210,000}{2} \cdot 0.10 = \qquad 10,500$$

$$_2N_w \cdot p = _2N_0 \cdot p = 140,000 \cdot 0.10 = \qquad\qquad\qquad 14,000$$

$$NHG_F = \qquad 24,500$$

Comment: This obviously contains, among other things, the fictitious gains resulting from cost of sales $(CS_w \cdot p = 80,000 \cdot 0.10/2 = 4,000)$, depreciation $(DE_w \cdot p = 14,000 \cdot 0.10 = 1,400)$, and sale of the old machine $(N_h \cdot (1 - d_2) \cdot p = 30,000 \cdot 0.90 \cdot 0.10 = 27,000 \cdot 0.10 = 2,700)$.

4. Inflationary Adjustment to Owners' Equity *(IA_{OE}):*

$$IA_{OE} = (N_w + _NM_w) \cdot p = NHG_F - MHG$$

$$N_w = (_1N_w + _2N_w) =$$

$$\frac{_1N_0 + (_1N_0 - CS_h) + _1P_c}{2} + _2N_w =$$

$$\frac{210,000}{2} + 140,000 = 245,000;$$

$$_NM_w = -85,000 \text{ (see item 1)};$$

$$IA_{OE} = NHG_F - MHG = 24,500 - 8,500 = (245,000 - 85,000) \cdot 0.10 = 16,000$$

Comment: For an explanation of the perhaps puzzling identity of $IA_{OE} = NHG_F - MHG$, compare the equity side of Table 6.2a with that of Table 6.3a.

The above results hold only under the FIFO method of inventory calculation. The following comparison of the inventory account under LIFO (Table 6.4f) with the inventory account under FIFO (Table 6.4g) reveals the pertinent variables affected and their differences:

Under the LIFO method (Table 6.4f), the only CVA adjustment required is that for holding the beginning inventory for a full year $(_1N_0 \cdot r_1)$ because $CS_c = _1P_c$. Under the FIFO method (Table 6.4g), one first must adjust the beginning inventory $(_1N_0)$ for the first half-year $(_1N_0 \cdot r_1/2)$, then for holding the rest of this inventory during the second half-year $[(_1N_0 - CS_h) \cdot r_1/2]$, and last for holding the newly purchased inventory during the second half-year $(_1P_c \cdot r_1/2)$. The result is a higher inventory value $(_1N_1 = 126,250$, compared to $_1N'_1 = 125,000$ under the LIFO method). Under the LIFO method, the CS'_h is not 80,000; rather, $CS'_h = CS_c = 90,000$, since all of CS_h is derived from the mid-year purchase $(_1P_c)$ thus the pertinent histori-

108   CRITIQUE OF ACCOUNTING

cal operating profit $\pi'_{ho} = 56,000$. This change would affect the balance sheet (under nominal CVA) by evaluating the ending inventory with $_1N_1 = 125,000$ (thus showing a decrease in value of 1,250, compared to FIFO) and a corresponding decrease of that part of the owners' equity section referring to (real and fictitious) nonmonetary holding gains by the same 1,250 to $N'_w \cdot r_w = 50,200$. In the case of the *real* CVA version, the situation is somewhat more complex for the owners' equity section, since the reduction in holding gain by 1,250 must be divided into its *real* portion $(1,250 \cdot (r_1 - p)/r_1 = 1,250 \cdot p/r_1 = 1,250 \cdot 0.10/0.25 = 750)$ and its *fictitious* portion $(1,250 \cdot p/r_1 = 1,250 \cdot 0.10/0.25 = 500)$. This means that NHG' = NHG - 750 = 26,950 - 750 = 26,200 (compare Tables 6.4f and 6.4g) and $IA'_{OE} = IA_{OE} - 500 = 16,000 - 500 = 15,500$, provided the balance sheet is based on the LIFO inventory method.

Furthermore, it must be borne in mind that this example is based on "the year's average dollar method" (evaluating the general price-level adjustment of the income statement and thus the income notion (π_{po}) in the pertinent year's average dollars, affecting even π_{co}). The alternative outcome in "year-end dollars" of the pertinent year results in somewhat different income figures (the balance sheet figures, except the transfers from the income statement are stated under both methods in year-end current costs). The year's average dollar method was preferred by the SFAS 33 of the United States and the Statement of Standard Accounting Practice (SSAP) 16 of the Institute of Chartered Accountants of England and Wales, or ICAEW (1980), in the United Kingdom, as well as the CVA regulation of the Canadian Institute of Chartered Accountants, or CICA (1982) in their *CICA Handbook* (Section 4510). The year-end dollar method was favored and illustrated by the American Institute of Certified Public Accountants (1963, especially 121–133).

Apart from FIFO versus LIFO, and year's average dollar versus year-end dollar methods, the difference between the nominal and the real CVA models lies in general in the following items:

a. Holding gains in the *nominal* CVA model are $N_w \cdot r_w$, thus containing real as well as fictitious holding items without any separation of the two. In contrast to Table 6.2a, we are using here (and in Table 6.4b) r_w instead of r, since *two* specific indexes, r_1 and r_2, now are used; hence, r_w indicates a kind of weighted r. Therefore,

$$r_w = (_1N_w \cdot r_1 + _2N_w)/(_1N_w + _2N_w) = (105,000 \cdot 0.25 + 140,000 \cdot 0.18)/245,000 = 0.21$$

and

$$N_w \cdot r_w = _1N_w \cdot r_1 + _2N_w \cdot r_2 = 105,000 \cdot 0.25 + 140,000 \cdot 0.18 = 51,450.$$

In the real CVA model, on the other hand, the additions to owners' equity, apart from the current operating profit π_{co}, consist of three items: the monetary holding gain (MHG); the real portion of the nonmonetary holding gains (NHG_R); and the inflationary adjustment (IA_{OE}) to the weighted OE, which contains the fictitious portion of the nonmonetary holding gains minus monetary holding gain (thus, the latter do not increase the total owners' equity and must be deducted here to balance the account).

b. The income statement of the nominal CVA model adjusts the historical cost income, (π_{ho}) for realized cost of sales and depreciation, and so on, supplying the current cost income (π_{co}), while the income statement of the real CVA model distinguishes between general inflation adjustments (($CS_w + DE_w$) $\cdot$ p) and separate adjustments for specific price changes ($CS_w \cdot (r_1 - p) + DE_w \cdot (r_2 - p)$). This results in a subtotal (π_{po}), the GPL (general price-level)-adjusted operating income.

ACCOUNTING MODELS FOR GENERAL PRICE-LEVEL ADJUSTMENTS

In the preceding section, I have tried to explain the basic structures of the nominal and the real CVA (current cost or value accounting) models, with some hint at the former SFAS 33 model of the United States, by schematic and algebraic presentations. Furthermore, I have discussed the distinction between three pairs of holding gains—monetary versus nonmonetary, real versus fictitious, and realized versus unrealized—and offered a concrete illustration with dollar figures. In this section, I shall deal with the structures of two models for general price-level GPL (also general purchasing power [GPP]) adjustment: a simple and a sophisticated one, comparing them to the nominal and real CVA models discussed earlier.

GPL accounting (for an "official" example, see American Institute of Certified Public Accountants 1963, and the penultimate column of Table 6.7) is based on the historical (or acquisition) cost approach but provides adjustment for GPL changes; yet in contrast to the CVA models, it makes no provision for adjustments to current cost. Similar to the second section, we begin with the same schematic "beginning balance sheet" (BS at t_0 [see Table 6.1a]) and assume, at first, that no transactions other than a *general* price-level change will occur. The result is the ending balance sheet of Table 6.5a, in which both the nonmonetary assets (N_0) as well as the owners' equity (OE_0) have been augmented by the inflation increase ($N_0 \cdot p$), while monetary assets and liabilities are unaffected and retain their nominal values ($M_1 = M_0$ and $L_1 = L_0$). The major characteristics of this first and, as I shall call it, simple (or unsophisticated) GPL model are (1) the neglect to show explicitly any possible gains (or losses) occurring from the holding of net monetary items ($_NM_0 = M_0 - L_0$ [as before]; these monetary holding gains are hidden in $N_w \cdot$ p), and (2) the fact that $N_0 \cdot$ p represents nothing but fictitious holding gains (or losses in the case that p < 0). Obviously, it is not possible to derive from mere inflation any real gains by holding nonmonetary assets, although it is possible to derive such real gains by holding negative monetary items (i.e., liabilities), as already pointed out in connection with Table 6.1c.

To reveal the (real) monetary holding gain (or loss), the fictitious holding gains ($N_0 \cdot$ p), as part of the ultimate owners' equity, are replaced by the monetary holding gain ($-_NM_0 \cdot$ p) and a residual (($_NM_0 + N_0$) $\cdot$ p $= IA_{OE}$). This replacement is the major feature of the sophisticated GPL model and is depicted in Table 6.5b.

So far, the corresponding income statement of the GPL model could be dispensed with for lack of any operating activity. The assumption of non-operation is now abandoned, and we obtain in Tables 6.5c and 6.5d schematic presentations

Table 6.5
GPL Models, without and with Operating Activity

Table 6.5a
BS at t_1 (Ending Balance Sheet,
GPL adjusted, without indication of monetary
holding gain, no operations)

$M_1 = M_0$	$L_1 = L_0$	
$N_1 = N_0 \cdot (1 + p)$	$OE_1 = \begin{cases} {}_N M_0 + N_0 \\ \quad + N_0 \cdot p \end{cases}$	Owners' Equity at t_0 Fict. Holding Gains
$M_1 + N_1$ $= M_0 + N_0 \cdot (1 + p)$	$L_1 + OE_1 =$ $L_1 + (M_0 - L_0) + N_0 + N_0 \cdot p$ $= M_0 + N_0 \cdot (1 + p)$	

Table 6.5b
BS at t_1
(GPL adjusted, with indication of monetary
holding gain, no operations)

$M_1 = M_0$	$L_1 = L_0$	
$N_1 = N_0 \cdot (1 + p)$	$OE_1 = \begin{cases} {}_N M_0 + N_0 \\ + ({}_N M_0 + N_0) \cdot p \\ - {}_N M_0 \cdot p \end{cases}$	Owners' Equity at t_0. Infl. Adjustment to OE. Monetary Holding Gain.
$M_1 + N_1 =$ $M_0 + N_0 \cdot (1 + p)$	$L_1 + OE_1 =$ $M_0 + N_0 \cdot (1 + p)$	

Table 6.5c
BS at t_1
(GPL adjusted, with indication of
monetary holding gain)

M_1	L_1	
$N_1 = N_w \cdot (1 + p)$	$OE_1 = \begin{cases} {}_N M_0 + N_0 \\ + ({}_N M_0 + N_w) \cdot p \\ - {}_N M_0 \cdot p \\ + \pi_{po} \end{cases}$	Owners' Equity at t_0. Infl. Adjustment to OE. Monetary Holding Gain. Oper. Profit Adj. for GPL.
$M_1 + N_1$	$L_1 + OE_1$	

Table 6.5d
Income Statement (GPL Accounting)
for period between t_0 and t_1

π_{ho}	Historical Cost (Operating) Profit (unadjusted).
$- CS_w \cdot p$	General Price Level Adjustment for Cost of Sales.
$- DE_w \cdot p$	General Price Level Adjustment for Depreciation (and Other Expenses; w = weighted).
π_{po}	(Operating) Profit, Adjusted for General Price Level Change.

of both financial statements for the sophisticated GPL model under ordinary operating conditions (an equivalent presentation for the simple GPL model is foregone, as its balance sheet corresponds to Table 6.1b under addition of π_{po} within OE_1).

The π_{po}, which is adjusted for GPL changes, is identical to the sub-profit concept (π_{po}) of Tables 6.3b and 6.5d. In the latter case as well as in the current, π_{po} arises from the unadjusted historical cost profit by eliminating the hidden but realized *fictitious* nonmonetary holding gains (as a result of cost of sales and depreciated assets, and so on). The main difference between the GPL models and the real CVA model lies in the fact that the former offers only inflation or GPL adjustments, whereas the latter supplies both, adjustments for inflation as well as for specific price changes above or below the general inflation rate (revealing in its income statement π_{po} as well as π_{co}, as shown in Table 6.3b). Thus, the nonmonetary holding gains in the OE section are limited to fictitious gains in the GPL models ($N_w \cdot p = -_N M_w \cdot p + (N_w + _N M_w) \cdot p$), while the real gains ($N_w \cdot (r - p)$) are revealed in the real CVA model. The latter thus offers more information than the GPL models as well as the nominal CVA model.

CONCEPTS OF CAPITAL MAINTENANCE

For a long time the notion of *capital maintenance* has played an important role in accounting and economics (for an excellent overview, see Sterling and Lemke 1982). The traditional view that income occurs only after the *original capital*[4] has been maintained is still accepted by most accountants; it found its best known economic expression in the famous income notion of Hicks, later Nobel laureate, who defined "a man's income as the maximum value which he can consume during a week, and still expect to be as well off at the end of the week as he was at the beginning" (Hicks 1946, 172). Since valuation and classification methods vary, it is by no means obvious what it means to maintain the capital. The same owners' equity at the beginning of an accounting period may lead under various capital maintenance notions to entirely different income and owners' equity figures at the end of the period. This may be a result of different methods of valuing assets and liabilities, different views of regarding certain holding gains as either income or owners' capital (beyond income), or both tendencies.[5] What kind of capital should one maintain, and under which circumstances?

If someone wants or is required (e.g., by the tax authorities) to maintain merely the nominal (or face) value of owners' equity, without regard for general inflation and specific price changes, then he or she must employ the *nominal financial capital maintenance* model. Obviously, this model is nothing but the historical cost model. On the other hand, if a "small investor" attempts to maintain the GPP of his original capital before recognizing any income, then one speaks of real financial capital maintenance (not to be identified with real CVA). Such a requirement is satisfied by both the GPL model (see Tables 6.5a to 6.5d) and the *sophisticated* GPL model (Table 6.6b). The hallmark of financial capital

Table 6.6
Owners' Equity Sections for Different Capital Maintenance Bases

Table 6.6a
Owners' Equity Section for Historical Cost Model
(Nominal Financial Capital Maintenance)

Beginning Owners' Equity (maint.)	OE_0		120,000
Historical Cost Operating Profit	π_{ho}	66,000	
Real and Fictitious Nonmonetary Holding Gains *realized* (Mach.sold)	$_{MS}NHG_{Rr}$	4,860	
Inclusive Historical Cost Income (comprehensive Income Statement)	$_N\pi_{ih}$		70,860
Total Ending Owners' Equity	$_hOE_1$		190,860

Table 6.6b
Owners' Equity Section for the Sophisticated GPL Model
(Real Financial Capital Maintenance)

Beginning Owners' Equity	OE_0	120,000	
Inflation Adjustment to OE	IA_{OE}	16,000	
Real Financial Capital Maintained	$_{RF}OE$		136,000
Monetary Holding Gain	MHG	8,500	
GPL-adjusted Operating Profit	π_{po}	60,600	
Inclusive GPL Income under Real Financial Capital Maintenance	$_R\pi_{ip}$		69,100
Total Ending Owners' Equity	$_pOE_1$		205,100

maintenance is inclusion of holding gains in the ultimate income concept. While $_R\pi_{ip}$ (of the GPL model in Table 6.6b) includes only monetary holding gains, the inclusive profit concept $_R\pi_{ic}$ (of the real CVA model in Table 6.6c) includes real nonmonetary as well as monetary or financial holding gains.

Last, investors or management may, in some situations, wish to maintain a capital based on the specific prices of individual assets or asset groups (machinery, plants and equipment, and the like). In this case, one speaks of physical capital maintenance; some even regard this as the "maintenance of capital goods."[6] The nominal CVA model usually satisfies this capital maintenance notion, but the real CVA model also contains the relevant information; that is, it exposes the noninclusive concept (π_{co} = $53,480) in Tables 6.6c and 6.6d, though only the latter table presents it as an ultimate income concept. The real CVA model can-

Table 6.6 (continued)

Table 6.6c
Owners' Equity Section for the Real CVA Model
(Real Financial Capital Maintenance)

Beginning Owners' Equity	OE_0	120,000	
Inflation Adjustment to OE	IA_{OE}	16,000	
Real Financial Capital Maintained	$_{RF}OE$		136,000
Monetary Holding Gain	MHG	8,500	
Real Nonmonetary Holding Gains	NHG_R	26,950	
CVA-adjusted Real Oper. Profit	π_{co}	53,480	
Inclusive CVA Income under Real Financial Capital Maintenance	$_R\pi_{ic}$		88,930
Total Ending Owners' Equity	$_cOE_1$		224,930

Table 6.6d
Owners' Equity Section for the Nominal CVA Model
(Physical Capital Maintenance)

Beginning Owners' Equity	OE_0	120,000	
Nonmonetary Holding Gains:			
Real, $NHG_R = 26,950$			
Fictitious, $NHG_F = 24,500$			
Total (also $IA_{OE} + MHG =$)	NHG	51,450	
Physical Capital Maintained	$_{PC}OE$		171,450
CVA-Adjusted Profit under Physical Capital Maintenance	π_{co}		53,480
Total Ending Owners' Equity	$_cOE_1$		224,930

not afford to do this, as it supplies information for both real financial as well as physical capital maintenance.

This discussion shows that the relation between various general and specific price-level models and different capital maintenance requirements, though being apparently analytical, is not a direct one. It requires an additional classificational decision as to which holding gains to include or exclude in its ultimate income concept. Thus, a particular inflation model may not automatically guarantee the maintenance of a specific capital—this apart from the empirical aspects, which determine the circumstances that require a specific capital maintenance, as shown later in this chapter. Tables 6.4d and 6.4e serve as a basis for our illustration of different capital maintenance concepts (in Tables 6.6a to 6.6d). These illustrations reveal which items of the total owners' equity must be regarded as adjustments for maintaining owners' capital, and which items constitute income assuring such capital maintenance.

1. *Nominal Financial Capital Maintenance* (Table 6.6a): As the traditional historical cost concept conforms particularly to this capital maintenance concept, the owners' equity to be maintained is $OE_0 = 120,000$; and the corresponding historical cost operating profit (assuring the maintenance of nominal capital) becomes π_{ho}, as encountered at the top of Tables 6.3b and 6.5d. This income notion includes (in a hidden form) real and fictitious realized holding gains from cost of goods sold, depreciation, and so on (i.e., $(CS_w + DE_w) \cdot r$), which, for this very reason, had to be deducted from π_{ho} (in Table 6.2b). This income notion does not include the holding gains from the realized portion of the real as well as fictitious holding gain from machinery ($_{MS}NHG_{Rr}$ [as a result of selling an old machine]); rather, it must be shown after the historical operating profit (π_{ho}) as a nonoperational increase to owners' equity. The calculation of this holding gain is as follows: The depreciated book value of the old machine at year's end ($N_h \cdot (1 - d_2) = 30,000 \cdot 0.90 = 27,000$) must be deducted from the cash sales value of this machine (incidentally also occurring at year's end), which is $N_c = 31,860$; hence,

$$_{MS}NHG_{Rr} = N_c - (N_h \cdot (1 - d_2)) = 31,860 - (30,000 \cdot 0.90) = 31,860 - 27,000 = 4,860$$

To include this holding gain, a comprehensive income statement must be chosen, and the result would be the inclusive historical cost income (of nominal financial capital maintenance):

$$_N\pi_{ih} = \pi_{ho} + {}_{MS}NHG_{Rr} = 70,860$$

The total owners' equity at year end is therefore

$$_hOE_i = OE_0 + \pi_{ho} + {}_{MS}NHG_{Rr} = 120,000 + (66,000 + 4,860) = 190,860$$

2. *Real Financial Capital Maintenance* (Tables 6.6b and 6.6c): As this concept requires the maintenance of the GPP of owner's equity, the capital in the ending balance sheet, maintaining original owners' equity, would have to be $OE_0 + (N_w + {}_NM_w) \cdot p = OE_0 + IA_{OE} = 120,000 + 16,000 = 136,000$ (see Table 6.6c). Hence, the corresponding income (assuring the real financial capital maintenance) would be $_R\pi_{ic} = MHG + NHG + \pi_{co} = 8,500 + 26,950 + 53,480 = 88,930$. Thus, the CVA-adjusted profit (π_{co}), differs from the inclusive income concept ($_R\pi_{ic}$), which would assure real financial capital maintenance. Many accountants still cling to some, if not all, aspects of the realization principle and thus are hesitant to include holding gains—especially unrealized holding gains—in their *major income concept*. The latter is usually taken to signal the maximum amount available for dividend distribution, a purpose for which the inclusion of holding gains, albeit real ones, does not seem to be advisable. Some theoreticians, like Edwards and Bell (1961), have taken a more radical stance. They have chosen for their real CVA model a concept like $_R\pi_{ic}$ as their major income concept, thus regarding income as comprehensive enough to include

all kinds of real holding gains. Table 6.6c demonstrates the separation of the total ending owners' equity ($_c$OE$_1$) into the "real financial capital maintained" ($_{RF}$OE = OE$_0$ + IA$_{OE}$) and the income ($_R \pi_{ic}$), which assures the maintenance of real financial capital. This also reveals the relation of the latter to the CVA-adjusted profit (π_{co}).

In contrast to the real CVA model, neither the nominal CVA model nor the simple GPL model (see Tables 6.2a, 6.4b, and 6.6d) reveals the inflation adjustment (IA$_{OE}$); thus, neither model can satisfy the real financial capital maintenance concept. The sophisticated GPL model (see Tables 6.5c and 6.6b), however, does make provision to reveal the inflation adjustment (IA$_{OE}$) and thus satisfies this capital maintenance concept. Indeed, the same figure of the real financial capital maintained ($_{RF}$OE = 136,000) is supplied by the real CVA as well as the sophisticated GPL model (compare Tables 6.6b and 6.6c). In this GPL model, the same real financial capital ($_{RF}$OE) is maintained; but since real nonmonetary holding gains have not been adjusted for, a different number emerges and a different symbol ($_R \pi_{ip}$, instead of $_R \pi_{ic}$) must be assigned to the inclusive GPL income, assuring real financial capital maintenance. Hence,

$$_R \pi_{ip} = 69,100 < {_R \pi_{ic}} = 88,930,$$

and the total ending owners' equity is

$$_p OE_1 = 205,100 < {_c OE_1} = 244,930.$$

3. *Physical Capital Maintenance* (Table 6.6d): Here, the task is not merely to maintain the general purchasing power of owners' equity, but to maintain the replacement value of assets of the enterprise (since the monetary assets and liabilities are usually expressed and to be repaid in nominal terms, the emphasis of this capital maintenance concept is on the specific price-level adjustments of all nonmonetary assets). The nominal CVA model is well suited for this physical capital maintenance concept (see Tables 6.4c and 6.6d), but the real CVA model may also satisfy this concept (see Table 6.6c).

To maintain the physical capital, in our case, a larger amount ($_{PC}$OE = 171,450) is required than to maintain the real financial capital ($_{RF}$OE = 136,000) because each of the specific price indexes, r_1 and r_2, exceeded the general inflation rate (p). Now the CVA-adjusted operating profit (π_{co}) assures the maintenance of physical capital. In the case of the real CVA model (Table 6.6c) a mere regrouping of some of the items of the owners' equity section is required; thus, the difference between those two presentations merely lies in the combination (in Table 6.6d) versus the separation (in Table 6.6c) of various holding gains and the inflationary adjustment to OE.

SIX NOTABLE VALUATION MODELS

We are now in a position to juxtapose and compare the six best-known accounting valuation models (Table 6.7, with explanations of symbols; most of them will already be known from the preceding discussion). Some simplifications (disregarding subtle

Table 6.7
Attempt of a Schematic Comparison of Income Statements (and Additions to Owners' Equity) under Different Valuation and Price-Level Adjustment Models

Alternative Models	Traditional Accounting (acquis. cost)	Fritz Schmidt (1921) CVA	Edwards and Bell (1961) nominal CVA	Edwards and Bell (1961) real CVA or curr./const. \$	AICPA (1963) ARS No. 6	FASB (1979) FAS No. 33
Components of Income Statement						
Sales Revenues	SR	SR	SR	SR	SR	SR
minus Expenses (historical)	(E_h)	(E_h)	(E_h)	(E_h)	(E_h)	(E_h)
General Price-Level Adjustment $RCS_F = \pi_{ho} \cdot p$	--	--	--	(RCS_F)	(RCS_F)	(RCS_F)
Diff. b. Curr. and Gen. P-L. Adjust. $RCS_R = \pi_{ho} \cdot (r-p)$	--	--	--	(RCS_R)	--	(RCS_R)
Current Price-Level Adjustment $RCS = \pi_{ho} \cdot r$	--	(RCS)	(RCS)	--	--	--
Operating Income Concepts	π_{ho}	π_{co}	π_{co}	π_{co}	π_{po}	π_{co}
plus Fictitious Nonmonetary Holding Gains	--	--	--	--	--	NHG_F
Real Nonmonetary Holding Gains	NHG_r	--	--	NHG_R	--	NHG_R
Mixed Nonmonetary Holding Gains, realized	--	--	NHG	--	--	--
Mixed Nonmonetary Holding Gains, real & fict.	--	NHG	--	--	--	--
Ultimate Income Concepts	$_N\pi_{ih}$	--	$_N\pi_{ic}$	$_R\pi_{ic}$	$_R\pi_{ip}$	--
Additions to Owners' Equity						
Monetary Holding Gains	--	--	--	MHG	MHG	MHG
Mixed Nonmonet. Holding Gains (real + fict.)	--	--	--	--	--	--
Inflationary Adjustment to Owners' Equity, etc.	--	--	--	IA_{OE}	IA_{OE}	$IA_{OE} - NHG_F$

Notes: Symbols in parentheses or preceded by a minus sign are being deducted (most symbols can assume negative values). Symbols above bold line belong to Income Statements. Symbols below bold line are excluded from Income Statements, but are taken into consideration under Owners' Equity. Ultimate (often "inclusive") income concepts are flanked by bold lines. All income concepts are before taxes.

116

Symbol	Definition
E_h	Expenses at historical cost (includes Cost of Sales, Depreciation and similar expenses)
IA_{OE}	Inflation (General Price-Level) Adjustment to Owners' Equity
MHG	Monetary Holding Gains as a result of holding net monetary items
NHG	Nonmonetary Holding Gains, Mixed (i.e., Real and Fictitious, realized and/or unrealized: $NHG = NHG_F + NHG_R$)
NHG_F	Nonmonetary Holding Gains (Fictitious) from fixed Assets (contained in MRU or IA_{OE})
NHG_R	Real (realized and unrealized) Nonmonetary Holding Gains to CS and ED, called "Realizable Holding Gains" by Edwards and Bell (1961)
NHG_r	Nonmonetary Holding Gains, realized from Fixed Assets. ($RCS = RCS_F + RCS_R = CS \cdot r + DE \cdot r = r \cdot (CS+DE)$)
RCS	Realized Cost Savings (Edwards and Bell 1961) resulting from Cost of Sales, Depreciation, and similar expenses
RCS_F	Realized Cost Savings, Fictitious (contained in RCS) = $p \cdot (CS + DE)$
RCS_R	Realized Cost Savings, Real (contained in RCS) = $(r - p) \cdot (CS + DE)$
$_R\pi_{ip}$	Inclusive Net Profit (real, i.e. GPL-adjusted; AICPA 1963)
SR	Sales Revenues
π_{co}	Current Operating Profit (Edwards and Bell 1961)
π_{ho}	Operating Profit (based on historical costs, nominal)
$_N\pi_{in}$	Inclusive profit, historical cost basis, nominal
π_{po}	Operating Profit, GPL adjusted
$_N\pi_{ic}$	(Inclusive) Business Profit (in nominal terms, i.e., with adjustment of specif. current (but not general) price-levels
$_R\pi_{ic}$	(Inclusive) Business Profit (in real terms, i.e., with general and current price-level adjustments)

Note: Real gains (or losses) are arising out of an excess (or deficiency) of current (i.e., specific) price change beyond that of the general inflation level, while fictitious gains are based solely on price changes in accord with the general price level. A realized gain derives from either the intermediate consumption (as cost of sales, depreciation, etc.) matching product sales or from the direct sale of fixed assets. Unrealized gains (or losses) derive from an increase (or decrease) in the value of inventories or fixed assets not yet sold.

conceptual differences, and the like) were unavoidable, but I hope the essence of each model has been preserved in order to render a genuine comparison (see also Mattessich 1982).

Apart from the text column, the first column shows the traditional historical cost income statement (for nominal financial capital maintenance [see also Table 6.6a] ending with the "inclusive" profit concept $(_N \pi_{ih})$. Monetary holding gains (or losses) would be hidden in the operating profit (π_{ho}) as soon as they are realized through repayment of credits (or debts) in nominal terms during inflationary times.

The second algebraic column represents the nominal CVA model of Schmidt ([1921] 1953); it corresponds to Table 6.6d. Here, the ultimate income concept (π_{co})—resulting from sales revenues minus cost of goods sold and "realized cost savings" (already clearly conceived by Schmidt in the early 1920s)—corresponds to the operating profit of the nominal as well as real CVA model of Edwards and Bell (1961). For Schmidt this ultimate income concept is noninclusive (of any holding gains) because he adheres to the physical capital maintenance concept. Nonmonetary holding gains can then be taken care of in the OE section outside the income statement. It seems that monetary holding gains are, surprisingly enough, hidden in NHG because of the previously explained relationship $(NHG = IA_{OE} + MGH$; see, for example, the equity side of Table 6.2a in $N_w \cdot r = NHG$, which, in Table 6.3a, turns out to be equal to inflationary adjustments plus MGH).

The third column reflects the nominal CVA model of Edwards and Bell (1961), which mainly deviates from Schmidt's model by choosing an ultimate income concept $(_N \pi_{ic})$, in which nonmonetary holding gains are included (compare with Table 6.2a in which real and fictitious holding gains are also combined).

The fourth column depicts the real CVA model of Edwards and Bell (1961) (see also Table 6.6c). Their real model deviates from their nominal model chiefly by the separation of the mixed realized cost savings into a fictitious and a real part as well as by the inclusion of monetary holding gains in their comprehensive income concept $(_R \pi_{ic})$. Only the inflation adjustment (IA_{OE}) lies, of course, in the OE section beyond the income statement. This model is in full conformity with the real financial capital maintenance concept (although its intermediate profit concept $[\pi_{co}]$ may serve the physical capital maintenance purpose).

The fifth column shows the attempt of the American Institute of Certified Public Accountants (1963) to introduce a GPL model in their Accounting Research Statement (ARS) No. 6, thus opting for physical capital maintenance. This is consistent with Table 6.6b and indicates the adjustment for fictitious realized cost savings in the GPL operating profit (π_{po}) as well as the later addition of monetary holding gains to attain the GPL inclusive income notion $(_R \pi_{ip})$, to which IA_{OE} is added in the remaining part of the OE section.

Last, the nominal CVA model of the Financial Accounting Standards Board (1979) is presented. Like the real model of Edwards and Bell, it shows in the operating income section the fictitious and real parts of realized cost savings separately; but it is satisfied with the noncomprehensive income concept (π_{co}). Some items of the OE were addressed by the FASB as follows: "gain from decline of purchasing power of net amounts owed" (here MHG), "increase in specific prices (current cost) of inventories and property, plant, and equipment held during the year" (here NGH), "Effect of increase in general price-level" (here NHG_F), and "excess of increase in specific prices over increase in general price-level" (here NHG_R).

Because of space limitations, I have abstained from discussing other models, such as the Institute of Chartered Accountants of England and Wales (1980) of the United Kingdom or the three versions of the Canadian Institute of Chartered Accountants (1982) approach, two models of which resemble the Edwards and Bell as well as the FASB models, and one showing some affinity with the ICAEW model and its somewhat complicated notion of financial or gearing adjustment (for details of the latter, see Lee 1982, 186; Scott 1982, 261–262; Lemke 1982, 313–314).[7] For similar reasons, I have omitted considerations of *exit values* (e.g., MacNeal 1939; Chambers 1967; Sterling 1970b), *present values* (e.g., Mattessich 1971a, 1971b), and related schemes, as this chapter aims at a better understanding of the notion of *instrumental hypotheses*, for which this discussion should be sufficient preparation.

CAPITAL MAINTENANCE AND
INSTRUMENTAL HYPOTHESES

Different information purposes obviously require different capital maintenance concepts; thus, it might be argued that no general accounting legislation should impose a particular capital maintenance concept upon the producers and users of financial statements. In regard to nominal financial capital maintenance, the traditional historical cost accounting approach (to which all past CVA regulations were merely complementary) will continue to provide the proper vehicle. The limitations of this nominal financial capital concept are obvious to everyone who struggles to safeguard his or her capital from the corrosive influence of inflation and who desires the information necessary to see if he or she has succeeded in this struggle. Thus, the major contenders are the real financial versus the physical capital maintenance concepts. At a first glance, the latter seems to be more appealing than the former, for reasons similar to those that make the CVA models nowadays more attractive than the GPL models. This first impression may be deceptive. Above all, as demonstrated, there is no perfect correlation between the various accounting models, on one side, and the three capital maintenance concepts, on the other. Furthermore, in many situations, there may be no reason for shareholders or other owners of an enterprise to maintain more (or less, in the case that $r_w < p$) than the general purchasing power of their investment beyond the profit derived from this enterprise. A third reason lies in the phenomenon of technological progress that defeats the logic of physical capital maintenance. Let us assume that the capital ($OE_0 = \$1,000,000$) invested in the beginning of period (t_0) in a specific enterprise went solely into computers and their components.

Assume the specific prices of those commodities have since decreased drastically, let us say to 50 percent of their original prices (hence, r_w = -0.50 per six years), while the inflation in those same six years may have increased by 50 percent (p_w = 0.50). On the basis of physical capital maintenance, management would have to maintain only $_{PC}OE_6 = OE_0 \cdot (1 + r_w) = 1,000,000 \cdot 0.50 = \$500,000$ (and could distribute the rest to shareholders during this time span), while on the basis of real financial capital, the firm would have to maintain the threefold amount of owners' equity, $_{RF}OE_6 = OE_0 \cdot (1 + p) = 1,000,000 \cdot 1.50 = \$1,500,000$, and thus could distribute much less as dividends.

Which capital maintenance notion is the appropriate one? Limperg (1964–1968) already recommended a *dual criterion* of real as well as physical capital maintenance. The answers given in a well-known symposium on capital maintenance (see Sterling and Lemke 1982) have been well summarized by Lemke:

If one had to categorize the Symposium authors and discussants, Sterling, Lee, Carsberg and probably Milburn would have to be described as unequivocal proponents of financial capital maintenance. Skinner and Ma come down more cautiously on the side of financial capital maintenance . . . . For Skinner, financial capital maintenance is a pragmatic choice. In terms of an "ideal," he is more in sympathy with Livingstone-Weil, Revsine and Scott, who take a catholic type of stance—a "different concepts for different purposes" approach. Revsine, however, is unequivocal in his advocacy of physical capital maintenance for macro-economic decisions. Hanna and Butterworth might best be described as neutrals—they want to see more research done before a choice is made. However, Hanna does favour financial capital maintenance in conjunction with his expanded funds-flow statement, and, as we shall see, Butterworth's agency theory approach also seems to point in direction of financial capital maintenance. (Lemke 1982, 288–289)

About one-third of the participants of this conference still believed in a single, correct capital maintenance method (all of whom opted for the "financial" one), while a considerable majority assumed more or less a pragmatic (or, if you like, a conditional–normative) approach. Butterworth (1982, 106), for example, points out that well-offness is a personal quality; and Livingstone and Weil assert that

no one measure serves all purposes. A debate about which measure is "right" must reduce to which of many purposes is to be served by the accountant and which are to be relegated to a secondary position. . . . Perhaps we will serve a higher professional goal if we demonstrate that there is no single measure of income that deserves attention, to the exclusion of others regardless of context, in policy matters. Accountants can broaden their professional responsibilities by understanding the various uses of the various definitions of capital maintenance and then reporting these measures with apt descriptions thereof. (Livingstone and Weil 1982, 255)

Revsine's (1982, 75–76) plea is hardly less pertinent, nor is Hanna's (1982, 282). Such ideas are in full conformity with the major thrust of the present book. Indeed, analysis for a specific case, namely, for macro-economic decisions, was pursued by Revsine; and he finds the physical capital maintenance approach appropriate for this specific purpose.

Why did the "decision usefulness approach" not generally succeed in accounting? I believe there are at least three reasons: First, the maxim that "separate analysis of each individual setting is required" is only a necessary but not a sufficient condition to establish an entire methodology. Second, the latter requires a framework that outlines the steps and procedures, the types of hypotheses, and their basic structure. Third, most of such "individual cases" require not only analysis but an empirical approach as well, though possibly one somewhat different from the traditional positive one. Skinner (1982, 127), for example, believes that maintenance of capital is defined such that it cannot be demonstrated empirically.

The approach needed, at least in my mind, is a conditional–normative methodology (CoNAM), supplying hypotheses capable of connecting efficient means with desired ends. What is the structure of such "instrumental hypotheses"? A simplified example of such an hypothesis is offered in Table 6.8. In contrast to positive hypotheses, the five major characteristic features of instrumental hypotheses are these:

a. They are goal-oriented and their simplest logical form is of the following *imperative* type: "To attain end E, under circumstances C, choose means M" (as compared to a positive hypothesis of a form like "If event A occurs, under circumstance C, then event B will occur").

b. They are highly efficiency responsive (i.e., cost–benefit and attainment sensitive).

c. Their acceptance criteria are based on the preceding two characteristics.

d. Their degree of generality is limited in comparison to law statements.

e. They are predominantly decision or action oriented.

In conformity with the spirit of this chapter, let me offer an example of an instrumental hypothesis from the area of capital maintenance. It is shown in Table 6.8 and assumes the viewpoint of a minority shareholder of, let us say, Company X. At a first glance this may not seem to reveal the fundamental difference between an instrumental versus a positive hypothesis. After all, the empirical and analytical relations (items 2 and 3) as well as the inductive inference (item 4) *appear* to be the same in both hypotheses. Hence, the question arises: Is CoNAM and the positive approach not pretty much the same? I do not deny the existence of a common basis; yet apart from the differences pointed out above (items a to e), CoNAM not only articulates the objective or norm within the argument proper but would actively support the search for an extended economic basis capable of accommodating a plurality of goals (beyond mere wealth maximization). Furthermore, it would make a concentrated effort toward developing an entire catalog of such instrumental hypotheses for more important eventualities arising in accounting. Depending on the specific preconceived objective, the appropriate instrumental hypothesis could be pulled from this catalog and applied in CoNAM.

Such means–end relations play an important role in everyday life as well as in

Table 6.8
Example of a Simplified Instrumental Hypothesis

1.	Minority Shareholder's Objective	To maintain a moderate standard of living (through regular dividends) without eroding his investment in Company X.
2.	Empirical Relationship	Maintenance of a moderate living standard is (under given circumstances) likely to be attained by maintaining "financial capital."
3.	Analytical Relationship	Maintaining "financial capital" implies measuring income adjusted for general inflation only.
4.	Inductive Inference	Measure income on the basis of general inflation adjustment.

business dealings. They also have a decisive place in the applied sciences, yet these relations are rarely explored by conventional empirical research—at least not openly or directly.[8] Why is this so, and what are the major difficulties in formulating means–end relations in a more "scientific" fashion? Some answers to this question may be found in the aforementioned criteria themselves, for example, in the limited degree of their generality (compared to truly positive law statements) and, therefore, in their restricted range of application. Another reason lies in the fact that means and ends *rarely* stand in one-to-one correspondence to each other (a specific tool may serve several purposes to various degrees, and a specific end can be achieved by various means—again, probably at various degrees of efficiency and effectiveness).

Last, let me illustrate the fundamental difference between the positive hypotheses of positive accounting theory (PAT) versus the instrumental hypotheses to be formulated under CoNAM. I shall juxtapose two hypotheses (4 and 7), formulated by Watts, to the corresponding instrumental hypotheses (IH 4 and IH 7):

"Hypothesis 4: The greater the value of a corporation's fixed assets, the greater the likelihood that its financial statements included an allocation of profits for renewals, repairs, maintenance or depreciation" (Watts 1992, 15).

"Hypothesis 7: The larger the size of a corporation whose net income is increased (decreased) by a proposed accounting standard, the greater the likelihood that its managers will lobby against (for) the standard" (Watts 1992, 22).

Such hypotheses say nothing about what management ought to do, but merely offer a vague picture of what is presently being done by some management, without confirming that this is the right way of doing things. If such confirmation can be obtained by extended empirical research, then the following instrumental hypotheses (IH) would follow from the positive hypotheses 4 or 7:

IH 4: The goal of Company X is only to maximize its wealth. The value of fixed assets of Company X is above such and such an amount (the sum would be stated as precisely as possible under the circumstances). Then it is recommended to include in its financial statements an allocation of profits for renewals, repairs, maintenance, or depreciation (perhaps even stating the magnitude of such allocations).

IH 7: The goal of Company X is only to maximize its wealth. The company's assets exceed a certain amount (to be stated as precisely as possible under the circumstances), and its net income would be increased (decreased) by a *proposed* accounting standard. Then it is recommended that its managers should initiate lobbying against (for) such standards (desirably together with an approximate amount to be spent on such lobbying).

Whereas the positive hypotheses are somewhat vague and of little use to the practitioner, the instrumental hypotheses give clear directions for attaining the stipulated end. Obviously, this is merely a sketch of how to attain formalized means–end relations. Just as the architect's drawing precedes the construction of a building, so the general conception of instrumental hypotheses must precede their specific formulation and testing. As to the argument that the ultimate basis of instrumental hypotheses—namely, their use or objective—may not always be obvious, to overcome this difficulty should not become an obstacle but rather a challenge. Where there is a genuine will to make those objectives more transparent, surely some way can be found to achieve this.

NOTES

This chapter is based partly on some new material, partly on the following publications of mine: "Major Concepts and Problems of Inflation Accounting," Parts I and II (Mattessich 1981a, 1981b), on some passages from "Fritz Schmidt (1882–1950) and His Pioneering Work in Current Value Accounting in Comparison to Edwards and Bell's Theory" (Mattessich 1986), and from "Conditional–Normative Accounting Methodology: Incorporating Value Judgments and Means–End Relations of an Applied Science" (Mattessich 1995).

1. Beaver and Landsman summarize their comparison between historical cost earnings and the current cost earnings, based on FASB Statement No. 33, with the following words:

The major findings are simple and dramatic: (1) Once historical cost earnings are known, the [FASB] Statement 33 earnings variables provide no additional explanatory power with respect to differences across firms in yearly stock price changes. (2) Even after any one of the Statement 33 earnings variables is known, knowledge of historical cost earnings still provides additional explanatory power. In this sense, historical cost earnings strictly dominate the Statement 33 earnings variables. (Beaver and Landsman 1983, 10)

These authors are fully aware of the discrepancy between their empirical findings and the theoretical or even common-sense expectations; this is manifested in their own words: "A theoretical analysis indicates that Statement 33 data potentially can provide information about the effects of unanticipated changing prices that historical cost accounting cannot" (1983, 8).

2. If $M_0 < L_0$ then it will be a genuine holding gain (instead of a loss) because $-_N M_0 \cdot p$ would become positive, since $_N M_0$ will be negative: For example, $M_0 = 100,000$, $L_0 = 150,000$, and $p = 0.10$; hence, $_N M_0 = M_0 - L_0 = 100,000 - 150,000 = -50,000$ and $-_N M_0 \cdot p = -(-50,000 \cdot 0.10) = 5,000$.

3. Apparently, Zappa (1957) envisaged a similar CVA model (compare Galassi 1980, 33).

4. For the sake of simplicity, we use original capital here in the sense of beginning owners' equity (in some cases adjusted for weighted general or specific price-level changes). In actual practice, however, the more realistic *weighted* owners' equity, adjusted also for new capital investments and withdrawals (including dividends) by the owners, might be chosen.

5. Schumacher, in his popular and best-selling book *Small Is Beautiful*, made the point that economists have traditionally mistaken a good deal of social capital as income by neglecting the crucial fact that most mining resources are nonrenewable. He says, for example, "First of all, and most obviously, there are the fossil fuels. No one, I am sure, will deny that we are treating them as income items although they are undeniably capital items" (Schumacher 1974, 12).

6. For me, the fundamental difference between capital goods and capital is similar to that between assets (usually nonmonetary ones) and equities. In Chapter 3, it has been pointed out that equities are claims (on property or debts); and it is regrettable that the confusion between capital goods and the claims on them is often perpetuated by asserting that physical capital maintenance is mainly concerned with capital goods, while it actually is concerned with maintaining the claim on them and its value (for details, see Chapter 3).

7. The "financing adjustment" (British, "gearing adjustment"), based on a firm's debt–equity ratio, is in essence a monetary holding loss or gain arising from weighted *net short-term monetary operating assets*. Scott (1982, 262) makes an interesting, though controversial, point in reference to this particular adjustment.

8. As commendable as the FASB's (1980a, 1985) attempt to encourage (conditional–)normative research is, it hardly aspires to the *epistemological* exploration of means–end relations. In the 1960s it was already recognized that "to advance knowledge significantly in normative accounting, the method of postulation and deduction cannot be dispensed with" (Hakansson 1969b, 39).

CHAPTER 7

What Has Post-Kuhnian Philosophy of Science to Offer?

The demise of positivism—and, to some extent, of Popper's falsificationism—some three decades ago created an epistemological vacuum which was, and still is, difficult to fill. Although there was no lack of candidates promoting alternative philosophies (e.g., Toulmin 1953; Hanson 1958; Kuhn 1962; Feyerabend 1965, 1975—for an overview, see Suppe 1974; Mattessich 1978a, 249–323), hardly any of them could inspire the confidence and respect that either neopositivism or falsificationism commanded from the 1920s to the 1960s. Nonetheless, there is one book which, for more than two decades, stirred the minds of philosophers and scientists more than any other: Thomas S. Kuhn's *The Structure of Scientific Revolutions* (1962). For readers unfamiliar with Kuhn's view of science, the following concise outline highlights its most essential points:

1. There exist anomalies and gaps of explanation in a specific theory or area of knowledge.

2. This is accompanied by an atmosphere of crisis or uncertainty concerning the dominant paradigm (i.e., something like a "belief system").

3. Potential rival paradigms are being developed ("revolutionary science") and begin to challenge the dominant one.

4. A battle of dominance between the potential rivals, as well as between each of them and the dominant paradigm, ensues.

5. The one potential paradigm that can explain the anomalies (or at least one of them) better than the competitors, including the previously dominant paradigm, pushes the latter aside and becomes the dominant paradigm.

6. This new paradigm is being consolidated, extended, and further developed ("normal science") until new anomalies emerge and the cycle starts all over again.

Kuhn's view certainly became the most widely quoted and debated of the novel epistemological theories of science and also found some response in the accounting literature (e.g., Wells 1976; American Accounting Association 1977; Mattessich 1978a, 1979b, 1984; Belkaoui 1981; Cushing 1989; Mouck 1993); however, it also created much reaction. At present, it seems that some choice or combination of the more recently developed views of Lakatos (1970, 1983), Stegmüller (1976, 1979, 1983, 1986), Laudan (1977), and Bunge (1983a, 1983b, 1985a, 1985b) could explain the epistemology and methodology of science on a more rational basis. Since these relatively recent views are rarely mentioned in the accounting literature, they deserve to be taken into consideration.

The newest methodological and epistemological trend does not necessarily reject Kuhn's theory but goes beyond it.[1] This trend rests on an important insight: *Specific theories must not be looked at in isolation but must be seen in the context of a larger unifying frame*, revealing the fundamental invariances of a certain research tradition or program. Such a view also helps to overcome the vagueness of the paradigm concept by linking it to a frame or net of specific theories all belonging to a common "research program." Laudan calls such a frame a research tradition, Lakatos refers to a "Research Programme," while Stegmüller speaks of a theory net or theory complex, and Bunge of a family of research fields. Although there may be some minor competition between specific scientific theories, the fierce paradigm competition (which Kuhn had in mind) takes place between entire research traditions—a view accepted among many contemporary philosophers of science. After discussing here this post-Kuhnian trend, we shall ask in Chapter 8 the following question: Does accounting possess such research traditions or programs, and can its recent evolution be represented as a competition between several of such traditions?

LAKATOS' EVOLUTIONARY PROGRAMMISM

For a quick understanding of Lakatos' (1983) view, the following five items might serve as a summary:

1. Lakatos' notion of a "scientific research program" is the basic unit of epistemological appraisal (amounting to an evolutionary interconnection of various related theories, in contrast to individual hypotheses or isolated theories).

2. The "hard core" (the set of basic laws) of a research program is either irrefutable or very hard to refute (negative heuristics). It is sheltered by a *protective belt* of auxiliary hypotheses (positive heuristics) that bear the brunt of the testing and get adjusted and readjusted (e.g., Newton's three laws of mechanics are regarded as such an irrefutable hard core). Therefore, it is not the emerging anomalies but the auxiliary hypotheses (similar to the "instrumental hypotheses") that dictate the choice of the problems to be solved, and continuing confirmations keep a research program going.

3. The distinction between "progressive" and "degenerative" research programs facilitates their appraisal and ultimate acceptance or rejection. While a progressive program can generate novel facts and auxiliary hypotheses, a regressive one lacks these features. It stagnates and finally must be rejected. However, since degenerating research programs occasionally have a comeback (see Lakatos 1983, 113; compare the return to the "stewardship program" discussed in Chapter 8), it is difficult to determine when a research program has ceased to "bud." Thus, Lakatos does not accept Popper's criterion of "crucial experiments" for rejecting a hypothesis on the basis of a single refutation.

4. Lakatos also prefers a "theoretical or methodological pluralism" to Kuhn's "theoretical monism." He regards Kuhn's scientific paradigms as approaching a dogmatic *Weltanschauung* which must be avoided through methodological tolerance (for further criticism of Lakatos' theory as well as Kuhn's, see Laudan 1977, 73–78).

5. A somewhat more complicated distinction of Lakatos is that between the "internal" and the "external" history (or influence) of a research program. What may be deemed as an external influence (e.g., priority disputes) for Popper, Kuhn, or others, may be interpreted as an internal influence for Lakatos (for him, priority disputes are vital internal problems).

Although Lakatos complains that for Kuhn there can be no logic but only a psychology of discovery, he adds that

Kuhn is right in objecting to naive falsificationism, and also in stressing the *continuity* of scientific growth, the *tenacity* of some scientific theories. . . . But Kuhn overlooked Popper's sophisticated falsificationism and the research programme he initiated. Popper replaced the central problem of classical rationality, *the old problem of foundations*, with *the new problem of fallible–critical growth*, and started to elaborate objective standards of this growth. In this paper I [Lakatos] have tried to develop his programme a step further. I think this small development is sufficient to escape Kuhn's strictures. (Lakatos 1983, 90–91, footnote omitted)

STEGMÜLLER'S EPISTEMOLOGICAL STRUCTURALISM

While Lakatos' proposal is admittedly an attempt to further develop and thus to rescue important aspects of Popper's view, Stegmüller's proposal might be interpreted as a refinement of Kuhn's exposition but is certainly much more than that. Apart from terminological differences and the degree of formalism, we find sufficient similarities between Lakatos' and Stegmüller's methodology (especially the similarities between research programs and theory nets) to regard them as closely related.[2] For this reason, I will address all those approaches as research programs or research traditions. This terminology fits best the particular situation of accounting where we are dealing with two or more major groups of research or "theories." Stegmüller admits that he seriously considered using the phrase "to hold a research programme" instead of his formulation of "holding a theory." As Stegmüller remarks at the same place, Lakatos in turn pointed out that "his [Lakatos'] concept of a research programme was 'reminiscent' of Kuhn's notion of normal science" (Stegmüller 1979, 61). Furthermore, Stegmüller emphasizes that in the sophisticated version of falsificationism (which Lakatos adopts from Popper and then adapts for his own purpose), neither individual hypotheses nor theories but "theory nets" (in Stegmüller's sense) are compared and related to each other.

There remains an epistemological, perhaps even an ontological, difference between Lakatos' research programs and Stegmüller's theory nets. The former contain theories that possess truth values, while the latter's theories, theory nets, and theory complexes (which are a further generalization) are all mathematical structures to which no truth values (only *preferences* based on specific goals) can be assigned. However, this difference is not as crucial as it might seem at first glance because, even in Stegmüller's scheme, the individual hypotheses contained in a theory do possess truth values.

OTHER MAJOR FEATURES OF STEGMÜLLER'S APPROACH

1. *Theoretical Core and Intended Applications*: The two components of a theory ("theory element") are considered to be a permanent theoretical *core* and a set of *intended* (empirical) *applications* (see formulas later in this section). The core, in turn, consists of a set of models containing the fundamental law as well as a set of possible models containing the conceptual apparatus, including the *theoretical terms* (which play such a crucial role in the Sneed–Stegmüller theory); a set of "partial" possible models excluding the theoretical terms (together with a reduction function enabling such exclusion); and a set of constraints linking various theory elements with each other. During Kuhn's phase of normal science, more and more theory elements emerge, all through specialization of the core, the intended applications, or both. A scientific revolution, however, would require a change of the fundamental law and hence of the core.

2. *Special Theories or Theory Elements*: Usually, there is not one intended application of a theory; but there are many such applications which often overlap to some degree. The idea of double classification, for example, did not only find application in financial and managerial accounting but was successfully applied in the matrix algebra of interindustry analysis, in national income accounting, and several other areas. In physics, Newton applied his theory not only to planetary motions but also to falling and pendulating objects on earth, as well as to ocean tides, and so on. He even hoped to apply it to optics. When Maxwell's electromagnetic wave theory of light proved this "intended" application of Newtonian mechanics as impermissible, it did not constitute a rejection of Newtonian physics but was considered merely an instance of limitation. The formulation of the special theories or theory elements for the purpose of specific applications bears similarity to the well-known notion of *interpretation* of the general theory.

3. The rejection of a theory does not depend on Popper's naive refutation; it occurs through dislodgement as soon as a better theory is available, but not before. This is another important instance where Stegmüller, Lakatos, and possibly Bunge approach each other.

4. *Theoretical versus Nontheoretical Terms:* The distinction between theoretical and nontheoretical terms is no longer taken to be absolute (in contrast to the neopositivistic distinction between theoretical and observational terms) but is now considered to be dependent on the specific theory (such terms as weight, mass, value, or utility may be theoretical notions in one theory but nontheoretical notions in another). Take, for example, an accounting theory T belonging to the stewardship program. Here, the *book value* arises as a residual (e.g., of acquisition cost minus depreciation) out of this very theory. Thus, the book value cannot be determined without this theory. Hence, the book value would, according to Sneed (1971) and Stegmüller (1975, 1979, 1986), be called a *T-theoretical* variable. The market value or the present value, however, may be a *T-nontheoretical* variable because it might be measurable without the aid of theory T. If we take an alternative accounting theory, let us say AT, belonging to the objective-oriented program (see Chapter 8), in which the *book value,* the *market value,* and the *present value* might arise out of this more comprehensive theory, then all three of these values would be *AT-theoretical* (although only the first remains T-theoretical*).* I am trying to re-interpret the Sneed–Stegmüller distinction between theoretical and nontheoretical terms in a somewhat different way, namely, such that nontheoretical variables include only concepts backed by reality (see Chapter 3), while theoretical variables contain pure concepts as well.

5. *Threefold Immunity:* There exists, according to Stegmüller (1975, 520–523), a threefold immunity of theories against empirical refutation: First of all, the core of a theory (representing the analytical aspects and corresponding to Kuhn's "theory matrix") can be expanded by further theory elements, thus creating a larger theory net. In a way, this net is open, since it cannot be known in advance how far it can be further expanded. If, at some intermediate stage, a theory element does not explain or predict satisfactorily, this may be a result of the fact that the researcher failed in correctly formulating the appropriate theory element (this refers to Kuhn's assertion that in normal science the skill of the researcher, not the theory, is being tested).

Second, the set of intended applications (reflecting the empirical aspects of a theory corresponding to Kuhn's "exemplars") also is an open set. Should the researchers consistently fail to apply such a theory to a particular area (e.g., Newton's theory as applied to the problem of electromagnetic waves), this would, in contrast to Popper's interpretation, not constitute a rejection of the theory but a mere setting of its boundary.

The third type of theory immunity is complex and can only be hinted at here. Its reason lies in Sneed's (1971) rejection of the absolute, positivistic criterion of theoreticity, and in accepting a relative criterion that is context dependent (as previously mentioned).[3] "This kind of theory-dependent T-theoretic variables make it impossible to empirically refute laws containing such variables" (Stegmüller 1975, 522, translated). He also mentions the irrefutability of Newton's second law (force = mass × acceleration) as an example of this third type of irrefutability.

Although accountants have, so far, paid little attention to these particular notions of research programs, theory nets, and so on, economists have found these ideas useful. The well-known historian of economic thought, Mark Blaug (1978, 1980), for example, sympathizes with the idea of research programs, while Hausman (1984, 22), an epistemologist of economics, points out that Lakatos' methodology has influenced many economists. Indeed, Stegmüller, who originally began as an economist, edited with some of his collaborators a book on the application of his ideas to economics (Stegmüller et al. 1982). For further economic applications of this theory see Balzer (1982), Hamminga (1983), Stegmüller (1986, Chap. 14), and Balzer et al. (1987). For an accounting application, see Balzer and Mattessich (1991).

To further clarify the problem of reality, more attention has to be paid to the distinction between theoretical and observational variables. As mentioned, this distinction—which was deemed to be absolute by the neopositivists—has been transformed by the structuralists (e.g., Sneed 1971; Stegmüller 1986) into a new and context-dependent distinction between theoretical and nontheoretical terms, while, according to the structuralists, the distinction depends upon the pertinent theory. Although this context dependence was appealing to many philosophers of science as well as scientists, major problems emerged:

a. Sneed's original criterion and definition of theoreticity was considered unsatisfactory by some scholars and was even abandoned by such a major structuralist as Balzer (1985) in favor of a more arbitrary criterion.[4]

b. The structuralists' distinction between T-theoretical and T-nontheoretical terms remained landlocked in a purely conceptual frame and thus excluded the realm of observation. This was heavily criticized by Bunge (1978, 1983a, 1985a) and others. To overcome this problem of "disregard for reality by structuralists" and to construct a bridge between structuralism and realism, I have extended the structuralist scheme in Figure 7.1 to include observational and non-observational levels of reality.

Structuralism regards an empirical theory (or "theory element") T as consisting of a theory core (K) and a set of intended applications (I) that we take to be closely related or identical to the set of *used* indicator hypotheses. The core, in turn, consists of the following components (I have deliberately chosen traditional terminology, but have added in quotes the terms used by structuralists wherever I deviate from them):

- A conceptual framework, F (the "set of potential models").
- The fundamental principles or law-statements, L ("set of models").
- The reduced framework, r(F), from which all the theoretical terms (i.e., those not backed by reality, in my view) have been eliminated ("partial potential models" or the set of all possible indicator hypotheses) by means of a reduction function, r (the "Sneed–Ramsey reduction"), to enable measurement.
- A set of constraints or cross-connections (C) connecting different applications with each other (e.g., the constraint that a 1988 U.S. $ must be the same whether applied to the accounting system of Company X, to U.S. National Income Accounting, or to any other kind of accounting model). Stegmüller (1986, 57) also calls these constraints "laws of higher generality."

Figure 7.1
Correspondence between Theory and Reality

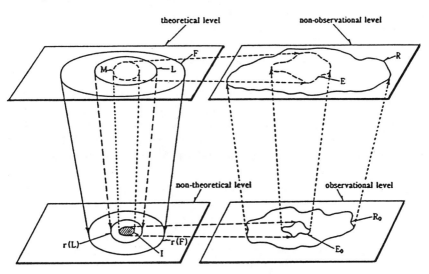

Sets (conceptual entities)		Concrete Aggregates	
F	conceptual framework	E_o	observational entities
L	fundamental principles [or law statements]	R_o	observational fragment [corresponding to r(F)]
M	interpreted models	E	empirical entities [incl. non-observ. items]
I	indicator hypotheses [or intend. applications]	R	fragment of reality
l(F)	reduced framework		
r(L)	reduced principles [without theor. terms]		

Thus, a theory T is considered to be a mathematical structure represented by the following vectors (ordered tuples), consisting of the core (K) and the intended applications (I):

$$T = \langle K, I \rangle$$

$$K = \langle F, L, r, r(F), C \rangle, \text{ hence}$$

$$T = \langle \langle F, L, r, r(F), C \rangle I \rangle.$$

This is expressed on the left-hand side of Figure 7.1 (the set of cross-relations [C] is here not depicted, but it would appear in a graph showing the power set of all pertinent models). Structuralists regard this purely formalistic presentation as sufficient because the set of "intended applications [I]" (as a subset of r(L), which, in turn, is L stripped of all T-theoretical terms) constitutes for them the "empirical" part of a theory. However, I is a set and thus is also a concept and hence not anything empirical. Because of the elimination of theoretical terms, the indicator hypotheses are merely "closer to reality" and better comparable to it but not reality itself. Thus, the vertical connections (e.g., from L to r(L)) belong to model theory, the semantics of mathematics, and not to empirical semantics. If we assume that the right-hand side of Figure 7.1 is a segment of reality that, in turn, is *represented* by theory T (on the left-hand side), the picture becomes much more complete.

The areas E_0 and R_0 are the empirical–observational referents of I and r(F), respectively, while the dashed horizontal line in the lower part of Figure 7.1 reveals the neglected but important semantic relations between the purely conceptual theory and the real objects, events, and their properties for which the theory stands. For the realist, in contrast to the positivist, reality goes beyond the observable, and possesses a nonobservational (or not yet observable) part, revealed by Figure 7.1 in its upper-right segment, called the "nonobservational plane." Here, the areas E and R correspond on the vertical side to E_0 and R_0, respectively. E and R are not only factual; they are also *potentially* factual and contain non-observable or not-yet-observable events that might (but need not) correspond on the *horizontal* level to the theoretical terms found in the set of interpreted models, M (a subset of L). That means that theoretical variables would be identical to pure concepts, and nontheoretical variables would be identical to concepts backed by reality (as discussed in Chapter 3). On the other hand, observational variables would be those accessible to observation, while nonobservational variables are not or not yet accessible (see Figure 7.1).

Let me discuss Figure 7.1 from an accountant's point of view. The theoretical level (upper-left side) might contain, among many variables, price–earnings ratios (which I consider as "pure concepts," like stellar constellations, as explained in Chapter 3), profit margins, and other coefficients that are all purely conceptual. The nontheoretical level (lower-left side) is stripped of the pure concepts but holds economic transactions and evaluations as well as other variables that correspond directly to the real manifestations mentioned in the next item. The observational level (lower-right side) presents physical, social, and other realities, for example, actual inventories, equipment, buildings, debts (owed as well as claimed), ownership claims, transfers of commodities, and their exchange values. Last, the nonobservational level could contain cash flows still to occur and other future events (not to be confused with an actual expectation, which is a present mental state and thus found on the preceding level).

Of course, one could argue that the right-hand side of Figure 7.1 is part of a picture, thus again a representation and not reality itself. Though this is correct, it hardly changes the situation: just as the left-hand side is a pictorial representation of a conceptual scheme, so is the right-hand side a pictorial representation of reality. With this realist interpretation of the structuralist view, we have introduced a further dichotomy, namely, that between T-observational and T-nonobservational entities in addition to that between T-nontheoretical and T-theoretical variables (each of those types of variables is contained in one of the four levels or planes of Figure 7.1).

This second dichotomy too is relative to theory T. An entity may prove to be nonobservational in one theory, while in another, perhaps more recent theory, that entity turns out to be observational (e.g., atoms have only recently been considered to be observable, and in the late nineteenth century they were regarded by many experts as purely theoretical concepts, and by others even as misleading notions). Last, this two-dimensional dichotomy also conforms to the structuralists' assertion that their notion of T-nontheoretical variables has a different meaning than the positivistic notion of observational (or, in our case, T-observational variables). Figure 7.1 reveals that, for me, this difference lies in the distinction between the conceptual structures on the left-hand side and the real structures on the right.[5] This also confirms the major realist task of a theory, namely, to create conceptual forms that represent, as truthfully as possible or necessary, structures inherent in a segment of reality (e.g., as crudely as a globe or geographical map represents essential features of the earth's surface or of a certain terrain). Let us not confuse a conceptual (e.g., mathematical) form with the *empirical structure* it describes.

BUNGE'S CRITICAL SCIENTIFIC REALISM

While most philosophers write primarily for other philosophers, Bunge's (1974a, 1974b, 1977, 1978, 1979, 1983a, 1983b, 1985a, 1985b) epistemological and methodological explorations seem to be directed primarily to empirical scientists. Since many of them, like Bunge, have a strong realist bias, his criticism of Lakatos and Stegmüller—as well as his own proposal—deserves some examination.

Bunge's attitude toward Thomas Kuhn's philosophy is fairly favorable. He agrees with most aspects of Kuhn's methodological dogmas; his notions of paradigm, exemplars, and their consequences; and with his distinction between normal versus extraordinary science (compare Bunge 1983a, 224–225; 1983b, 129, 163–164, 175). Bunge criticizes Kuhn's insufficient clarity or precision:

Kuhn's (1962) modern classic had the merit of bringing it [extraordinary research] to the fore. What remain problematic are the very notions of a conceptual framework and of a paradigm, and of a revolution in it. Neither of these notions has been elucidated carefully, either by Kuhn or by his followers or critics (see, e.g., Lakatos and Musgrave 1970). . . . Kuhn's most important contributions to methodology are perhaps his ideas that in every science there is a permanent tension between tradition and change, and that negative evidence is treated differently by normal research and by extraordinary research. . . . The second idea is more original: it is that, whereas normal research attempts to *accommodate* negative evidence to the ruling conceptual framework, extraordinary research uses such anomalies to *undermine* the framework. (Bunge 1983b, 175–176 and 178–179)

Indeed, Bunge subsequently presents his own answer according to which extraordinary research need not be revolutionary: "It may ensue in an epistemic counterrevolution, i.e., a partial return to an earlier conceptual framework" (Bunge 1983b, 178)—note the similarity with Lakatos' "comeback" of a research program. The ensuing examples from accounting theory (particularly the emergence of agency-information analysis as a partial return to the traditional stewardship paradigm) offers an excellent illustration for such a counterrevolution or comeback (see Chapter 8).

Another aspect of Kuhn's work that Bunge criticizes is the acclaimed "incommensurability" between different paradigms. Kuhn believes that "operations and measurements are paradigm-determined" (Kuhn 1962, 125), and that "after a scientific revolution many old measurements and manipulations become irrelevant and are replaced by others instead" (Kuhn 1962, 128). This point has been contemplated by Stegmüller (1986, Chap. 10), but Hacking's pertinent analysis offers the best illustrations. Hacking (another realist) distinguishes different kinds of incommensurabilities: The first kind is topic incommensurability. It occurs when the successor theory (T*) completely replaces the topics, concepts and problems of T, the preceding theory. He calls his second category dissociation. Here, he points out that some theories manifest so radical a change that one needs something far harder than the mere learning of a theory. He compares, for example, our modern theories to those of Paracelsus (1493–1541) and states that "the contrast between ourselves and Paracelsus is *dissociation*. . . . Paracelsus lived in a different world from ours" (Hacking 1983, 71). Last, he presents his meaning incommensurability, according to which such theoretical variables and unobservable entities as, for example, "'mass' in Newtonian theory would not mean the same as 'mass' in relativistic mechanics. 'Planet' in Copernican theory will not mean the same as 'planet' in Ptolemaic theory, and indeed the sun is a planet for Ptolemy but not for Copernicus" (Hacking 1983, 72).

Bunge's attitude toward Lakatos' methodology is much less enthusiastic than toward Kuhn's; above all, Bunge criticizes Lakatos' "hazy notion of research programme" (Bunge 1983b, 163). Of greater interest is Bunge's reaction toward the Sneed–Stegmüller approach. It begins with a short review of Stegmüller's (1976) book and raises the following complaint about the Sneed–Stegmüller theory:

1. It eschews metamathematical considerations.
2. It identifies theories with uninterpreted theories and defines their applications as models in the model–theoretic sense.
3. It cannot explain how one and the same formalism can be assigned a number of different factual interpretations.
4. It sees no need to provide a semantic theory elucidating factual interpretation.
5. Its dogmatism and neglect of evidence (e.g., narrowness of illustrations) for or against this structuralist view.
6. It takes unwarrantedly for granted that Kuhn's hypotheses have been borne out by historical case studies.

This review closes with the following words: "The new philosophy of science advanced in this work [Stegmüller 1976] is at least as remote from living science as any of the rival views criticized in it" (Bunge 1978, 330). Five years later, Bunge—in referring to both Sneed (1971) and Stegmüller (1976)—continues in a similar tone:

The models built in factual science and technology are radically different from those studied by model theory, a branch of logic. . . . This, the *logical* concept of a model, must be sharply distinguished from the *epistemological* concept of model as a conceptual representation of concrete things of a narrow kind. But, whether logical or epistemological, all such models are conceptual: real things are not models of anything, but instead the objects of modeling. (The statement that the real world is a model of some theory makes sense only in a Platonic ontology.) This terminological remark had to be made in view of the widespread confusion between the two kinds of model introduced by the so-called set–theoretic semantics of science. (Bunge 1983a, 337)

And a few pages afterwards:

A related view is *formalism,* according to which model theory, i.e., the semantics of mathematics, suffices to analyze factual theories (Sneed, 1971; Stegmüller, 1976). The upholders of this view have probably been misled by the ambiguity of the term 'model', which in mathematics designates an example of an abstract theory, whereas in science and technology it designates a specific theory....Consequently they ignore the concepts of reference and representation, central to the semantics of factual theories, and they cannot explain why factual theories cannot be validated or invalidated by purely mathematical considerations." (Bunge 1983a, 355)

Two further years later: "The failure to distinguish the logical from the epistemological concepts of model (as in Sneed 1971 and Stegmüller 1976) has given rise to an utterly artificial philosophy of science. (See Truesdell 1984 for proof that this philosophy is remote from real science)" (Bunge 1985a, 47).

Truesdell's (1984) often sarcastic remarks and objections toward the approach of Sneed, Stegmüller, and other "Suppesians"[6] are primarily based on their (according to Truesdell) inadequate understanding of classical particle mechanics, its mathematical structure, and its proper representation. Thus, Truesdell's review is hardly based on a general epistemological inadequacy that necessarily would affect the application of the Sneed–Stegmüller framework to other disciplines. Some of Bunge's objections to structuralism might be a result of misunderstandings, and others a result of a different philosophic outlook (realist versus idealist).

Bunge envisages for every theory a "conceptual framework" containing not only the general, formal, and specific background but also other aspects such as the problematic, the fund of knowledge, and the research goals. This affords a richer vision and can further be extended to what Bunge calls a *family of research fields* by taking into consideration (in addition to the conceptual framework) the research community, the society, and the universe of discourse (see Bunge 1983b, 176–198). It must be pointed out that in a later version, Stegmüller

(1986, Chap. 3) refers to a structuralistic research that has already taken into consideration several of those aspects.

Further aspects of Bunge's criticism might also be redundant in the face of a later presentation by Stegmüller (1986). This revised and expanded version of the structuralist theory and the work by Balzer et al. (1987) offer a fairly up-to-date overview, taking recent contributions by many structuralists—as well as some criticism by others—into consideration. Although neither such major criticism as Bunge's (1978, 1983a, 1983b, 1985a) nor Truesdell's (1984) is mentioned by Stegmüller, some of this criticism seems to have been taken into account.

STRUCTURALISM VERSUS REALISM?

As for the broad philosophic differences between realists and structuralists, no reconciliation—as, for example, attempted by Niiniluoto (1984)—is made by Stegmüller (1986). On the contrary, his pertinent chapter (Chapter 11)—with major reference to some works by Sneed (1981, 1983), Putnam (1980, 1982), Niiniluoto (1981, 1983), and others—is devoted to discuss those differences. According to Stegmüller the conflict between scientific realism and structuralism can be found in the following three items (K1 to K3):

"K1   The structuralist reconstruction of theories is such that the empirical claims of those theories contain logical forms which considerably deviate from the logical forms encountered in the traditional literature. This degree of divergence is deemed to be strong enough by realists to reject structuralistic reconstructions" (Stegmüller 1986, 328, translated).

A major thesis of epistemic structuralism is the claim that the traditional term *theory* is too vague, as it can mean at least three different things:

1. A set of empirical claims or hypotheses
2. A theory element consisting of a logical structure called the core, and of a set of "intended applications"
3. A *theory net* (or "theory complex") consisting of many connected theory elements

The structuralists try to clarify the situation by imposing a very specific logical structure upon a "theory" (see K1) and make a strict distinction not only between logical and descriptive variables but also between the theoretical core and its "intended applications" (the latter are supposed to be the empirical part; but as they form the subset of a set of conceptual models, this subset as well as its members appear to be purely conceptual and rather should be called "partial models intended for application"). Furthermore, a structure is imposed upon the core (an ordered tuple or vector) consisting of a set of models (M, containing the fundamental laws), a set of possible models (M_p, containing the conceptual framework including the theoretical terms), a set of partial possible models (M_{pp}, excluding theoretical terms), a reduction function (r, reducing M_p to M_{pp}), and a set of constraints (C or Q, connecting various theory elements with each other). Thus, they reject the traditional and simplistic logical form in which empirical claims are presented.

"K2   The structuralist difference between theoretical and non-theoretical elements (of the models of a theory) contain an ontological distinction of the entities or properties (magnitudes) which the theory discusses. Realism rejects the idea of such a distinction" (Stegmüller 1986, 128–129, translated).

K2 is admittedly imprecise; but as I see it, the ontological controversy between structuralists and realists pivots only on the nontheoretical terms (which the structuralists, in contrast to the realists, seem to take as real).

"K3   According to the structuralist view, it is possible that the meaning of theoretical terms changes in the course of 'normal' as well as 'revolutionary' development. Realism rejects this view" (Stegmüller 1986, 328–329, translated).

This refers to the context dependence of the structuralistic notion of theoretical terms previously discussed. I wonder whether scientific realists such as Bunge, Hacking, and Niiniluoto would agree to this threefold characterization (K1 to K3) and its arguments. Furthermore, if philosophers would succeed in finding a common realist ground (with regard to theory nets or research traditions), the new methodology might have better chance of acceptance in the scientific community. To what extent all this is relevant to accountants will be shown in Chapter 8.

NOTES

This chapter is based partly on "Epistemological Aspects of Accounting," in *Keiri Kenkyu* (Mattessich 1990), partly on "Paradigms, Research Traditions and Theory Nets of Accounting," from *Philosophical Perspectives on Accounting* (Mattessich 1993b), as well as some new material.

1. Epistemology deals with the foundations and boundaries of knowledge and is, together with methodology, the main constituent of the philosophy of science.

2. Stegmüller, for example, points out that "Lakatos anticipated the distinction [made by Stegmüller] between theories and empirical claims of theories *in our sense,* but that he was not consistent in his terminology. Whenever he speaks of *theories as members of a sequence* with the sequence representing a research programme his 'theories' correspond to our 'empirical–hypothetical claims'" (Stegmüller 1979, 60–61).

3. Sneed (1971) regards a variable as "T-theoretical" if it can be measured within the frame of theory T; but if one has to step outside of T to measure this variable, the latter is called "T-nontheoretical." Thus, the nature of the variable is dependent upon the pertinent theory (e.g., T) and no longer absolute (i.e., either "theoretical" or "observational" for all theories), as the neopositivists have claimed.

4. Balzer states, "Originally, Sneed introduced a class M_{pp} of 'partial potential models' by cutting off the 'theoretical components' from members of M_p. Thus the definition of M_{pp} hinged on the distinction between theoretical and non-theoretical terms. I will propose a more general definition of M_{pp} which is not relativized to theoreticity and which yields a frame for precise investigations of theoreticity. We will introduce partial poten-

tial models as arbitrary 'substances' of potential models... it is usually difficult to determine which terms of a theory are theoretical and which are non-theoretical. The reconstruction of some theory in Sneed's original terms is possible only if this difficulty is overcome. My present approach avoids the problem: a theory-element can be completely reconstructed without drawing a distinction between theoretical and non-theoretical terms. This distinction can of course be introduced later on" (Balzer 1983, 5–7).

5. Alternatively, one may speak of the theoretical/nonobservational versus the nontheoretical/observational levels, bearing in mind that the expression before the slash refers to the conceptual aspects and the expression after the slash to the real aspects involving a theory. This does not mean that the relation between theoretical variables and unobservable entities, if such a link exists at all, is as strong or fundamental as that between nontheoretical variables and observable entities.

6. Sneed was a student of Patrick Suppes, the spiritual father of the logical or epistemic structuralists.

CHAPTER 8

Research Traditions of Accounting

During the last two decades or more, distinct research tendencies manifested themselves in accounting. These tendencies rest partly on ideas developed in Germany and the United States during the early part of this century and partly on ideas introduced more recently on the American continent. To survey these research trends, I start from the following paradigms postulated by Butterworth,[1] but will elaborate and transform them into various phases of three distinct research traditions, taking the pertinent German literature into account as well:

a. Valuation I (present value and current cost theories)

b. Valuation II (theory of risk sharing)

c. Valuation III (theory of financial markets)

d. Stewardship I (historical acquisition cost theory)

e. Stewardship II (descriptive agency theory)

f. Stewardship III (agency-information theory, and so on)

Previous attempts to formulate different accounting paradigms can be found by Wells (1976); by the American Accounting Association (1977);[2] and, above all, by Belkaoui (1981), who, apparently inspired by the AAA, distinguished in both editions of his textbook the following six paradigms:

1. *The Inductive–Anthropological Paradigm*: Hatfield (1927), Gilman (1939), Littleton (1953), Paton and Littleton (1940), Ijiri (1975), Gordon (1964), Watts and Zimmerman (1978).

2. *The Deductive Ideal Income Paradigm*: Paton (1922), Canning (1929), Sweeney (1936), MacNeal (1939), Alexander (1950), Edwards and Bell (1961), Moonitz (1961), Sprouse and Moonitz (1962).

3. *The Decision Theoretic Paradigm*: Sterling (1970b, 1972), Beaver et al. (1968).

4. *The Capital Market Paradigm*: Gonedes (1972), Gonedes and Dopuch (1974), Beaver (1972).

5. *The Behavioral Paradigm*: Bruns (1968), Hofstedt and Kinard (1970), Birnberg and Nath (1967).

6. *The Information Economic Paradigm*: Feltham (1968), Crandall (1969), Feltham and Demski (1970).

As interesting as this categorization is, it is based on different perspectives from which accounting has been illuminated during recent decades rather than on more fundamental criteria. In contrast, Butterworth and Falk (1986) chose a different classification criterion with a smaller number of categories. Such a scheme is more convenient for deriving a limited number of global theories or research programs in the sense of Lakatos (1983), theory nets by Stegmüller (1979, 1983, 1986), the families of research fields by Bunge (1983b, 1985a), or the like (see also Mattessich 1987a).

More recent attempts at applying Kuhn's approach to accounting can be found by Cushing (1989) and Mouck (1993). Cushing not only offers the most comprehensive survey of various Kuhnian interpretations of accounting—despite missing some pertinent publications such as Belkaoui (1981) and Mattessich (1978a, 249–272; 1979a)—but also presents his own interpretation. Cushing concludes that (1) the double-entry model, through its resilience during many centuries, has become the focus of the traditional accounting paradigm[3]; (2) in the twentieth century, governmental pressure and the process of setting uniform accounting standards drastically changed the nature of our discipline and precipitated a profound crisis, which, in turn, prompted the search for the foundations of accounting and a commitment to a more scientific approach; (3) there is a possibility that fundamental accounting problems may not be solvable within the original paradigm of double entry, and hence a Kuhnian revolution may occur; and (4) Kuhn's approach is certainly relevant to accounting.

Mouck (1993, 35), although deviating in several respects from Cushing's ideas, acknowledges a certain concordance with this view; but he attributes the crucial accounting changes of the 1960s more to social, political, and technical forces from outside than to an internal paradigm crisis in the Kuhnian sense. Furthermore, he believes that Kuhn's ideas are not applicable to accounting thoughts before the "awakening" of the 1960s. Above all, Mouck characterizes the differences between Chambers, Devine, Edwards and Bell, Mattessich, and Sterling during this pivotal decade as "pre-paradigmatic."

Compared to this view, the post-Kuhnian scheme, presented in the following sections, regards Chambers, Edwards and Bell, and Sterling as belonging to the first phase of the valuation program; Ijiri (who must also be included) as belonging to the first phase of the stewardship program; and Devine and Mattessich as belonging to the objective-oriented program. This indicates that the differences between those categories (and pertinent authors) are fundamental enough to be regarded as paradigmatic, provided that the notion of "accounting paradigm" is acceptable at all.

Mouck, however, believes to find a paradigm change in the apparent victory of the "informational perspective" of the empirical and positive accounting theorists over the "economic income perspective" of the *apriorists* (Chambers, etc.). This is a tempting thought indeed, but it can be maintained only by putting such diverse views (as those between Chambers, Sterling, and Edwards and Bell vs. Devine and Mattessich vs., possibly, Ijiri, and so on) into a single pot. As Mouck is clearly aware of those differences, he finds no other way out but to label them as "pre-paradigmatic." One wonders whether for Mouck this expression has the semiderogatory connotation (which Kuhn imparted to it); elsewhere, Mouck (1989) speaks highly of those authors, reiterating Gaffikin's (1988) emphasis on their primary influence on modern accounting research.

Nevertheless, Mouck believes that the "normative apriorists" failed to offer young academics a paradigm with clear-cut research opportunities and the appropriate methods, while the proponents of the competing paradigm provided well-defined normal science problems and their exemplars, though all borrowed from financial economics. Despite this, he sees a growing and widespread disenchantment with the "informational perspective" and points out that a series of studies have began to undermine the very basis of this paradigm—which rests on the efficient market hypothesis (EMH), the capital–asset pricing model (CAPM), and portfolio analysis (PA).[4] He mentions, first, the functional fixation hypothesis (FFH) and the paper by Harris and Ohlson (1990), both critical of—or even contradictory to—EMH; Mouck (1989) then refers to other studies, all damaging to the validity of the CAPM; last, he asserts that the rationality of the PA would be in doubt if EMH and CAPM would fall. Mouck, therefore, sees a new crisis and continuing paradigm struggle.

Apart from such considerations, and returning to Butterworth and Falk (1986), the question arises whether these two authors were dealing at all with paradigms in the commonly understood sense.[5] Although the theoretical representation of accounting has been beset by conflicts between various camps, it is doubtful whether all of those differences were crucial or basic enough to speak of rivaling paradigms in the Kuhnian sense. Such paradigmatic rivalry may exist between one or the other of those Butterworth paradigms, but hardly between all six. Even more decisive is the fact that several of these paradigms are so closely connected with each other that the gaps between them are rather minor evolutionary jumps than revolutionary upheavals. The recent development of accounting can possibly be better understood by organizing the Butterworth paradigms into a small number of research programs (theory nets), each subdivided into various phases (theory elements) in accordance with the post-Kuhnian trend outlined in Chapter 7. The combination of the first three Butterworth paradigms (Valuations I, II, III) seems to make sense, since all three cases regard the valuation of assets, equities, and income as the primary function of accounting. We may, therefore, speak of a valuation research tradition. Similarly, it should be possible to combine the last three Butterworth paradigms to a stewardship research tradition, since all of them regard allocation and the monitoring as well as the evaluation of stewardship as the primary function of accounting. Such a classification is not only based on the fundamental distinction between valuation and allocation (as competing primary functions of accounting) but would reduce the fragmentation of accounting theory to a single dichotomy between two camps: On one side would be those who find the major function of financial accounting in the income and profitability measurement by means of discounted net cash flows or the current valuation of assets and equities. This program would serve foremost the temporary investors, developers, and speculators. In the other camp would be those who regard financial accounting as monitoring the stewardship of management for the sake of shareholders, in particular, the more permanent and major shareholders. Therefore, priority is given to income measurement on the basis of accrual accounting and the matching of costs against revenues.

However, the urgent quest to give accounting a purpose orientation rather than imposing upon it a monolithic goal limitation suggests or even necessitates a third alternative: the objective-oriented program. Instead of focusing on a single major accounting goal, it emphasizes the need for different accounting models matched to different information objectives. This third program would, for example, pay equal attention to the stewardship–allocation, the valuation–investment, and other functions. Above all, it would put stronger emphasis on the examination of means–end relations. Toward the end of this chapter this third program is briefly mentioned, though its corresponding methodology will be discussed in chapter 11. We must first concentrate on the competition between the stewardship research tradition—so significant for conventional accounting practice—and the valuation research tradition, which, during the last two decades, succeeded in replacing the former in many academic circles. In accordance with the post-Kuhnian view and actual manifestations, I will discuss each of those two traditions in three phases, each one of which approximates one of the Butterworth paradigms and constitutes a theory element in Stegmüller's (1979, 1986) sense.

Some experts may argue that there exist many more research traditions than here indicated, for example, that behavioral accounting is such a neglected special tradition. Such an objection is based on a misunderstanding of this presentation as well as on the nature of behavioral accounting. The latter is not a research tradition in the sense of a theory net consisting of a variety of interrelated theory elements but an empirical methodology to complement the theoretical or analytical approach. Above all, it is independent of the particular research tradition involved. Although specific methodologies may depend on certain research traditions, the two should not be confused with each other. For further details, see Chapter 11, which shifts the emphasis to the methodological level.

THE FIRST RESEARCH TRADITION: STEWARDSHIP PROGRAM

Accounting, being an applied science, must replace the structuralists' "fundamental law" by the primary function (and its basic principles). This function, according to the first research tradition, is the principal's monitoring of stewardship. This stewardship is the task of various managerial and submanagerial echelons. Thus, the information provision for short- and middle-term investment is relegated to financial analysis including capital budgeting and becomes a mere secondary function of accounting. For the realization of this first tradition, a model type emerged that Butterworth originally called "stewardship paradigm I" and which shall be discussed and elaborated as the first phase (or "theory element") of the stewardship tradition.

First Phase: The Plain Periodization Approach

This approach arose out of the view that the monitoring of managerial stewardship can be fulfilled best by the "appropriate" allocation of cost and revenues to a particular period. Hence, we find the following well-known principles in the foreground of this model:

1. The historical or acquisition cost basis
2. The periodical allocation of costs and revenues via matching one with the other
3. The allocation of depreciable asset costs over an estimated time of useful life
4. The assumption of ongoing enterprise
5. The stewardship function, which dominates this and the other two phases of this particular program or tradition

The periodization approach has been dominating accounting practice for a considerable time and was supported and elaborated by Schmalenbach (1919a) and his followers (e.g., Kosiol 1956, 1970, and 1978) in the German literature, and by Paton (1922) in the Anglo-American literature. Further interpretations of this model type are to be found by the AAA (1936, 1941, 1948), by Sanders et al. (1938), and by Paton and Littleton (1940). In more recent times, Ijiri (1967, 1981) has been its most prominent proponent. Butterworth and Falk also counted Mattessich (1964a) into this category; but I regard this publication as belonging to the third research program (see the last section of this chapter), which Butterworth and Falk (1986) did not treat as a separate paradigm.

An essential aspect of the periodization approach lies in the fact that valuation is perceived as the primary function of the market but not of accounting. This manifests itself in various slogans such as "the accountant is not an appraiser" or "the accountant ought to report facts and not opinions." The function of accounting, therefore, lies in the accountability and the necessary "digestion" of data resulting from various business transactions. Hence, cost aggregates become the cornerstone, and consistency, objectivity, cost verification, and the like, its basic principles.

In reference to Paton's (1922) postulation attempt, Butterworth and Falk (1986) raise the question: From whence are the foundations of accounting derived? Since it is difficult to find an empirical–scientific basis, those authors speak of the "excathedra character" of such foundations. This characterization is understandable in the face of accounting theory as generally practiced, but the proponents of the third research program might disagree (see the penultimate section of this chapter). Some of them believe that a general accounting theory can be developed that will permit them to match a specific information purpose to a specific accounting model on the basis of analytical as well as empirical foundations.

Second Phase: The Original Agency Approach

The first publications analyzing systematically the problems of work and management contracts seem to be those of Coase (1937) and Herbert Simon (1951). These publications found little echo originally; it took some two decades until a more widely accepted theory of the principal–agency relations evolved. In economics, it was the paper by Alchian and Demsetz (1972); and in business administration, a subsequent paper by Jensen and Meckling (1976) that provided the actual launching basis. Shortly before, special aspects of similar contracts were analyzed in two fundamental papers by Mirrlees (1971, 1976) as well as Spence and Zeckhauser (1971). The integration of all those and a considerable number of later research efforts led to what nowadays is known as "agency (contract) theory." There is an essential difference between this *original*, predominantly descriptive agency theory and the subsequent, analytical agency theory that I will address as agency-information analysis, to be discussed under the third phase of the stewardship research program.

The central issue of the original agency theory is to be found in the costs caused by the potential goal conflict between principal and agent (e.g., monitoring of agent's activity, profit reduction resulting from a different value judgment between the two parties, foregoing of actions preferred by agent in consideration of the principal's different preferences—in the last case, for example, the agency costs are borne by the agent). Closely related to this problem is the search for a motivational contract that enables a risk sharing between principal and agent that hopefully is Pareto optimal (no party is worse off than before, but some parties may be better off). Therefore, the accounting-information system employed plays a vital role. In this way the agent (whose activity cannot always be observed) shall be motivated such that his interest coincides with that of the principal (self-enforcing contract); and furthermore, the "agency costs" shall be reduced to a minimum. Last, it is to be expected that the agency costs grow to a lesser degree than the agency's share in the firm; but the more the motivational incentive decreases, the higher the costs of monitoring the agent will be. In the realm of finance, agency theory tried to analyze the motivations and relations caused by certain shifts between internal and external financing in order to search for an optimal financing ratio. In this connection arises the question whether such a finance theory might be more realistic than the theory of Modigliani and Miller (1958), which seems to deny such an optimization possibility.

Butterworth and Falk (1986) have pointed out that within the predominantly descriptive approach of Jensen and Meckling (1976), it was neither possible to examine the equilibrium conditions of such a contract model nor to examine certain consequences (e.g., bonding and monitoring features voluntarily accepted by the agent) that might possibly arise from this theory. Butterworth also includes two well-known publications by Watts and Zimmerman (1978, 1979) in this second phase or paradigm. These two authors put special emphasis on the "positive" nature of their theory to distinguish it strictly from the preceding normative phase. Although positive accounting theory is strongly oriented toward "political phenomena" (as, for example, the legislation of accounting standards), it tries for this very reason to connect agency theory with accounting and the political costs connected with it. Last, Butterworth and Falk (1986) included the publication by Holthausen and Leftwich (1983), that supplied early empirical tests to the agency theory in this phase. For a detailed survey of this "positive" research, in the broad sense, see the paper by Abdel-khalik et al., which concludes as follows:

First, evidence about the income-smoothing hypothesis continues to elude researchers. . . . Second, corporations and accounting firms do lobby for their preferred accounting standards. Researchers have speculated on possible motives for such lobbying. There has been no recent critical synthesis of theory in this area or review of the extent to which evidence is inconclusive. Again hard evidence is difficult to obtain, and there is no adequate analysis of the effect of lobbying on the quality of accounting standards or on resource allocation. Third, the role of contractual arrangements in affecting the choice of accounting methods and accounting accruals have been brought to the forefront with the advent of popular articles on agency theory. Various accounting surrogates have been developed to proxy for the presumed impact of debt contractual arrangements. Accounting numbers assume more relevance as they constitute benchmarks and bases for contractual provisions. The state-of-art in this area has progressed somewhat slowly. Little hard evidence is collected and examined. Anecdotal evidence and recent research results suggest that accounting researchers have given the role of debt covenants in the choice and determination of accounting measurements more credence than is warranted. Better understanding of the relevant institutional arrangements appears to be necessary for progress in this area. (Abdel-khalik et al. 1989, 175)

Third Phase: The Agency-Information Approach

This third phase of the stewardship paradigm arose out of the combination of descriptive agency theory, on one side, and information economics, on the other. The latter was developed by Marschak (1974) and others in the 1950s and 1960s and applied to accounting by Butterworth (1967, 1972), Demski (1980), Demski and Feltham (1972, 1976, 1978), Feltham (1967, 1968, 1972), Feltham and Demski (1970), and others (for further details, see last section of Chapter 5).

For years there did not exist much contact between descriptive agency theory and information economics, but disciples of the latter searched for new fields of application and noticed that agency theory offers a rich potential for further formalization. Thus, an amalgamation of both areas came about. For this reason, we speak in the following of agency-information analysis when referring to the analytical approach of agency theory. Its core is to be found in the contractual relations and the risk sharing between the principal and the agent, but it is more than a mere extension of the second phase discussed earlier. Some authors (e.g., Abdel-khalik et al. 1989, 155) believe that this analytical version of agency theory has not helped produce much testable material, while the descriptive version has done much better in this regard. Indeed, there seems to be some minor (nonparadigmatic) competition occurring between these two phases. This is confirmed by the last sentence of the following quote from Jensen—one of the major proponents of the descriptive version (who calls it "positive theory of agency," in contrast to the analytical "principal–agent literature"):

Both literatures address the contracting problem between self-interested, maximizing parties and both use the same agency cost minimizing tautology (although not necessarily in the same form). They differ, however, in many respects. . . . The principal–agent literature has generally concentrated on modeling the effects of three factors on contracts between parties . . . (1) the structure of the preferences of the parties of the contracts, (2) the nature of uncertainty, and (3) the information structure in the environment. . . . The positive agency literature has generally concentrated on modeling the effects of additional aspects of the contracting environment and the technology of monitoring and bonding on the form of the contracts and organizations that survive. . . . Tractability problems seem to limit the richness of the principal–agent models. . . . The positive agency literature proceeds on the assumption that the variables emphasized in the principal–agent literature are relatively unimportant in understanding the observed phenomenon when compared with the richer specifications of information costs, other aspects of the environment, and the monitoring and bonding technology. (Jensen 1983, 334–335)

In the end, Jensen hopes for a closer cooperation of the two agency approaches and expects mathematics (toward which he first expressed suspicion, at least as far as its application to organizational theories is concerned) to be of great help.

Depending on the type of employment contract, management's share (of the total enterprise profit before its own remuneration) lies between two extremes: (a) on the one side, we find a *fixed managerial salary* (under full monitoring of the manager's activity by the principal), whereby the total remaining profit goes to the principal who bears all the risk (principal is risk neutral, agent is risk averse); whereas the other extreme is found in (b) the *renting of the business by the agent* such that the principal receives a fixed rent and the agent who bears all the risk receives the remaining profit (principal is risk averse, agent is risk neutral; see items [a] and [b] in Table 8.1).

There exist many types of contracts between these extremes, one of which is shown in item (c) of Table 8.1. It leads to a Pareto optimal profit and risk sharing between the two parties in accordance with classical marginal economic theory (principal and agent are both either risk neutral or risk averse). All these are "first-best solutions" and are of less interest than the so-called "second-best solutions" because only the latter offer means to cope with two crucial issues (already mentioned in Chapter 5):

Table 8.1
First-Best Solutions of Agency Contracts

Principal P can observe action a of agent A as well as result x; P also knows A's utility function and shares his beliefs with respect to the probability of x, hence, there exists complete information.

(a) P is risk neutral, } Pareto optimal contract:
     A is risk averse.   } P bears all risk,
     $z(x) = c$ } A receives constant wage c.

This represents the simple situation in which the Pareto optimal contract and reward z for A is a fixed wage, and full monitoring of A's activity by P is possible. In this case, the full risk rests on the shoulders of P.

(b) P is risk averse } Pareto optimal contract:
     or risk neutral,   } action a need not be observable.
     A is risk neutral. } A bears all the risk.
     $z(x) = x - r$ } P receives constant rent r.

Here, the situation is reversed, as the full risk now rests on A, since he pays a fixed amount r for renting the enterprise from P. This situation makes P's monitoring of A's activity redundant.

(c) A and P are both } Pareto optimal contract:
     risk averse.   } Action a must be observable.
                        } P and A efficiently share the outcome.

In between the above two extremes lies situation (c), in which A's reward depends upon his effort as well as upon the firm's total profit, provided A's activity can be fully monitored by P.

Symbols used:

A	agent	r	constant rent
a	effort of A	x	profit of enterprise (before
c	constant wage		payment of c or r)
P	principal	$z(\cdot)$	reward of A

I gratefully acknowledge advice given by Prof. G. A. Feltham in designing this table and writing the related description in the text, including equations.

1. The problem of *moral hazard:* Since the full monitoring of the agent's activity by the principal is often infeasible (and since agency-information analysis assumes that each party maximizes its own expected utility), the agent's optimal actions may not coincide with those actions optimal for the principal.

2. The problem of *adverse selection* of revealed information: In many situations, there exists an asymmetry of information between principal and agent (usually, but not always, in favor of the agent); so, for example, the manager may have an information advantage over the principal because of the former's better or more specialized training and experience; or, in the case of an insurance contract, the insured person (principal) may have better information about his own health than the insurer (agent) in spite of the required medical examination. (Another favored example is the second-hand car market [see Akerlof 1970].) Therefore, if one party withholds some information which otherwise would lead the other party to choose a different contract or action, namely, one less favorable to the first but more favorable to the second party, then this adverse selection leads to distrust— hence lesser market participation—and impedes a first-best solution.

A major task of agency-information analysis, therefore, is to find conditions under which a Pareto optimal contract between both parties can be obtained; that is, one searches for an incentive and risk-sharing scheme that is mutually satisfactory for both parties. Such an analysis would take care of both—the problem of moral hazard as well as that of adverse selection. This literature, dealing with both, has become comprehensive enough to speak of a "theory of asymmetric information" as well as of a "contract theory," both of which are closely related or a part of agency-information analysis. Butterworth and Falk (1986) even speak occasionally of an "asymmetric information paradigm" as well as a "contracting paradigm." Here again, the aim is to find the efficient contract that leads to a compromise between two opposing tendencies: On the one side, one must find an efficient risk sharing between principal and agent; on the other side, it is necessary to motivate the manager sufficiently to act in the interest of the principal. However, research has shown that contracts which are risk-efficient are inefficient in regard to motivation (compare Butterworth and Falk 1986, 22).

For the further understanding of this phase or theory element, we illustrate— by means of three simplified models—how the information-economic approach and the original agency theory were synthesized in agency-information analysis. Information economics is taken to be the natural extension of statistical decision theory, whereby the decision theoretical model has become enriched by the notion of information (signal). This yields the first model:

I. Basic Model of Information Economics

$$E(u|\eta^*) = \max_{a(y),\ \eta} \sum_s \sum_y u(a(y), s) \cdot p(y|s, \eta) \cdot p(s)$$

$$= \max_\eta \sum_y \max_a \sum_s u(a, s) \cdot p(s|y, \eta) \cdot p(y|\eta)$$

Explanation of symbols for this and the following two models:

a	action or effort of agent (* refers to optimal action or other variable), often as a function of y
argmax	refers to the actions that maximize the subsequent expression (which can be a set or a singleton [see models II and III])
d (a)	agents disutility caused by effort a
$E(u|\eta^*)$	expected value of utility u, given optimal information system η^*
$E_p(u_p|\cdot)$	principal's expected utility given some variables
η	information system
$p(y|s, \eta)$	probability of information y, given state s, and η
p(s)	probability of state s (sometimes conditioned on y and η)
s	state
y	information
u (a (y), s)	utility as a function of y and s
u_p or u	utility of principal (usually as a function of some variables)
u_A or u	utility of agent (usually as a function of some variables)
u_A^{min}	agent's minimum acceptable utility
x (a, s)	outcome (profit) as a function of a and s
z (·)	agent's reward for effort a (usually as a function of some variables)

II. Basic Agency Model

$$E_p(u_p|a^*, z^*) = \max_{a,z} \sum_s u_p(x(a,s) - z(x(a,s))) \cdot p(s)$$

subject to

$$\sum_s u_A(z(x(a,s))) \cdot p(s) - d(a) \geq u_A^{min}$$

$$a \in \text{argmax} \sum_s u_A(z(x(a,s))) \cdot p(s) - d(a)$$

This agency model regards the situation from the point of view of the principal; but it is possible to formulate it similarly from the agent's point of view, whereby the goal function and constraints become reversed and slightly modified. In our situation, the principal's utility (i.e., after deduction of the agent's reward) is to be maximized. The constraints refer to the agent's opportunity costs (offering his services in a free market) and to the maximization of his own utility, respectively (assuming his or her action is not observable by the principal).

III. Basic Model of Agency-Information Analysis:

$$E_p(u_p|a^*, z^*, \eta) = \max_{a,z,\eta} \sum_s \sum_y u_p(x(a,s) - z(y)) \cdot p(y|a,s,\eta) \cdot p(s)$$

subject to

$$\sum_s \sum_y u_A(z(y)) \cdot p(y|a,s,\eta) \cdot p(s) - d(a) \geq u_A^{min}$$

$$a \in \text{argmax} \sum_s \sum_y u_A(z(y)) \cdot p(y|a,s,\eta) \cdot p(s) - d(a)$$

The third presentation reveals the amalgamation of the original agency model with information economics, discernible through the enrichment with the information signal variable (y) and the information system variable (η), as shown in the agency-information model. The goal function of principal (P) maximizes his or her utility expectation through the choice of an optimal contract with the agent (A), stipulating the optimal information system (η^*) and the optimal agent's reward (z^*) in such a way that the optimal action (a^*) will be chosen by A. The constraints correspond to the previous model, modified by the enrichment mentioned previously. Through elimination of more and more restrictions, on one side, and further enrichment of the model, on the other, many variations of this basic agency-information model are possible.

This stewardship research program (which, during the 1970s, seemed to be pushed aside by the valuation–investment program) has now in its third phase, as a consequence of agency-information analysis, experienced a genuine Renaissance (compare Gjesdal 1981). This return to the stewardship program illustrates Lakatos' belief in the new "budding" of what was believed to be an already "degenerate" research program; it also is an admission that stewardship or accountability (i.e., the provision of information for establishing an efficient contractual basis) belongs to accounting's most important functions (compare Butterworth et al. 1982). Such a contract should be capable of reducing the agency costs to a minimum (including from residual costs, which do not necessarily need to be carried by the principal) and enable a mutually satisfactory position for both parties. It must be taken into consideration that the capital risk need not only rest on the shoulders of principal and agent; it may also rest on those of other investors and creditors. The contracts with the latter (e.g., bond indentures) might possibly be incorporated into a sophisticated agency-information model under consideration of market equilibrium. Credit contracts may be represented as contingent claims toward the assets of the borrowing person or firm. This is the starting point of contingent claims analysis, in which the price of the assets is determined by such stochastic processes as logarithmic–normal diffusion.[6] For a survey of contingent claims analysis, we refer to Hughes (1984); for the application of agency theory to the area of finance, we refer to Barnea et al. (1985); and for the application to accounting, several papers in Mattessich (1984, 1991d) offer an appropriate overview: Feltham (1984), Baiman (1982), and Butterworth et al. (1982). In each of these areas the agency–information analysis was instrumental in clarifying specific problems.

THE SECOND RESEARCH TRADITION:
VALUATION–INVESTMENT PROGRAM

This tradition regards the "correct" economic evaluation of the assets and equities as the primary purpose of accounting. Behind this, however, stands the quest for an economically correct *income determination* and *optimal capital disposition*. The capital theory of Böhm-Bawerk and Irving Fisher was applied to accounting in Canning's (1929) fundamental work and in a somewhat modified way through the current value theory of Schmidt ([1921] 1953). The latter can be interpreted as an objectified approximation of a basically subjective approach. Again, we encounter three phases (or theory elements) within this tradition.

First Phase: The Present Value and Current Value Approach

The opposition to the historical cost and accrual approach (of the stewardship tradition) had practical as well as theoretical roots: The latter is to be found in capital theory, the former in the promotion of replacement costs by American as well as German railway companies (for details, see Seicht 1970, 511; Boer 1966; and Mattessich 1982, 349–350). In the accounting and business literature, this approach seems first to be discussed by Fäs (1913); later, we find it by Paton (1918) and possibly by Limperg (see Van Seventer [1975, 68] who claims that Limperg conceived this approach between 1917 and 1918). The first systematic exponent of it is Schmidt ([1921] 1953) and, after him, Canning (1929), who regards replacement value as a kind of objective substitute for the true economic present value. Apart from serving short-term investors (compare Staubus 1961), this approach is split into two camps. On one side stand the defenders of the current *entry value* approach (replacement value)—such as the American Accounting Association (1957), Edwards and Bell (1961), and Sprouse and Moonitz (1962)—such as well as those of the current *exit value* approach—such as MacNeal (1939), Chambers (1966), and Sterling (1970b). On the other side are the proponents of the *capital theoretic* approach, for whom the present value is the center of attention (e.g., Hansen 1962; Honko 1959; Albach 1965; Seicht 1970, 558–619; and, more recently, Ohlson and others [see next subsection]).

Butterworth and Falk (1986) characterize this "paradigm" through the present value, which, as they point out, may be substituted in situations of uncertainty by the current value (if markets are perfect or at least efficient). The objection to this characterization or substitution possibility lies in the notion that every investment or disinvestment decision requires a subjective as well as an objective evaluation (i.e., the juxtaposition of a personal estimation with a market situation). This means that, at least in such situations, the latter cannot be regarded as a substitute for the former. This is in agreement with other authors (e.g., Chambers, Sterling, and the like), who, for example, would *object* to the use of net realizable values (NRV) as a substitute for present values (PV).

Second Phase: The Risk-Sharing Approach

This phase is also based on neoclassical economic theory and its extension by Arrow and Debreu (1954) but, above all, on modern portfolio theory (Markowitz 1952; Fama 1965) as well as on the capital–asset pricing theory of Sharpe (1963, 1964) and Lintner (1965). Within the area of accounting, Butterworth originally emphasized the research by the following authors: Hakansson (1969a), Demski (1973), Garman and Ohlson (1980), and Ohlson and Buckman (1980). This second phase also stresses the valuation of market predictions and similar information as well as its effect upon our discipline. Furthermore, it introduces uncertainty and stochastic processes into accounting. Last, it takes into consideration the evaluation of securities in accord with modern finance theory with its distinction between *unsystematic risk*—which is unique to each security and can be eliminated by portfolio diversification—on one side, and *systematic risk*, on the other side.

Other works significant in this context are those by Hakansson et al. (1982) and Ohlson (1987, 1988, 1990). Previous publications concerning the value of public information contradicted each other: For example, Hirschleifer (1971) showed that public information has no value under perfect competition; whereas Marshall (1974) and others demonstrated that (under certain assumptions) public information may have value even under perfect competition. The papers by Hakansson et al. (1982) and Ohlson (1987, 1988, 1990) not only reveal the necessary and sufficient conditions under which public information (for perfectly competitive markets) has value but also unite and reconcile in an elegant mathematical way the literature that previously appeared to be contradictory.

Third Phase: The Capital Market Approach

This phase is closely tied to the preceding one. While Butterworth originally tried to distinguish these two phases by two paradigms, he later combined them (see Butterworth and Falk 1986). The basic premises are those of the preceding approach but enriched by empirical research and further assumptions (e.g., that the pertinent security yield possesses a probability distribution, which, however, need not be observable). The information of the security market is considered to have value if it helps to improve the estimation of the yield, together with the underlying assumption that the capital market is efficient with regard to the financial statement information. Above all, the pioneering works of Ball and Brown (1968) and Beaver (1968) ought to be mentioned in this connection. These were the first well-grounded accounting publications that took into consideration the correlation between published profits and stock prices. Benston (1967) presented similar ideas, but his empirical research was not yet sufficiently carried out. Therefore, this third phase is mainly an application of newer, especially empirical, insights of finance literature gained in the wake of further developments of the Sharpe–Lintner capital–asset pricing models.

Ball and Brown (1968) and Beaver (1968) showed that the changes of stock prices highly correlate with the (unexpected) profit changes of the pertinent firms. More precisely, in Dopuch's formulation:

The Ball and Brown study allowed us to conclude that historical cost income numbers captured the effects of events the stock market uses to estimate firms' values (i.e., their equilibrium security prices). But the experimental design did not enable them to determine whether the numbers were actually used by the stock market. Indeed, their results suggested that the information contained in firms' income numbers appeared to be processed by the market in establishing equilibrium security prices before the numbers were actually released. In contrast, Beaver attempted to directly test whether market agents used the [numbers] at the time of their release. He did so by assessing whether trading volume and the variances of security returns increased beyond their expected values around the time firms' earnings numbers were released. The variances of returns metric used by Beaver is basically the squared value of the residual from the market model of firms' expected returns (or abnormal returns squared), standardized to remove heteroscedastic problems. This metric has intuitive appeal, but as noted by Phil Brown and Bill's workshop, the statistical properties of the metric were not known. For this reason, Phil suggested that Bill drop the residual metric and merely rely on the behavior of unexpected volume to determine whether the market used accounting income numbers. What is interesting is that for a few years after the paper appeared, researchers were willing to accept the intuition underlying the squared residual metric, but they questioned the meaning of the evidence about unexpected volume. Subsequently Patell (1976) was able to derive some of the statistical properties of the residual square metric and certain researchers at Berkeley and UCLA provided a (limited) rationale for assessing unexpected volume. As a result, both measures of information content continued to be used in current studies in accounting. (Dopuch 1989, 45–46)

The last sentence of this quote may hint at, but does not fully reveal, how precarious the notion of "information content" actually is. Further publications to be taken into consideration are those by Ball (1972), Foster (1973), Sunder (1973), Gonedes and Dopuch (1974), and Beaver (1981). For concise surveys, see Lev and Ohlson (1982), Clarkson and Mattessich (1984), and Dopuch (1989). Despite impressive efforts, this research still suffers from a lack of general credibility, and no phase of the program offers well-formulated relations for choosing the optimal accounting system. A major difficulty lies in the use of what these scholars call the "concept of information content." Perhaps the reason lies in the fact that information content is neither an observable notion nor one in conformity with the more precise concept (bearing even the same name) that is used in computer science and is measurable in bits.

THE THIRD RESEARCH TRADITION:
OBJECTIVE-ORIENTED PROGRAM

Whether one is justified to talk in this case about a "tradition" may be a point of controversy, but it is appropriate to call it a program. Although one repeatedly encounters in the literature the quest for different accounting models suited to different information needs, there hardly exists agreement on how such a purpose-oriented theory can systematically be developed and in which way the system structure can be matched to the pertinent information objective. We seem to be in a dilemma: On one side, experts agree that so-called general-purpose systems satisfy only very simple accounting needs; on the other side, many experts join opposing groups, each of which pursues only a single, one-sided direction. The major impediment toward the development of such a purpose-oriented theory seems to be the "arbitrariness" or "excathedra character" of most foundations of accounting, which Butterworth and Falk (1986) criticize explicitly. However, to understand our objection to this criticism, it must be taken into consideration that the foundations of science in general are subject to a similar excathedra aspect (as the next paragraph shows). Furthermore, the justification for the use of any instrument lies in the fulfillment of its purpose. The construction and evaluation of this instrument must begin and end with the purpose and the degree of its fulfillment within a long-range cost–benefit context. No special philosophy is required to recognize that both accounting and science in general are instruments in this sense.

Bertrand Russell (1948), for example, who endeavored to formulate the foundations of science and of knowledge in general had to abandon the quest for an absolute foundation of science and had to be satisfied with formulating fairly pragmatic postulates.[7] In other words, he had to substitute the epistemic question "What are the foundations of science?" with the pragmatic question, "Which assumptions do we accept when doing science?" (compare Mattessich 1978a, 176–179). Similarly, I abandoned the search for any absolute foundation of accounting some thirty years ago, and tried to answer the following question: "Which assumptions do we accept when applying any kind of double-classification accounting system?" (compare Mattessich 1964a; for further details, see Chapter 5 in this volume).

To a modest degree, a purpose orientation for accounting has been available for a considerable time; the distinction between financial accounting and cost or managerial accounting is the most obvious example. The objective-oriented program aims not only at a richer diversification but, above all, at a much better theoretical justification of its diverse categories and articulations (compare Mattessich 1978b) as well as an appropriate methodology (for suggestions about the latter see Chapter 11). J. M. Clark (1923) might be regarded as the father or precursor of this third research program.[8] His slogan "different costs for different purposes" sets the stage and points in the direction that I (among others) have tried to pursue. Other authors who occasionally emphasized purpose orientation (in one way or the other) are Le Coutre (1949), Spacek (1962), Backer (1966), Heinen (1978), possibly Schneider (1981, particularly 405ff.), Hamel (1984), and Devine (1985)—apart from those mentioned in the last section of Chapter 6. Special cases are the works of three notable Japanese scholars: Kurosawa (1932), who pleaded for three different kinds of balance sheets; Iwata (1954), who proposed two different income determination models—one with the emphasis on the income statement (for management decisions), the other on the balance sheet (for auditing work); and Kimura (1954), who emphasized that accounting cannot escape from subjective income measurement.

Further publications about objectives of accounting are to be found by Stützel (1967); Beaver and Demski (1974); Cyert and Ijiri (1974); Cramer and Sorter (1974); the Financial Accounting Standards Board (1979); Stamp (1980, 32–38); and Griffin (1982), and, above all, the Trueblood Report of the American Institute of Certified Public Accountants (1973). Most recently, Boritz has stated, "However, there is unlikely to be a single set of measurements to suit all purposes. Which value/goals should accounting academe serve? Unfortunately, practitioners and standard setters have not been clear about their goals/motives/values, have not spoken with a united voice, and are not consistent cross-sectionally or longitudinally" (Boritz 1994, 37).

Since the early 1960s, I have attempted to bring some clarity into this third research program and tried to distinguish strictly between the basic uninterpreted or semi-interpreted theory, on one side, and the purpose-oriented interpretations for different intended applications, on the other side (see Mattessich 1964a; 1970a; 1972; 1979a; 1984, 1–45; 1992; 1995). The introduction of additional auxiliary hypotheses in the case of new applications of a basic theory is generally accepted in modern science and may correspond to the introduction of new theory elements in the Sneed–Stegmüller methodology discussed in Chapter 7. This kind of "specific interpretation" or expansion of the theory net assumes particular significance in the applied sciences. The purpose orientation of all applied sciences creates methodological problems hitherto insufficiently explored (e.g., instead of the "fundamental law," the "objective" may serve as the invariant nucleus of a theory net). Surprisingly, those endeavors took little root in the academic community in spite of the fact that the need for purpose orientation is often acknowledged in the literature and even materialized in actual practice. The standards on price-level adjustments (originally established but now abandoned) by the Financial Accounting Standards Board (1979, 1984a, 1984b), Canadian Institute of Chartered Accountants (1982), and so on, resulted in the introduction of greater purpose orientation into the accounting systems of American business (as shown in Chapter 6). These current cost accounting standards were much more than mere inflation accounting; they also reflected shifting prices between commodities and served other information purposes (e.g., income measurement on the basis of nominal and real financial capital maintenance, as well as physical capital maintenance, each serving a different information objective and decision goal). However, the pertinent regulations of the FASB and CICA were abandoned after some five years or so.

CONCLUSION

Accounting research can be illuminated from different angles and classified in a great variety of schemes. It may seem that this exposition is but another such attempt of classification. I hope it is more than that. The crucial point of the distinction between three accounting research programs is the connection to recent insights in methodology and the philosophy of science. This goes beyond Thomas Kuhn's popular but somewhat simplistic picture of a dominating paradigm. It is important to recognize two things: First, accounting, like many other scientific endeavors, consists of different research traditions that compete with and complement each other, instead of a single, dominating paradigm (emerging from the struggle between a preceding, obsolete paradigm and several new competitors). Second, and perhaps more important, each research tradition constitutes an entire network of theory elements. The latter compete with each other as well, but in a more moderate or secondary fashion; first, because those theory elements are based on one and the same fundamental set of premises, and second, because each element is a further specialization or articulation of the basic theory from which it evolves chronologically.

Attempts of more rigorous structuralist reconstructions of theories and their nets from various fields, including accounting, have been undertaken (see Stegmüller 1986; Balzer et al. 1987; Balzer and Mattessich 1991). The current presentation is informal, but a more formal treatment is feasible. Indeed, the best chance for a rigorous treatment of accounting networks might be the close cooperation between a philosopher of science, with expertise in the logical reconstruction of theories, and an accountant versed in formalization and axiomatization. The paper by Balzer and Mattessich (1991) is such an attempt, but it deals mainly with the input–output aspects of accounting without any expansion into finance and agency theory, and the like. Hopefully, the project can be extended in the way sketched in the present exposition. Such an interdisciplinary effort could further improve upon the search for the appropriate axiomatization of accounting theory by revealing its logical structure as well as its empirical claims in a clearer and more generally acceptable way than previously done.

APPENDIX

Dimensions of Multiperson Information Economic Models

1. Number of Persons
    Small number (game–theoretic model)
    Large number (equilibrium model)

2. Transferability of Claims to Outcomes
    Transferable
    Nontransferable (transferability either prohibited or not enforceable)

3. Variety of Transferable Claims Available
    Complete (security market is sufficiently flexible to satisfy all combinations of investment needs)
    Incomplete because of exogenous restrictions
    Incomplete because of insufficient information

4. Alternative Actions in Transferable Claims Models
   Pure exchange models (no choices)
   Firm's actions are exogenously determined and cannot be influenced by
      creating new information
   Production models (actions are collective choices, e.g., manager and principal
      decide in cooperation, or decisions in a planned economy)
   Agency Models (individual choice, e.g., by manager)

5. Direct Preferences for Actions in Agency Models
   None (manager has no particular preferences)
   Disutility expressing manager's efforts is taken into consideration

6. Similarity of Preferences for Actions in Nontransferable Claims Models
   Strictly independent (e.g., manager has different preferences than principal)
   Strictly identical (e.g., principal and agent have same preference structure)
   Strictly opposite (preferences of agent harm preferences of principal and vice versa)

7. Action Commitments in Nontransferable Claims Model
   Nonfeasible
   All feasible (purely cooperative model)
   Some feasible

8. Similarity of Prior Beliefs
   Homogeneous (principal and agent use same probability distribution)
   Heterogeneous (principal and agent use different probability distributions)

9. Timing of Information Distribution
   Precommitment (see also Baiman 1982, 276–277)
   Predecision (see also Baiman 1982, 277–278, 279–280)
   Postdecision (see also Baiman 1982, 270–276, 278–279)

10. Extent of Information Distribution
    Public report
    Private acquisition
    Private acquisition prior to public report

11. Extent to Which Private Information Is Revealed
    None revealed
    Fully revealed
    Partially revealed

12. Selection of Information System
    Exogenous
    Endogenous

13. Number of Periods
    Single period
    Multiple periods

NOTES

This chapter is partly based on the second part of "Paradigms, Research Traditions and Theory Nets of Accounting" (Mattessich 1993b, 192–220) and partly on new material. The Appendix is a somewhat extended version of Feltham's (1984, 183–184) Table 1, adapted with permission of the CGA-Canada Research Foundation (previously, The Canadian Certified General Accountants Research Foundation).

1. Those six paradigms were presented by Butterworth in an Accounting Faculty Seminar in Fall 1983 at the University of British Columbia. Since then, different drafts of this paper (by Butterworth and Falk) have appeared until its ultimate version was published as Chapter 2 ("Information Attributes of the Contractual Paradigm") of Butterworth and Falk (1986, 9–29). However, in this last version, only the following four paradigms are mentioned: (1) the Discounted Money–Value Paradigm (corresponding to Valuation I), (2) the Stewardship Paradigm (corresponding to Stewardship I), (3) the Capital Market Paradigm (combining Valuations II and III, and, quite unexpectedly, Stewardship II), and (4) the Contracting Paradigm (corresponding to Stewardship III). From the viewpoint of our paper, the original presentation is more meaningful, but since it is not available in print, I will either refer to the original presentation as "Butterworth" or to the ultimate publication as "Butterworth and Falk (1986)."

2. Two excellent review articles of this report were written by Peasnell (1978) and Hakansson (1978).

3. If this "double-entry model" could be regarded as a means to attain proper stewardship, Cushing's (1989) accounting paradigm might approach the "stewardship program" (particularly its first phase) discussed in the second section.

4. For a definition or explanation of *efficient market hypotheses*, *capital–asset pricing model*, and *portfolio analysis*, see such reference works as Cooper and Ijiri (1983).

5. As for the possibilities and difficulties of formulating paradigms in accounting and business administration, see Mattessich (1979b) and the different contributions of the anthological proceedings by Fischer-Winkelmann (1982).

6. Black and Scholes (1973) have pioneered an equilibrium model for stock options under simple capital structure of the pertinent enterprise. This work was extended and further developed by Merton (1973a, 1973b, 1974, 1976), Brennan and Schwartz (1977, 1978, 1979), Cox and Ross (1976a, 1976b), and others and was also applied to other areas.

7. Russell (1948) deals with the scientific–empirical foundations—in contrast to the more-renowned *Principia Mathematica* by Whitehead and Russell, which deals with the foundations of modern mathematics and with which the work of 1948 must not be confused.

8. Staubus (1987) blames J. M. Clark for our "dark ages of cost accounting," but this hardly affects our issue. Staubus merely concludes "that instead of different costs for 'different purposes,' Clark should have stressed proper identification of the object of costing in each case" (Staubus 1987, 7).

CHAPTER 9

Empirical Research and Positive
Accounting Theory

THE EMPIRICAL REVOLUTION IN ACCOUNTING

During the second half of the 1960s some revolutionary papers (Benston 1967; Ball and Brown 1968; Beaver 1968) appeared that led accounting theory into the direction of a full-fledged empirical discipline. The best-known among these publications is that by Ball and Brown (1968); yet, when it was submitted to *The Accounting Review*, the paper was rejected by reviewers and the editor with the argument that it did not deal with accounting but finance. The editor of the *Journal of Accounting Research*, on the other hand, was of a different mind. He tells us that "I did not have the paper reviewed by anyone on the editorial board since the members at the time would not have understood the paper any more than I initially did" (Dopuch 1989, 45). He accepted the paper merely on the trust he had in the motivation and talents of Ball and Brown whom he knew well from the time they spent at Chicago.

Thus came to be published the work which, twenty years later, received the most prestigious of the literature prizes of the AAA, the Award for Seminal Contributions to Accounting Literature (short only of the Nobel Prize, which in accounting was granted only once, namely, in 1984 for work in "national income accounting" to Richard Stone, an economist). It was the first time that this relatively rare award was conferred. In 1991, Beaver received for his empirical work the same prestigious AAA Award for Seminal Contributions to Accounting Literature; and in 1994, this award was, for the first time, granted for analytical research (see Chapter 5).

Publication of those papers also introduced the overlordship of financial economics (with such notions as efficient capital markets, market-based research, capital–asset pricing models, portfolio theory, cross-sectional valuation perspective, and so on) over accounting—a trend that continued until recently. Hence, relatively few fundamental innovations arose during the last two decades from the very core of traditional accounting. Ijiri's (1989) "momentum accounting" is such a rare example. Our field became the playground of the behavioral sciences, economics, and finance, as well as statistics and decision theory. This had the advantage of bringing accounting more in line with the general scientific trend manifested in other disciplines; but it had the disadvantage of drawing resources from traditional areas such as managerial accounting, accountability and ethics, inflation accounting, analysis of accounting objectives and their hierarchy, and the like. If it were feasible, it would be interesting to assess the opportunity costs of this shift away from accountability issues. Another difficulty arose from the failure to draw clear boundaries between such pure sciences as the sociology of accounting and the economics of accounting, on one side, and accounting proper (i.e., as an applied science), on the other side (for a definition of applied science, see Chapter 11, note 1).

Empirical accounting research has since been applied in innumerable papers to many problems. Its foremost area is earnings research (i.e., investigating the relationship between share prices and corresponding "excess earnings").[1] This is followed by other information-content studies (assessing the information inferred from such events as voluntary changes in accounting techniques, management's forecasts on the basis of the effect that such occurrences have on security prices, and so on) and the question whether or to what extent accounting regulations affect wealth distribution. All of these problems arose out of financial accounting, while the area of managerial accounting was more influenced by experimental and behavioral–organizational research (referred to in Chapter 10). The major results of the first phase of those nonexperimental empirical studies (apart from "positive accounting research," to be discussed subsequently) may be summarized by quoting Dopuch:

Taken overall, the years from 1968–74 provided evidence consistent with the following broad inferences: first, both annual and interim earnings announcements have information content, with the association between unexpected returns and unexpected earnings tending to increase with the magnitude of the latter. Second, the market seems willing to rely on managements' forecasts of earnings even though such numbers are not formally "audited." Third, other financial data reported in annual reports are not as highly associated with unexpected returns, which may reflect deficiencies in the expectations models applied to non-earnings data. Fourth, no significant associations between voluntary accounting method changes and unexpected returns could be documented except when the auditing changes related directly to changes in firms' expected future cash flows (e.g., moving from FIFO to LIFO). The later inference is important, because it raised the questions of the need for regulatory bodies, such as APB [Accounting Principles Board], to impose uniform accounting methods on firms. It also casts doubt on any benefits managements might achieve through attempts to "manage earnings" by judiciously selecting accounting methods. (Dopuch 1989, 46)

Apart from several anthologies, this first phase (and the beginning of the second one) was consolidated and summarized in the well-known book by Beaver (1981). As for the results of the second phase (i.e., after 1974), Dopuch points at several studies confirming that the FASB regulations do not affect stockholders' wealth and that the market is apparently in a position to see through any "cosmetic" changes in the presentation of financial statements.

In evaluating that type of empirical accounting research, the results may seem to be modest to the outsider and hardly in proportion to the considerable and highly sophisticated research effort invested. This is compounded by the provisional nature of most of those results. Empirical accountants themselves admit this and point at frequent contradictions of evidence and research findings and the need for further studies. Considering the statistical–empirical vacuum in our discipline before 1970 or so, the results may be seen in a very different light. Above all, grand schemes are of little use if they are not being materialized by the meticulous, step-by-step work typical for *normal* empirical research. The question is merely whether these steps do follow an overall plan and, if so, whether it is the appropriate one. Empirical research has been criticized mainly on two grounds, or as Daley formulates it:

It is legitimate to attack existing research on at least two points. First, it has often been so focused on repetitively documenting the same phenomenon (such as the fact that firm size and debt covenants always appear to be important "partial" determinants of the choice of accounting standards, early adoption of new standards, and share value consequences of new standards) that it has failed to address more substantive measurement issues. Second, it often has documented phenomena so far removed from the specific measurement issues at hand (such as most of the work on the information content of earnings conditional of firm size) that it contributes little to a rich understanding of the benefits that different measurement alternatives might provide. (Daley 1994, 44)

My own major regret is that no empirical attempts were made to relate directly specific goals to the means for attaining them and to test the efficiency of those means. However, I fully realize the difficulties of such an undertaking and also admit that plenty of indirect relations have been established, in particular, through positive accounting theory (see next section). Those attempts were made at the price of excluding value judgments from the theory proper.

POSITIVE ACCOUNTING THEORY AND ITS CONTROVERSY

Confusing Terminology

The scientific and philosophic meaning of *positive* implies a theory free of value judgments (except for "prescientific" ones, necessary for scientific research in general). In other words, a pure science cannot accept value judgments as premises but can only encapsulate them in observed facts. Means–end relations are thus automatically excluded from the theory itself, since the goal or "end" is a value-laden premise for determining the means. Attention to value judgments gives way to a concern with presumed causalities based on statistical association. This predisposes academic accountants to think in terms of positive hypotheses (cause-and-effect relations) instead of instrumental hypotheses (means–end relations), often without awareness of the logical gap and other differences between them (although presumed *truth* is important for both types of hypotheses, presumed *usefulness* is a further ingredient of instrumental hypotheses).

The expression "positive accounting theory" (PAT) has assumed several meanings. In the most comprehensive sense, it is identified with empirical accounting research in general. In Europe, the term is often identified with the leading North American accounting research, produced during the last two decades or so. It would be no less an oversimplification to identify the research efforts on this continent with PAT than to identify the efforts of the British critical–interpretive school with European accounting research in general; yet the view is not quite as absurd since both PAT and the critical–interpretive views reveal features characteristic of the pertinent continents. The philosophy behind each approach (e.g., materialism versus humanism) appears to reflect in significant ways the tradition prevalent in America or Europe, respectively. Even in America, "positive accounting theory" or similar expressions are frequently applied to a wide context of empirical accounting research. The paper by Abdel-khalik et al. (1989, 153–180), for example, includes a diverse array of empirical topics under the heading of "positive theory," such as income smoothing, lobbying for accounting standards, price-level disclosures, foreign currency transactions, costing issues for the oil and gas industry, pension issues, debt covenant restrictions, agency theory together with compensation and performance evaluation issues, and the like.

Nonetheless, to identify PAT, as presented by Watts and Zimmerman, with empirical research in accounting in general, is like asserting that every bird is a sparrow. To confuse a subset with the universal set is obviously a logical error, yet it seems to occur all too often. While empirical research is by no means inconsistent with a conditional–normative accounting methodology, PAT seems to reject categorically any kind of theory that attempts to incorporate value judgments in its premises. If accounting is an applied discipline, as I try to show in Chapter 11, then the term positive has no place in it, except when referring to the pure mother disciplines of economics and the behavioral sciences on which accounting rests. Observing the obsession with which many of the younger researchers (particularly during the 1980s) were trying to cling to the term positive, one cannot help suspecting an overcompensation for a professional inferiority complex. The adepts of more prestigious applied sciences, such as medicine and engineering, are not burdened with such a curse. They realize that theirs is a mission-oriented science and would hardly dream of addressing its theories as "positive," being well aware that the pertinent mother disciplines carry this venerable attribute.

In a less comprehensive but still relatively broad sense, the expression PAT has, since the late 1970s, referred to most of the research undertaken by Watts and Zimmerman and other members of the Rochester School, as well as their disciples. This usage may be acceptable by sheer convention; but apart from the fact that the term refers more to theory elements (see Chapter 7) than an overall theory, this interpretation fails to separate the respectable empirical accounting research of these authors from the extreme methodology they promote. This methodology does not possess a monopoly over accounting and is not necessarily suited to every kind of empirical research. Nonetheless, psychologically the slogan "positive" seems to have achieved the intended effect. After all, it conveys not only the opposite of "normative" but also that of "negative." Another *ambiguity* hanging over the Watts and Zimmerman methodology is their attitude to norms or value judgments. On one side, they and their disciples are truly concerned with policy issues that require the very prescriptions their methodology renounces. A reasonable choice would be to abandon such a methodology and with them the precious term *positive*. After all, nobody can keep his or her pie and eat it at the same time.

Last, in the narrow sense, the term refers to no theory at all but to a special methodology that forbids normative premises even to a theory of accounting, the very essence of which consists of prescriptions. It is mainly in this narrow sense that my own criticism of PAT applies. There is no denying that the major accounting trend during the last decade or two found its manifestation in PAT. Whether it was Ball and Brown's (1968) use of the expression "positive accounting" or Jensen's (1976, 13) call for a "Positive Theory of Accounting" which launched this trend, the ultimate force behind it were two well-known papers by Watts and Zimmerman (1978, 1979). Many articles followed in their wake until the book and subsequent paper by Watts and Zimmerman (1986, 1990) summarized and consolidated this particular position. Though PAT has been so well entrenched in the English-language accounting literature, one does find growing opposition to PAT (e.g., Tinker et al. 1982; Christenson 1983; Lowe et al. 1983; Mattessich 1984; Schreuder 1984; Whittington 1987; Demski 1988; Whitley 1988; Hines 1988; Mouck 1990; Sterling 1990; Boland and Gordon 1992; Ballwieser 1993; Chambers 1993), ranging from mild misgivings to vehement rejection. Watts and Zimmerman (1990) tried to respond to some of this criticism. This response, no less than their former publications, is still a point of controversy, as Watts and Zimmerman (1990, 131) themselves seem to admit quite freely. They may even have reflected on changing their brand name to "economic consequence literature," conceding that "the term 'positive' generated more confusion than we anticipated" (Watts and Zimmerman 1990, 148). To illuminate these issues from my own perspective, I will first refer to the empirical results of PAT and then list major features of its methodology, together with some comments and criticism.

Empirical Results of PAT

As for the empirical results growing out of PAT, there is foremost the first paper by Watts and Zimmerman (1978). It deals with voting and lobbying activity at the FASB concerning the issue of disclosure of price-level changes. It led to the conclusion that only firm size (as an indirect yardstick for measuring political costs) is a statistically significant variable, such that managers of larger firms would lobby for standards that have a chance of reporting smaller income figures. The explanation given for this behavior is the entrepreneur's desire to distract attention of regulating authorities that levy taxes from the firm or grant contracts to it. A later and more refined study by McKee et al. (1984, 658), along similar lines, raised doubts about some conclusions of the Watts and Zimmerman (1978) study, though Watts and Zimmerman (1986, Chaps. 11 and 12; see also 1990, 143) claim that some twenty-one other studies are consistent with their theory. On the other hand, the case method (e.g., as used by Geneen 1984; see Abdel-khalik et al. 1989, 169–172) seems to supply further instances contradicting some conclusions of PAT.

The other, less popular, empirical study of these two authors is found in Watts and Zimmerman (1979). It, too, is concerned with lobbying behavior but on a more general level. It concludes that in an economy without obligatory auditing of its corporations, the auditor's report is still desirable for the entrepreneur if there is a chance of lowering his or her agency costs. This being the case, the entrepreneur voluntarily accepts accounting and auditing clauses in his or her debt (or other) contracts. However, in an economy with obligatory auditing, the demand for accounting theories and related services is likely to rest on a very different basis. There, accounting theories are deemed to justify the self-interest of entrepreneurs and managers. Thus, "Government intervention produces a variety of theories, because each group affected by an accounting change demands a theory that supports its position. The diversity of positions prevents general agreement on a theory of accounting, and accounting theories are normative because they are used as excuses for political action (i.e., the political process creates a demand for theories which prescribe, rather than describe, the world)" (Watts and Zimmerman 1979, 273).

No one will deny that the political process needs prescriptions; that is precisely why it is political. Nor is it surprising that anyone with an axe to grind will use it as long as it serves his or her vested interest. The implication seems to be that academics have prostituted themselves in supplying those normative (i.e., unscientific) tools to vested interest groups in compensation for financial favors such as research grants, fees for consulting or expert witnesses, and the like; yet to put part of the blame—let us say, for a murder committed with a "general" instrument—upon those who designed that instrument, seems to go too far (see also Peasnell and Williams 1986).

The authors admit that their evidence "is 'casual' and not as 'rigorous'" as they would like it to have been. No wonder that many experts have taken issue with this "theory for excuses." Watts and Zimmerman also had to admit that their own theory can be abused no less than any normative theory. Even if the empirical value of this second study is limited, it has (like the first one) important methodological implications. One of these is the argument that the abuse of theories, referred to previously, could be greatly reduced if the actual goals were clearly exposed, as I have recommended all along. This can be best done through a conditional–normative theory.

In general, Watts and Zimmerman (1990, 138–139) claim that over the years PAT has succeeded in disclosing important empirical regularities and explanations, as manifested in the following hypotheses:

- *Bonus plan hypothesis*. In firms with managerial bonus plans, the manager is more likely to choose "income-increasing" accounting methods, that is, those *reporting* a "relatively higher" income figure.
- *Debt–equity hypothesis*. The higher a firm's debt–equity ratios, the more likely it is that its management will choose "income-increasing" accounting methods.
- *Political cost hypothesis*. In larger firms, the manager is more likely to choose "income-decreasing" accounting methods.

Typical variables used in those hypotheses (associated with choice of accounting methods) are managerial compensation or other incentives, leverage, firm size, risk, interest coverage, and dividend constraints. As for the "empirical regularities," it must be pointed out that they are based on statistical correlations (that are occasionally contradicted) and often without any firm establishment of the causal nexus. Again, the conclusion is that measured on the *input*, the sophisticated empirical research of PAT is impressive, but measured on the *output*, it seems to be much less so.

The major argument in favor of PAT is "the lack of an alternative model with greater explanatory power, not the low explanatory power of the extant theory" (Watts and Zimmerman 1990, 140). This does not mitigate the fact that PAT has, so far, covered only a very narrow segment of accounting. It can hardly be regarded as the core of accounting as some experts seem to make us believe. These limitations should incite academics to extend this theory toward inclusion of normative premises.

The Methodology of PAT

This subsection outlines concisely what I take to be the main methodological features of PAT. In doing so, I may run the risk of possibly misinterpreting Watts and Zimmerman (1978, 1979, 1986, 1990), since they do not systematically spell out all their methodological assumptions and often shift their philosophical stance, as shown by Boland and Gordon (1992). After having stated each feature, I will add my own comments or criticism:

1. Accounting theory should not be concerned with prescription but only with explanation and prediction because prescriptive (i.e., normative) theories are unscientific.

Comment: Whether the last phrase also refers to theories based on a conditional–normative accounting methodology is difficult to surmise.[2] Such a methodology has not even been considered as an alternative by those authors. This is surprising, as they obviously deal with motives and value judgements and expressively state that the "usefulness of positive theories depends on their predictive and explanatory power and on *the user's preference or objective function. . . .* A positive theory can have normative implications once the objective function is specified" (Watts and Zimmerman 1990, 147, 148, italics added). Why then should a discipline like accounting not incorporate in its premises those objective functions? All other applied sciences seem to do it. Are some academics so desperate in their desire to make a pure or positive science out of accounting that they would disregard the basic goals and principles of their discipline?

Promoting the exclusion of norms and prescriptions from accounting theory means abrogating the foremost goal of any applied science, namely, supplying different ready-made models for different specific situations and purposes. Even the pure sciences recognize theoretical frameworks for their applied counterparts (e.g., engineering for physics, medicine and genetic engineering for biology, chemical engineering for chemistry). Most typical, positive economists admit normative economics (economic policy and welfare economics) as a legitimate academic discipline. Why should one not also tolerate a normative theory in accounting?

2. Chicago-based neoclassical economics as the major foundation for accounting.

Comment: The authors admit that their "economics-based research methodology may be fundamentally flawed in ways we do not now understand. But, accounting research using this methodology has produced useful predictions of how the world works (e.g., association between earnings and stock prices, random walk model of earnings, contracting and size variables associated with accounting choice)" (Watts and Zimmerman 1990, 147). I believe that accountants and even economists have a fair idea of the limitations of neoclassical economics. As for predictions, both groups have much reason to be humble. The close connection between the conservative economics of the Chicago School and PAT of the Rochester School—as well as the shortcomings of both—have been emphasized by Whittington (1987), who also hints at the illusion that PAT might be objective and free of norms. Above all, he stresses the "extreme methodological stance" of Watts and Zimmerman (1986) and says that the same "lack of respect for alternative views was, ironically, one of the faults of the 'normative' theorists of the 1960's" (Whittington 1987, 329).[3] This critic also casts a glance at the "efficient market hypothesis" so crucial for PAT and makes the following interesting remark:

If, as Beaver (1981) correctly points out, market efficiency is defined with respect to a specific information set, then if we are concerned with fundamental characteristics, it is possible to improve the market's valuation process by widening the information set. By making possible better forecasts of the long-run returns of individual firms, such information might improve the decisions of investors who were interested in the long-run income rather than short-term capital gains, and lead to a better allocation of resources... both between individual firms and between the equity of firms and other forms of investment. This type of argument is the justification for the theoretical work of such writers as Chambers (1966) and Edwards and Bell (1961), who are summarily dismissed by Watts and Zimmerman. (Whittington 1987, 332)

Another disadvantage of the "economics-based accounting" is the overriding influence of a single objective, namely, wealth maximization. In the real world, there exist many other objectives; but they are suppressed under this restricting assumption. A related issue is the neglect of environmental and social issues. In the face of such neglect, the economists' wealth maximization becomes short-term instead of long-term maximization; and the disastrous consequence of this can be seen everywhere in the economic life on this continent.[4] Obviously, such questions open a hornets' nest for further inquiries. Alone, the clarification of the notions of long-run versus short-run wealth maximization could fill volumes. For a long time, economists swept such problems under the rug, reminiscent of Keynes's slogan that "in the long-run we are all dead." No longer can we afford to be so smug.

The fact that the United States and Canada are the two leading countries in corporate fraud (as evidenced in a recent survey of six countries by the public accounting firm Peat Marwick Thorne, Inc. 1993)—not to speak of the fraud, waste, and incompetence in the governments of those countries—should be reason enough to shift again to the more basic issues of ethics and accountability. Whatever the opportunity costs arising out of the past neglect of those crucial problems are, one can hardly deny the immense economic and social damage incurred by all this detected as well as undetected fraudulent activity.

3. Overemphasis of predictions as the fundamental goal of accounting theory.

Comment: The repeated emphasis of prediction seems to be exaggerated in the fact that most economists nowadays concede that their discipline can supply, at best, only preliminary explanations but very little reliable prediction. Economics must be highly praised for its elegant models and basic insights; but when it comes to realistic issues as, for example, the very serious ones confronting present-day accounting, economics usually proves wanting. This does not mean we should abandon this subject altogether, but accountants must be clear about their priorities. Above all, they should realize that neither the simple-minded nor the muddle-headed approach alone will do; both must be used.

Even in modern physics, the traditional notions of explanation and prediction had to be constrained in the face of such new discoveries as the empirically confirmed theory of chaos and the closely associated fractal geometry.[5] The phenomena underlying the latter play a particularly important role in the biological as well as social sciences. This makes, in spite of all significance tests, the correlational notions of explanation and prediction particularly suspect in areas like accounting.

4. To regard methodological disputes as fruitless.

Comment: If methodological disputes are in vain, how do those authors defend their own methodology? One way of answering this question is found in the passage quoted under item 2; the two authors brush off the question with a nondescript reference to the "usefulness argument" of economics. In reading their various publications one has the impression they firmly believe that theirs is the only proper methodology for accounting, and thus there is no need to further probing. This may be gathered from the following quote: "To most researchers, debating methodology is a 'no win' situation because each side argues from a

different paradigm with different rules and no common ground. . . . The methodology we and the subsequent literature use is the methodology of economics, finance, and science generally" (Watts and Zimmerman 1990, 149, 150). As for the
beginning of this passage, let me remind you that from the time of Descartes's
(1637) *Discourse on Methods* to this very day, methodological questions have
played a crucial role in science. Often enough, they have created a bridge between
different points of view (e.g., the combination of arithmetic and geometry in
Descartes's system of coordinates). As far as the end of the previous quote is concerned, Watts and Zimmerman may be correct, but only if one excludes the applied sciences from "science." Who would dare to do that when such prestigious
disciplines as medicine and engineering belong to the former?

5. Predominant reliance on statistical procedures to test hypotheses.

Comment: Despite its increasing significance, the testing of statistical hypotheses is only part of the arsenal of empirical science to come to grips with the truth,
acceptability, or usefulness, be they hypotheses of the pure or applied sciences
(compare Bunge 1983b, 59–154). Particularly in an applied discipline, where
conjectured means–end relations are commonplace, a broader basis for testing
hypotheses becomes inevitable.

Above all, the empirical regularities referred to by Watts and Zimmerman
(1990) resemble the ones familiar from such applied sciences as medicine where,
for example, a decade ago or so, a sequence of statistical studies led to the urgent
recommendation of using margarine (instead of butter) in our diet, while new
studies recommend even more urgently to abstain from margarine.[6] I do not want
to belittle this kind of statistical research and its results; it still may be the best we
have. But one must never forget the fragility of those results, for rarely is there an
assurance that all the critical variables have been taken into consideration.

6. Exclusion of value judgments from the premises of PAT and disregard for
means–end relations.

Comment: This issue has already been discussed in connection with item 1, but
some further remarks are appropriate. Watts and Zimmerman state, "While individuals want a theory which prescribes procedures conducive to their own interest, they do *not* want a normative theory which has their self-interest as its stated
objective" (Watts and Zimmerman 1979, 275). I much agree with this view; I even
think it is valid to "self-interest" in the broadest sense, but I draw very different
conclusions from it than do the two authors.

First, if a person wants to conceal the true goal behind the means he has
adopted, at least he himself should have a clear vision of the pertinent ends–means
relation. More important, it seems that, at least to some extent, the "accounting
crisis" is rooted in frequent attempts to conceal the true objectives pursued. If a
conditional–normative methodology of accounting can prevent such hypocrisy
and concealment, this in itself would be a strong argument to defend such an approach.

7. The attempt to make a positive science out of accounting.

Comment: The criticism that PAT is not a theory of accounting but one of "accounting sociology" has been raised repeatedly (e.g., by Christenson 1983; Whittington 1987; Sterling 1990; Ballwieser 1993). This means, on one side, that Watts and Zimmerman and their disciples are blurring the line between the pure sciences—on which accounting is ultimately based—and academic accounting proper; on the other side, they try to substitute the sociology and economics of accounting for accounting as an applied science. Since Watts and Zimmerman (1990, 147) emphasize that people matter in accounting, one may point out that this is the very reason why most, or even all, of the pure sciences dealing with human beings are accompanied by corresponding normative academic subjects with their own theories.

Further Criticism of PAT in the Accounting Literature

My aforementioned objections may be partly supplementary to and partly overlapping with previously raised criticism. At any rate, there are many ways to criticize PAT; and there are several possibilities to categorize such criticism. Boland and Gordon (1992), for example, distinguish three types of criticism launched against PAT and their authors:

1. *Technical limitations* about their research, raised by such authors as Lev and Ohlson (1982), Ball and Foster (1982), Holthausen and Leftwich (1983), McKee et al. (1984), and Christie (1987, 1990)

2. *Objections against their philosophy of science attitude*, raised partly by Tinker, Merino, and Neimark (1982); Christenson (1983); Mattessich (1984, 21–22, 77–78; 1991c, 14); Schreuder (1984); partly by Whittington (1987) and Whitley (1988); partly by Sterling (1990) and Mouck (1990); and to some extent by Boland and Gordon (1992) themselves

3. *Objections against the assumptions of their neoclassical economic basis*, raised by Demski (1988) and partly by Tinker, Merino, and Neimark (1982); Whittington (1987); and Sterling (1990)

As far as the objection to the particular methodology of PAT is concerned, Boland and Gordon make it quite clear that "the methodological question here is whether it is easier to build models that assume personal utility maximization than to build models in which the individuals have a concern for the social consequences of their actions" (Boland and Gordon 1992, 163). These authors also point out that

methodologists can perform an important and marketable service of revealing and explaining the limitations of the ideological and methodological preferences embodied in any research. If, for example, one wishes to follow the lead of Watts and Zimmerman and assume that the markets are sufficiently in equilibrium so that one has equilibrium prices available for the calculation of one's cost and benefits of adopting any particular accounting procedure, one would be wise to recognize the limitations of such an approach *if being wrong matters*. For consumers shopping in the methodology market, it certainly can be useful to know exactly what they are buying. (Boland and Gordon 1992, 166)

These authors put particular emphasis on Whitley's (1988) doubt about the application of natural science methodology to the social sciences (which could be extended to the applied sciences). Then there are such arguments as Demski's (1988) that Watts and Zimmerman's assumption of perfect markets may not generally hold.

After this critical look at PAT, it must be repeated that my own criticism is primarily directed against Watts and Zimmerman's methodological stance rather than their empirical research. PAT and the whole empirical movement (from the late 1960s onward) was probably an inevitable reaction of a younger generation of academic accountants to the views, questions, and approaches of an older generation, not so well trained in modern financial economics, sophisticated statistical hypotheses testing, and other technical fields. Meanwhile, this "younger" generation has become older; and one begins to discern a more reconciliatory and tolerant attitude, perhaps even a realization, that we all stand but on the shoulders of our academic forebears. Thus, there are signs that this phase of excessive confrontation between generations is coming to an end and, even more important, that the pendulum of academic fashion (that moved away from the *a priori* research of pragmatic–normative accounting in the late 1960s and early 1970s) is reversing its direction. But if this is the case, one should not expect the pendulum to move back into the groove of three decades ago.

NOTES

This chapter is not based on any previous publication of mine. It constitutes the "empirical link" between the more historical and analytical aspects of preceding chapters and the more methodological considerations to follow. It reflects my view of present-day empirical accounting research and its methodological underpinning. In this overview I have drawn on several surveys, including my own (Mattessich 1984, 1991a), and Ball and Smith (1992), and the conference proceedings by Frecka (1989b). I would like to express my gratitude to Prof. Moustafa F. Abdel-Magid for bringing the last of these publications to my attention.

1. *Excess earnings* (or "abnormal earnings") is defined in the empirical literature as the anticipated earnings, as simplified by some expectations model or forecast. In the analytical literature (e.g., Feltham and Ohlson 1993, 1994), this term (in both versions) refers to a firm's earnings beyond the interest that could be attained by investment in riskless bonds. To avoid terminological confusion, the analytical notion might better be addressed as *residual earnings*.

2. "We would prefer to reserve the term 'theory' for principles advanced to explain a set of phenomena, in particular for sets of hypotheses which have been confirmed. However, such a definition would exclude much of the prescriptive literature and generate a semantic debate" (Watts and Zimmerman 1979, 273, footnote 1). From this quote, one might possibly infer that Watts and Zimmerman would exclude CoNAM from their criticism of normative accounting.

3. I wholeheartedly agree with Whittington (1987). During the 1960s, those promoting current exit values derided those pleading for current entry values, while the latter, in turn, attacked those defending historical cost values, and so on. Out of disillusion with such quarrels, I began to plead for a more tolerant approach according to which each valuation concept (or each notion of income, or of wealth, or the like) may be justified, depending on the objective to be pursued (see, for example, Mattessich 1964a, 215–231; 1972, 471–472, 478–479, 484–487).

4. The annals of economic events of the last decade are filled with cases of short-run and short-sighted wealth maximizers—from Campeau's department stores conglomerate and Keating's Lincoln Savings and Loan Association to Maxwell's industrial empire or the Reichmann brothers' Olympia and York Developments. Compare the maximizing policies of these enterprises to the investment strategies of major Japanese corporations that are often willing to forego higher momentary profits for the sake of wealth creation in the long run.

5. See Gleick (1987) and, above all, Edward Lorenz (1993) who, working at first with weather-simulation models, is considered to be the founder of the *empirical* science of chaos—one of the most exciting recent discoveries. Its famous "butterfly effect" demonstrates that even a minute change in initial conditions will, in time, make a system *unpredictable*. The new geometry of fractals (see Mandelbrot 1983), suitable to such dynamic situations, can at least predict the boundaries of this unpredictability.

6. There exists, of course, statistical research in medicine, which after decades of innumerable studies, could establish something like causal links. The best known of this kind of research is the one establishing the connection between smoking and lung cancer. Not until experimental research on mice was combined with statistical research on humans could a causal link between nicotine and cancer be confirmed. The tobacco industry still tries to submit counterevidence to the courts.

CHAPTER 10

Normative Accounting and the Critical–Interpretive School

After more than a decade of preoccupation with "positive accounting theory"—during which time the use of the notion of normative accounting has been slighted by the inner sanctum of leading American accounting researchers—the mood, in favor of a more realistic assessment, seems to be slowly changing. In the face of the growing gap between practitioners and academics, the time may be ripe for a historical examination as well as a revival of interest in normative accounting (see also Mattessich In press).

EARLY GERMAN ETHICAL–NORMATIVE THEORIES

The literature dealing systematically with normative accounting theory begins in the first decade of our century with two German scholars, Johann Friedrich Schär (1846–1924) and Heinrich Nicklisch (1876–1946).[1] This early approach was, in an important aspect, quite different from the normative theories of the post–World War II period, flourishing in the Anglo-American accounting literature from the late 1950s to the early 1970s. The theory of Schär (e.g., 1890, 1914) and, even more so, that of Nicklisch (e.g., 1912, 1915–1916, 1923, 1929–1932) had a definite ethical slant, according to which businessmen ought to optimize efficiency and performance for the general benefit of society rather than maximize profit for the primary benefit of individual firms or persons.

The rise of this early ethical–normative accounting or business theory[2] seems to have been intimately connected with the dispute of value neutrality or

Werturteilsstreit (during the first decade of the twentieth century), between two opposing factions of German economists.[3] This is confirmed by the following quote from Schneider:

In the aftermath of the value-neutrality dispute, an ethical–normative economist accuses other economists (who plead explicitly for value-free research) that they were about to proclaim an economics promoting the special interests of entrepreneurs. Though not directly addressed (but not yet sufficiently secure as university teachers), some professors of commercial science take this opportunity, instead of opting for a value-free science, to pledge themselves, for this very reason, to an ethical–normative point of view. (Schneider 1981, 137, translated)

The economist Karl Bücher seems to have gone even farther, implicating the emerging discipline of business studies (*Privatwirtschaftslehre*) directly for being primarily profit oriented. Lujo Brentano even attacked Schär, who had emphasized that he also defends an approach to business in which not profit making, but the minimization of production costs to the ultimate benefit of consumers is the actual goal (see Schär 1911, 73). After 1915, Nicklisch became the leader in the defense of ethical–normative business studies and asserted that "also the representatives of business studies see in their work, first of all, the human being. . . . He is the link to the whole. His activity or inactivity must be dominated by the relation of the individual to the totality" (Nicklisch 1915–1916 102, 104, translated).

What used to be less well known is the fact that, for a limited time after World War I (probably from 1919 to 1930 or later), the renowned Eugen Schmalenbach (1873–1955) also adopted an ethical–normative stance for accounting and business administration (*Betriebswirtschaftslehre*, more accurately translated as "business economics") in general. Traditionally, Schmalenbach is regarded as an empiricist (although modern representatives of PAT might dispute this). But Schneider points out that

the socio-economic, ethical–normative reference of Schmalenbach is first encountered in the original edition of his *Dynamic Accounting [Dynamische Bilanz]* and his *Cost Accounting [Selbstkostenrechnung]*.[4] . . . *This confirms that Schmalenbach wants to develop an accounting theory containing a purpose which definitely is not the purpose of [either] financial or tax accounting*. Particularly, Schmalenbach's most lasting scientific work is not at all empirical–realistic and practical–normative. (Schneider 1981, 140–141, translated)

This author also mentions that

the ethical–normative science goal of Nicklisch (as already manifested by Schär) remains essentially a good intention or merely wishful thinking. As soon as he goes into details, for example in his discussions of cost accounting or wage policy of the firm, in the later editions of his *Wirtschaftliche Betriebslehre* (footnote omitted), he hardly reaches farther than some literature of the 19th century, e.g., Emminghaus (1868). The reason for this failure is obvious: What distinguishes an ethical–normative microeconomic theory from social hogwash are the foundational steps (conceptual explication, reflections on measurement) that infer, from the basic ethical–normative value judgment, the goal of the individual case and the consequent actions. Such an analysis is lacking in Nicklisch. Schmalenbach, at least hints at it in his theory of the "proportionalen Satz." (Schneider 1981, 140, translated)

Schneider regards even Schmalenbach's ethical–normative scientific endeavor to be a failure:

He [Schmalenbach] asserted himself in the original editions of his major works and failed in both cases on the inner contradictions of his theory, which to a large extent was due to Schmalenbach's disinterest in thorough conceptualization, and also due to the deviation of his action recommendations—based on insufficiently precise socio-economic elaborations—from the actions and desires of actual practice. Thereby he is unwilling to maintain the ethical–normative reference in the face of business opposition. Later even he expresses himself not more concretely than merely referring to the trivial maxim "avoid waste." (Schneider 1981, 142, translated)

The ethical aspect of the normative paradigm fell into oblivion after World War II, and a major German reference work emphasizes that

his [Nicklisch's] universalistic system results in the teaching of the "community of the enterprise" [Betriebsgemeinschaft] through which the opposition between work and capital should be eliminated (defender of workers' profit sharing!). Though his theory and demands are becoming nowadays again increasingly acute, Nicklisch has not yet found a successor to continue his work. (Sellien and Sellien 1956, 2: 2073, translated)

PRAGMATIC–NORMATIVE THEORIES

In contrast to the aforementioned ethical–normative trend, the normative accounting theories, as developed from the 1950s to early 1970s (in many countries), may be regarded as pragmatic–normative. The distinction between ethical–normative theories versus pragmatic–ethical theories is by no means novel. As we have seen, Schneider pointed out that "Schmalenbach worked [even] before 1919 in a 'practical–normative' [i.e., pragmatic–normative instead of an ethical–normative] way" (Schneider 1981: 142, translated). Obviously, there exist different kinds of norms (prescientific, ethical, social, methodological, technical, legal, administrative, and so on) that can be incorporated into a theory or other system.[5] With regard to normative (i.e., pragmatic–normative) theories, Hendriksen (1982, 56–86) mentions mainly the following authors in his chapter on "The Normative Deductive Approach—Concepts, Measurements, and Structure": Paton (1922), Moonitz (1961), Sprouse and Moonitz (1962), Mattessich (1964a), Goldberg (1965), Chambers (1966), Ijiri (1967), and Sterling (1970b).[6] For Hendriksen, as for many other accountants, the term "normative" seems to be almost synonymous with "deductive" (something to which I object). Even the milder statement by Wolk et al. may lead to misunderstandings: "Although there are exceptions, deductive systems are usually normative, and inductive approaches usually attempt to be descriptive" (Wolk et al. 1992, 33). First, empirical theories require deductive as well as inductive inferences. Second, conditional–normative theories cannot exist without (at least implied) empirical means–end relations (gained through inductive reasoning). Third, the statement under quote would imply that mathematics and logic (which both deal exclusively with deductive inferences) are normative disciplines. This would violate the agreement that pre-scientific value judgments do not make a discipline normative. As for Hendriksen, he does not make any distinction between different categories of the normative paradigm. Such a representation blurs the picture, not only because it neglects the distinction between ethical–normative and pragmatic–normative but because it altogether neglects a third and, to my mind, most important category: the conditional–normative approach.[7]

Although it is easy to blame academic accountants for not *seeing the need* for the crucial place that means–end relations occupy, it is much more difficult to blame either normative or positive accounting theorists for not formalizing the instrumental hypotheses themselves. In the applied sciences in general, means–end relations are usually treated informally and are too often taken for granted. The reason for this is one of the least-understood points in the entire controversy be-tween normative and positive accountants. The explanation may lie, at least in part, in the peculiar logic and methodology (underlying an explicit formulation of instrumental hypotheses) that is still insufficiently explored. A more important reason seems to be the fact that instrumental hypotheses are difficult to press into the mold of positive hypotheses. The former do not obey the same logic and may even require different (i.e., supplementary) testing procedures.

THE BEHAVIORAL–ORGANIZATIONAL DIRECTION

Just as finance arose from accounting (and partly from economics) more than thirty years ago and came to dominate a good deal of accounting, so during the last few decades, a similar trend is noticeable in the relationship between the area of Management Information Systems vis-à-vis Accounting.[8] Accounting, not un-like philosophy, seems to have been a mother hen breeding new areas, some of which have already matured enough to become independent subjects. In our age of increasing specialization, such "cell divisions" and bifurcations are as natural and inevitable as is any growth process; yet such newly created and separate sub-jects have repercussions upon the mother discipline (see McCarthy 1987). For instance, some accountants who became MIS experts behaved as if they were leaving a sinking ship; others asserted that the time was not far off when account-ing would be torn apart, with the spoils to be divided between the economics of finance, on one hand, and MIS, on the other. However, our concern in this sec-tion is not with that part which belongs to MIS but, rather, with the residual that runs under the flag of behavioral–organizational accounting.

Following Chua (1986), the organizational–behavioral direction may be con-ceived as consisting of the following three subdivisions:

1. Behavioral accounting (mainstream behavioral research, [see Table 10.1]), also called "experimental research" (compare Libby 1989, 126)
2. Organizational accounting (interpretive perspective, [see Table 10.2])
3. Critical radicalism (critical perspective or Marxism, [see Table 10.3])

The first subdivision follows traditional scientific methodology, and is no less frequently encountered in America as in other countries; the other two subdivisions (here referred to as the "critical–interpretive school," or "interpretative" [see Chua 1986, 615]) are more typical endeavors of the British critical–interpretive school, and rest on different philosophical foundations. Although the two latter directions have spread from England to Australia, Canada, and other places—even to the United States—nowhere is their influence stronger than in the United Kingdom. Of course, normative considerations have been a long-standing concern of European accounting academics, as indicated in the first few pages of this chapter.

Behavioral Research

The emergence of behavioral accounting is one of the main features of the adolescent phase of our discipline. Already Argyris (1952), a psychologist, undertook

Table 10.1
Dominant Assumptions of Mainstream Accounting

A. Beliefs About Knowledge

Theory is separate from observations that may be used to verify or falsify a theory. Hypothetico-deductive account of scientific explanation accepted.

Quantitative methods of data analysis and collection which allow generalization favored.

B. Beliefs About Physical and Social Reality

Empirical reality is objective and external to the subject.   Human beings are also characterized as passive objects; not seen as makers of social reality.

Single goal of utility-maximization assumed for individuals and firms. Means-end rationality assumed.

Societies and organizations are essentially stable; "dysfunctional" conflict may be managed through the design of appropriate accounting control.

C. Relationship Between Theory and Practice

Accounting specifies means, not ends. Acceptance of extant institutional structures.

Reproduced from Chua (1986), Table 2, page 611, with the permission of the editor of *The Accounting Review*.

Table 10.2
Dominant Assumptions of the Interpretative Perspective

A. Beliefs About Knowledge

Scientific explanations of human intention sought. Their adequacy is assessed via the criteria of logical consistency, subjective interpretation, and agreement with actors' common-sense interpretation.

Ethnographic work, case studies, and participant observation encouraged. Actors studied in their everyday world.

B. Beliefs About Physical and Social Reality

Social reality is emergent, subjectively created, and objectified through human interaction.

All actions have meaning and intention that are retrospectively endowed and that are grounded in social and historical practices.

Social order assumed. Conflict mediated through common schemes of social meanings.

C. Relationship Between Theory and Practice

Theory seeks only to explain action and to understand how social order is produced and reproduced.

Reproduced from Chua (1986), Table 3, page 615, with the permission of the editor of
The Accounting Review.

highly original behavioral studies in budgeting; but it probably was Stedry's (1960) award-winning dissertation which gave the signal to the new trend of looking at accounting from a behavioral point of view. From this time onward, many publications appeared on the behavioral aspects of our discipline (for references, see, for example, Caplan et al. 1971; Gibbins and Hughes 1982; Richardson and Gibbins 1988). There is little doubt that this subarea should inquire into the sociological, psychological, perhaps even economic foundations of accounting, and into the related behavioral traits of the users of accounting information. Less unanimity exists whether it also should inquire into the behavior of the producers of accounting statements and systems or even into the behavior of accounting theorists. A further issue of behavioral accounting arises from its interdisciplinary character and concerns the problem of reduction: "The ideal would be to express the foundations of accounting measurement in terms of economics and administrative behavior, to express the foundations of the latter in terms of psychology and sociology, the foundations of these again in terms of biology, then in terms of chemistry, and finally in terms of physics" (American Accounting Association 1971d, 48).

Table 10.3
Dominant Assumptions of the Critical Perspective

A. Beliefs About Knowledge

Criteria for judging theories are temporal and context-bound. Historical, ethnographic research and case studies more commonly used.

B. Beliefs About Physical and Social Reality

Human beings have inner potentialities which are alienated (prevented from full emergence) through restrictive mechanisms. Objects can only be understood through a study of their historical development and change within the totality of relations.

Empirical reality is characterized by objective, real relations which are transformed and reproduced through subjective interpretation.

Human intention, rationality, and agency are accepted, but this is critically analyzed given a belief in false consciousness and ideology.

Fundamental conflict is endemic to society. Conflict arises because of injustice and ideology in the social, economic, and political domains which obscure the creative dimension in people.

C. Relationship Between Theory and Practice

Theory has a critical imperative: the identification and removal of domination and ideological practices.

Reproduced from Chua (1986), Table 4, Page 622, with the permission of the editor of
The Accounting Review.

The major thrust of this area is toward improving decision-making procedures in accounting and particularly in auditing (see Libby 1989). Two of the necessary conditions to achieve this are (1) evaluating current decision making, and (2) understanding its underlying determinants. While in the 1970s and early 1980s this research relied to a considerable extent on Brunswik's *lens model* and on probability judgments, new impetus came in the mid-1980s by a change of direction, namely, exploring the differences between the ill-structured decision making in accounting versus the decision making as explored in psychology.

A related sub-area is the "disclosure issue," where, in spite of a great diversity of the research perspectives, some central issues (e.g., searching for the determinants of accounting policy choice) seem to be crystallizing. In the "analysis area," the search for the appropriate decision models and the overcoming or control of bounded rationality are considered to be promising; and in the "area of use," Richardson and Gibbins (1988) emphasize the shift from the decision making to the stewardship task of accounting. Furthermore, the general trend in these areas seems to be away from grand theories toward theories of the mid-range.

The chief criticism is not so much launched against behavioral accounting as such, but against faulty or superficial applications. In spite of interesting contributions, representative authors of this subarea (e.g., Dyckman et al. 1978; Gibbins and Hughes 1982; Richardson and Gibbins 1988) are well aware of, and freely admit, the difficulties encountered in this kind of endeavor. Behavioral scientists from areas beyond accounting have also repeatedly complained about methodological deficiency as well as the lack of sufficient generality of the behavioral research carried out by accountants. Furthermore, the question of where to draw the boundaries of behavioral accounting has been left unanswered. They emphasize, for example, the paucity of results of much of this research, lack of critical mass and the fragmentary nature of much of this research activity, and inadequate exploration of the underlying (or presumed) theories. Although there exist examples of close cooperation between behavioral–empirical and analytical research, such cooperation is still too rare and requires further promotion.[9] For a more detailed study of this area, the award-winning book by Libby (1981) and that by Ashton (1984) are recommended (see also the pertinent surveys in Mattessich 1984, 1991a). For the sake of comparison, Chua (1986) summarizes the major assumptions of this mainstream (behavioral) accounting (see Table 10.1).

The British Critical–Interpretive School

Scotland and England are the countries where the science of economics was born, and the United Kingdom has a particularly outstanding tradition in this field. Strangely enough, in academic accounting (and business administration in general) this country seemed to have initially lagged behind those of Continental Europe as well as the United States.[10] What are the reasons for such a delay? Is it because of the deeply ingrained commercial instinct of the British people for whom all business matter comes so naturally that an academic investigation of this subject was difficult to accept? Or was it because of the old humanistic and "scientific" tradition of the two dominating universities of Oxford and Cambridge, which resisted the teaching of such a "vulgar" subject as business administration for considerable time?[11] Or is it a combination of several such reasons?

I have pointed out that accountancy, as an academic subject, was already vigorously pursued in many European countries as well as in America during the first decade of this century. After World War I, many accounting articles and books appeared in America and on the European continent. Scholars such as Sprague, Hatfield, Paton, Canning, D. R. Scott, Littleton, Sweeney, Gillman, MacNeal, G. O. May, and many others made their reputation in the United States, while Schär, Nicklisch, Schmalenbach, Schmidt, Mahlberg, Rieger, Le Coutre, Sommerfeld, Walb, and a host of epigones gained renown in Germany. In other continental countries, academics such as Limperg in Holland; Besta, Rossi, Zappa, and others in Italy; Quesnot, Léautey and Guilbaut in the French-language area; and Gomberg and Tödury in Switzerland also contributed substantially to this childhood phase of our discipline.

Some accounting research activity can, of course, be found in Great Britain *before* World War II (e.g., Edwards 1937, 1938; Baxter 1938). Pertinent articles are contained in such anthologies as Solomons (1952) and Baxter and Davidson (1962), but the high tide of British academic accountancy came after World War II. A particular role in this trend is played by the British critical–interpretive school.[12] This movement became a driving force in emphasizing ethical and other normative aspects; it developed during the 1970s under the leadership of Anthony Hopwood and the journal of *Accounting, Organizations and Society*, which he founded.[13] The title of this journal reveals an emphasis of the organizational–behavioral direction as well as a social concern. Some experts might hesitate to regard this trend as leading to a "theory." Indeed, to a considerable extent, it is concerned with a critique of traditional and current accounting and its way of constructing theories. Nevertheless, it is the closest to a successor of normative accounting theory as developed in pre–World War II Germany, in spite of the fact that references to either Nicklisch or Schär (or their theories) are hardly ever made in the vast literature that has come forth from this particular quarter. The critical–interpretive school may itself be divided into two related directions (one could say a more moderate and a more radical one). The first has been called by Chua (1986) the interpretive perspective (also organizational accounting); the second, the critical–radical perspective (or Marxian accounting).[14]

Organizational Accounting (Interpretive Perspective)

Representative works from the *interpretive perspective* are Burchell, Clubb, and Hopwood (1985); Hopwood (1987, 1988); Cooper (1983); Cooper, Scapens, and Arnold (1983); Hopper and Powell (1985); Roberts and Scapens (1985); and others, often following the sociological work of Burrell and Morgan (1979), Giddens (1976, 1979, 1981), and Morgan (1983a, 1983b) and the social philosophies of Schutz (1962–1966, 1967), Foucault (1972, 1979, 1980), Derrida (1981), Culler (1985), Felperin (1985), and others. The philosophic outlook of this literature is opposite to that of the positive camp. The former rejects the notion that accounting represents reality and emphasizes that it rather creates reality and has a strong "ritualistic significance."[15] According to this view, accounting cannot be neutral and must be held responsible for the social consequences it helps to engender. This branch is more often oriented toward managerial accounting than the behavioral research mentioned previously. It relies on a different set of assumptions, shown in Table 10.2 (Chua 1986).

The entire area of organizational accounting has come to prominence only during the last two decades or so, and its publications are occasionally shrouded in the veil of sociology as practiced in Europe. Some of the pertinent papers are critical and emphasize the "ritualistic significance" of accounting. Some recent books that might be counted to this area are Ashton (1982), the anthology by Cooper et al. (1983), and MacIntosh (1985). Other articles worth mentioning, and dealing with organizational control and normative models, are Flamholtz et al. (1985) and Waller and Jiambalvo (1984), respectively.

A special version of interpretive organizational accounting has been promulgated and applied to accounting by Roberts and Scapens (1985). This "structural dualism," as one might call it, follows the social theories of Giddens (1976, 1979, 1981), putting special emphasis on the relationship between subject and object, and stressing interdependence between system and its structure. Other important papers in this area are Hopwood (1987), which investigates accounting systems changes (with some references to the last 150 years or so) and their preconditions digging through the sediments of organizational and accounting history (even recent ones) in order to trace the footsteps that lead to the present; and Swieringa and Weick (1987), which is geared toward the dynamic and motivational aspects of management accounting and thus touches both the organizational as well as behavioral aspects. The latter paper also shows that such notions and procedures as "return on investment," "cost–volume profit analysis," and "variance analysis" may induce short-term vision among management. The paper by Kren and Liao (1988) offers a survey of the pertinent literature with some ties to agency theory. Much more vociferous is a small group of accountants that follow the Marxist tradition, discussed in the next subsection.

The Critical–Radical Perspective

Representative papers of this trend are by Tinker et al. (1982); Tinker (1984); Lehman and Tinker (1985); Chua (1986); and possibly Lowe et al. (1983), Cooper et al. (1985), and Hopper et al.(1987). Their philosophic basis is to be found primarily in Habermas (e.g., 1971, 1974, 1978), Marcuse (e.g., 1941, 1968), and other Marxist writers. Some of these authors also seem to be enamored with modern French philosophy, even with deconstructionalism, which seems to reject the notion of truth, substituting for it that of ideology.[16] The dominant epistemic and ontological premises of this camp are concisely stated in Table 10.3. This group emphasizes that accounting is not a neutral instrument but is actively involved in the social conflict and control between classes. They plead for accounting research as a social critique and stress the inseparability of social, economic, and political interest. Chua (1986, 626), however, admits that in such research it is still debatable what constitutes an acceptable theory or explanation.

In the face of the difficulties in which business and public accounting presently find themselves, and aggravated by the relentless environmental onslaught, it is hardly surprising that critical voices find a growing echo. To what extent moderate-objective and radical-subjective views will influence accounting research during the next decades may well depend on the political and economic climate a social and ecological crisis might bring about.[17]

THE SYNTHESIS: ANOTHER OPTION

If we regard PAT and the critical–interpretive approach as two extremes that manifest themselves in present-day accounting, the question arises whether one could conceive of some middle ground on which a genuine synthesis might flourish—a basis that combines desirable features of both approaches but minimizes their shortcomings. If academic accounting is an applied science (and Chapter 11 offers supporting evidence that it is), then the inclusion of norms and means–end relations in its theories seems to be inevitable. On the other hand, this discipline is hardly feasible without empirical research and procedures for testing its hypotheses. A conditional–normative approach seems to constitute a synthesis that satisfies those requirements.

The hallmark of any conditional–normative theory is the inclusion of the objective as well as the instrumental hypotheses within its theoretical frame. This makes the pertinent theory "conditional" insofar as the norms, to be incorporated and clearly revealed, constitute the conditions under which such a theory is valid. Academic accounting—like engineering, medicine, law, and so on—is obliged to provide a range of tools for practitioners to choose from, depending on preconceived and actual needs. The user rarely possesses the inferential means of connecting his or her own goal with the scientific propositions that enable him or her to attain his or her objective in an optimal or satisfactory way. One may say that actual practice expects the researchers at professional schools to offer different sets of ready-made tools for different purposes. This is justified because it would be most inefficient to force practitioners to forge for themselves those tools from the material supplied by positive accounting theory. If this holds for medicine, engineering, and other applied sciences, it holds no less for accounting.

Thus, a theoretical framework offering the choice of different instrumental hypotheses dependent on the specific information purpose or goal pursued seems to be, in the long-run, indispensable in our discipline.[18] Academic accountants may still have difficulty in grasping the need for a conditional–normative approach as long as they want to be "social scientists" instead of "social engineers" (see quote of Milburn 1994, in Chapter 11). The present gap between practice and academia is bound to grow as an increasing number of academics are being absorbed in either the modeling of highly simplified (and thus unrealistic) situations or the testing of empirical hypotheses (most of which are not even of instrumental nature). Both of these tasks are legitimate academic concerns, and this book must not be misinterpreted as opposing those efforts. What must be opposed is the one-sidedness of this academic concern and, even more so, the intolerance of positive accounting theorists toward attempts of incorporating norms (objectives) into the theoretical accounting framework.

Once the insight is widely accepted that academic accounting goes beyond a pure science, a more tolerant academic policy can be expected. Those who believe in the mission of a conditional–normative accounting methodology should be prepared for the right moment. However, a general state of readiness may only be attainable if a large enough number of high-level theorists get involved in both the analytical aspects of normative accounting research and the empirical search for relevant instrumental hypotheses.

If a rigorous solution to this problem is not feasible at this stage, perhaps a preliminary, less rigorous approach might be easier to attain and yet capable of clarifying the present confusion about means–end relations. It, too, would bridge the gap between practice and academia and reveal the actual goals pursued (instead of the pretended ones). After all, accountants make many choices that are as yet unexplained. A conditional–normative theory could not only uncover hidden objectives; it would also be the most rational way to connect the means to the desired ends. This could bring us a long way toward finding out why practitioners do what they do. Last, a conditional–normative framework could be applied equally well to ethical as to pragmatic goals, thus clarifying the means–end relations in both areas.

What is at stake is the scientific illumination of an activity that is going on in everyday business life. Even positive accounting theorists admit that someone must adapt the positive theory to the objectives of actual practice. Why should this important task—which is nothing but a process of deductive and inductive inference (as outlined in Chapter 6)—be excluded from scientific investigation? Why do so many prominent accounting theorists try to brand it with the term *unscientific*? In the hope to overcome at least some of the present preconceptions, Chapter 11 offers a closer look at CoNAM and its general setting.

NOTES

This chapter is based partly on "On the History of Normative Accounting Theory: Paradigm Lost, Paradigm Regained?" (Mattessich 1992), partly on some pages of "Editor's Commentary: A Decade of Growth, Sophistication, and Impending Crisis" (Mattessich 1991c, 10–13), and partly on new material.

1. Schär obtained the first academic chair of commercial science (*Handelswissenschaft*) at the University of Zürich in 1903 and later accepted an offer of the University of Berlin. Nicklisch taught first as lecturer at the Commercial University (*Handelshochschule*) of Leipzig and eventually also became Professor at the University of Berlin.

2. Although this normative theory was not restricted to accounting, but was proclaimed for business in general, it must be borne in mind that at this time the major (though by no means only) constituent of business studies was accounting.

3. With Lujo Brentano (1844–1931), Werner Sombart (1863–1941) and Max Weber (1864–1920) pleading for a value-neutral economics, while Gustav Schmoller (1838–1917), Richard Ehrenberg (1857–1921), and others were promoting the normative approach.

4. Schmalenbach (1919a, 1919b).

5. "A system is called 'normative' with respect to a certain property or activity. . . . Whether a system (e.g., Management Science) is free of values or not, depends on the location of the value judgment in relation to the boundaries of the system . . . , the bound-

aries might be manipulated in such a way as to include or exclude those value judgments which causes us to regard a science as normative or positive respectively" (Mattessich 1978a, 40, 44). For further details, see other passages of this previous book.

6. Obviously, there are many more authors who could be put into the normative category (indeed, the adherents of "positive accounting theory" might label the work of almost every accounting scholar before 1968 or so as normative). In this chapter, however, I am concerned only with major trends and not with an enumeration of all the publications falling into this or that category.

7. With some stretch of imagination, many more eminent authors could be regarded as belonging to the normative–pragmatic camp (for additional names, see last section of Chapter 6). For example, the dispute between Solomons (1991a, 1991b) and Tinker (1991) shows that Solomons regards himself as a "neutralist," while Tinker takes him to be no less normatively biased.

The major characteristic of the ethical–normative direction is its explicit commitment to a social equity (e.g., environmental, consumer, income, and wealth distributional concerns) beyond the individual or merely economic principles, while the pragmatic–normative direction relies (implicit or explicit) on value judgments, constituting methodological, technical, legal, or administrative norms.

8. Obviously, both finance, on one side, and MIS, on the other side, have a plurality of roots beyond accounting (e.g., economics and computer science, respectively). The remarks in the text are not intended to deny this but refer more to the changes in the departmental structure of business schools.

9. For an example of such cooperation, see the empirical work on FIFO/LIFO research by Sunder (1975, 1976), Abdel-khalik (1985), R. M. Brown (1980), Hunt (1985), Johnson and Dhaliwal (1986) and the corresponding analytical work by Jung (1985), Amershi and Sunder (1987), and Hughes, et al. (1988), which offer a theoretical explanation why in the United States the LIFO method is usually rejected by "high-quality" firms (i.e., those least likely to go into bankruptcy) in spite of certain tax advantages (see also Dopuch and Pinkus 1988).

10. Italy's "National Accounting Academy" goes back to 1813 (with subsequent changes of names; today, it has a somewhat broader basis and is called Accademia di Economia Aziendale); and Italy's first higher business school, in Venice, seems to date back to 1868 or so. The United States opened the Wharton School (apparently its first academic business school) in 1881. In Germany, the *Handelshochschulen* of Leipzig and Aachen opened in 1898; and in the same year, the *Hochschule für Welthandel* (now University of Economics) of Vienna as well as the *Handelshochschule St. Gallen* (now a Graduate School of Economics, Business, and Public Administration) in Switzerland opened.

11. After World War II, Cambridge University did establish a chair supported by a public accounting firm (yet called "applied economics"). It was occupied by an economist, Richard Stone, who was primarily concerned with national income accounting, for which he received in 1984 the Nobel Memorial Prize. It seems that this university did not establish its first proper chair of accountancy until the late 1980s.

12. Some readers may wonder about this big jump (from the Germany of the 1930s to Great Britain of the 1970s or 1980s); but during those four or five decades, no major accounting trend that could be regarded as "ethical–normative" (in the sense of supplementing economic principles with those of social equity) seems to have existed. During this

time, most accounting research was either descriptive or analytical, or it fell into the "pragmatic–normative" or "statistical–empirical" categories.

13. A more recent journal, *Critical Perspectives in Accounting* (founded in 1990 and edited from New York and Edmonton), pursues a similar goal.

14. See Chua (1986) and Mattessich (1991c, 12–14). For further references, see the review article on financial accounting by Whittington (1986) and the review by Roslender (1990).

15. This is something that I suspected a long time ago: "Whether it [accounting] is a trivial or a sophisticated means, whether it furthers the cognitive process of science, or whether it is a dogmatic body for pursuing the *ritual* of an industrial age, are still controversial questions" (Mattessich 1964a, 3, italics added).

16. See Descombes (1980). Ehrenreich—in an essay referring to the alleged misrepresentations of Nobel laureate David Baltimore and, in particular, his co-worker Thereza Imanish Kari makes the following ironic remark about the relation of deconstructionalist philosophy to the contemporary way of life: "What does one more lie matter anyway? Politicians 'misspeak' and are forgiven by their followers. Pop singers have been known to dub in better voices. *Literary deconstructionists* say there's no truth anyway, just ideologies and points of view. Lies, you might say, are the great lubricant of our way of life. They sell products, flatter the powerful and appease the electorate" (Ehrenreich 1991, 86).

17. I am aware of the difficulty of attaining complete objectivity in the social sciences. For me, objectivity is a matter of degree; and I am prepared to accept different shades of objectivity. Since we can hardly attain absolute truth, our objectivity (even in the sciences) is rarely, if ever, pure but usually tainted by one or the other human element. Newton's corpuscular theory of light was accepted as highly objective during the eighteenth century, whereas today, in light of the quantum–wave theory of light, Newton's theory appears to be less objective and only partially true.

18. At least if two conditions are fulfilled: (1) if one can convince accountants that academic accounting is an *applied* science, and (2) if academic accountants continue their aspirations of a scientific–empirical treatment of their subject matter. There is no contradiction between the conditional–normative and the scientific–empirical approach. Though the latter can be carried out without the former, the reverse does not hold (because conditional value judgments are introduced only on this second level). The following quote indicates that I have held such convictions for three decades: "But one of the important tasks of accounting theory is the formulation of various alternative sets of hypotheses required for specific purposes" (Mattessich 1964a, 45).

CHAPTER 11

Conditional–Normative
Accounting Methodology

"The value judgments which are forbidden to enter through the front door
of political science, sociology or economics, enter these disciplines through
the back door."

(Strauss 1959, 23)

Wherever a purpose is to be fulfilled, one must find the means for attaining this
purpose satisfactorily. Accounting systems, as well as accounting standards, are
meaningless without such purpose orientation. Indeed, the long-established tradition in search for those objectives (compare Backer 1966; American Institute
of Certified Public Accountants 1973; Financial Accounting Standards Board
1976b, 1978, 1980a) gives testimony to the importance of such an undertaking.
Purpose orientation has led to one of the pivotal issues of this book, namely, that
academic accounting is an applied rather than a pure science.

One would assume that this concern for objectives directly translates into the
investigation of the means for attaining those objectives. However, rarely are such
means–end relations discussed explicitly in the accounting literature. These relations, although vital for accounting practice, are usually obscured by layers of
standards, principles, rules, constraints, and the like. Often, even the value judgments inherent in the objectives are not clearly perceived.

This attitude is aggravated by the positive trend in accounting that contributes
to the bewilderment of many accountants when confronted with a paradigm that
focuses on the direct relations between means and ends. Indeed, nothing appears

to be more difficult to change than a preconception established by training, professional habits, or a lifelong way of thinking. Anyone looking at the practice of accounting must admit that its objective is not to represent economic reality in a purely scientific way but to approximate it pragmatically on the basis of particular norms. However, just as the opponents of Galileo refused to look through his telescope to see the evidence in favor of the heliocentric theory, so some academics seem to be unwilling to see the evidence supporting the view that academic accounting is an applied discipline.

The situation is different in other applied sciences. Physicians, for example, have emphasized means–end relations from the very inception of their discipline. Even today, medicine officially recognizes innumerable effective treatments or remedies merely on the basis of their effectiveness but without complete cause-and-effect explanation in the scientific sense. Of course, it is better to know the cause-and-effect nexus, even for finding the means–end relation; but to abandon the search for the latter merely because the former has not been found runs contrary to most applied disciplines. There is further similarity with medicine: Physicians are beseeched, these days, by patients who clamor for alternative choices to the one-sided and exclusive treatment with high-powered but potentially dangerous drugs. If there is a parallel with accounting, it is this: Just as a good physician will inform the patient about alternative treatments (including natural remedies), indicating for each alternative the pros and cons, so a good accounting academic or practitioner is the one who offers the client a spectrum of alternatives together with pertinent information to help make an intelligent choice, depending on the latter's needs and values.

Finance, a discipline close to ours, also begins to put greater emphasis on norms and means–end relations. Take the case of choosing one among various portfolios (say, from a family of mutual funds offered by a single company); each portfolio (model) has a different risk characteristic clearly revealed to the investor. This is a typical situation in which each model *incorporates* another value judgment (e.g., the type of risk to be chosen by the investor [on how to incorporate value judgments in systems and theories, see Mattessich 1974; 1978a, 17–52]). Such arguments, together with the fact that the practice of accounting is purpose oriented, should be convincing enough to analyze accounting issues (like the choice of a valuation method or of some accounting standard) in a similar means–end fashion. Take the reader of a particular set of financial statements (as outlined in Chapter 6). If he or she is concerned with the maintenance of "real financial capital," would he or she not choose a different income and valuation model than when concerned with maintaining the value of "physical capital"?

As repeatedly emphasized, one purpose of this book is to outline a methodology that, first, pays more attention to value judgments; second, promotes accounting theories flexible enough to accept a variety of exchangeable objectives; and third, tries to relate those objectives directly to the pertinent means. Whether such an approach is worth pursuing is up to each individual researcher to decide; but one hardly can afford to close one's mind to an unaccustomed point of view merely because it requires thinking in unfamiliar terms. If there is any barrier to this view, it does not lie in the difficulty of grasping it nor in its presentation but in the break with a deeply rooted academic tradition that hesitates to contemplate value judgments and their relations to means. Since means–end relations abound in accounting practice, there should be enough justification for trying to analyze and understand those relations in a systematic but normative way.

The second section of this chapter clarifies the historical background for the need of taking value judgments more seriously in our discipline, while the third section supplies evidence in support of the premise that academic accounting is an applied science and elaborates on the need for means–end analysis. The fourth section clarifies essential features of the conditional–normative methodology (CoNAM) and shows how it is considered to be objective. The fifth section (choosing accounting objectives) discusses accounting objectives, their choice, and the need for broadening the range of objectives and for articulating a hierarchy of accounting goals. The sixth section casts a glance at the current state of the conditional–normative approach, while the seventh offers some further discussion of reality issues. It distinguishes between the rigorous *positive* representation and the *pragmatic* representation of reality; it also explains two issues: (1) how the two representations are connected, and (2) why a pragmatic representation cannot be "realistic" in the positive sense of the word but is perhaps more reasonable from a practical point of view. The eighth section emphasizes future requirements as well as difficulties to be overcome before all aspects of CoNAM can be implemented; it also offers a short recapitulation.

VALUE JUDGMENTS IN ACCOUNTING

Among the many changes that accounting research experienced during the second half of this century, none was more influential than the shift of emphasis from analytical concerns (lasting from about the late 1950s to the early 1970s) to empirical–statistical research which slowly began in the late 1960s and gathered momentum in the 1970s and 1980s. The "empirical revolution" could not prevent the fragmentation of accounting into several opposing camps, though. In the wake of mounting criticism of business practices (including those of public accountants) during the 1980s, many normative and particularly ethical questions have arisen (e.g., Briloff 1981, 1986, 1987, 1990; Belkaoui 1984, 1989; Gaa 1988a, 1988b, 1994; Hopwood 1988; Mozes 1992). Such a shift may affect neither the analytical insights gained since the late 1950s nor the empirical achievements attained during the last twenty-five years, but it suggests that normative issues (originally dominating academic accounting) can no longer be pushed to the fringe.

Which alternatives are available for accommodating normative aspects in accounting? There seem to be at least four major options:

One possibility would be a return to the traditional normative approach of the 1960s and early 1970s, as found in the works of Edwards and Bell (1961), Chambers (1966), Sterling (1970b), and others. This would mean the implicit incorporation of some absolute pragmatic value judgments (acceptance of a specific valuation approach, realization criterion, and the like). Such a return to old times seems to be implied in Chambers (1993), if I correctly interpret his criticism of "positive accounting theory." Would this be a viable proposition? Would it not be an attempt to turn the wheel of time backward? It certainly would ignore both the call for better explication of value judgments and the critical–interpretive camp's emphasis on ethical and social issues. It also might constitute a rejection of the new empirical methods introduced to accounting in the late 1960s and dominating it during the last decade or more.

The second possibility lies in emphasizing ethical (instead of pragmatic) norms, in particular, those in accord with social goals. This might lead to a predominantly interpretive and critical methodology, which argues that no accounting theory is value free. Chua (1986) has summarized this position, which ranges over a wide spectrum of researchers—from Hopwood (1988) to more radical authors such as Tinker (1985) (See Tables 10.2 and 10.3.) Although this critical–interpretive camp fulfills an important function in present-day accounting, it does not seem to offer enough flexibility in the choice of competing value judgments arising from the considerable variety of accounting objectives. The advantage of the critical–interpretive approach lies in the openness with which it reveals its underlying ethical value judgments. In its less radical form, it may even converge with the conditional–normative methodology promoted in this book (see the fourth alternative).

A third possibility is the continuing embrace of PAT or related empirical approaches, which implies the exclusion of norms (as long as they are not hidden) from the set of premises, relegating them to a category beyond the theory proper. Although the choice of most value judgments is ultimately with the user, a truly "positive accounting theory" leaves the user on his or her own to infer the appropriate means from the positive theory plus the chosen norms. Although this approach is based on empirical and often statistical methods and lays claim to objectivity (in the traditional scientific sense), in the view of some experts (e.g., the critical–interpretive camp), this approach possibly hides value judgments inherent in its neoclassical economic basis which, from a practical point of view, proved so inadequate as far as environmental and social issues are concerned.

Last, there is the possibility of incorporating value judgments into the theory proper and offering a broad range of alternative purpose-oriented models to the users of accounting information; this is the conditional–normative accounting methodology outlined in this book. Its ultimate vision is the creation of a considerable number of accounting models, each with specific hypotheses tailor-made to a specific accounting objective or *standardized* (just as cars or shirts, and the like, are standardized) yet offering a considerable choice to "consumers." This methodology lays claim to a kind of objectivity that is justified, in part, by the disclosure of its value judgments and, in part, by empirical procedures confirming the relationship between the purpose and the means to attain it. Although such a synthesis uses normative as well as empirical elements, it is, in crucial aspects, different from the "positive approach" (see also Chapter 6). As we have seen, the latter term is irreconcilable with the presence of value judgments in any premise of the pertinent theory or model; CoNAM, on the other hand, requires normative premises. Since applied sciences are not concerned with gaining pure or disinterested knowledge (in the sense of the natural, biological, or positive social sciences) but with applying this knowledge to the attainment of practical goals, CoNAM should be well suited to accounting as an applied science. Although many features of such a program can easily be implemented, the realization of the entire program would require mastering many obstacles, as the analysis in this book has indicated. Where would science and technology be today without having overcome obstacles, applied novel methods, and aimed for difficult targets?

ACCOUNTING AS AN APPLIED SCIENCE[1]

The need for a conditional–normative methodology cannot be comprehended without the notion of accounting as an applied or "mission-oriented" discipline (see, for example, Archer 1993; Milburn 1994). The latter, addressing the economics of accounting as the "social science approach" and applied science as the "engineering approach," expresses this in the following words:

A few years ago I raised some of these issues with a prominent agency theorist, who eloquently dismissed my criticisms. He drew an analogy between an "engineer" and a "social scientist." He views himself as a social scientist who is interested in rigorously assessing the goodness/value of accounting information by examining its logical effects within the agency theory model. The engineer, on the other hand, is primarily concerned with the engine itself (the underlying measurement system(s) in accounting). By this I would infer that the engineer is concerned with a rigorous understanding of the specifications of the system, exactly how it works, what it is capable of, what its limitations are, and how it might be most efficiently designed to fulfill its purpose.

Both the social scientist and engineering approaches are, in my view, necessary to achieving a useful financial accounting product. The problem, I submit, is that academic accounting research over the past two or three decades has emphasized the social science perspective—and in so doing has neglected the engineering side. (Milburn 1994, 19)

Archer, too, accepts the position that academic accounting is ultimately an applied science[2]; and the following presents supporting evidence for the applied nature of academic accounting:

1. The major task of an applied science is the application of law statements and other research findings (of the corresponding pure science) to practical goals. Contrary to pure science, its task is not to find but to apply those law statements.[3] I do not suggest that accounting lacks basic laws, but these are the ones belonging to pure science (just as the natural laws underlying engineering and medicine are found in physics, chemistry, biology, and so on). Thus, the question arises whether there exist any positive laws pertaining to accounting beyond economics

192 CRITIQUE OF ACCOUNTING

or the behavioral sciences. One would have to demonstrate, first, that the regularities inferred by empirical accounting research are genuine scientific laws, and second, that they are laws of accounting instead of economics or other pure disciplines.

Chambers (1991) tried to conceptualize a series of "accounting laws." Neither does the postulation of the law statements follow stringent scientific inductive and deductive requirements, nor do those statements enjoy general recognition as reflecting scientific laws. Despite some attempts to declare ad hoc hypotheses as empirical laws of accounting, I have not yet encountered a single "accounting law" that enjoys general scientific consensus. This "vacuum" might even jeopardize the entire enterprise of a positive theory of accounting. Of course, one could always tinker with the semantics and speak of a "positive economic–behavioral theory of accounting" as part of either economics or the behavioral sciences in general (compare Mouck 1993, who seems to regard PAT as belonging to the "normal" scientific effort, in the Kuhnian sense, of economics). Such an alternative might remove a good deal of the controversy around PAT. The fact that some accounting researchers engage in pure economic research does not make accounting a pure science, just as the pure research of some physicians does not change the applied status of medicine. To speak of a "positive theory of medicine" or a "positive theory of engineering" would bear little meaning because the initiate knows that the positive theories of those subjects are to be found in biology, chemistry, physics, and so on. Would it not be equally meaningful to find the positive basis of accounting in such pure disciplines as economics and the behavioral sciences?

2. Accounting cannot be practiced without accepting certain norms and frequent value judgments (beyond "prescientific" ones). An academic discipline claiming to explore and serve such a practical field as accounting can no less afford to ignore those norms than the sciences of medicine and engineering could disregard the norms handed down to them and applied by their practitioners. It is no coincidence that one has begun to realize that "agency theory. . . forms a (possible) basis for a positive as well as a normative [i.e., conditional–normative] theory of cost accounting. . . [and that, in the case of the latter,] cost accounting is dependent of the user and thus of the goal" (see Wagenhofer 1993, 169, 164, translated). While value judgments (other than prescientific ones) are strictly prohibited as premises in any pure science, normative premises are an indispensable requirement for all applied sciences. Among the many value judgments of accounting, one category is special and important enough to be discussed separately in the next item.

3. Some of the most crucial value judgments entering accounting stem from cost–benefit considerations. The norm that the long-run benefit of an information system must exceed its long-run costs should be trivially obvious; yet despite paying lip service to it, accountants ignore this maxim often enough, particularly when asking why financial statements and their valuations are so "unrealistic." Take, for example, a fairly realistic but highly sophisticated valuation procedure that costs more than it benefits in the long run. Obviously, it must be rejected in practice. The difficulty of measuring those costs and, even more so, of estimating

the corresponding benefits is a separate problem which, in principle, does not change the issue or need for cost–benefit criteria.

4. Accounting is taught and researched predominantly at faculties of commerce, business administration, management, and the like. The latter are considered to be professional schools, such as those of medicine, engineering, and law. These are called "professional" because their task is to teach and research primarily the application of scientific insights to specific professional goals. These are factual premises that can be confirmed. Thus, the claim that accounting is an applied science is supported (but not necessitated) by the probabilistic inference following from these premises. This neither excludes pure and basic research from being pursued at such schools, nor does it mean that the applied sciences themselves are not amenable to foundational research. It merely means that the major research goal of those institutions is found in the creation of knowledge and theories directly applicable to practical or professional problems. Such schools arose out of the very need to spare the practitioner the toil of adapting for himself or herself positive hypotheses to his or her objectives.

NORMATIVE THEORIES AND OBJECTIVITY

The major criticism directed against normative accounting theories—and the reason for their dismissal by many leading accounting researchers during the past decades—lies in the claim that such theories are subjective, hence "unscientific." Indeed, value judgments, which underlie every normative theory, are neither objective nor accessible to empirical refutation or verification. A conditional–normative methodology can circumvent this limitation and impart a degree of objectivity to a normative framework. The objectivity claim of the conditional–normative methodology is to be found in the following circumstances:

1. CoNAM recognizes that different groups or individuals pursue different goals in accounting, management, finance, and business in general. It thus rejects the notion of "absolute" values or objectives but tries to comprehend the entire spectrum and hierarchy of competing as well as complementary objectives. This methodology does not regard any single norm or goal (profit maximization, current exit valuation, equal access to information, and so on) as the only one valid but offers a free choice of value judgment to the decision maker. Above all, it insists on the disclosure of the value judgments incorporated in any accounting theory, model, or system. In opting for one of those alternative objectives, a certain objectivity is attained by openly disclosing the value judgment behind it. This is no novel insight; and it has been expressed best by Myrdal, the Nobel laureate, with the following words: "The only way in which we can strive for strict 'objectivity' in theoretical analysis is to expose the valuations into full light, make them conscious, specific and explicit, and permit them to determine the theoretical research" (Myrdal 1970, 55).

Therefore, the first objective aspect of a conditional–normative theory lies in the clear exposition of its underlying value judgment (or set of value judgments) and in the admission that the pertinent norm is but one among many possible alternatives. Thus, a conditional–normative methodology makes a pragmatic–scientific approach possible (the empirical aspects of means–end relations, discussed below will reinforce this claim). This is confirmed by such views as that of Mozes, who interprets the FASB's call for normative research,[4] obviously, in the conditional–normative sense: "The Board's call for normative research can be interpreted as a request for accounting researchers to investigate whether the user-specific and decision-specific qualities that standard-setters require are present in accounting data. Such research can be conducted in accordance with the scientific method since a normative research hypothesis addresses only the issue of whether an accounting rule maximizes the standard-setter's objective function, and not the issue of whether the accounting rule maximizes societal welfare" (Mozes 1992, 94).

2. In a conditional–normative theory, the recommended means are predicated on the underlying norms or value judgments. This requires expressing the relationship between those norms and their means in an appropriate analytical as well as empirical way. The structure of such formalized means–end relations is different from that of scientific law statements of pure science, and it is crucial to recognize the relevant structure. Kaplan seems to stress this particular point:

A knowledge of the underlying structure is necessary if researchers wish to make normative recommendations to change some aspect of the environment. . . . But occasionally researchers are not as careful in this regard and fail to recognize that even when they obtain a model that predicts well, the model does not provide a basis for making normative recommendations about preferences among accounting methods. . . . But it is knowledge of the underlying structure that is required if we are to consider the impact of alternative actions within the context of the assumed structure. (Kaplan 1983, 345)

Occasionally, the relations connecting ends to pertinent means are formulated purely analytically (e.g., the relationship between valuation model and capital maintenance basis); but, in general, means–end relations should lend themselves to some kind of *empirical* testing, confirming statistically or otherwise that the inferred means can "satisfactorily" attain the desired end. Conventional accounting research, following the path of pure science, cannot formulate means–end relations in any direct way; it must bridge the gap between "is" and "ought" in some indirect fashion. Let me illustrate this through a quote from Watts and Zimmerman, who say that "normative propositions are concerned with prescriptions. They take the form 'Given the set of conditions C, alternative D should be chosen.'. . . This proposition is not refutable. Given an objective, it can be made refutable. . . . Thus given an objective, a researcher can turn a prescription into a conditional prediction and assess the empirical validity. However, the choice of the objective is not the theorist's, it is the theory user's" (Watts and Zimmerman 1986, 9).

At first glance, these sentences seem to conform to the maxims of CoNAM; but there is an important difference, and it lies in the expression "conditional prediction" that would be "conditional *prescription*" under CoNAM. This should be obvious, as a positive theory is concerned with statements of fact (e.g., descriptions), while the latter is concerned with recommendations (prescriptions) based on revealed norms. This structural difference indicates that a positive theory cannot make recommendations in a direct way; it requires additional steps, outside the theory proper, to transform the description into a recommendation. Therefore, whenever a positive theory is tempted to aim at policy recommendations, it cannot do this but in the indirect way just pointed out. Hence the decisive question is this: Who is to make the jump from *is* or *will be*, to *ought to be* (i.e., from description to prescription)? According to Watts and Zimmerman, it seems to be the practitioner (who gets from the academic "conditional *descriptions*" at best); but under CoNAM, it is the academic who formulates the means–end relations and is supposed to present the practitioner with prescriptions for alternative ends. In other words, the question is this: Shall the recommendations for actions be done within the theoretical framework, or outside of it?

My answer is that the very essence of an applied science lies in preparing "in advance" theoretical solutions for an entire battery of alternative objectives. Only then can the user—be he or she a medical practitioner, engineer, lawyer, or accountant—take the theory and apply it to actual practice without getting himself or herself involved in cumbersome inferences. The crucial question is this: To what extent can practitioners rely on academic accounting to supply them with appropriate models and systems for their particular information requirements? I believe one cannot expect practitioners to build, in each situation anew, a bridge between a statement of positive accounting theory and the means required for attaining a specific objective. This may be one reason why many practitioners have lost interest in the results of modern accounting research and why there exists such a gap between the theory and practice of accounting.

As academic accountants are not used to dealing with means–end relations directly, considerable research and training will be required before such a methodology will be fully operational. It also must be borne in mind that testing procedures of CoNAM may not always be as rigorous as those of PAT. Any applied science must supplement its testing by trial and error and other nonstatistical procedures (depending on the situation, such empirical testing may be statistical or nonstatistical: questionnaires, interviews, coherence testing, and the like). One may bear in mind that even in the pure sciences, statistical testing (the "reliability" of which may be overrated by some academics) constitutes a relatively small, though increasing, part in the arsenal of evaluating empirical hypotheses (for further details, see, for example, Bunge 1983b, 132–154).

3. Another programmatic feature of CoNAM is the estimation of the degrees of efficiency and effectiveness of the means fulfilling a specific end. This is an important secondary goal, but to attain it rigorously may prove to be even more difficult than the determination and testing of means–end relations themselves. Such difficulties imply neither that a conditional–normative approach is arbitrary nor that measurement or estimation of its effectiveness and efficiency is impossible.

I pleaded earlier for greater emphasis on objectives as well as a better insight into the connection between those objectives and the means to attain them. This may not be enough. To overcome the shortcomings of present-day accounting, the range of objectives itself may have to be extended. An essential feature of a relevant methodology is the identification and incorporation of different macro- and micro-objectives pursued by society in general or a specific group or an individual. Obviously a whole *hierarchy* of objectives and other concepts will have to be conceived. The first to have conceived and presented such a hierarchy (at least as far as "costs" are concerned), seems to have been Saario (1950)—considered by Honko (1966, 10) one of Saario's most significant scientific works. As my examples in Chapter 6, referring to capital-maintenance methods and enterprise context, have indicated, the objectives would range far beyond those presented in Financial Accounting Standards Board (1976a, 1976b, 1978, 1980a) and preceding studies, such as "the Trueblood Report" of the American Institute of Certified Public Accountants (1973). Also, goals beyond financial accounting and profit maximization would have to be included. Above all, a better distinction between short- and long-term wealth maximization, as two distinct goals, might need to be made.[5] There is a growing tendency to extend the economic basis of accounting from neoclassical economics to ecological economics (compare Belkaoui 1984).[6]

CHOOSING ACCOUNTING OBJECTIVES

A conditional–normative accounting methodology is the basis for a *general* framework that relates accounting objectives to the means capable of attaining those objectives. It would provide a framework capable of accommodating many specific normative theories of accounting. Such a framework is in conformity with the notion of "theory" in the post-Kuhnian philosophy of science, which (as shown in Chapter 7) regards a theory as an entire network of more specific theory elements.

While a *methodology* provides the guidelines and basis for developing theories, a *theory* offers the structure and network of sentences and models for the description, explanation, and (at times) prediction of phenomena. The choice of an objective may occur on a fairly general level, as, for example, in the setting of accounting and auditing standards, or on a more specific level when, for instance, choosing one among several competing valuation and capital-maintenance concepts. The latter example is well suited to illustrate this issue.

Some scholars, for instance, have persistently argued that current exit values are the only proper evaluation for most assets (e.g., Chambers 1980; Sterling 1970b). Contrary to such an "absolute" value notion, CoNAM regards the valuation method as a condition of, among others, the capital-maintenance approach to be chosen. The latter, in turn, depends (as shown in Chapter 6) on the type of enterprise and similar circumstances. Why did those experts, who regarded the current-value method as the only valid one, not perceive this connection between context and valuation method? First, they may have accepted too narrow an economic basis; and second, they may have neglected cost–benefit considerations and other practical constraints. As accountants argued for several decades in vain which valuation approach is the only proper one, it is no surprise that the younger generation turned its back to those kinds of "measurement" problems. CoNAM abandons the search for an absolute valuation method and may thus be considered superior.

An example illustrating the traditional tendency toward "single" objectives in conventional accounting is taken from Lev (1988). This is one of the most praised accounting policy papers of the 1980s, and is also concerned with such problems as the relativity of information relevance, the effectiveness with which certain means attain an objective, and the general difficulty of handling policy issues:

What is highly useful information for some investors might be irrelevant or even damaging. . . for others. So what public interest criterion *does* and/or *should* determine the choices made by accounting regulators. Or, yet another largely unanswered policy question—how should the social consequences of accounting regulation be evaluated and the effectiveness of these policies determined? . . . One must conclude, therefore, that despite increasing awareness of these issues involved, little progress has thus far been made in addressing the basic accounting policy issues. (Lev 1988, 2–3)

Ultimately, Lev's paper pivots on a single objective, namely, "equal access to information relevant for asset evaluation" (p. 3). Other objectives, such as "fairness, eliminating fraud, protecting the uninformed investor against exploitation by insiders" are brushed aside as "vague, anachronistic, and unattractive notions" (p. 1). Lev presents forceful arguments that his "*ex ante* equality of opportunity concept" is state of the art as well as operational. Indeed, the fact that it can be better operationalized (than so-called "moralistic" notions) is a strong incentive for adopting it. However, a conditional–normative methodology aims for a framework in which the user freely chooses among a variety of objectives—not only where *competing* objectives are involved, but also in cases like Lev's, where *complementary* objectives (as fairness, and so on) do not necessarily exclude the one promoted by a specific expert. In the future, some of those other objectives might also become easier to operationalize—apart from the fact that the difficulty of operationalization may (for a particular decision maker) not be critical for excluding a specific objective. Most important, the choice of the objective should remain with the decision maker (i.e., the ultimate user of the financial information). The applied scientist is obliged to submit the relevant range of objectives to the user and inform him or her about the means for reaching each of those objectives as well as its consequences. Thus, the academic (or, in his or her place, the practitioner) will offer a palette of accounting models from which one can choose according to one's information needs. Based on such stipulation, or in anticipation of it, the academic may recommend certain strategies, but *he or she must not impose any objective* upon the user.

Another example of a single objective overriding all others is the FASB's tendency to put decision-relevant information over other goals such as accountability. Even if Mozes (1992, 96) points out that the Financial Accounting Standards

Board (1980c, 1985) accepts the following six normative categories (qualities of accounting information) in establishing accounting rules, these categories are subordinated to the making of investment decisions: (1) consistency (with other accounting rules), (2) understandability, (3) relevance, (4) neutrality, (5) representational faithfulness, and (6) cost–benefit relation. Mozes (1992) subsequently discusses pertinent literature dealing with these issues, thus pointing to a potentially important research area for conditional–normative accounting research.

As for the conditional–normative approach in cost accounting, an example is found in the German literature, first by Riebel (1978), who developed a decision-oriented cost concept different from the "pagatoric" (see Kosiol 1956) as well as the opportunity cost notions, and later by Schneeweiß, who, continuing Riebel's endeavors, sketches this methodology in the following way:

> Embedding the cost problem in the general frame of a prescriptive administrative decision theory, one sees that decision-oriented and value-based cost notions belong to different levels of abstraction and relaxation. These notions are therefore not to be used in an independent but in a complementary way. . . . The adaptation of parameters will then be such that the decision-maker employs goal-values [*Zielwerte*] which constitute for him an acceptable compromise. . . . The entire problem of valuation can then be represented as follows: the decision-maker first specifies the goal-system [*Zielsystem*] . . . and the value-preferences [*Höhenpräferenzen*]. Then he designs a decision generator and evaluates the pertinent cost parameter k (together with the non-cost parameter a) in the goal-system of the reality model [*Realmodell*]. (Schneeweiß 1993, 1025, 1028, 1031, translated, footnote omitted)

As for the past success or failure in solving major issues of accounting, Beaver and Demski are pointing out that

> the nature of income and valuation remains as elusive as when we were graduate students. Yet issues of income measurement and valuation remain at the heart of the institutional setting of financial reporting, not to mention the practice and use of accounting throughout the economy. . . . Clearly we have not been successful in resolving or even reducing the set of specialized notions of income or accounting value. This is hardly surprising, since under these market conditions [imperfect and incomplete] it is possible to generate illustrations or examples where any notion of accounting will fail to capture some supposedly relevant aspect of the entity's life. This follows from the fact [that] valuation is not fully defined in the absence of perfect and complete markets, except in special cases (e.g., derivative securities). . . . More deeply, our understanding here is limited by the fact [that] we have not developed a theory of accounting measurement in which demand for accounting measurement is endogenous. (Beaver and Demski 1994, 1–3)

If the valuation issue has been intractable for such a long time, might it not be that traditional accounting methodology has been inadequate or that the conventional approach with its neoclassical economic basis—on which these attempts rest—is too narrow? Perhaps both of these are at fault? The economic basis is still dominated by the single goal of wealth maximization; it rarely allows consideration of other purposes and norms.

Last, Ijiri (1980, 33), Griffin (1987), Gaa (1988a) and, above all, Swieringa (1989, 182), emphasize that the FASB, or standard setters in general, need from researchers not only facts, concepts, theories, and frameworks but also identification and evaluation of alternatives as well as justifications. In other words, they need application of a conditional–normative methodology. Bernard (1989, 73–74), referring to the disenchantment with "economic consequent studies," indicates, as Frecka confirms, that "our existing research technology is not adequate for addressing economic consequences issues" (Frecka 1989a, 15).

Thus, we need a different "research methodology," which, as I believe, ought to consist of two major steps: (1) the incorporation of norms or value judgments into accounting models (or theories), which then are predicated on the pertinent objectives; and (2) statistical and related empirical techniques for inferring not only deductively but, above all, inductively means from ends. The first step has abundantly been discussed in this book; the other step requires no less than a second empirical accounting revolution. Even before such a revolution has occurred, accountants can go a far way to forge CoNAM into a practical tool. They can use the very same statistical techniques that are presently available in empirical accounting and then convert the positive hypotheses into instrumental (i.e., conditional–normative) hypotheses, as indicated in the last section of Chapter 6. This is neither a cop-out nor a rueful return to PAT. The latter excludes value judgments from the premises of accounting theory, while CoNAM insists on their incorporation into accounting theories. Thus, the decisive difference between these two methodologies remains intact. How do we know which methodology is the appropriate one? This question can be answered, over time, only by a procedure of trial and error. There is no guarantee that the most glamorous or technically refined methodology will win; it is more likely that it will be the one which proves most useful in solving the problems of an applied science.

PRESENT STATUS OF CONDITIONAL–NORMATIVE METHODOLOGY

Philosophers have been working for decades on the formal analysis of normative logic that includes the logic of commands and other imperatives, as well as that of means–end relations.[7] That this is an excruciatingly complex problem area is manifested by some quotes from von Wright, one of the great pioneers of normative logic:

Dissatisfaction with my earlier attempts to deal with practical inference urged me to return to the topic time and time again. . . . Ever since the appearance of my first paper on deontic [i.e., normative] logic in *Mind* in 1951 I felt that there was some philosophically essential aspect of norms (normative concepts and discourse) which the formal system I had constructed either did not capture at all or tried to capture in the wrong way. In the 30 years which have passed I have again and again returned to the topic—often with a new idea which I thought would at last put things essentially right. But always, so far, to be disappointed. . . . For my part I regard my passage through the wilderness of deontic logic as terminated. I hope the feeling I now have will last, that the new essay "Norms, Truth and Logic" has eventually removed the uneasiness I felt about advancing with instruments of logic beyond the frontiers of truth and falsehood. (von Wright 1983, vii–ix)

It is a common misconception to believe that normative inferences obey the same formal laws as conventional logic. Can accountants afford to disregard the efforts made in clarifying the problems of practical inferences? This does not mean that accountants must receive formal training in normative (i.e., deontic) logic, but they should be better informed about the difference between the traditional (i.e., declarative) logic governing positive propositions and the deontic logic governing normative statements (for details, see Mattessich 1978a, which deals with the deductive as well as inductive determination of instrumental hypotheses). Here, I can merely draw attention to the existence of pertinent differences and offer some instances and references. There are several reasons why declarative logic cannot be applied to normative arguments. Ross, for example, points out that "according to the usually accepted definition of a logical inference, an imperative is precluded from being a constituent part of such inference" (1944, 32). Rescher, in dealing with commands (one of the most common groups of imperatives), states that "The giving of a command is a performance. From this angle, a 'logic of commands' is difficult to envisage. Performances cannot stand in logical relations to one another, and specifically, one performance cannot entail or imply another, nor can the description of one performance entail that of another" (Rescher 1966b, 8).

Aristotle, realizing the limitations of conventional logic, hinted in his *Nicomachean Ethics* (Book 7, Chap. 3) at a logic of action. Modern logicians have devised various alternative schemes to deal with this problem (for details, see Mattessich 1978a, 128–140). Some of these approaches use declarative sentences but construct an extended logic of action (e.g., von Wright 1968, 1983). In the applied disciplines, it is legal science which—under the eminent legalistic scholar Hans Kelsen (e.g., 1967 [1934], 1991)—has taken leadership in exploring the application of normative logic. In this connection, Archer (1993, 69) even suggests some association between Kelsen's work and my own efforts (Mattessich 1964a, 1972), though at this time, I was not aware of the details of Kelsen's work, merely of his reputation (the social science library at the University of California at Berkeley has been named after him—"Hans Kelsen Library").

The Nobel laureate Herbert Simon (1965, 1966) also has been deeply concerned with normative aspects and their role in the applied sciences. He opposes a separate logic of action and recommends simple conversion rules to supplement declarative logic for the purpose of "practical reasoning." Binkley succinctly summarizes Simon's procedure as follows:

Simon says, roughly, that decisions are made in the following way. (Or perhaps that they are to be made in the following way. . . .) We begin with an imperative which specifies the end. We convert this to a declarative; that is, we assume that the end is achieved. Combining this with other declaratives which define the circumstances, we draw an inference about what actions must have been done. These action declaratives are finally converted to imperatives which tell us to perform the means to our end. It is a logical process with imperatives at the top and imperatives at the bottom, but with a lot of declarative reasoning in between.

A theory of decision is mainly interested in the intervening declarative reasoning. . . . However, from the point of view of the philosopher concerned with the problem of practical reason, it is *the links with imperatives at top and bottom* that hold the interest. . . . And, given this interest, the philosopher will focus his attention on the rules *connecting imperatives to the means-end statement*, Simon's "conversion rules." These rules will have so great an importance for the philosopher that he will be bound to refer to them as a special logic of imperatives. (Binkley 1966, 22–23, italics added)

Figure 11.1 (see penultimate section of this chapter) may further indicate that the connection between imperatives (objectives) and means–end statements are relevant not only to philosophers but also to applied scientists as well as practitioners. Of lesser priority to the latter might be the controversy whether Simon's "conversion rules" or a similar system should be regarded as a special kind of logic. The fact remains that traditional logic, without some supplementation (be it a full-fledged logic of action or only some conversion rules), cannot properly master means–end relations.

Conditional–normative theories are quite common in the economic and management sciences. Ultimately, such theories depend no less on empirical research than the cause-and-effect relations of positive theory; but they clearly reveal the underlying goals and value judgments. In operations research (OR) the essence of conditional–normative theories is best manifested and most concisely characterized by Luce and Raiffa, who emphasize that "it is crucial that the social scientist recognize that game theory is not *descriptive*, but rather (conditionally) *normative*. It states neither how people do behave nor how people should behave in an absolute sense, but how they should behave if they wish to achieve certain ends" (Luce and Raiffa 1957, 63).

In OR (and occasionally in other management and economic sciences) the empirical aspect is often hidden because the only goals considered are those of profit or wealth maximization, usually assumed to be prescientific. Then, the problem of optimizing this single objective is amenable to a purely mathematical solution without much need for either a deontic logic or the empirical testing of means–end relations.

First steps toward a conditional–normative accounting approach can be found in Mattessich (1964a, 8–9, 232–291, 429–431). There, the need for more purpose orientation (and a series of "mono-purpose" or "limited-purpose" accounting systems) is repeatedly mentioned. Above all, this book introduced to accounting the notion of "pragmatic hypotheses" (i.e., formalized means–end relations, called "instrumental hypotheses" in Mattessich 1978a), distinguishing them clearly from the "positive" hypotheses of the pure sciences. Furthermore, this work separates unequivocally the more permanent basic assumptions of accounting from those specific, pragmatic and purpose-oriented hypotheses (see Mattessich 1964a, 30–45, 232–239, 419, 424–430).[8] Despite the fact that some experts began (during the 1960s and 1970s) to see that each valuation method might serve a different objective (e.g., as far as capital maintenance is concerned), many accountants seem to have continued their search for the "one and only correct" valuation method.

The next step was an article in which the separation between basic assumptions and their purpose-oriented interpretation was further analyzed. This article emphasized that *"the heart of the problem might rest in the difficulty to formulate specific well-defined purposes, and to match them to a set of specific hypotheses"* (Mattessich 1972, 478–479). As this article was accorded an official recognition (AICPA/AAA Award), there was some hope that the notion of a purpose-oriented (i.e., conditional–normative) accounting theory might now receive wider attention. Indeed, during the late 1970s and early 1980s, the complementary price-level adjustment standards promulgated by the Financial Accounting Standards Board (1979) and the Canadian Institute of Chartered Accountants (1982) could be interpreted as a step toward such a conditional–normative approach, as statement readers were offered a current-cost model, in addition to the historical-cost model. The *CICA Handbook* went even further by offering (in addition to the traditional basis) an option from three different valuation models. Although such options are still recommended in countries such as Canada and the United States, the "legislations" themselves have been abandoned under the impact of politics as well as the positive accounting trend (compare Beaver and Landsman [1983], whose publication may well have influenced the pertinent FASB decision).

Some reasons for the accountants' reluctance toward such an approach are the previously mentioned lack of training, insufficient background research, and too little interest in the pertinent philosophical foundations. The decisive factor, however, seems to have been the application of empirical–statistical methods (because of the quantitative revolution in the social sciences), which, during the 1970s absorbed the attention of most of the bright young accounting researchers. In the 1990s, the urgency of settling ethical and other normative problems in accounting offers new opportunities to explore a purpose-oriented approach, its norms, and means–end relations.

A glance at other applied sciences shows that, for example, practicing physicians, engineers, and so on, routinely apply means–end relations no less than practicing accountants do. This gave rise to investigating the nature of means–end relations from a more general point of view. It was done in Mattessich (1978a), where the epistemological problems of applied sciences in general were explored. This book (*Instrumental Reasoning and Systems Methodology*) was preceded by several papers (e.g., Mattessich 1974, 1977), all of which foreshadowed related ideas.

Hopefully, this section has dispelled the belief that CoNAM is merely a vision without any roots in present-day academic research. Although this book has a programmatic component, the conditional–normative methodology is based on a long-standing tradition in related disciplines and even in accounting literature. Here, one might add that the advent of *expert systems* in accounting may impart particular urgency to the search for the underlying norms and means–end relations. In medicine, for example, expert systems are capable of diagnosing diseases and recommending corresponding therapies. However, they do this not on a purely positive basis but by means of principles typical for an applied science. In these expert systems, objectives and means–end relations play a decisive role. The successful operation of expert systems in medicine, engineering, meteorology, and other applied sciences is irrefutable evidence that those systems are based on practical inference and some kind of conditional–normative methodology. In designing an expert system, one must first have a clear picture of the goal or goals which a particular system is to achieve. Furthermore, one must know the means to achieve this purpose efficiently, for example, whether it requires the maintenance of nominal financial capital, or real financial capital, physical capital and which inflation accounting model satisfies the particular capital maintenance required. Thus, the need for viable accounting expert systems may stimulate the interest in CoNAM and could become a welcome ally in the promotion of the latter.

ACCOUNTING REPRESENTATION AND REALITY

The problem whether accounting can or does represent reality and to what extent it may do so has engendered much controversy. Above all, one must make clear the meaning of *reality*. I have tried to explain this through the so-called "onion model" (see Chapter 3), which envisages reality as a hierarchy, consisting of many layers (from ultimate to physical, chemical, biological, mental, and social reality), each of which is characterized by its emergent properties, whereby a lower or more basic layer is enveloped by the next higher layer, as in an onion. Thus, it becomes essential to distinguish, for example, between physical and social reality and to qualify a certain manifestation of reality either as physical, social, and so on.

The second question concerns the distinction between a specific segment of reality and the attempt to represent it conceptually. As shown in Chapter 3, accountants occasionally confuse these two stages. Another problem, sometimes raised by members of the critical–interpretive camp, concerns the assertion that "accountants do not represent reality but create it." My answer is that they do both. Obviously, reality changes with every event and with every human thought and action. Hence, we are faced with a choice: either to abandon any kind of science (or other conceptual representation, like speaking and writing), out of fear that by doing so we might influence reality to such an extent that those representations are no longer accurate enough, or, alternatively, go ahead with our conceptualizations but later check and describe to what extent a particular measure or representation has influenced the situation, though sometimes this is not possible (compare the Heisenberg Principle of quantum mechanics). Thus, there is no reason to deny that accountants create new realities nor that they try to represent them; the two are not exclusive.

However, it is crucial to distinguish that segment of reality which serves as a tool of representation from the one that is the object of cognition and representation. This duality is so deeply rooted in our mental and linguistic habits that, without it, we could understand neither the nature of language nor that of science. Let us not forget that the conceptual structures which usually serve to represent reality always have some kind of physical manifestation (e.g., ink and paper, air and sound waves, tapes with magnetized dots, neurons and electric charges as well as neurons and neural transmitters, and so on). In other words, we cannot represent some parts of reality without employing other parts of it. Prehistoric people did this when they represented "real" economic goods and events by transferring "real" clay tokens from one container into another (a typical example of the transition from figurative or pictorial to conceptual thinking).

Humans simply cannot do without constantly representing the world around us by all kinds of things—foremost, by pictures and concepts—even if this reality is not static but dynamic. This includes accountants who try to represent segments of economic reality by accounts, financial statements, and so on. Take the following situation in which there is hardly a problem of distinguishing between observable economic phenomena and equally observable accounting abstractions describing such phenomena, for example, the economic phenomenon of a cash purchase of merchandise in the amount of $1,000. This is observable by the handing over of cash and merchandise and the accompanying bill. The accountant's abstraction is observed by his debiting in the ledger the inventory account and crediting the cash account in the amount of $1,000. Each is part of a different segment of "reality," but there is hardly any danger of confusing the two.

A more challenging question is whether the distinction between reality and its conceptual representation does not smack of Cartesian mind–body duality, untenable in the fact that mind itself is but a function of the body. I am far from invoking the Cartesian duality. In this book, the distinction between reality and its conceptual representation is based merely on the fact that the human mind, as physical as it might be, is a mirror for reflecting our environment and envisioning new possibilities for this environment. If there exists a pertinent fundamental question in accounting, it concerns the extent to which accountants can and do represent segments of reality. Is it a representation in a rigorous positive sense, in a pragmatic sense, or merely in the intuitive sense of everyday life? Let us try to answer this question.

The argument pivots on the schematic outline of Figure 11.1 in which the conceptual representation (as a special part of total reality) is shown on the left-hand side. Let us assume that positive accounting theory or any similar "pure" economic theory is capable of representing economic reality in a rigorous scientific sense by means of probabilistic present-value models or other sophisticated procedures. This positive representation is depicted in the small box at the top-left of Figure 11.1. Obviously, this is neither the way practical accountants represent

Figure 11.1
Conditional–Normative Accounting Theory and Reality

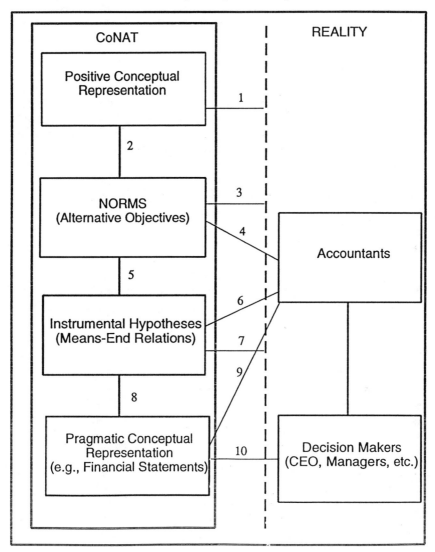

reality nor the way most academics recommend that it ought to be done. Accountants actually represent reality *pragmatically*, and this is depicted in the small box at the bottom (left).[9]

It seems that an explanation is required why and to what extent this pragmatic representation deviates from the positive one. Since a conditional–normative accounting theory (CoNAT, i.e., the large vertical rectangle on the left of Figure 11.1) embodies both such representations, it should be possible to reconcile the two, perhaps even analyzing where and why such a discrepancy occurs. In other words, one should be able to answer the perennial question, "Why does accounting practice seem to be so 'unrealistic' or inconsistent with a rigorous academic view?" Understanding the transition from the positive to the pragmatic representation (here indicated in several steps) may shed light on this important question. Figure 11.1 reveals concisely the major elements and relations involved in those kinds of representations.

For a "critical realist," the primary task of any positive science is the representation (i.e., the approximation) of the structure of a segment of reality as accurately as possible under the optimal research conditions available at a certain time. In the case of an applied science, an additional constraint is imposed on such a representation. Its accuracy is subject to the cost–benefit criterion and other norms (see relations 2 to 4 that follow). This assures, for example, that in the long-run, the costs of such representation do not exceed the expected benefits.

Relation 1 (between positive conceptual representation and reality) must be established by empirical research and corresponds in its broad features to the factual research of the received view. It corresponds to all the relations shown in Figure 7.1, which, in turn, can be regarded as presenting further and more formal details of the same process. To illustrate the situation, let us assume that the scientifically correct valuation model is some kind of "present-value model" (be it deterministic or probabilistic), even if unknown for situations of imperfect and incomplete markets. This model might be applied for positive representation but not for a pragmatic representation (the latter is shown at the bottom-left side of Figure 11.1). Such a positive representation is supposed to bathe the pertinent segment of reality in a fairly objective light and in all of its facets. But can it do that; is it not based on too many simplifying assumptions?[10]

Relation 2 (between positive representation and the set of feasible norms or objectives) contains various competing as well as complementary value judgments. From this pool of relevant norms, some will be chosen to determine (in relations or steps 5 and 8) the pragmatic representation suitable to a specific information purpose and managerial objective. Among these norms are constraints such as cost–benefit and "lower of cost or market value," for example.

Relation 3 (between norms and reality) is necessary to ensure the incorporation of a feasible set of objectives (during the standard-setting process or while choosing the relevant capital maintenance concept, and so on). The objectives are found in the social reality of the needs and desires of individuals as well as of entire groups of persons.

Relation 4 (between norms and accountants) is merely an extension or subdivision of relation 3, but focuses on norms arising from accountants rather than the public.

Relation 5 (formulating means–end relations on the basis of chosen norms) is particularly important. Everyday life constantly operates informally with such means–end relations, yet the logical gap between "ought" and "is" (to be bridged in step 2) has always been an impediment to the direct scientific formulation of those relations. Another reason for the traditional neglect of empirical means–end research may be concisely described by paraphrasing a saying of Bertrand Russell: It is easier to scientifically discover truth than usefulness. In everyday life, one handles those means–end problems by trial and error; but the challenging question is whether there exist more systematic ways to analyze and solve those problems. This becomes possible only by including value judgments in the pertinent theory or model.

Relation 6 (between instrumental hypotheses and accountants) arises from the empirical search for and testing of formalized means–end relations. It also refers to their use by practitioners. In present-day accounting practice, these relations are often implied rather than explicitly stated.

Relation 7 (between means–end relations and reality in general) arises out of the fact that the implicit or explicit means–end relations of accounting are determined by a wide setting that may reach far beyond the accounting community.

Relation 8 (between means–end relations and pragmatic conceptual representation) constitutes the last link in the chain of possibly reconciling the positive to the pragmatic representation of financial reality. This leads to the box reflecting actual accounting records and financial statements, all of which are, obviously, normatively tainted.

Relation 9 (between accountants and the pragmatic conceptual representation) is familiar. It constitutes the keeping of accounts and the construction of financial statements, as well as the pertinent auditing activity. Such a pragmatic representation, in contrast to the positive one (discussed in relation 1), does not aim at an objective and all-illuminating picture. It is satisfied with shedding light only on certain facets, illuminating the pertinent segment from a single side. That is the very reason why we need different accounting models for different purposes, why we must illuminate "our" reality separately from many sides. Through such variety of viewpoints, we may reveal more of this segment than a positive representation could ever do. This metaphor might be worth careful contemplation. In Figure 7.1, we saw (on the representational side) a reduction from the "theoretical" to the "nontheoretical" level, while here we see a further restriction (through the preceding introduction of value judgments and other constraints) from the nontheoretical level to the more specific, pragmatic level.

Relation 10 (between other decision makers and the pragmatic representation) is nothing but an extension of relation 9. Here, accounting records and financial statements are connected with management and the financial community at large.

FUTURE REQUIREMENTS

1. The fact that means–end relations are multi-ended and often difficult to analyze, formulate, and confirm by supporting evidence should be a challenge for science rather than a deterrent. The confirmation of such instrumental hypotheses may be statistical but need not be so. The kind of testing will depend on the circumstances and must be in accord with the required degree of rigor and the methodology appropriate for the specific purpose.[11]

Apart from some limited mathematical techniques, as offered in operations research and decision theory, in most cases one will have to rely on empirical methods. Although statistical techniques may prove most helpful, nonstatistical methods—such as case and field studies, heuristics, systematized trial-and-error procedures, and systems methodology—can hardly be dispensed with in any applied science. The solutions of the latter are rarely perfect; their degree of accuracy, for example, is always constrained by cost–benefit and other considerations.

2. The analysis of value judgments and objectives and the formulation of an entire hierarchy of goals is another important requirement. There exist numerous attempts along these lines (compare Backer 1966; Heinen 1978; American Institute of Certified Public Accountants 1973; Financial Acccounting Standards Board 1976b, 1978, 1980a), but most of those efforts were limited to financial accounting, and none of them express any awareness of the problems involved in means–end relations. Those previous studies could possibly be adapted, revised, or extended for the purpose of CoNAM.

3. A major argument for pursuing such a methodology is the simple fact that (wherever accounting objectives are concerned) the practitioners usually find means to achieve their goals, however imperfect this may be. If such means–end relations exist in actual practice, then science should be able to analyze the process of their creation, to show whether the means are effective, how to formalize the relations, and hopefully, how to improve them.

4. The crucial prerequisite for any success along those lines will be the cooperation of leading accounting academics. This kind of research requires a great variety of empirical and analytical expertise, as well as elaborate investigations, often of an unconventional sort. A single person or even a small group cannot master such a task. Ultimately, it will depend on the entire accounting community whether they can muster the will to bring the persistent normative problems of their discipline under an "objective" umbrella.

Recapitulation: Absolute normative theories (e.g., ethical–normative or pragmatic–normative ones) might be considered as "unscientific," since they are neither confirmable nor refutable. This can be remedied by a conditional–normative methodology. The latter reveals the specific objective as only one among several alternatives and requires the formulation of means–end relations, indicating the means that lead (under specific circumstances) to a stipulated goal. These relations, so characteristic for the applied sciences, must be found and empirically confirmed. Usually, their determination and confirmation is difficult and imprecise and goes beyond the bounds of positive methodology.

While other applied sciences have taken advantage of exploiting conditional–normative methodology, the received view of accounting has spurned any attempt to go beyond its positive basis. In medicine, for example, expert systems reflect the value judgments and means–end relations; and in legal science, the logic of norms has been explored and applied. Can accounting afford to shut itself off from this trend and behave as though it were a pure science? Have our leading researchers learned nothing from the history of science and the price to be paid for a narrow outlook? Who believes that mathematical models and statistical empiricism can solve all accounting problems? Are not the many contradictions between theory and practice vivid evidence that in accounting we have *not* done enough to serve the practitioner, the stockholder, and, above all, society at large? Have accountants lost their initiative to experiment? Do they not see that an applied science cannot be conducted in the same fashion as a pure science, or do they really believe that accounting is an instance of the latter?

Accounting shows the major characteristics of an applied science (resting only on law statements of other disciplines, such as economics and the behavioral sciences; containing many norms; depending on cost-benefit considerations; and being researched at professional faculties). Therefore, a general framework of accounting requires more than a positive basis. The normative extension (means-end relations, and so on) of accounting, though practiced and taught informally, is neglected in conventional accounting theory. Furthermore, there are many present and future accounting needs (particularly those not satisfied by neoclassical economics) that may encourage the application of a conditional-normative accounting methodology, for example, those expressed by the FASB: closing the gap between practice and theory, ethical considerations, greater emphasis of policy research, the endeavor to construct accounting and auditing expert systems, the quest for the most realistic representations permitted under a cost-benefit criterion, the revelation of hidden value judgments in standard setting, and so on.

Obviously, the implementation of such a methodology would have to be step by step, but even that of the first step—clear disclosure of all the pertinent value judgments—would already constitute a major advance. The resulting conditional-normative framework would conform to the requirements of the applied sciences in general; it thus may have to be satisfied with less rigorous testing procedures than those of the pure sciences, though the resulting theories need not forego objectivity.

NOTES

This chapter is (with some modifications) mainly based on my paper "Conditional-Normative Accounting Methodology: Incorporating Value Judgments and Means-End Relations of an Applied Science" in *Accounting, Organizations and Society* (Mattessich 1995).

1. I accept Bunge's definition of an applied science as "the investigation of cognitive problems with possible practical relevance. . . . Doing applied science, like doing basic science, is conducting research aiming at acquiring knowledge. The differences between applied research and basic research are differences in intellectual debt to basic science in scope, and in aim. . . . That is, applied research employs knowledge acquired in basic research. . . . The applied scientist is supposed to make discoveries but is not expected to discover any deep properties or general laws. He does not intend to" (Bunge 1983b, 208–209).

2. Archer, for example, states:

Insistence on intellectual autonomy for accounting would, however, be unrealistic and stultifying, as was recognized by Canning (1929) and others many years ago. . . . Finally the proposal [for what Archer calls the "gross balance approach"] can be regarded as reductionist only if *the status of accounting as an applied discipline* is denied, which is hardly possible. Numerous accounting thinkers have recognized that the conceptual foundations of accounting are to be sought in economics, law, social psychology, socio-linguistics and other branches of the social sciences. (Archer 1993, 108–109, italics added)

3. To avoid semantic confusion one distinguishes between "scientific laws," which are presumed structures of reality (related to the ontological question) and "law statements," which are attempts of the pure sciences to conceptualize those structures (the epistemic question).

4. The Financial Accounting Standards Board conceptual framework contains, according to Mozes, a methodology for selecting accounting rules of which "the first provides the standard-setters' objective and the second provides the accounting data qualities necessary to achieve that objective" (Mozes 1992, 94). The FASB, in contrast to the present study, focuses mainly on one major objective, namely, to procure in the financial statements information that helps to assess the amounts, timing, and uncertainty of future cash flows to an enterprise.

5. This must not be misinterpreted as promoting indiscriminately long-term over short-term wealth and profit maximization. There are situations, particularly on the microeconomic level, where short-term maximization is appropriate.

6. Ecological economics could be regarded as an extension of traditional economics (see such early attempts as those by Hotelling 1931; Arrow and Fisher 1974; and Dasgupta and Heal 1979, as well as later works, such as Daly et al. 1989; Pearce and Turner 1989; Constanza 1991; and others) and environmental accounting as its counterpart in our field (see Ahmad et al. 1989).

7. Normative (or deontic) logic comprises the logic of actions, imperatives, commands, and other normative statements. For an overview of deontic logic, see the anthologies edited by Rescher (1966b) and Hilpinen (1971); for individual contributions to deontic logic, practical inferences, and the logic of action, see von Wright (e.g., 1968, 1983); and for the logic of commands, see Rescher (1966a).

8. If *Accounting and Analytical Methods* (Mattessich 1964a) found wide response in the accounting literature (particularly in the 1960s and 1970s), it was partly because of its introduction of rigorous analytical methods and financial simulation models to our discipline and partly because of the formulation of "basic assumptions" and their axiomatization. *However, the crucial aspect of this book, that of launching a purpose-oriented and hence conditional–normative theory of accounting, aroused little attention,* though the need for a functional and purpose-oriented approach was emphasized in the Introduction (pp. 8–9) and elaborated in Chapter 7 (namely, pp. 232–239) of the book.

9. Murphy (1992) calls such pragmatic accounting representation "instrumentalism," which he juxtaposes to "realism." Figure 11.1 and the pertinent discussion try to show that these two ways of representing financial reality are not unconnected and that the relation between them (i.e., involved in the transition from a positive to a pragmatic one) is at least as important as the gap that separates them.

10. Compare Scott, who remarks with reference to *present-value accounting* and *market-value accounting*: "The problem is that in a non-ideal world these valuation bases need not be well defined and, indeed, market value cannot be relied upon to equal present value" (Scott 1994, 64).

11. Mattessich (1978a, namely: 1–51, 247–323) explains the nature of "systems methodology" and why applied sciences are more amenable to it than to a positive methodology.

CHAPTER 12

Summary and Conclusion

ACCOUNTABILITY, TOLERANCE, AND SYNTHESIS

In this book, I have tried to present a critical analysis of those accounting issues that I consider fundamental, even at the risk of returning to a few questions that some experts may deem to be obsolete or irrelevant. The problems of accountability and disclosing value judgments have been the main themes (in many variations), just as the aim toward a *synthesis* of extreme positions (as that between American positive accounting theory and the British critical–interpretive school) was the underlying base that sustained the entire composition. This led to the choice of different goals by the information user and, in turn, to a research methodology suitable for finding and testing the means that could effectively attain those goals. Such a "tolerant" solution would encourage accountants to design models for different situations, offering "customized" or even "tailor-made" wares.

The first chapter drew attention to the fairly widespread feeling that accounting might be in a crisis. Thus, it was advisable to listen to various experts on this very issue. My own preliminary diagnoses pointed at three related predicaments: first, a legislative and social exigency (e.g., in corporate governance, the auditor's dependence on the management of the client–firm instead of its shareholders, and the trend of public accounting firms to shift from the risky business of auditing into the safe havens of management consulting); second, a moral and spiritual exigency (rapidly declining business morality, including that in public accounting, insufficient research and teaching in ethical conduct and professional responsibility, and so on); and third, an *academic exigency* (intolerance and disunity among academic ranks and allocating disproportionate resources to the attempt of converting a basically applied discipline into a positive science). This led to a neglect of other research areas (in accounting objectives, means–end relations, accountability issues, and the like) and created an ever-widening gap between practice and academia.

10,000 YEARS HENCE

I cannot speak for the reader, but for me this was not a passage through the dry and forlorn desert of a technical field; rather, it was an adventurous journey with unexpected turns and a glimpse of the cultural depth illuminating significant aspects of our subject matter. All too often, such features are hidden beneath a plain surface that lends credence to the proverbial picture of the "dusty accountant" with a quill pen behind a large ear befitting an "auditor." As distorted as this picture may be, it is correct insofar as accounting literally arose out of the clay or dust of Mesopotamia and the Fertile Crescent on the border of a vast desert during the 5,000-year period between 8000 B.C and 3000 B.C.

This relatively recent archeological discovery was discussed in Chapter 2, almost at the beginning of our wandering or even our "wondering"; for only an unimaginative soul can fail to marvel about the immense consequences that token accounting—with its simple clay symbols—had upon the invention of writing, abstract counting, the permanent representation of physical as well as social reality, socioeconomic and legalistic behavior, and humanity's cultural development in general. As an additional bonus, we even learned that the ancient Sumerians already had a prototype of *double-entry* record keeping 5,000 years ago. In prehistoric times, mankind started out to make its members *accountable* by keeping enduring records; but 10,000 years hence, we are still struggling with this task—now with highly sophisticated means yet still unable to maintain a satisfactory degree of accountability.

INCOME AND OWNERS' EQUITY ARE REAL

Chapter 3 tried to show that accountants can escape from reality issues no less than from reality itself. How can one understand the representation of something if one lacks a clear notion of that which is to be represented? The first step to a more satisfactory solution is to ask what one means by the expression "reality" when dealing in the market, when buying and acquiring property or selling it, and when incurring debts or granting credits. Out of this quest arose my metaphor of the onion model of reality. This expression conveys that total reality may be compared to an onion consisting of many layers—from the ultimate reality (of pure energy or quantum gravity), to physical, chemical, biological, mental, and social reality. Each of these layers envelops the preceding one but possesses its own emergent properties (i.e., new "specific chunks" of reality). For accountants, the distinction between the physical reality of commodities, machineries, buildings, and so on, versus the social reality of debt and ownership claims seems to be particularly important. Such a distinction removes the misconception that an ownership claim and income (as one of its possible increments) are nothing but concepts without any underlying reality. It also helps to resolve the problem of values and valuation in accounting because it interprets subjective values as conceptual representations of personal preferences (belonging to psychic reality) and objective values as market manifestations, hence representing a social reality. The existence of those values is independent of the skill or refinement with which they are determined; hence, the claim that the values contained in financial statements do not represent anything real is based in the confusion between the ontological issue of whether something is real (e.g., the price one paid or the preference one possesses) and the methodological issue concerning the accuracy with which those values can be determined. Deficiency in the process of "measurement" does not mean that reality suddenly vanishes; it merely means that reality is too roughly approximated or represented. Besides, accounting practice can hardly aspire to any precise or scientific representation of reality; we must be satisfied with pragmatic representation that depends on the cost–benefit criterion and other value judgments. The question of how much one can afford to spend in determining accounting values obviously depends on the objective and the benefit one expects from such measurement.

For all too long, accountants (and I do not exclude myself) had the vague notion that the asset side of the balance sheet (with the exception of such claims as "accounts receivable," and the like) points to concrete things, hence to reality, while the *equity side* is abstract, hence purely conceptual. This confusion of taking the dichotomy of "physical versus social" for that of "real versus conceptual" may have led to the assertion by some scholars that capital and income are purely abstract notions that have no reality behind them. As for *accountability*, it too requires the comparing of reality with the representation that gives account of those events. Pictures are one such form of representation, and it is no coincidence that Sumerian accountants experimented with this mode before converting it into a conceptual one.

The conclusion of all this is that there is little use pondering about the essence of ultimate reality but a great need to clarify the layers of physical, mental, and social reality with their emergent properties that relate to accounting. Only then will accountants be spared the confusion of those different dichotomies. Only then will they cease to doubt that such variables as income and owner's equity (including their valuations) are not mere fictions but notions backed by reality. Only then may they agree that the methodological problem of measurement must be separated from the ontological problem of existence.

FOUNDATIONS ON SAND OR ROCK?

In drawing conclusions from Chapters 4 and 5, the more obvious aspect is that most of the conceptual and foundational issues of accounting were laid during the last one hundred years or so, though this process has hardly been brought to an end. Our discipline cannot claim to have reached its adulthood, but the adoption of analytical methods, empirical and statistical techniques, computer simulation methods, and so on, has created an impressive arsenal for mastering a challenging future. All this requires firm foundations, and we can hardly be satisfied with what has been achieved thus far.

Apart from attempting to clarify important conceptual and measurement issues, the emphasis in Chapter 4 is on the need for specific interpretations in accounting (as a preparation for later chapters) and the discussion of the concept of *duality*. To understand this notion in all of its dimensions, one must begin by distinguishing physical duality (e.g., the transfer of concrete goods) from two social dualities (debts and ownership claims) and examine the relations between those dualities as manifested in the three principles of input–output, symmetry, and conservation.

This and the related task of formalization is pursued in Chapter 5, which begins with an overview of postulational and axiomatic attempts made in accounting during this century. The main emphasis is on purpose-oriented interpretation, made possible by separating placeholder assumptions from other basic assumptions. The former provide the flexibility which exchangeable instrumental hypotheses (formalized relations connecting efficient means to the desired ends) afford. To illustrate this distinction, major accounting axioms and theorems were presented (as well as a lengthy proof in the Appendix). The axiomatic approach of accounting, sidetracked in recent years, is only one major aspect of the progress of analytical methods in our discipline. Another is the application of information economics as well as formalized agency theory to accounting. For this reason, a concise historical overview has been presented; it reaches from the pioneering works of Jacob Marschak and the Nobel laureate George Stigler to Demski and Feltham, the two most recent recipients of the prestigious AAA Award for Seminal Contributions to Accounting Literature.

An Appendix presented the detailed sketch for a proof of the "double-classification theorem," relating to the duality notion of Chapter 4. This proof is important, not so much because it shows a previously deemed axiom to be a theorem—and certainly not because it proves that the value of all debits equals the value of all credits—but because it traces, in a strictly logical way, the conceptual abstraction of accounting transactions of a single entity, to real economic transactions (transfers of goods and the creation or redemption of ownership and debt claims) between two or more entities. As this proof is somewhat esoteric, I relegated it to an Appendix yet hope that it may be appreciated by some of the readers.

FROM VALUATION MODELS TO
INSTRUMENTAL HYPOTHESES

Chapter 6 aimed at explaining the notion of instrumental hypothesis (a formalized means–end relation), which is crucial for understanding subsequent discussions, particularly those of Chapter 11. This concept was illustrated through a discussion of various valuation and capital maintenance models, each of them serving a different purpose. Such an approach fulfilled a secondary objective, the recapitulation of current-value and inflation accounting with its subtle concepts. First, there is the distinction between various capital gains, such as real versus fictitious, monetary versus nonmonetary, and realized versus unrealized. Furthermore, there is the distinction between various capital-maintenance concepts: nominal financial versus real financial versus physical, and so on. This "secondary" discussion seemed to be desirable for three reasons: (1) the neglect of inflation accounting issues during the last decade, (2) the basic nature of those valuation issues for accounting issues in general, and (3) the enduring importance of inflation accounting in international comparisons (e.g., with Latin American countries, particularly Mexico, where regulations of inflation accounting play an important role).

After discussing a schematic comparison of six famous valuation models— such as (1) acquisition cost accounting, (2) Schmidt's ([1921] 1953) current-value accounting (CVA), (3 and 4) Edwards and Bell's (1961) nominal and real CVA, (5) the American Institute of Certified Public Accountants (1963) general price-level accounting (GPL), and (6) the Financial Accounting Standards Board (1979) CVA—the chapter showed the connection between valuation models and capital maintenance models, on one side, and between the latter and different contexts and objectives of the firm, on the other side. While the former relationship may be analytical, the latter is empirical. The future challenge is to express those relations in form of instrumental hypotheses which should become as testable as are positive hypotheses. While the latter are based only on cause and effect, the former also take into account relations of ends to means. The need for such purpose-oriented hypotheses is frequently manifested in the literature (e.g., in the "decision-usefulness approach"). For example, in a conference dealing with the problem of capital maintenance (organized by Sterling and Lemke [1982]), the majority of participants expressed themselves in favor of a plurality of capital-maintenance concepts, each concept being dependent on a different context or objective. The chapter tried to articulate this issue by comparing two positive hypotheses, presented by Watts (1992), with "corresponding" instrumental hypotheses. The latter are richer and are endowed with objectives (objective functions), which makes them suitable candidates for a conditional–normative theory (see Chapter 11).

POST-KUHNIAN PHILOSOPHY AND ACCOUNTING RESEARCH PROGRAMS

Chapters 7 and 8 belong together. Chapter 7 explained recent trends in the philosophy of science, in particular, with regard to paradigms and research programs (or traditions), while Chapter 8 investigated to what extent different research traditions are manifested in accounting. The former concerns different views on what constitutes a theory and how various paradigms or, more precisely, "research programs" (and their subunits) compete among each other. Chapter 7 offers such a survey, reaching from Kuhn's notion of scientific paradigms to Lakatos' evolutionary programmism, Stegmüller's epistemological structuralism, and other approaches. Those later developments not only have extended or even superseded Kuhn's view but show *some* agreement among each other. They regard a theory not as simply being a set of definitions, axioms, and theorems but as a complex network of many theory elements (i.e., subtheories). Each theory may stand in fierce competition with other such theories, while competition between theory elements (within one theory) seems to be less significant.

Epistemic structuralism (not to be confused with linguistic and anthropological structuralism), developed by Sneed, Stegmüller, Balzer, and others, rejects the positivistic tradition of regarding the distinction between theoretical and observational variables as absolute (i.e., if a variable is theoretical in one theory, it must be so in all theories; the same would hold for observational variables). The structuralists regard "theoretical" and "nontheoretical" variables as being theory dependent (i.e., a variable may be theoretical in one theory but could be nontheoretical in another). Apart from this, most epistemic structuralists share a Platonist view and regard all concepts (even empty ones) as real or—what amounts to the same—see all reality as conceptual. This may explain why they speak of "nontheoretical" instead of "observational" variables.

From a realist standpoint (which the majority of scientists seem to share), such a view is untenable. Therefore, I tried to extend the structuralist's distinction between "theoretical versus nontheoretical" (on the conceptual side) by a second dichotomy, that of "observational versus nonobservational" (on the reality side). That means, on one hand, theoretical variables would be identical to pure concepts, and nontheoretical variables would be identical to concepts backed by reality (as discussed in Chapter 3); on the other hand, observational variables would be those accessible to observation, while nonobservational variables are not or are not yet so (see Figure 7.1). From an accountant's point of view, typical theoretical variables would be price–earnings ratios (one cannot observe the ratios, only prices and earnings), profit margins, and other purely conceptual coefficients; nontheoretical notions would be accounting transactions, evaluations, and other variables that have a direct correspondence to reality. Typical observational variables would be actual inventories; equipment; buildings; debt relations, as well as property claims and their increments; commodity transfers; and even the values expressing real preferences and exchange transactions. Last, to the nonobservational variables would belong cash flows still to occur, other future events or indirectly observable realities, or even those beyond our present power of observation.

In Chapter 8, I started from previous attempts of distinguishing between various accounting paradigms, such as Wells (1976), Belkaoui (1981), and Butterworth and Falk (1986). The last-mentioned effort became my basis for making the transition from the Kuhnian to the post-Kuhnian approach in accounting. Accordingly, we may discern between three major research traditions: the stewardship program, the valuation–investment program, and the less-developed objective-oriented program. The first two programs are each divided into three phases.

The *stewardship program* sees accountability and its monitoring as the primary task of accounting. Its first phase, the "plain periodization approach," is characterized by such well-known principles as the acquisition cost basis, the cost–revenue matching or accrual basis, the ongoing enterprise assumption, and the stewardship function. This phase has covered most of accounting practice until now; but in academic circles, it was largely pushed aside since the early 1970s. In the 1980s and 1990s, the stewardship program experienced a revival in its second and third phase. This is not a continuous sequence; in the meantime, the valuation–investment program (see next paragraph) became quite prominent. The revival, or even renaissance, of the stewardship program was a result of the introduction of agency theory to accounting. Experts became aware that the basic goal of this theory, namely, accountability, coincides with that of the plain periodization phase, even if assumptions differed. A further extension occurred by merging information economics with the agency approach, leading to the analytical agency–contract theory, which constitutes the third phase of the stewardship program. Although there may exist minor competition between those phases, the actual struggle for a dominant paradigm is the one between the three research programs. I have tried to convey the essence of agency theory (e.g., Figure 8.1) as well as the transition from the basic information-economic model to the basic agency model and, finally, to the basic agency-information model by means of concise equations.

The second, or valuation–investment, program sees the primary task of accounting not in accountability but in evaluating assets, equities, and income, all for the ultimate purpose of proper resource allocation, hence investment decisions. This program goes back to the economics of Böhm-Bawerk, Irving Fisher, and others and begins in accounting with Canning (1929), or possibly even with Schmidt (1953 [1921]). The first phase of the second program, the present-value and current-value approach, developed relatively slowly from the 1920s to the 1970s. The real break came through financial economics in the second phase, which Butterworth and Falk (1986) called the "risk-sharing approach." Such financial achievements as modern portfolio theory, capital–asset pricing theory, and so on, played a decisive role in this development. Above all, it changed the deterministic basis of the present-value model to a probabilistic one, introducing the notion of risk (and its distinction between systematic and unsystematic risk) as an essential factor. The last phase, the capital-market approach (compare Butterworth and Falk 1986), is a natural continuation of the previous phase. It pivots on the efficient-market hypothesis (and its various interpretations), and is based on the statistical–empirical accounting research introduced in the late 1960s by Ball and Brown (1968), Beaver (1968), and further developed by many others.

The third, or objective-oriented, approach is more a program than a tradition— in spite of going back more than seventy years to Clark (1923) and his call:

"different costs for different purposes." Although the need for such purpose orientation made itself repeatedly felt in the accounting literature, little systematic development has occurred. My own modest efforts toward the realization of such a program can be found in the following suggestions: (1) to separate placeholder assumptions from other basic accounting assumptions (Mattessich 1964a, 1972; see also Chapter 5 of this volume); (2) the introduction of instrumental hypotheses (for which placeholder assumptions provide the basis [see also Chapter 6]); and (3) the outline of a conditional–normative accounting methodology (Mattessich 1995; see also Chapter 11). Such an approach could even eliminate the perceived conflict between the stewardship program and the valuation–investment program. Since both pursue legitimate accounting goals, the objective-oriented program would tolerate each program as a kind of "phase," provided neither of the two would claim sole dominion. This not only sounds more reasonable but is pretty much in accord with present-day accounting practice where, among many other objectives, the goals of both programs are being pursued.

THE EMPIRICAL–POSITIVE WAVE

To create an "empirical link" between the historical and analytical presentation of Chapters 1 to 8 and the more methodological considerations of Chapters 10 and 11, I inserted this concise reflection on statistical–empirical research and positive accounting theory (PAT). In a way, it offers a view from the "outside," even if the statistical–empirical revolution in accounting of the late 1960s has always fascinated me from a historical point of view. The sections dealing with PAT, and my reservations about its methodology, are a necessary introduction for a better understanding of Chapter 11, which (be it now controversial or not) might become the most important part of this book.

I could not refrain from drawing the reader's attention to the "roundabout way" in which the crucial paper by Ball and Brown (1968) was published and how, despite some resistance from the editor and reviewers of a leading journal, it—together with some other works—not only revolutionized accounting but also put it under the joint suzerainty of financial economics and the behavioral sciences. Thus, I tried to summarize succinctly the highlights of empirical accounting research.

I offered a similar summary for PAT, so closely associated with empirical–statistical research that it can be distinguished from it only by its radical methodology. Indeed, for me, PAT is interesting mainly because of this extreme position. The latter is diametrically opposed to my own view (despite some overlap [see Chapter 11 on CoNAM]). At the risk of some possible misinterpretation, I considered the following items crucial for Watts and Zimmerman's methodological position (each, in the main text, followed by some critical remarks):

1. *The rejection of prescriptions in accounting theory.* A pure or positive science can afford to concentrate solely on prediction and explanation; whether accounting theory can imitate this is another question. Above all, this depends on the scientific status; and it is far from certain that accounting is, or can ever be, a

positive science. This is by no means a settled issue because it cannot be decided by a small group of accounting academics. The decision depends on many circumstances, not least on the verdict of the scientific community in general. Considering the need of accounting practice for prescriptions, it seems strange that leading theorists should want to exclude objectives and objective functions from the premises of accounting theories.

2. *Chicago-based economics as the most desirable basis for accounting theory.* This raises several questions, the most crucial of which is whether or to what extent this economics takes care of the many social, ethical, and environmental issues, as well as multiple goals, all relevant to accounting. It appears to me that such issues are insufficiently taken care of, which would make this neoclassical basis useful, at best, for short-term but not for long-term considerations.

3. *Overemphasis on prediction as the fundamental goal of accounting and its theory.* This overemphasis seems critical in the face of new insights about the precarious nature of predictions in science in general, in particular, in the biological and social sciences. It seems to me that the predictions of PAT, for example, are as fragile as some predictions made by other applied sciences (e.g., medicine).

4. *To regard methodological disputes as fruitless (and the implication that PAT might possess the only methodology appropriate for accounting).* Such considerations and disputes are necessary in every scientific discipline as none has a claim to absolute truth in methodology, for the latter itself is a normative field. The need for such disputes becomes all the more urgent when scholars try to impose the methodology of basic science upon an applied one.

5. *Predominant reliance on statistical procedures in testing hypotheses.* Although statistical procedures are prominent these days, most sciences have a vast arsenal of methods for testing (i.e., verifying, confirming, refuting, and so on) their theories. An example of an important nonstatistical testing procedure is the "coherence test." It checks how well a hypothesis fits into the overall scheme of a theory or entire discipline. Rarely is such a test emphasized in present-day accounting theory.

6. *Exclusion of value judgments from premises of accounting theory.* This is related to item 1, and the objections made there hold here as well. Additional dangers of excluding value judgments from accounting theory are (a) the concealing of the actual objectives pursued, substituting for them pretended goals; (b) ignorance about means–end relations; and (c) burdening practitioners with the difficult task of creating the connection between a positive theory and the ultimate prescriptions needed in accounting.

7. *The attempt to make a positive science out of a basically applied discipline such as accounting.* This inevitably leads to the confusion of accounting proper with sub areas of pure sciences such as "accounting sociology," the "behavioral science of accounting," the "economics of accounting," or the like. Pure sciences dealing with human beings (as in economics) are usually accompanied by prescriptive branches and theories (e.g., normative economics). Thus, it is surprising that a similar scientific status should be denied to accounting, the very essence

of which is normative. To ban the latter from our discipline would be as nonsensical as declaring medicine to be a nonprescriptive science.

FROM TRADITIONAL NORMATIVE THEORIES TO A CONDITIONAL–NORMATIVE APPROACH

Again, I grouped two chapters together. Chapter 10 sketched the evolution of various approaches to normative accounting issues, while Chapter 11 tried to outline the need for a conditional–normative accounting methodology and the problems faced in developing it. I have distinguished between three types of normative accounting theories (ethical, pragmatic, and conditional ones). Ethical–normative theories can be found by Schär and Nicklisch (and fleetingly also by Schmalenbach) in the first two or three decades of the twentieth century—something less known in North America than on the European continent.

The pragmatic–normative accounting theories (from the 1950s to the 1970s) of the Anglo-American literature are still well known and, in some circles, even notorious. They are connected with such prominent names as Chambers, Edwards and Bell, Ijiri, Sprouse and Moonitz, Sterling, and others. These theories are called normative by Watts and Zimmerman and other disciples of PAT, but some experts might question whether they are not actually nonstatistical empirical theories. However, they do seem to contain pragmatic value judgments—often hidden ones. Above all, each theory seems to have clung to a particular predominant valuation hypothesis: *current exit value*, in the case of Chambers and Sterling; *current entry value*, by Edwards and Bell as well as Sprouse and Moonitz; and *acquisition cost*, in Ijiri's case.

During the 1970s two branches of the behavioral–organizational trend returned to the ethical–normative direction. While the mainstream of this trend belongs to the empirical approach, two branches (the more moderate "interpretive perspective" and the "critical–radical perspective"), both summarized under the heading, "The British critical–interpretive school," have displayed a distinctive ethical–normative flavor, even if its disciples showed little awareness of the earlier German ethical–normative school.

Normative theories are subjective by the very fact that they favor a specific set of norms that is in competition with other such sets. This loss of objectivity has led to a rejection of "absolute" normative theories by the scientific community, the prestige of which is built on the claim to provide objective theories. To cope with this dilemma, an applied science must clearly stipulate the specific objective to be pursued and then search (along analytical as well as empirical lines) for efficient means to attain this particular end. To outline such a possibility for accounting has been the task of Chapter 11.

In Chapter 11, I tried to outline a conditional–normative accounting methodology, the major features of which are (1) recognition that academic accounting is an applied science, (2) more attention to value judgments and the peculiarities of the hypotheses that relate means to ends, (3) recognition that the neoclassical economic basis of present accounting theory is too narrow to accommodate the many goals and subgoals pursued in accounting, and (4) the need for a comprehensive catalog of objectives and the corresponding (empirically determined) means–end relations. This catalog might serve the "customers" of accounting either in a "tailor-made" or "customized" (standardized or semistandardized) way, supplying them information that fits their particular needs and value judgments.

To convey this, I first showed that, in spite of the occasional talk about objectives in academic accounting, accountants rarely think in terms of means–end relations in any direct way. The prime prerequisite to reach any kind of goal is either to know the means required to attain it or to find them. Second, some reflections were made on different attitudes (of the pragmatic–normative, the ethical–normative, the positive, and the conditional–normative camps) toward value judgments in academic accounting. Third, I presented arguments offering strong evidence for the applied nature of academic accounting: the absence of accounting laws in the truly scientific sense, the need for norms and prescriptions in accounting, the importance of cost–benefit and similar considerations, and the predominance of professional faculties in the teaching and research of accounting. Fourth, I tried to show that a conditional–normative theory can be regarded as being objective (despite possessing value judgments as premises): first, by clearly revealing the value judgments or objective pursued, and second, by employing scientific (i.e., analytical and, above all, empirical) methods in determining the means capable of attaining those objectives.

Further consideration was given to (a) the need for recognizing the plurality of accounting objectives and the development of a systematic hierarchy of accounting goals, objectives, subobjectives, and so on; (b) the present status of CoNAM and its relation to the search for a logic of norms (deontology or related attempts) in such disciplines as jurisprudence, operations research, and philosophy; (c) a comparison with other applied sciences which, apparently, have no need to convert their own theories into positive ones, as they recognize that their positive basis can be found only in such pure sciences as physics, chemistry, biology, economics, the behavioral sciences, and the like.

The penultimate section tried to expose two different ways in which the financial and economic aspects of social reality can find conceptual representation. First, there is the attempt of economics (including the economics of accounting) toward a positive representation of values and similar realities; second, there is the endeavor of a pragmatic representation in accounting and its everyday practice (see Figure 11.1). It is particularly important to explore the difference between these two modes of representation and whether or how they are linked to each other. According to my preliminary explorations, the major links are the norms or value judgments introduced by the pragmatic process, as well as its means–end relations.

The last section of Chapter 11 summarizes and points at some difficulties that CoNAM would need to overcome or cope with (e.g., inferring the proper means from ends; the multi-endedness of means–end relations; development of a proper hierarchy of objectives; systematization of what practitioners often do instinctively; cooperation among academics, as well as between town and gown).

Apart from having tried to clarify a series of basic concepts and relations in this book, I have presented arguments and evidence in support of the following *main hypotheses*:

1. There is a fundamental difference between, on one side, the economics (and sociology) of accounting, which may be positive, and, on the other side, accounting as an applied science. The latter can be understood only from a conditional–normative point of view and is academically not *negative* but has its criteria of objectivity no less than any other science.

2. Economics of accounting alone cannot explain the rationality of accounting practice. To elucidate the gap between the positive representation and the pragmatic representation of economic transactions requires an analysis and comprehension of the pertinent value judgments and means–end relations that are sandwiched between those two modes of representation.

3. To find a solution to the dilemma of academic accounting, the hierarchy of accounting objectives must be clarified; norms must be incorporated as conditional premises into accounting models and theories; and means–end relations must be formulated and empirically tested—not unlike ordinary cause-and-effect relations being tested in the pure sciences.

These are the major methodological insights to be gleaned from this work. To go beyond them is not possible at this stage. The direct inference of means from ends requires another empirical revolution, one beyond the pale of not only analytical but also positive accounting. The *indirect* inference, based on traditional empirical methods, might do, provided that accounting is recognized as an applied science in which value judgments are incorporated as premises.

I can only hope that this book has fulfilled the promise of giving a critical analysis of foundational problems crucial for a proper understanding of our discipline, of surveying and exploring the possibility for dealing with means–end relations in a more direct way, and of outlining a conditional–normative theory. An architect's sketch is, of course, something different from that of the ultimate edifice. To create the latter will require the support and effort of the entire accounting community. This will not come about without resistance. After all, many academics may resist an approach that shatters the illusion of a pure science of accounting; yet reality must be faced, as painful as it may be.

NOTE

I found this chapter more difficult to write than originally expected. The reason for this seems to lie in the pitfalls of summarizing or conveying conclusions without being able to call upon all the supporting details. Hence, I must warn the reader not to regard the reading of any one of these sections as a convenient substitute for reading the corresponding chapter.

References

Abdel-khalik, A. Rashad. 1985. The effect of LIFO—Switching and firm ownership on executives' pay. *Journal of Accounting Research* 23(Autumn): 427–447.

Abdel-khalik, A. Rashad, and B. B. Ajinkya. 1983. An evaluation of "The everyday accountant and researching his reality." *Accounting, Organizations and Society* 8(4): 375–384.

Abdel-khalik, A. Rashad, P. R. Regier, and S. A. Reiter. 1989. Some thoughts on empirical research in positive theory. In *The state of accounting research as we enter the 1990's*, ed. T. J. Frecka, 153–180. Urbana: University of Illinois at Urbana–Champaign, Department of Accountancy.

Ackoff, Russell L. 1962. *Scientific method—Optimizing applied research decisions*. New York: John Wiley & Sons.

Ahmad, Yusuf J., Salah el Serafy, and Ernst Lutz. 1989. *Environmental accounting for sustainable development*. Washington, D.C.: World Bank.

Akerlof, G. 1970. The market for "lemons": Qualitative uncertainty and the market mechanism. *Quarterly Journal of Economics* 84(August): 488–500.

Albach, Horst. 1965. Grundgedanken einer synthetischen Bilanztheorie. *Zeitschrift für Betriebswirtschaft* 35: 21–31.

Alchian, Armon A., and Harold Demsetz. 1972. Production, information costs, and economic organization. *American Economic Review* 62(December): 777–795.

Alexander, Sydney S. 1950. Income measurement in a dynamic economy. In *Five monographs on business income*. New York: Study Group on Business Income, American Institute of Accountants. Reprinted in 1973. Lawrence, Kans.: Scholars Book Co.

American Accounting Association (AAA). 1936. A tentative statement of broad accounting principles underlying corporate financial statements. *The Accounting Review* 11(June): 187–191.

American Accounting Association. 1941. Accounting principles underlying corporate financial statements. *The Accounting Review* 16(June): 133–139.

American Accounting Association. 1948. Accounting concepts and standards underlying corporate financial statements. *The Accounting Review* 23(October): 339–344.

American Accounting Association. 1957. Accounting and reporting standards for corporate financial statements: 1957 revision. *The Accounting Review* 32(October): 536–547.

American Accounting Association. 1971a. Report of the committee on accounting and information systems. *The Accounting Review* 46(Supplement): 289–350.

American Accounting Association. 1971b. Report of the committee on accounting theory construction and verification. *The Accounting Review* 46(Supplement): 51–79.

American Accounting Association. 1971c. Report of the committee on behavioral science content of the accounting curriculum. *The Accounting Review* 46(Supplement): 247–285.

American Accounting Association. 1971d. Report of the committee on foundations of accounting measurement. *The Accounting Review* 46(Supplement): 1–48.

American Accounting Association. 1977. *A statement on accounting theory and theory acceptance.* Sarasota, Fla.: AAA.

American Accounting Association. 1993. How would research be effected by more emphasis on the stewardship role of accounting. A panel presentation at the 78th Annual Meeting of the AAA, San Francisco. (Moderator: Robert Ashton. Panelists: Rick Antle, Robert Ashton, John Dickhaut, Yuji Ijiri, and Katherine Schipper.)

American Institute of Certified Public Accountants (AICPA). 1961. *Accounting terminology bulletin no. 1.* New York: AICPA.

American Institute of Certified Public Accountants. 1963. *Reporting the financial effects of price level changes.* New York: AICPA.

American Institute of Certified Public Accountants. 1973. *Objectives of financial statements: Report of the study group on the objectives of financial statements* (Trueblood report). New York: AICPA.

Amershi, A. H., and S. Sunder. 1987. Failure of stock prices to discipline managers in a rational expectations economy. *Journal of Accounting Research* 25(Autumn): 177–195.

Amiet, Pierre. 1966. Il y a 5000 ans les Elamites inventaient l'écriture. *Archeologia* 12: 20–22.

Andersen, Arthur. 1970. *Behind the figures—Addresses and articles by Arthur Andersen 1913–1941.* Chicago: Arthur Andersen & Co.

Archer, Simon. 1993. On the methodology of constructing a conceptual framework for financial accounting. In *Philosophical perspectives on accounting—Essays in honour of Edward Stamp*, ed. M. J. Mumford and K. V. Peasnell, 62–122. London: Routledge.

Argyris, Chris. 1952. *The impact of budgets on people.* Ithaca, N.Y.: School of Business and Public Policy—Controllership Foundation.

Aristotle (of Stagira). 1943. Nicomachean ethics [based on translation by J. E. C. Welldon]. In *On Man in the Universe*, ed. L. R. Loomis, 84–242. Roslyn, N.Y.: Walter J. Black.

Arrow, Kenneth J. 1973. Information and economic behavior. A presentation to the Federation of Swedish Industries, Stockholm. Reprinted in Arrow, Kenneth J. 1984. *The economics of information—Collected papers of Kenneth J. Arrow*, vol. 4, pp. 136–152. Cambridge: Harvard University Press.

Arrow, Kenneth J. 1979. The economics of information. In *The computer age: A twenty year view*, ed. M. L. Dertouzos and J. Moses, 306–317. Cambridge: MIT Press.

Arrow, Kenneth J. 1984. *The economics of information—collected papers of Kenneth J. Arrow*, vol. 4, pp. 303–307. Cambridge: Harvard University Press.

Arrow, Kenneth J. and G. Debreu. 1954. Existence of an equilibrium for a competitive economy. *Econometrica* 22: 256–290.

Arrow, K. J., and A. C. Fisher. 1974. Environmental preservation, uncertainty and irreversibility. *Quarterly Journal of Economics* 88(May): 312–319.

Ashton, Robert H. 1982. *Human information processing in accounting*. Sarasota, Fla.: American Accounting Association.

Ashton, Robert H., ed. 1984. *The evolution of behavioral accounting research*. New York: Garland.

Avilà, H. E., G. Bravo, and E. R. Scarano. 1988. An axiomatic foundation of accounting. Working paper. Buenos Aires: Institute of Accounting Research, University of Buenos Aires.

Backer, Morton. 1966. Accounting theory and multiple reporting objectives. In *Modern accounting theory*, ed. M. Backer, 439–463. Englewood Cliffs, N.J.: Prentice-Hall.

Baiman, Stanley. 1982. Agency research in managerial accounting: A survey. *Journal of Accounting Literature* 1: 154–213. Reprinted in 1984. *Modern accounting research: History, survey and guide*, ed. Richard Mattessich, pp. 251–294. Vancouver, B.C.: Canadian Certified General Accountants Research Foundation.

Ball, Raymond. 1972. Changes in accounting techniques and stock prices. *Journal of Accounting Research* [Empirical Research in Accounting: Selected Studies] 10(Supplement): 1–38.

Ball, Raymond, and Philip Brown. 1968. An empirical evaluation of accounting income numbers. *Journal of Accounting Research* 6(Autumn): 159–178.

Ball, Raymond, and George Foster. 1982. Corporate financial reporting: A methodological review of empirical research. *Journal of Accounting Research* 20(Supplement): 161–234.

Ball, Raymond, and Clifford W. Smith, Jr., eds. 1992. *The economics of accounting policy choice*. New York: McGraw Hill.

Ballwieser, Wolfgang. 1993. Die Entwicklung der Theorie der Rechnungslegung in den USA. *Zeitschrift für betriebswirtschaftliche Forschung* 32(Special issue). In *Ökonomische Analyse des Bilanzrechts*, ed. F. W. Wagner, 107–138.

Balzer, Wolfgang. 1982. Empirical claims in exchange economics. In *Philosophy of economics*, ed. W. Stegmüller, W. Balzer, and W. Spohn, 16–40. New York: Springer-Verlag.

Balzer, Wolfgang. 1983. Theory and measurement. *Erkenntnis* 19: 3–25.

Balzer, Wolfgang. 1985. The proper reconstruction of pure exchange economics. *Erkenntnis* 23: 185–200.

Balzer, Wolfgang, and Richard Mattessich. 1991. An axiomatic basis of accounting: A structuralist approach. *Theory and Decision* 30: 213–243.

Balzer, Wolfgang, C. U. Moulines, and J. D. Sneed. 1987. *An architecture for science*. Boston: D. Reidel.

Barnea, Amir, R. A. Haugen, and L. W. Senbet. 1985. *Agency problems and financial contracting*. Englewood Cliffs, N.J.: Prentice-Hall.

Bartusiak, Marcia. 1986. *Thursday's universe*. New York: Times Books.

Baxter, W. T. 1938. A note on the allocation of oncosts between departments. *The Accountant*, November 5: 633–636. Reprint. 1952. *Studies in costing*, ed. David Solomons, 267–276. London: Sweet & Maxwell, Ltd.

Baxter, W. T., and Sidney Davidson, eds. 1962. *Studies in accounting theory*. Homewood, Ill.: Richard D. Irwin.

Beaver, William H. 1968. The information content of annual earnings announcements—Empirical research in accounting. *Journal of Accounting Research* 6(Supplement): 67–92.

Beaver, William H. 1972. The behavior of security prices and its implication for accounting research methods. In American Accounting Association. Report of the committee on research methodology in accounting. *The Accounting Review* 47(Supplement): 407–437.

Beaver, William H. 1981. *Financial reporting: An accounting revolution.* Englewood Cliffs, N.J.: Prentice-Hall.

Beaver, William H., and Joel S. Demski. 1974. The nature of financial accounting objectives: A summary and synthesis. *Journal of Accounting Research* [Studies in Financial Accounting Objectives] 12(Supplement): 170–187.

Beaver, William H., and Joel S. Demski. 1994. Income measurement and valuation. Working paper presented on April 28. Vancouver, B.C.: Faculty of Commerce and Business Administration, University of British Columbia.

Beaver, William H., J. W. Kennelly, and W. M. Voss. 1968. Predictive ability as a criterion for the evaluation of accounting data. *The Accounting Review* 43(October): 675–683.

Beaver, William H., and W. R. Landsman. 1983. *Incremental information content of Statement 33 disclosures.* Stamford, Conn.: Financial Accounting Standards Board.

Bedford, Norton. 1965. *Income determination theory.* Reading, Mass.: Addison-Wesley.

Belkaoui, Ahmed. 1981. *Accounting theory.* San Diego: Harcourt Brace Jovanovich.

Belkaoui, Ahmed. 1984. *Socio-economic accounting.* Westport, Conn.: Quorum Books.

Belkaoui, Ahmed. 1985. *Accounting theory.* 2nd ed. San Diego: Harcourt Brace Jovanovich.

Belkaoui, Ahmed. 1989. *The coming crisis in accounting.* New York: Quorum Books.

Benston, George J. 1967. Published corporate accounting data and stock prices. *Journal of Accounting Research* [Empirical Research in Accounting] 5(Supplement): 1–14, 22–54.

Bernard, V. L. 1989. Capital market research in accounting during the 1980's: A critical review. In *The state of accounting research as we enter the 1990's,* ed. T. J. Frecka, 72–120. Urbana: University of Illinois at Urbana–Champaign, Department of Accountancy.

Besta, Fabio. 1891. *La ragioneria.* Milan: Francesco Vallardi. (A one-volume pamphlet by this author, under the same title, seems to have appeared in 1880 with the publisher Coletti in Venice.)

Bhattacharyya, Anjan Kumar. 1988. *Modern accounting concepts in Kautilya's Arthaśāstra.* Calcutta: Firma KLM Private Ltd.

Bierman, Harold. 1963. Measurement and accounting. *The Accounting Review* 38(July): 501–507.

Binkley, R. 1966. Comments on H. Simon's "The logic of heuristic decision making." In *The logic of decision and action,* ed. Nicholas Rescher, 21–27. Pittsburgh: University of Pittsburgh.

Birnberg, J. G., and Raghu Nath. 1967. Implications of behavioral science for managerial accounting. *The Accounting Review* 42(July): 468–479.

Black, F., and M. Scholes. 1973. The pricing of options and corporate liabilities. *Journal of Political Economy* 81(May–June): 637–659.

Blaug, Mark. 1978. *Economic theory in retrospect.* 3rd ed. Cambridge: Cambridge University Press.

Blaug, Mark. 1980. *The methodology of economics*. Cambridge: Cambridge University Press.

Boer, Germain. 1966. Replacement cost: A historical look. *The Accounting Review* 41(January): 92–97.

Boland, L. A., and I. M. Gordon. 1992. Criticizing positive accounting theory. *Contemporary Accounting Research* 8(Fall): 142–170.

Bonini, Charles P. 1963. *Simulation of information and decision systems in the firm*. Englewood Cliffs, N.J.: Prentice-Hall.

Boritz, J. E. 1994. Comments for workshop on measurement research. In *Measurement research in financial accounting*, ed. Ernst & Young Foundation, 35–39. Workshop proceedings, September 30 to October 1, 1993. Waterloo, Ontario: Ernst & Young Foundation and Waterloo University, School of Accountancy.

Brandes, Mark A. 1980. Modelage et imprimerie aux débuts de l'écriture en Mésopotamie. *Akkadica* 18: 1–30.

Brennan, Michael, and Eduardo Schwartz. 1977. Convertible bonds: Valuation and optimal strategies for call and conversion. *The Journal of Finance* 32(December): 1699–1715.

Brennan, Michael, and Eduardo Schwartz. 1978. Finite difference methods and jump processes arising in the pricing of contingent claims: A synthesis. *Journal of Finance and Quantitative Analysis* 13(September): 461–474.

Brennan, Michael, and Eduardo Schwartz. 1979. A continuous time approach to the pricing of bonds. *Journal of Banking and Finance* 3(July): 133–155.

Briloff, Abraham J. 1972. *Unaccountable accounting*. New York: Harper & Row.

Briloff, Abraham J. 1981. *The truth about corporate accounting*. New York: Harper & Row.

Briloff, Abraham J. 1986. Standards without standards/principles without principles/fairness without fairness. *Advances in Accounting* 3: 22–50.

Briloff, Abraham J. 1987. Do management services endanger independence and objectivity? *CPA Journal* 57(8): 22–29.

Briloff, Abraham J. 1990. Accountancy and society, a covenant desecrated. *Critical Perspectives in Accounting* 1: 5–30.

Brown, Philip R. 1988. Review of Ian Griffiths' *Creative accounting*, 1986. *The Accounting Review* 63: 538–539.

Brown, Robert M. 1980. Short-range market reaction to changes to LIFO accounting using preliminary earnings announcement dates. *Journal of Accounting Research* 18(Spring): 38–73.

Bruns, William J., Jr. 1968. Accounting information and decision making: Some behavioral hypotheses. *The Accounting Review* 43(July): 469–480.

Buckley, John W., Paul Kircher, and Russell L. Mathews. 1968. Methodology in accounting theory. *The Accounting Review* 43(April): 274–283.

Bunge, Mario. 1967a. *Scientific research I—The search for system*. New York: Springer-Verlag.

Bunge, Mario. 1967b. *Scientific research II—The search for truth*. New York: Springer-Verlag.

Bunge, Mario. 1974a. *Treatise on basic philosophy: Semantics I—Sense and reference*. Vol. 1. Boston: D. Reidel.

Bunge, Mario. 1974b. *Treatise on basic philosophy: Semantics II—Interpretation and truth*. Vol. 2. Boston: D. Reidel.

Bunge, Mario. 1977. *Treatise on basic philosophy: Ontology I—The furniture of the world*. Vol. 3. Boston: D. Reidel.

Bunge, Mario. 1978. Review of Stegmüller, Wolfgang: *The structure and dynamics of theories*, 1976. *Mathematical Review* 55(2): 330, item 2480.

Bunge, Mario. 1979. *Treatise on basic philosophy: Ontology II—A world of systems*. Vol. 4. Boston: D. Reidel.

Bunge, Mario. 1983a. *Treatise on basic philosophy: Epistemology and methodology I— Exploring the world*. Vol. 5. Boston: D. Reidel.

Bunge, Mario. 1983b. *Treatise on basic philosophy: Epistemology and methodology II— Understanding the world*. Vol. 6. Boston: D. Reidel.

Bunge, Mario. 1985a. *Treatise on basic philosophy: Epistemology III—Philosophy of science and technology*. Vol. 7, Part I. Boston: D. Reidel.

Bunge, Mario. 1985b. *Treatise on basic philosophy: Epistemology III—Philosophy of science and technology*. Vol. 7, Part II. Boston: D. Reidel.

Burchell, S., C. Clubb, and A. G. Hopwood. 1985. Accounting in its social context: Towards a history of value added in the United Kingdom. *Accounting, Organizations and Society* 10(4): 381–414.

Buros, O. K., ed. 1978. *[The eighth] Mental measurement yearbook*. Vols. 1 and 2. Highland Park, Newfoundland: Gryphon Press.

Burrell, G., and G. Morgan. 1979. *Sociological paradigms and organisational analysis*. London: Heinemann.

Butterworth, John E. 1967. *Accounting systems and management decision: An analysis of the role of information in the managerial decision process*. Ph.D. dissertation. Berkeley: University of California.

Butterworth, John E. 1972. The accounting system as an information function. *Journal of Accounting Research* 10(Spring): 1–27.

Butterworth, John E. 1982. Discussion. In *Maintenance of capital: Financial versus physical capital*, ed. Robert R. Sterling and Kenneth W. Lemke, 105–113. Houston: Scholars Book Co.

Butterworth, John E., and Haim Falk. 1986. Information attributes of the contractual paradigm. In *Financial reporting—Theory and application to the oil and gas industry in Canada*, pp. 9–29. Hamilton, Ontario: Society of Management Accountants of Canada. (Originally by Butterworth, J. E. 1983. The methodological implications of a contractual theory of accounting. Working paper. Vancouver, B.C.: University of British Columbia.)

Butterworth, John E., Michael Gibbins, and R. D. King. 1982. The structure of accounting theory: Some basic conceptual and methodological issues. In *Research to support standard setting in financial accounting: A Canadian perspective*, pp. 1–65. Toronto: Clarkson–Gordon Foundation. Reprint. 1984. *Modern accounting research: History, survey and guide*, ed. Richard Mattessich, pp. 209–250. Vancouver, B.C.: Canadian Certified General Accountants Research Foundation.

Butterworth John E., and Berndt A. Sigloch. 1971. A generalized multi-stage input–output model and some derived equivalent systems. *The Accounting Review* 46(October): 700–716.

Campbell, D. T. 1966a. Evolutionary epistemology. In *The philosophy of Karl Popper*, ed. P. A. Schilpp, 413–463. La Salle, Ill.: Open Court.

Campbell, D. T. 1966b. *Pattern matching as an essential in distal knowing*. New York: Rinehart & Winston.

Campbell, N. R. 1928. *An account of the principles of measurement and calculation*. London: Longmans Green.

Canadian Institute of Chartered Accountants (CICA). 1982. Reporting the effects of changing prices. In *CICA Handbook*, Section 4510. Toronto: CICA.

Canning, J. B. 1929. *The economics of accountancy*. New York: Ronald Press.

Caplan, E. H., J. G. Birnberg, T. J. Burns, J. J. Cramer, T. R. Dyckman, W. N. Gentry, and R. J. Swieringa. 1971. Report of the committee on behavioral science content of the accounting curriculum. *The Accounting Review* 46(Supplement): 247–285.

Carlson, M. L., and J. W. Lamb. 1981. Constructing a theory of accounting—An axiomatic approach. *The Accounting Review* 56(July): 554–573.

Carnap, Rudolf. 1942. *Introduction to semantics*. Boston: Harvard University Press.

Cayley, Arthur. 1894. *The principles of book-keeping by double entry*. Cambridge: Cambridge University Press.

Chambers, Raymond J. 1955. Blueprint for a theory of accounting. *Accounting Research* 6(January): 17–25.

Chambers, Raymond J. 1965. Measurement in accounting. *Journal of Accounting Research* 3(Spring): 32–62. Reprint. Chambers, R. J. 1969. *Accounting, finance, and management*, pp. 125–132. Sydney: Arthur Andersen & Co.

Chambers, Raymond J. 1966. *Accounting, Evaluation and Economic Behaviour*. Englewood Cliffs, N.J.: Prentice Hall. Reprint. 1975. Accounting Classics Series. Houston: Scholars Books.

Chambers, Raymond J. 1967. Continuously contemporary accounting—Additivity and action. *The Accounting Review* 42(October): 751–757.

Chambers, Raymond J. 1971a. Asset measurement and valuation. *Cost and Management* 45(March–April): 30–35.

Chambers, Raymond J. 1971b. Measurement and valuation again. *Cost and Management* 45(July–August): 12–17.

Chambers, Raymond J. 1980. *Price variation and inflation accounting*. Sydney: McGraw Hill.

Chambers, Raymond J., 1991. Metrical and empirical laws in accounting. *Accounting Horizons* 5(December): 1–15.

Chambers, Raymond J., 1993. Positive accounting and the PA cult. *Abacus* 29(March): 1–26.

Charnes, Abraham, W. W. Cooper, and Y. Ijiri. 1963. Breakeven budgeting and programming to goals. *Journal of Accounting Research* 1(Spring): 16–41.

Chatfield, Michael. 1974. *A history of accounting thought*. Hindsdale, Ill.: Dryden Press.

Chatfield, Michael, and R. G. Vangermeersch, eds. In press. *Encyclopedia of the history of accounting and accounting thought*. New York: Garland.

Chi, S. K. 1989. Ethics and agency theory. Ph.D. dissertation. Seattle: University of Washington.

Christenson, C. 1983. The methodology of positive acounting. *The Accounting Review* 58(January): 1–22. Reprint. 1984. *Modern accounting research: History, survey and guide*, ed. Richard Mattessich, 131–163. Vancouver, B.C.: Canadian Certified General Accountants Research Foundation.

Christie, Andrew A. 1987. On cross-sectional analysis of accounting research. *Journal of Accounting and Economics* 9: 231–258.

Christie, Andrew A. 1990. Aggregation and test statistics: An evaluation of contracting and size hypotheses. *Journal of Accounting and Economics* 12: 15–36.

Chua, W. F. 1986. Radical developments in acounting thought. *The Accounting Review* 61(4): 601–632.

Churchill, Neil C. 1964. Linear algebra and cost allocations: Some examples. *The Accounting Review* 39(October): 894–904.

Clark, J. M. 1923. *Studies in the economics of overhead costs.* Chicago: University of Chicago Press.

Clark, Kenneth. 1969. *Civilisation: A personal view.* New York: Harper & Row.

Clarkson, Peter, and Richard Mattessich. 1984. A review of market research in financial accounting. In *Modern accounting research: History, survey and guide,* ed. Richard Mattessich, 361–389. Vancouver, B.C.: Canadian Certified General Accountants Research Foundation.

Coase, R. H. 1937. The nature of the firm. *Economica* 4(November): 386–405.

Coase, R. H. 1960. The problem of social cost. *Journal of Law and Economics* 3(October): 1–44.

Columbia University Press. 1983. *The concise Columbia encyclopedia.* New York: Columbia University Press and Avon.

Constanza, Robert, ed. 1991. *Ecological economics.* New York: Columbia University Press.

Cooper, David J. 1983. Tidiness, muddle and things: Commonalities and divergences in two approaches to management accounting research. *Accounting, Organizations and Society* 10(2–3): 269–286.

Cooper, D. J., A. Lowe, A. E. Puxty, and H. Willmott. 1985. The regulation of social and economic relations in advanced capitalistic societies: Towards a conceptual framework for a cross national study of the control of accounting policy and practice. Paper presented at the Interdisciplinary Perspectives in Accounting Conference, University of Manchester, July 8–10.

Cooper, D. J., R. Scapens, and J. Arnold, eds. 1983. *Management accounting research and practice.* London: Institute of Cost and Management Accountants.

Cooper, William W., and Yuji Ijiri, eds. 1983. *Kohler's dictionary for accountants.* Englewood Cliffs, N.J.: Prentice-Hall.

Corbin, Donald A. 1962. The revolution in accounting. *The Accounting Review* 37(October): 626–635.

Cotrugli, Benedetto. [1573] 1990. *Della mercatura e del mercante perfetto.* Modern reprint, with Introduction by Ugo Tucci. Venice: Arsenale Editrice.

Cox, J., and S. Ross. 1976a. A survey of some new results in financial option pricing theory. *The Journal of Finance* 31(May): 383–402.

Cox, J., and S. Ross. 1976b. The valuation of options for alternative stochastic processes. *Journal of Financial Economics* 3: 145–166.

Cramer, Joe J., Jr., and George H. Sorter, eds. 1974. *Objectives of financial statements.* Vol. 2, *Selected papers.* New York: American Institute of Certified Public Accountants.

Crandall, Robert H. 1969. Information economics and its implications for the further development of accounting theory. *The Accounting Review* 44(July): 457–466.

Culler, J. 1985. *On deconstruction: Theory and criticism after deconstruction.* Ithaca, N.Y.: Cornell University Press.

Cushing, Barry E. 1989. A Kuhnian interpretation of the historical evolution of accounting. *The Accounting Historians Journal* 16(December): 1–41.

Cyert, Richard M., and H. Justin Davidson. 1962. *Statistical sampling for accounting information.* Englewood Cliffs, N.J.: Prentice-Hall.

Cyert, Richard M., and Yuji Ijiri. 1974. Problems of implementing the Trueblood objectives report. *Journal of Accounting Research* [Studies on Financial Accounting Objectives] 12(Supplement): 29–42.

Cyert, Richard M., and R. M. Trueblood. 1957. *Sampling techniques in accounting*. New York: Prentice-Hall.

Daley, L. A. 1994. Measurement, information, and academic research. In *Measurement research in financial accounting*, ed. Ernst & Young Foundation, 40–48. Workshop proceedings, September 30 to October 1, 1993. Waterloo, Ontario: Ernst & Young Foundation and Waterloo University, School of Accountancy.

Daly, Herman E., John B. Cobb, and Clifford W. Cobb. 1989. *For the common good*. Boston: Beacon Press.

Dasgupta, Partha, and Geoffrey Heal. 1979. *The economic theory of exhaustible resources*. Cambridge: Cambridge University Press.

Davies, P. C. W. 1979. *The forces of nature*. Cambridge: Cambridge University Press.

Dean, Joel. 1951. *Managerial economics*. New York: Prentice-Hall.

Deguchi, H., and B. Nakano. 1986. Axiomatic foundations of vector accounting. *Systems Research* 3(1): 31–39.

De Morgan, August. 1846. *Elements of arithmetic*. 5th ed. London: Taylor & Walton.

Demski, Joel S. 1973. Rational choice of accounting method for a class of partnerships. *Journal of Accounting Research* 11(Autumn): 176–190.

Demski, Joel S. 1980. *Information analysis*. 2nd ed. Reading, Mass.: Addison-Wesley.

Demski, Joel S. 1988. Positive accounting theory: A review. *Accounting, Organizations and Society* 13(6): 623–628.

Demski, Joel S., Nicholas Dopuch, Baruch Lev, Joshua Ronen, Jerry Searfoss, and Shyam Sunder. 1991. Statement on the state of academic accounting. Mimeo.

Demski, Joel S., and Gerald A. Feltham. 1972. Forecast evaluation. *The Accounting Review* 47(July): 533–548.

Demski, Joel S., and Gerald A. Feltham. 1976. *Cost determination—A conceptual approach*. Ames, Iowa: Iowa State University Press.

Demski, Joel S., and Gerald A. Feltham. 1978. Economic incentives in budgetary control systems. *The Accounting Review* 53(April): 336–359.

Denman, John. 1994. Comments on measurement research and financial accounting. In *Measurement research in financial accounting*, ed. Ernst & Young Foundation, 83–87. Workshop proceedings, September 30 to October 1, 1993. Waterloo, Ontario: Ernst & Young Foundation and Waterloo University, School of Accountancy.

de Pree, C. M. 1989. Testing and evaluating a conceptual framework in accounting. *Abacus* 25(September): 61–73.

Derrida, Jacques. 1981. *Dissemination*. Trans. B. Johnson. Chicago: University of Chicago Press.

Descartes, René. 1637. *Discours de la méthode*. Paris.

Descombes, Vincent. 1980. *Modern French philosophy*. Trans. L. Scott-Fox and J. M. Harding. Cambridge: Cambridge University Press.

de Ste. Croix, G. E. M. 1956. Greek and Roman accounting. In *Studies in the history of accounting*, ed. A. C. Littleton and S. Yamey, 14–74. Homewood, Ill.: Richard D. Irwin.

Devine, Carl T. 1966. Some conceptual problems in accounting measurements. In *Research in accounting measurement*, ed. R. K. Jaedicke, Y. Ijiri, and O. Nielson. Menasha, Wis.: American Accounting Association.

Devine, Carl T. 1985. *Essays in accounting theory*. 5 vols. Sarasota, Fla.: American Accounting Association.

Dicksee, L. R. 1892. *Auditing*. London.

Dopuch, Nicholas. 1989. The auto- and cross-sectional correlations of accounting research. In *The state of accounting research as we enter the 1990's*, ed. T. J. Frecka, 40–59. Urbana: University of Illinois at Urbana–Champaign, Department of Accountancy.

Dopuch, Nicholas, and Morton Pincus. 1988. Evidence on the choice of inventory accounting methods: LIFO versus FIFO. *Journal of Accounting Research* 26(1): 28–59.

Dopuch, Nicholas, and Shyam Sunder. 1980. FASB's statements on objectives and elements of financial accounting: A review. *The Accounting Review* 55(January): 1–21.

Dumarchey, J. 1925. *La comptabilité moderne: Essay de constitution rationelle d'une discipline comptable du triple point de vue philosophique, scientifique et technique*. Paris: Gauthier-Villars.

Dyckman, Thomas R., Michael Gibbins, and Robert J. Swieringa. 1978. Experimental and survey research in financial accounting: A review and evaluation. In *The impact of accounting research on practice and disclosure*, ed. A. Rashad Abdel-khalik and Thomas L. Keller, 48–105. Durham, N.C.: Duke University Press. Reprint. 1984. *Modern accounting research: History, survey and guide*, ed. Richard Mattessich, 299–323. Vancouver, B.C.: Canadian Certified General Accountants Research Foundation.

Dyckman, Thomas R., and D. Morse. 1986. *Efficient capital markets and accounting: A critical analysis*. 2nd ed. Englewood Cliffs, N.J.: Prentice-Hall.

Edey, H. C. 1959. *Business budgets and accounts*. London: Hutchinson.

Edwards, Edgar O., and Philip W. Bell. 1961. *The theory and measurement of business income*. Berkeley: University of California Press.

Edwards, J. Richard, ed. 1994. *Twentieth century accounting thinkers*, with a Foreword by David Solomons. London: Routledge.

Edwards, R. S. 1937. The rationale of cost accounting (a lecture delivered at the London School of Economics). In *Some modern business problems*, ed. Sir A. Plant, 277–299. London: Longmans Green. Reprint. 1952. *Studies in costing*, ed. David Solomons, 87–104. London: Sweet & Maxwell.

Edwards, R. S. 1938. The nature and measurement of income. *The Accountant* 98(July–October). Reprint. 1977. *Studies in accounting theory*, ed. W. T. Baxter and Sidney Davidson, 96–140.

Ehrenreich, Barbara. 1991. Science, lies and the ultimate truth. *Time*, June 3: 86.

Emminghaus, K. B. A. 1868. *Allgemeine Gewerkslehre*. Berlin.

Ernst & Young Foundation, ed. 1994. *Measurement research in financial accounting*. Workshop proceedings, September 30 to October 1, 1993. Waterloo, Ontario: Ernst & Young Foundation and Waterloo University, School of Accountancy.

Falkenstein, A. 1964. *Keilschriftforschung und die alte Geschichte Vorderasiens*. Leiden: E. J. Brill.

Fama, Eugen F. 1965. The behavior of stock market prices. *Journal of Business* 38(January): 34–105.

Farag, Shawki M. 1967. *Input–output analysis: Application to business accounting*. Urbana: Center for International Education and Research in Accounting, University of Illinois.

Fäs, Emil. 1913. *Die Berücksichtigung der Wertverminderung des stehenden Kapitals in den Jahresbilanzen der Erwerbswirtschaft*. Tübingen.

Felperin, H. 1985. *Beyond deconstruction: The uses and abuses of literary theory*. Oxford: Claredon Press.

Feltham, Gerald A. 1967. A theoretical framework for evaluating changes in accounting information for managerial decisions. Ph.D. dissertation. Berkeley: University of California.

Feltham, Gerald A. 1968. The value of information. *The Accounting Review* 43(October): 684–696.

Feltham, Gerald A. 1970. Some quantitative approaches to planning for multiproduct production systems. *The Accounting Review* 45(January): 11–26.

Feltham, Gerald A. 1972. *Information evaluation.* Sarasota, Fla.: American Accounting Association.

Feltham, Gerald A. 1984. Financial accounting research: Contributions of information economics and agency theory. In *Modern accounting research: History, survey and guide*, ed. Richard Mattessich, 179–207. Vancouver, B.C.: Canadian Certified General Accountants Research Foundation.

Feltham, Gerald A., Amin H. Amershi, and William T. Ziemba, eds. 1988. *Economic analysis of information and contracts.* Boston: Kluwer Academic.

Feltham, Gerald A., and Joel S. Demski. 1970. The use of models in information evaluation. *The Accounting Review* 45(October): 623–640.

Feltham, Gerald A., and James A. Ohlson. 1993. Valuation and clean surplus accounting for operating and financial activity. Working paper. Vancouver, B.C.: Faculty of Commerce and Business Administration, University of British Columbia.

Feltham, Gerald A., and James A. Ohlson. 1994. A no arbitrage model of the relation between accounting numbers and market value. Working paper. Vancouver, B.C.: Faculty of Commerce and Business Administration, University of British Columbia.

Feyerabend, P. K. 1965. Problems of empiricism. In *Beyond the edge of certainty*, ed. R. Colodny, 145–150. Englewood Cliffs, N.J.: Prentice-Hall.

Feyerabend, P. K. 1975. *Against method.* London: New Left Books.

Filios, P. V. 1984. The transition of systematic accounting from ancient to Byzantine Greece. In *Fourth International Congress of the History of Accountancy, Congress proceedings*, ed. T. Antoni, 171–191. Pisa: ETS Editrice.

Financial Accounting Standards Board (FASB). 1974. *Conceptual framework for accounting and reporting: Consideration of the report of the study group on objectives of financial statements.* Discussion memorandum. Stamford, Conn.: FASB.

Financial Accounting Standards Board. 1976a. *Conceptual framework for financial accounting and reporting: Elements of financial statements and their measurement.* Discussion memorandum. Stamford, Conn.: FASB.

Financial Accounting Standards Board. 1976b. *Tentative conclusions on objectives of financial statements.* Stamford, Conn.: FASB.

Financial Accounting Standards Board. 1978. *Objectives of financial reporting by business enterprises.* Report of the study group on objectives: Statement of financial accounting concepts no. 1. Stamford, Conn.: FASB.

Financial Accounting Standards Board. 1979. *Statement of financial accounting standards no. 33, Financial reporting and changing prices.* Stamford, Conn.: FASB.

Financial Accounting Standards Board. 1980a. *Objectives of financial reporting by nonbusiness organizations.* Report of the study group on objectives: Statement of financial accounting concepts no. 4. Stamford, Conn.: FASB.

Financial Accounting Standards Board. 1980b. *Reporting funds, flows, liquidity, and financial flexibility.* Discussion memorandum. Stamford, Conn.: FASB.

Financial Accounting Standards Board. 1980c. *Statement on financial accounting concepts*. Report of the study group on objectives: Statement of financial accounting concepts no. 2. Stamford, Conn.: FASB.

Financial Accounting Standards Board. 1984a. *Proposed statement of financial accounting standards, Financial reporting and changing prices: Current cost information*. Stamford, Conn.: FASB.

Financial Accounting Standards Board. 1984b. *Statement of financial accounting standards no. 82, Financial reporting and changing prices: Elimination of certain disclosures* [amendment of FASB statement no. 33]. Stamford, Conn.: FASB.

Financial Accounting Standards Board. 1985. *Elements of financial statements*. Report of the study group on objectives: Statement of financial accounting concepts no. 6. Stamford, Conn.: FASB.

Fischer-Winkelmann, Wolf F., ed. 1982. *Paradigmenwechsel in der Betriebswirtschaftslehre*. Munich: Institut für Kontrolling, Hochschule der Bundeswehr.

Fisher, Irving. 1906. *The nature of capital and income*. London: Macmillan.

Flamholtz, E. G., T. K. Das, and A. S. Tsui. 1985. Toward an integrative framework of organizational control. *Accounting, Organizations and Society* 10(1): 35–50.

Flegg, G. 1983. *Numbers—Their history and meaning*. New York: Schocken Books.

Foster, G. 1973. Stock market reaction to estimates of earnings per share by company officials. *Journal of Accounting Research* 11(Spring): 25–37.

Foucault, Michele. 1972. *The archeology of knowledge*. London: Travistock.

Foucault, Michele. 1979. *Discipline and punish: The birth of the prison*. Harmondsworth, U.K.: Penguin.

Foucault, Michele. 1980. *Power/knowledge: Selected interviews and other writings 1972–1977*, ed. C. Gordon. New York: Pantheon.

Frecka, T. J. 1989a. Editor's summary. In *The state of accounting research as we enter the 1990's*, ed. T. J. Frecka, 7–27. Urbana: University of Illinois at Urbana–Champaign, Department of Accountancy.

Frecka, T. J., ed. 1989b. *The state of accounting research as we enter the 1990's*. Urbana: University of Illinois at Urbana–Champaign, Department of Accountancy.

Gaa, James C. 1986. User primacy in financial reporting rulemaking: A social contract approach. *The Accounting Review* 61(3): 435–454.

Gaa, James C. 1988a. The auditing profession and society: Prisoners of a dilemma. In *A profession in transition: The ethical and legal responsibilities of accountants, Proceedings of the third annual research symposium*. Chicago: De Paul University, School of Accountancy.

Gaa, James C. 1988b. *Methodological foundations of standard setting for corporate financial reporting*. Sarasota, Fla.: American Accounting Association.

Gaa, James C. 1994. *The ethical foundations of public accounting*. Vancouver, B.C.: Canadian Certified General Accountants Research Foundation.

Gaffikin, Michael J. R. 1987. The methodology of early accounting theorists. *Abacus* 23(1): 17–30.

Gaffikin, Michael J. R. 1988. Legacy of the golden age: Recent developments in the methodology of accounting. *Abacus* 24(1): 16–36.

Gaffikin, Michael J. R., and Michael J. Aitken, eds. 1982. *The development of accounting theory: Significant contributors to accounting thought in the 20th century*. New York: Garland.

Galassi, Giuseppe. 1978. *Sistemi contabili assiomatici e sistemi teorici deduttivi*. Bologna: Patron Editore.

Galassi, Giuseppe. 1980. Capital–income relations, A critical analysis. In *Gino Zappa, Founder of concern economics*, pp. 28–49. Bologna: Accademia Italiana di Economia Aziendale.

Gambling, Trevor E. 1968. A technological model for use in input–output analysis and cost accounting. *Management Accounting* 50(December): 33–38.

Garman, M. B., and J. A. Ohlson. 1980. Information and the sequential valuation of assets in arbitrage-free economies. *Journal of Accounting Research* 18(Autumn): 420–440.

Geneen, Harold. 1984. *Managing*. New York: Avon Books.

Gibbins, Michael. 1994. Social complexity and judgment in accounting measurement. In *Measurement research in financial accounting*, ed. Ernst & Young Foundation, 49–61. Workshop proceedings, September 30 to October 1, 1993. Waterloo, Ontario: Ernst & Young Foundation and Waterloo University, School of Accountancy.

Gibbins, Michael, and Patricia Hughes. 1982. Behavioral research and financial accounting standards. In *Usefulness to investors and creditors of information provided by financial reporting: A review of empirical accounting*, ed. P. A. Griffin, 99–134. Stamford, Conn.: Financial Accounting Standards Board. Reprint. 1984. *Modern accounting research: History, survey and guide*, ed. Richard Mattessich, 347–360. Vancouver, B.C.: Canadian Certified General Accountants Research Foundation.

Giddens, A. 1976. *New rules of sociological methods*. London: Hutchinson.

Giddens, A. 1979. *Central problems in social theory*. London: Hutchinson.

Giddens, A. 1981. *A contemporary critique of historical materialism*. London: Hutchinson.

Gilman, S. 1939. *Accounting concepts of profit*. New York: Ronald Press.

Gjesdal, Froystein. 1981. Accounting for stewardship. *Journal of Accounting Research* 19(1): 208–231.

Gleick, J. 1987. *Chaos: Making a new science*. New York: Viking Press.

Goldberg, L. 1965. *An inquiry into the nature of accounting*. Menasha, Wis.: American Accounting Association.

Gomberg, Léon. 1908. *Grundlegung der Verrechnungswissenschaft*. Leipzig.

Gomberg, Léon. 1927. *Eine geometrische Darstellung der Buchhaltungsmethoden*. Berlin: Wien.

Gonedes, N. J. 1972. Efficient capital markets and external accounting. *The Accounting Review* 47(January): 11–21.

Gonedes, N. J., and N. Dopuch. 1974. Capital–market equilibrium, information production, and selecting accounting techniques: Theoretical framework and review of empirical work. *Journal of Accounting Research* 12(Supplement): 48–129.

Gordon, M. J. 1964. Postulates, principles, and research in accounting. *The Accounting Review* 39(April): 251–263.

Gorelik, George. 1975. On the nature of information. *International Journal of Accounting and Education Research* 10(2; Spring): 109–125.

Gorelik, George. 1994. The setting of accounting standards: Canada, the United Kingdom, and United States. *The International Journal of Accounting* 29(1): 95–122.

Greenball, M. N. 1971. The predictive-ability criterion: Its relevance in valuating accounting data. *Abacus* 7(1): 1–7.

Griffin, Paul A. 1982. *Usefulness to investors and creditors of information provided by financial reporting—Review of empirical accounting research*. Stamford, Conn.: Financial Accounting Standards Board.

Griffin, Paul A. 1987. *Usefulness to investors and creditors of information provided by financial reporting*. 2nd ed. Stamford, Conn.: Financial Accounting Standards Board.

Griffiths, I. 1986. *Creative accounting*. London: Sidgwick & Jackson.

Guo, Dao Yang. 1982. *History of Chinese accounting* (in Chinese). Vol. 1. Bejing: Chinese Finance and Economics Publishing House.

Guo, Dao Yang. 1988. *History of Chinese accounting* (in Chinese). Vol. 2. Bejing: Chinese Finance and Economics Publishing House.

Guo, Dao Yang, and Yang Shi Zhan, eds. In preparation. *Hundred notable accountants and their historical contributions* (in Chinese). ShengYang: Liao Lin Province Publishers.

Habermas, J. 1971. *Toward a rational society*. London: Heinemann.

Habermas, J. 1974. *Theory and practice*. London: Heinemann.

Habermas, J. 1978. *Knowledge and human interest*. 2nd ed. London: Heinemann.

Hacking, Ian. 1983. *Representing and intervening*. Cambridge: Cambridge University Press.

Hakansson, Nils H. 1969a. An induced theory of accounting under risk. *The Accounting Review* 44(July): 495–514.

Hakansson, Nils H. 1969b. Normative accounting theory and the theory of decision. *International Journal of Accounting Education and Research* 4(Spring): 33–47.

Hakansson, Nils H. 1978. Where we are in accounting: A review of "Statement on accounting theory and theory acceptance." *The Accounting Review* 53(July): 717–725. Reprint. 1984. *Modern accounting research: History, survey and guide*, ed. Richard Mattessich, 69–76. Vancouver, B.C.: Canadian Certified General Accountants Research Foundation.

Hakansson, Nils H., J. G. Kunkel, and J.A. Ohlson. 1982. Sufficient and necessary conditions for information to have social value in pure exchange. *Journal of Finance* 37(December): 1169–1181.

Haller, Axel. 1991. *Die Grundlagen der externen Rechnungslegung in den USA*. 2nd ed. Stuttgart: C. E. Poeschel.

Hallo, William W. 1992. Foreword. In Denise Schmandt-Besserat. *Before writing*. Vol. 1, *From counting to cuneiform*, ix–xi. Austin: University of Texas Press.

Hamel, Winfried. 1984. Ansatzpunkte Strategischer Bilanzierung. *Zeitschrift für betriebswirtschaftliche Forschung* 36(November): 903–911.

Hamminga, Bert. 1983. *Neoclassical theory structure and theory development*. New York: Springer-Verlag.

Hanna, John R. 1982. Discussion. In *Maintenance of capital: Financial versus physical capital*, ed. Robert R. Sterling and Kenneth W. Lemke, 267–283. Houston: Scholars Book Co.

Hansen, Palle. 1962. *The accounting concept of profit: An analysis and evaluation in the light of the economic theory of income and capital*. Copenhagen.

Hanson, N. R. 1958. *Patterns of discovery*. Cambridge: Cambridge University Press.

Harris, T. S., and J. A. Ohlson. 1990. Accounting disclosures and the market's valuation of oil and gas properties: Evaluation of market efficiency and functional fixation. *The Accounting Review* 65(October): 764–780.

Hartmann, Nicolai. 1940. *Der Aufbau der realen Welt*. Berlin: de Gruyter.

Hatfield, Henry R. 1909. *Modern accounting: Its principles and some of its problems*. New York: D. Apple.

Hatfield, Henry R. 1927. *Accounting: Its principles and problems*. New York: D. Apple.

Hausman, Daniel M., ed. 1984. Editor's introduction. *The philosophy of economics—An anthology*. Cambridge: Cambridge University Press.

Hawking, Stephen. 1988. *A brief history of time*. New York: Bantam Books.

Heath, L. C. 1987. Accounting, communication, and the Pygmalion Syndrome. *Accounting Horizons* 1(March): 1–8.

Heinen, Edmund. 1978. Supplemented multi-purpose accounting. *The International Journal of Accounting* 14(1): 1–15.

Henderson, M. S., and G. Peirson. 1983. *Accounting theory—Its nature and development.* Melbourne: Longman Cheshire.

Hendriksen, E. S. 1982. *Accounting theory.* 4th ed. Homewood, Ill.: Richard D. Irwin.

Hendriksen, E. S., and M. F. van Breda. 1991. *Accounting theory.* Homewood, Ill.: Richard D. Irwin.

Herde, Georg. 1992. *Präzisierung dreier axiomatischer Theorien des Rechnungswesens in einer formalen Typentheorie.* Ph.D. dissertation. Bamberg: Otto-Friedrich-Universität.

Hicks, J. R. 1946. *Value and capital.* 2nd ed. Oxford: Claredon Press.

Hilpinen, Risto, ed. 1971. *Deontic logic: Introductory and systematic readings.* Boston: D. Reidel.

Hines, Ruth D. 1988. Popper's methodology of falsificationism and accounting research. *Accounting Research* 63(4): 657–662.

Hirschleifer, Jack. 1971. The private and social value of information and the reward to inventive activity. *American Economic Review* 61(September): 561–574.

Hofstadter, D. R. 1981. Reflections. In *The mind's I,* ed. D. R. Hofstadter and D. C. Dennett, 144–146. New York: Bantam Books.

Hofstedt, T. R., and J. C. Kinard. 1970. A strategy for behavioral accounting research. *The Accounting Review* 45(January): 38–54.

Holthausen, R., and R. Leftwich. 1983. The economic consequences of accounting choice: Implications of costly contracting and monitoring. *Journal of Accounting and Economics* 5(August): 77–117.

Honko, Jaakko. 1959. *Yrityksen vuositulos: The annual income of an enterprise and its determination, A study from the standpoint of accounting and economics.* Helsinki: Oy Weilin & Göös Ab.

Honko, Jaakko. 1966. Esipuhe (Introduction). In *Suomalaista liiketaoustiedettä 1966* (Finnish Research on Business Studies 1966), ed. J. Honko and J. Lehtovuori. Helsinki: Weilin & Göös Ab.

Hopper, T., and A. Powell. 1985. Making sense of research into organizational and social aspects of management accounting: A review of its underlying assumptions. *Journal of Management Studies* 22(September): 429–465.

Hopper, T., J. Storey, and H. Willmott. 1987. Accounting for accounting: Towards the development of a dialectical view. *Accounting, Organizations and Society* 12(5): 437–456.

Hopwood, Anthony G. 1987. The archeology of accounting systems. *Accounting, Organizations and Society* 12(3): 207–234.

Hopwood, Anthony G. 1988. *Accounting from the outside: The collected papers by Anthony G. Hopwood.* New York: Garland.

Hotelling, Harold. 1931. The economics of exhaustible resources. *Journal of Political Economy* 39: 137–175.

Hughes, John S. 1984. *A contracting perspective on accounting valuation.* Sarasota, Fla.: American Accounting Association.

Hughes, P. J., E. S. Schwartz, and A. V. Thakor. 1988. Capital structure and the FIFO/LIFO choice. Working paper. Los Angeles: Anderson Graduate School of Management, University of California.

Hunt, H. 1985. Potential determinants of corporate inventory accounting decisions. *Journal of Accounting Research* 23(Autumn): 448–467.

Ijiri, Yuji. 1965a. Axioms and structures of conventional accounting measurement. *The Accounting Review* 40(January): 36–53.

Ijiri, Yuji. 1965b. *Goal oriented models for accounting and control.* Amsterdam: North-Holland.

Ijiri, Yuji. 1967. *The foundations of accounting measurement.* Englewood Cliffs, N.J.: Prentice-Hall. Reprint. 1978. Accounting Classics Series. Houston: Scholars Book Co.

Ijiri, Yuji. 1968. An application of input–output analysis to some problems in cost accounting. *Management Accounting* 49(April): 49–61.

Ijiri, Yuji. 1975. *Theory of accounting measurement.* Sarasota, Fla.: American Accounting Association.

Ijiri, Yuji. 1980. A dialogue on research and standard setting in accounting. In *Perspectives on research: Proceedings of the 1980 Beyer Consortium*, ed. R. D. Nair and T. W. Williams, 26–39. Madison, Wis.: School of Business, University of Wisconsin.

Ijiri, Yuji. 1981. *Historical cost accounting and its rationality.* Vancouver, B.C.: Canadian Certified General Accountants Research Foundation.

Ijiri, Yuji. 1982. *Triple-entry bookkeeping and income momentum.* Sarasota, Fla.: American Accounting Association.

Ijiri, Yuji. 1989. *Momentum accounting and triple-entry bookkeeping: Exploring the dynamic structure of accounting measurements.* Sarasota, Fla.: American Accounting Association.

Ijiri, Yuji, F. K. Levy, and R. C. Lyon. 1963. A linear programming model for budgeting and financial planning. *Journal of Accounting Research* 1(Autumn): 198–212.

Institute of Chartered Accountants of England and Wales (ICAEW). 1980. *Current cost accounting—Statement of standard accounting practice 16.* London: ICAEW, Accounting Standards Committee.

Iwata, Iwao. 1954. Rijun-keisan no nigenteki-kozo (Dual structure of income determination). *Sangyo-keiri* 14: 1, 6.

Jaedicke, R. K., Y. Ijiri, and O. Nielson, eds. 1966. *Research in accounting measurement.* Menasha, Wis.: American Accounting Association.

Jensen, Michael C. 1976. Reflections on the state of accounting research and the regulation of accounting. Stanford Lectures in Accounting. Palo Alto, Calif.: Stanford University Press.

Jensen, Michael C. 1983. Organization theory and methodology. *The Accounting Review* 58(April): 319–339.

Jensen, M. C., and W. M. Meckling. 1976. Theory of the firm: Managerial behavior, agency costs, and ownership structure. *Journal of Financial Economics* 4(October): 305–360.

Johnson, B., and D. Dhaliwal. 1986. LIFO abandonment. Working paper. Chicago: Kellogg Graduate School of Management, Northwestern University.

Johnson, R. A., F. E. Kast, and J. E. Rosenzweig. 1964. Systems theory and management. *Management Science* 10(2): 367–384.

Johnston, J. 1960. *Statistical cost analysis.* New York: McGraw Hill.

Jung, W. 1985. Accounting decisions under asymmetric information. Ph.D. dissertation. Los Angeles: University of California.

Kam, Vernon. 1990. *Accounting theory.* 2nd ed. New York: John Wiley & Sons.

Kaplan, R. S. 1983. Comments on Wilson and Jensen. *The Accounting Review* 58(April): 340–346.

Kaplan R. S., and Gerald L. Thompson. 1971. Overhead allocation via mathematical programming models. *The Accounting Review* 46(April): 352–364.

Kelsen, Hans. 1967. *Pure theory of law*. Berkeley: University of California Press.

Kelsen, Hans. 1991. *General theory of norms*. Oxford: Claredon Press.

Kimura, Wasaburo. 1954. *Kaikeigaku-kenyu* (Research in accounting theory). Tokyo: Yuhikaki.

Kline, Morris. 1980. *Mathematics—The loss of certainty*. Oxford: Oxford University Press.

Koguchi, Yoshiaki, trans. 1992–1993. Richard Mattessich: Foundational research in accounting—Professional memoirs and beyond (in Japanese). *Chuo Hyoron* (April 1992): 154–162; (July 1992): 146–159; (October 1992): 112–120; (January 1993): 124–134; (April 1993): 136–148. Extended English version in press. Tokyo: Chuo University Press.

Kohler, Eric. 1952. *A dictionary for accountants*. Englewood Cliffs, N.J.: Prentice-Hall.

Kolmogoroff, A. N. 1933. *Grundbegriffe der Wahrscheinlichkeitsrechnung*. Berlin: Springer Verlag.

Kosiol, Erich. 1956. Pagatorische Bilanz. *Lexikon des kaufmännischen Rechnungswesens* 3: 2085–2120.

Kosiol, Erich. 1970. Zur Axiomatik der Theorie der Pagatorischen Erfolgsrechnung. *Zeitschrift für Betriebswirtschaft* 40: 135–162.

Kosiol, Erich. 1978. *Pagatoric theory of financial income determination*. Urbana: Center for Education and Research in Accounting, University of Illinois.

Kotlikoff, Lawrence J. 1992. *General accounting*. New York: The Free Press.

Kren, Leslie, and W. M. Liao. 1988. The role of accounting information in the control of organizations: A review of the evidence. *Journal of Accounting Literature* 7: 280–309.

Kuhn, Thomas S. 1962. *The structure of scientific revolutions*. Chicago: University of Chicago Press.

Kunkel, J. G. 1982. Sufficient conditions for public information to have social value in a production and exchange economy. *Journal of Finance* 37(4): 1005–1013.

Kurosawa, Kiyoshi. 1932. Taisha-kutaishohyo hyojunka no igi ni tsuite (On the meaning of standardization of the balance sheet). *Kaikei* (Accounting) 13: 340–366.

Laffont, J. J. 1989. *The economics of uncertainty and information*. Translated from French by J. Bonini and H. Bonini. Cambridge: MIT Press.

Lakatos, Imre. 1970. Falsification and the methodology of scientific research programmes. In *Falsification and the methodology of scientific research programmes*, ed. I. Lakatos and A. Musgrave, 91–196. Cambridge: Cambridge University Press.

Lakatos, Imre. 1983. The methodology of scientific research programmes. In *Collected philosophical papers*, vol. 1, ed. J. Worrall and G. Currie. 2nd ed. Cambridge: Cambridge University Press.

Lakatos, Imre, and A. Musgrave, eds. 1970. *Falsification and the methodology of scientific research programmes*. Cambridge: Cambridge University Press.

Lall Nigam, B. M. 1986. Bahi-Khata: The pre-Pacioli double-entry system of bookkeeping. *Abacus* 22(2): 148–161.

Lambert, Maurice. 1966. Pourquoi l'écriture est née en Mésopotamie. *Archeologia* 12: 30.

Laudan, Larry. 1977. *Progress and its problems*. Berkeley: University of California Press.

Le Coutre, W. 1949. *Grundzüge der Bilanzkunde—Eine totale Bilanzlehre*. Vol. 1. 4th ed. Wolfenbüttel.

Léautey, E., and A. Guilbault. 1885. *La science de compt à la porte de tous*. Paris: Guillaumin.

Lee, Ronald M. 1981. *CANDID, description of commercial and financial concepts: A formal semantics approach to knowledge representation.* Laxemburg, Austria: International Institute of Applied Systems Analysis.

Lee, Thomas A. 1982. U.K. current cost accounting and physical capital. In *Maintenance of capital: Financial versus physical capital*, ed. Robert R. Sterling and Kenneth W. Lemke, 171–194. Houston: Scholars Book Co.

Lehman, C., and A. M. Tinker. 1985. A semiotic analysis of "The great moving right show" featuring the accounting profession. Paper presented at the Interdisciplinary Perspectives in Accounting Conference. University of Manchester, July 8–10.

Lemke, Kenneth W. 1982. Financial versus physical capital. In *Maintenance of capital: Financial versus physical capital*, ed. Robert R. Sterling and Kenneth W. Lemke, 287–323. Houston: Scholars Book Co.

Leonardo (Fibonacci) da Pisa. 1202. *Liber abbaci.* In *Scriti di Leonardo da Pisa*, ed. Baldassare Boncompagni. Rome: Tipographia delle Science Mathematiche e Fisiche [published 1857–1862].

Leontief, Wassili W. 1951. *The structure of the American economy 1919–1939.* 2nd ed. New York: Oxford University Press.

Lev, Baruch. 1969. *Accounting and information theory.* Sarasota, Fla.: American Accounting Association.

Lev, Baruch. 1988. Toward a theory of equitable and efficient accounting policy. *The Accounting Review* 63(January): 1–22.

Lev, Baruch, and James A. Ohlson. 1982. Market-based empirical research in accounting: A review, interpretation, and extension. *Journal of Accounting Research* [Studies on Current Research Methodologies in Accounting: A Critical Examination] 20(Supplement): 249–322.

Libby, Robert. 1981. *Accounting and human information processing: Theory and applications.* Englewood Cliffs, N.J.: Prentice-Hall.

Libby, Robert. 1989. Experimental research and distinctive features of accounting settings. In *The state of accounting research as we enter the 1990's*, ed. T. J. Frecka, 126–147. Urbana: University of Illinois at Urbana–Champaign, Department of Accountancy.

Lieberman, Stephen J. 1980. Of clay pebbles, hollow clay balls, and writing: A Sumerian view. *The American Journal of Archeology* 84(3): 339–358.

Limperg, Theodor, Jr. 1964–1968. *Bedrijfseconomie—Verzameld werk van Prof. dr. Th. Limperg Jr.* 7 vols. Deventer, The Netherlands: E. E. Kluwer.

Lin, Jun Z. 1992. Chinese double-entry bookkeeping before the nineteenth century. *The Accounting Historians Journal* 19(December): 103–122.

Lintner, J. 1965. The valuation of risky assets and the selection of risky investments in stock portfolios and capital budgets. *Review of Economics and Statistics* 47(February): 13–37.

Littleton, A. C. 1953. *Structure of accounting theory.* Menasha, Wis.: American Accounting Association.

Littleton, A. C., and V. K. Zimmerman. 1962. *Accounting theory: Continuity and change.* Englewood Cliffs, N.J.: Prentice-Hall.

Livingstone, John L. 1968. Matrix algebra and cost allocation. *The Accounting Review* 43(July): 503–508.

Livingstone, John L. 1969. Input–output analysis for cost accounting, planning and control. *The Accounting Review* 44(January): 48–64.

Livingstone, John L., and Roman L. Weil. 1982. Accounting for changing prices in the U.S.: An explication and evaluation of SFAS 33. In *Maintenance of capital: Financial versus physical capital*, ed. Robert R. Sterling and Kenneth W. Lemke, 225–257. Houston: Scholars Book Co.

Lodge, G. C. 1991. *Perestroika for America*. Boston: Harvard Business School Press.

Lorenz, Edward N. 1993. *The essence of chaos*. Seattle: University of Washington Press.

Lorenz, Konrad. 1977. *Behind the mirror*. Trans. Ronald Taylor. New York: Harcourt Brace Jovanovich.

Lowe, E. A., A. G. Puxty, and R. C. Laughlin. 1983. Simple theories for complex processes: Accounting policy and the market for myopia. *Journal of Accounting and Public Policy* 2(Spring): 19–42.

Luce, R. D., and Howard Raiffa. 1957. *Games and decisions: Introduction and critical survey*. New York: John Wiley & Sons.

Machlup, Fritz. 1962. *The production and distribution of knowledge in the United States*. Princeton: Princeton University Press.

Machlup, Fritz. 1980. *Knowledge, Its creation, distribution, and economic significance*. Vol. 1, *Knowledge and knowledge production*. Princeton: Princeton University Press.

Machlup, Fritz. 1982. *Knowledge, Its creation, distribution, and economic significance*. Vol. 2, *The branches of learning*. Princeton: Princeton University Press.

Machlup, Fritz. 1984. *Knowledge, Its creation, distribution, and economic significance*. Vol. 3, *The economics of information and human capital*. Princeton: Princeton University Press.

Machlup, Fritz, and Una Mansfield, eds. 1983. *The study of information—Interdisciplinary messages*. New York: John Wiley & Sons.

MacIntosh, Norman B. 1985. *The social software of accounting and information systems*. New York: John Wiley & Sons.

MacNeal, Kenneth. 1939. *Truth in accounting*. Philadelphia: University of Pennsylvania Press.

Mandelbrot, B. B. 1983. *The fractal geometry of nature*. Rev. ed. New York: W. H. Freeman.

Manes, Rene P. 1965. Comment on matrix theory and cost allocation. *The Accounting Review* 40(July): 640–643.

Marcuse, H. 1941. *Reason and revolution*. 2nd ed. London: Routledge & Kegan Paul.

Marcuse, H. 1968. *Negations: Essays in critical theory*. Boston: Beacon Press.

Markowitz, Harry. 1952. Portfolio selection. *Journal of Finance* 7(March): 77–91.

Marschak, Jacob. 1954. Towards an economic theory of organization and information. In *Decision processes*, ed. R. M. Thrall, C. H. Coombs, and R. L. Davis, 187–220. New York: John Wiley & Sons.

Marschak, Jacob. 1964. Problems in information economics. In *Management controls: New directions*, ed. C. P. Bonini, E. K. Jaedicke, and H. M. Wagner, 38–90. New York: McGraw Hill.

Marschak, Jacob. 1974. *Economic information, decision and prediction*. 3 vols. Boston: D. Reidel.

Marschak, Jacob, and K. Miyasawa. 1968. Economic comparability of information systems. *International Economic Review* 9(2): 137–174.

Marschak, Jacob, and Roy Radner. 1972. *Economic theory of teams*. New Haven, Conn.: Yale University Press.

Marshall, John M. 1974. Private incentive and information. *The American Economic Review* 64(June): 373–390.

Mattessich, Richard. 1956. The constellation of accountancy and economics. *The Accounting Review* 31(October): 551–564.

Mattessich, Richard. 1957. Towards a general and axiomatic foundation of accountancy— With an introduction to the matrix formulation of accounting systems. *Accounting Research* 8(October): 328–355. Reprinted in Zeff, Stephen A. 1982. *The accounting postulates and principles controversy of the 1960s*, pp. 328–355. New York: Garland.

Mattessich, Richard. 1959. Messung, Vorausberechnung und Buchhaltung. *Zeitschrift für handelswissenschaftliche Forschung* 11(April): 179–194.

Mattessich, Richard. 1961. Budgeting models and system simulation. *The Accounting Review* 36(July): 384–397.

Mattessich, Richard. 1964a. *Accounting and analytical methods, measurement and projection of income and wealth in the micro- and macro-economy.* Homewood, Ill.: Richard D. Irwin. Reprint. 1977. Accounting Classics Series. Houston: Scholars Book Co.

Mattessich, Richard. 1964b. *Simulation of the firm through a budget computer program.* Homewood, Ill.: R. D. Irwin. Reprint. 1979. Reprints on Demand Series. Ann Arbor, Mich.: Microfilms International.

Mattessich, Richard. 1970a. *Die Wissenschaftlichen Grundlagen des Rechnungswesens.* Düsseldorf: Bertelsmann Universitätsverlag.

Mattessich, Richard. 1970b. On the perennial misunderstanding of asset measurement by means of "present values." *Cost and Management* 44(March–April): 29–31.

Mattessich, Richard. 1971a. Asset measurement and valuation—A final reply to Chambers. *Cost and Management* 45(July–August): 18–23.

Mattessich, Richard. 1971b. On further misunderstandings about "measurement" and valuation: A rejoinder to Chambers' article. *Cost and Management* 45(March–April): 36–42.

Mattessich, Richard. 1972. Methodological preconditions and problems of a general theory of accounting. *The Accounting Review* 47(July): 469–487.

Mattessich, Richard. 1973. On the axiomatic formulation of accounting: Comment on Prof. S. Saito's considerations (in Japanese). *Sangyo Keiri* 33(3): 70–77. English trans. in *The Musashi University Journal* 21(1–2): 77–94.

Mattessich, Richard. 1974. The incorporation and reduction of value judgements in systems. *Management Science* 21(September): 1–9.

Mattessich, Richard. 1977. Normative vs. positive systems: On the relation between normativity, teleology, and mentalistic aspects. In *Proceedings of the 8th International Congress of Cybernetics*, pp. 221–231. Namur, Belgium: International Association of Cybernetics.

Mattessich, Richard. 1978a. *Instrumental reasoning and systems methodology.* Boston: D. Reidel.

Mattessich, Richard. 1978b. Instrumentelle Bilanztheorie: Voraussetzungen und erste Ansätze. *Zeitschrift für betriebswirtschaftliche Forschung* 30(10–11): 792–800.

Mattessich, Richard. 1979a. Instrumental aspects of accounting. In *Accounting for a simplified firm: Seventeen essays based on a common example*, ed. R. R. Sterling and A. L. Thomas, 335–351. Houston: Scholars Book Co.

Mattessich, Richard. 1979b. Konfliktresolution in der Wissenschaft—Zur Anwendung der Methoden von Thomas Kuhn, Sneed und Stegmüller in den Sozial- und Wirtschaftswissenschaften. In *Unternehmungsbezogene Konfliktforschung: Methodologische und forschungsprogrammatische Grundfragen*, ed. G. Dlugos, 253–272. Stuttgart: Poeschel Verlag.

Mattessich, Richard. 1980. Management accounting: Past, present and future. In *Management accounting 1980*, ed. H. Peter Holzer, 209–240. Champaign: University of Illinois, Department of Accountancy.

Mattessich, Richard. 1981a. Major concepts and problems of inflation accounting: Part I. *CGA Magazine* 15(May): 10–15.

Mattessich, Richard. 1981b. Major concepts and problems of inflation accounting: Part II. *CGA Magazine* (June–July): 20–27.

Mattessich, Richard. 1982. On the evolution of inflation accounting—With a comparison of seven models. *Economia Aziendale* 1(3): 349–381.

Mattessich, Richard, ed. 1984. *Modern accounting research: History, survey and guide*. Vancouver, B.C.: Canadian Certified General Accountants Research Foundation.

Mattessich, Richard. 1986. Fritz Schmidt (1882–1950) and his pioneering work in current value accounting in comparison to Edwards and Bell's theory. *Contemporary Accounting Research* 2(Spring): 157–178.

Mattessich, Richard. 1987a. An applied scientist's search for a methodological framework: An attempt to apply Lakatos' research program, Stegmüller's theory-nets, and Bunge's family of research fields to accounting theory. In *Logic, philosophy of science and epistemology*, ed. P. Weingartner and G. Schurz, 243–262. Vienna: Hölder-Pichler-Tempsky.

Mattessich, Richard. 1987b. Prehistoric accounting and the problem of representation: On recent archeological evidence of the Middle East from 8000 B.C. to 3000 B.C. *The Accounting Historians Journal* 14(2): 71–91. Reprint. 1990. *The closure of the accounting profession*, vol. 1, ed. T. A. Lee, 246–266. New York: Garland Press.

Mattessich, Richard. 1988. Wittgenstein and archeological evidence of representation and data processing from 8000 B.C. to 3000 B.C. In *Philosophy of law, politics and society*, ed. Ota Weinberger, P. Koller, and A. Schramm, 254–263. Vienna: Hölder-Pichler-Tempsky.

Mattessich, Richard. 1989. Accounting and the input–output principle in the prehistoric and ancient world. *Abacus* 25(2): 74–84.

Mattessich, Richard. 1990. Epistemological aspects of accounting. *Keiri Kenkyu* 34(Autumn): 3–30.

Mattessich, Richard, ed. 1991a. *Accounting research in the 1980s and its future relevance*. Vancouver, B.C.: Canadian Certified General Accountants Research Foundation.

Mattessich, Richard. 1991b. Counting, accounting, and the input–output principle— Recent archeological evidence revising our view on the evolution of early record keeping. In *The costing heritage—Studies in honor of S. Paul Garner*, ed. O. Finley Graves, 25–49. Harrisonburg, Va.: Academy of Accounting Historians.

Mattessich, Richard. 1991c. Editor's commentary: A decade of growth, sophistication, and impending crisis. In *Accounting research in the 1980s and its future relevance*, ed. Richard Mattessich, 1–72. Vancouver, B.C.: Canadian Certified General Accountants Research Foundation.

Mattessich, Richard. 1991d. Social reality and the measurement of its phenomena. In *Advances in Accounting*, vol. 9, ed. Bill N. Schwartz, 3–17. Greenwich, Conn.: JAI Press.

Mattessich, Richard. 1991e. Social versus physical reality in accounting, and the measurement of its phenomena. In *Contemporary issues of accounting research*, ed. Bhabatosh Banerjee, 1–30. Calcutta: Indian Accounting Association's Research Foundation.

Mattessich, Richard. 1992. On the history of normative accounting theory: Paradigm lost, paradigm regained? *Accounting, Business and Financial History* 2(2): 181–198.

Mattessich, Richard. 1993a. On the nature of information and knowledge and the interpretation in the economic sciences. *Library Trends* 41(Spring): 567–593.

Mattessich, Richard. 1993b. Paradigms, research traditions and theory nets of accounting. In *Philosophical perspectives on accounting—Essays in honour of Edward Stamp*, ed. M. J. Mumford and K. V. Peasnell, 177–220. London: Routledge.

Mattessich, Richard. 1994a. Accounting as a cultural force: Past, present and future. *The European Accounting Review* 3(2): 354–374.

Mattessich, Richard. 1994b. Archeology of accounting and Schmandt-Besserat's contribution. *Accounting, Business and Financial History* 4(1): 5–28.

Mattessich, Richard. 1994c. The number concept in business and "concern economics." In *Leonardo Fibonacci—Il tempo, le opere, l'eredità scientifica*, ed. Marcello Morelli and Marco Tangheroni, 109–135. Pisa: Pacini Editore.

Mattessich, Richard. 1995. Conditional–normative accounting methodology: Incorporating value judgments and means–end relations of an applied science. *Accounting, Organizations and Society* 20(4): 259–284.

Mattessich, Richard. In press. Normative accounting. In *Encyclopedia of the history of accounting and accounting thought*, ed. M. Chatfield and R. G. Vangermeersch, New York: Garland.

Mautz, R. K., and H. A. Scharaff. 1961. *The philosophy of auditing*. Madison: American Accounting Association.

McCarthy, William E. 1987. Accounting information systems: Research directions and perspective. *Journal of Information Systems* 2(1): 29–32.

McKee, A. James, T. B. Bell, and J. R. Boatsman. 1984. Management preferences over accounting standards: A replication and additional test. *The Accounting Review* 59(October): 647–659.

McKinsey, James O. 1922. *Budgetary control*. New York: Ronald Press.

Merton, R. 1973a. An intertemporal capital asset pricing model. *Econometrica* 41(September): 867–887.

Merton, R. 1973b. Theory of rational option pricing. *The Bell Journal of Economics* 4(Spring): 141–182.

Merton, R. 1974. On the pricing of corporate dept: The risk structure of interest rates. *Journal of Finance* 29: 449–470.

Merton, R. 1976. Option pricing when underlying stock returns are discontinuous. *Journal of Financial Economics* 3: 125–144.

Milburn, J. Alex. 1994. Towards new directions in financial accounting research. In *Measurement research in financial accounting*, ed. Ernst & Young Foundation, 14–26. Workshop proceedings, September 30 to October 1, 1993. Waterloo, Ontario: Ernst & Young Foundation and Waterloo University, School of Accountancy.

Miller, Jonathan. 1982. *The body in question*. London: Papermac.

Mirrlees, J. 1971. An exploration in the theory of income taxation. *Review of Economic Studies* 38(April): 175–201.

Mirrlees, J. 1976. The optimal structure of incentives and authority within an organization. *The Bell Journal of Economics* 7(1): 105–131.

Mock, T. J. 1971. Concepts of information value and accounting. *The Accounting Review* 46(October): 765–778.

Mock, T. J. 1976. *Measurement and accounting information criteria*. Sarasota: Fla.: American Accounting Association.

Modigliani, F., and M. Miller. 1958. The cost of capital, corporation finance, and theory of investment. *American Economic Review* 48(June): 261–297.

Moonitz, Maurice. 1961. *The basic postulates of accounting*. New York: American Institute of Certified Public Accountants.

Moonitz, Maurice. 1986. *History of accounting at Berkeley*. Berkeley: University of California, Professional Accounting Program.

Moonitz, Maurice. 1993. *Selected writings of Maurice Moonitz*. Vols. 1 and 2. New York: Garland.

Moonitz, Maurice, and Charles C. Staehling. 1950–1952. *Accounting: An analysis of its problems*. Vols. 1 and 2. Brooklyn: Foundation Press.

Morgan, Gareth. 1983a. *Beyond methods: Strategies for social research*. Beverly Hills, Calif.: Sage.

Morgan, Gareth. 1983b. Social science and accounting research: A commentary on Tomkins and Groves. *Accounting, Organizations and Society* 8(4): 385–388.

Most, Kenneth S. 1982. *Accounting theory*. 2nd ed. Columbus: Grid Publishing.

Mouck, Tom. 1989. The irony of "the golden age" of accounting methodology. *The Accounting Historians Journal* 16(December): 85–106.

Mouck, Tom. 1990. Positive accounting theory as a Lakatosian research programme. *Accounting and Business Research* 20(Summer): 231–239.

Mouck, Tom. 1993. The "revolution" in financial reporting theory: A Kuhnian interpretation. *The Accounting Historians Journal* 20(June): 33–56.

Mozes, H. 1992. A framework for normative accounting research. *Journal of Accounting Literature* 11: 93–120.

Mueller, G. G., ed. 1971. *A new introduction to accounting—A report of the study group sponsored by the Price Waterhouse Foundation*. New York: Price Waterhouse Foundation.

Murphy, G. J. 1992. The changing interrelationships amongst financial statements: Instrumentalism vs. realism. Working paper. Saskatoon, Saskatchewan: University of Saskatchewan.

Myrdal, Gunnar. 1970. *Objectivity in social research*. London: Gerald Druckworth.

Nehmer, Robert A. 1988. Accounting informations systems as algebras and first order axiomatic models. Ph.D. dissertation. Urbana–Champaign: University of Illinois; and Ann Arbor, Mich.: University Microfilms.

Neter, John 1952. Some applications of statistics for auditing. *Journal of the American Statistical Association* 47(March): 6–24.

Nicklisch, H. 1912. *Allgemeine kaufmännische Betriebslehre als Privatwirtschaftslehre des Handels*. Leipzig: C. E. Poeschel.

Nicklisch, H. 1915–1916. Rede über Egoismus und Pflichtgefühl. *Zeitschrift für Handelswissenschaft und Handelspraxis* 8: 101–104.

Nicklisch, H. 1923. *Revising and extending Wilhelm Osbahr's* Die Bilanz vom Standpunkt der Unternehmung. 3rd ed. Berlin: Haude & Spenersche Buchhandlung.

Nicklisch, H. 1929–1932. *Die Betriebswirtschaft*. 3 vols. Stuttgart: C. E. Poeschel.

Niiniluoto, I. 1981. The growth of theories: Comments on the structuralist approach. In *Pisa Conference on the History and Philosophy of Science, Proceedings 1978*, ed. J. Hinitkka, D. Gruender, and E. Agazzi, 4–47. Boston: D. Reidel.

Niiniluoto, I. 1983. Theories, approximations, and idealizations. *Proceedings of the 7th International Congress of Logic, Methodology, and Philosophy of Science*. Vol. 3, *Abstracts of section 6*, pp. 4–7. Salzburg: The Congress.

Niiniluoto, I. 1984. *Is science progressive?* Boston: D. Reidel.

Nissen, H. J., Peter Damerow, and R. K. Englund 1993. *Archaic bookkeeping—Early writing techniques of economic administration in the ancient Near East*. Trans. Paul Larsen. Chicago: University of Chicago Press.

Nobes, C.W. 1987. The pre-Pacioli Indian double-entry system of bookkeeping: A comment. *Abacus* 23(2): 182–184.

Noreen, Eric. 1988. The economics of ethics: A new perspective on agency theory. *Accounting, Organizations and Society* 13(4): 259–369.

Ohlson, James A. 1987. On the nature of income measurement: The basic results. *Contemporary Accounting Research* 4(Fall): 1–15.

Ohlson, James A. 1988. The social value of public information in production economies. In *Economic analysis of information and contracts*, ed. G. A. Feltham, A. Amershi, and W. T. Ziemba, 95–119. Boston: Kluwer Academic.

Ohlson, James A. 1990. A synthesis of security valuation theory and the role of dividends, cash flows, and earnings. *Contemporary Accounting Research* 6(Spring): 648–676. Reprint. 1991. *Accounting research in the 1980s and its future relevance*, ed. Richard Mattessich, 157–181. Vancouver, B.C.: Canadian Certified General Accountants Research Foundation.

Ohlson, James A., and A. G. Buckman. 1980. Toward a theory of financial accounting. *Journal of Finance* 35(May): 537–547.

Olenick, Richard, Tom M. Apostol, and David L. Goodstein. 1985. *The mechanical universe: Introduction to mechanics and heat*. Cambridge: Cambridge University Press.

Oppenheim, Leo A. 1959. On an operational device in Mesopotamian bureaucracy. *Journal of Near Eastern Studies* 18(2): 121–128.

Orbach, Kenneth Ned. 1978. Accounting as a mathematical measurement theoretic discipline. Ph.D. dissertation. College Station, Tex.: Texas A & M University; and Ann Arbor, Mich.: University Microfilms.

Pacioli, Luca. 1494. *Summa de arithmetica, geometria, proportioni et proportionalita*. Venice.

Pagels, Heinz R. 1983. *The cosmic code*. New York: Bantam Books.

Pagels, Heinz R. 1986. *Perfect symmetry—In search of the beginning of time*. New York: Bantam Books.

Parker, Sybill P., ed., 1983. *McGraw-Hill encyclopedia of physics*. New York: McGraw-Hill.

Patell, James M. 1976. Corporate forecasts of earnings per share and stock price behavior: empirical tests. *Journal of Accounting Research* 14(2): 246–276.

Patell, James M. 1979. The API and the design of experiments. *Journal of Accounting Research* 17(August): 528–549.

Paton, William A. 1918. The significance and treatment of appreciation in the accounts. In *Michigan Academy of Science, twentieth annual report*, ed. G. H. Coons. Ann Arbor, Mich.: Michigan Academy of Science. Reprint. 1976. *Asset appreciation, business income and price-level accounting: 1918–1935*, ed. Stephen A. Zeff, 35–49. New York: Arno Press.

Paton, William A. 1922. *Accounting theory—With special reference to the corporate enterprise*. New York: Ronald Press. Reprint. 1972. Accounting Classics Series. Lawrence, Kans.: Scholars Book Co.

Paton, William A., and A. C. Littleton. 1940. *An introduction to corporate accounting standards*. Sarasota, Fla.: American Accounting Association.

Pearce, D. W., and R. K. Turner. 1989. *Economics of natural resources and the environment*. Baltimore: Johns Hopkins University Press.

Peasnell, Kenneth V. 1978. Statement of accounting theory and theory acceptance: A review article. *Accounting and Business Research* 8(Summer): 217–225.

Peasnell, K. V., and D. J. Williams. 1986. Ersatz academics and scholar-saints: The supply of financial accounting research. *Abacus* 22(2): 121–135.

Peat Marwick Thorne, Inc. 1993. *KPMTG international fraud survey report*. Toronto, Ontario: KPMTG Peat Marwick Thorne, Chartered Accountants.

Pellicelli, Giorgio. 1969. The axiomatic method in business economics: A first approach. *Abacus* 5(December): 119–131.

Peragallo, William A. 1938. *Origin and evolution of double entry bookkeeping*. New York: American Institute.

Philips, G. Edward. 1963. The revolution in accounting theory. *The Accounting Review* 38(October): 696–708.

Phlips, Louis. 1988. *The economics of imperfect information*. Cambridge: Cambridge University Press.

Plato. 1963. *The collected dialogues including the letters*, ed. E. Hamilton and H. Cairns. Princeton: Princeton University Press.

Ponemon, Lawrence A., and David R. L. Gabhard. 1993. *Ethical reasoning in accounting and auditing*. Vancouver, B.C.: CGA-Research Foundation.

Power, Michael K. 1992. From common sense to expertise: Reflections on the prehistory of audit sampling. *Accounting, Organizations and Society* 17(1): 37–62.

Prakash, Prem, and Shyam Sunder. 1979. The case against separation of current operating profit and holding gain. *The Accounting Review* 54(January): 1–22.

Putnam, Hilary. 1980. Models and reality. *The Journal of Symbolic Logic* 45: 462–482.

Putnam, Hilary. 1982. *Vernunft, Wahrheit und Geschichte*. German trans. by J. Schulte, Frankfurt. Originally published in 1981 as *Reason, truth and history*. New York: Cambridge University Press.

Rescher, Nicholas. 1966a. *The logic of commands*. London: Routledge & Kegan Paul.

Rescher, Nicholas, ed. 1966b. *The logic of decision and action*. Pittsburgh: University of Pittsburgh Press.

Revsine, Lawrence. 1982. Physical capital maintenance: An analysis. In *Maintenance of capital: Financial versus physical capital*, ed. Robert R. Sterling and Kenneth W. Lemke, 75–103. Houston: Scholars Book Co.

Richardson, A. J., and M. Gibbins (with the assistance of John Wilson). 1988. Behavioral research on the production and use of financial information. In *Accounting research: A critical analysis*, ed. K. R. Ferris, 15–45. New York: Century VII.

Riebel, P. 1978. Überlegungen zur Formulierung eines entscheidungsorientierten Kostenbegriffs. In *Quantitative Ansätze der Betriebswirtschaftslehre*, ed. H. Müller-Merbach, 127–146. Munich: Vahlen Verlag.

Rieger, W. 1928. *Einführung in die Privatwirtschaftslehre*. Nuremberg.

Roberts, J., and R. Scapens. 1985. Accounting systems and systems of accountability— Understanding accounting practices in their organizational contexts. *Accounting, Organizations and Society* 10(4): 443–456.

Rosenblatt, David. 1960. On some aspects of models of complex systems. In *Information and decision processes*, ed. R. E. Machol. New York: McGraw Hill.

Roslender, R. 1990. Sociology and management accounting research. *British Accounting Review* (December): 351–372.

Ross, A. 1944. Imperatives and logic. *Philosophy of Science* 11(April): 30–46.

Russell, Bertrand. 1948. *Human knowledge: Its scope and limits*. New York: Simon & Schuster.

Russell, Bertrand. 1960. *Introduction to mathematical philosophy*. 10th ed. London: George Allen & Unwin.

Saario, Martti. 1950. Om preoritetsordningen för costnarder (On the priority order of costs). *Affärsekonomi*, pp. 1183–1186, 1193–1194.

Saint Augustine. 1991. *Confessions*. Trans. Henry Chatwick. Oxford: Oxford University Press. (Originally published about A.D. 400.)

Saito, Shizuki. 1972. Some considerations on the axiomatic formulation of accounting (in Japanese). *Kaikei* 101: 45–65; English trans. in *The Mushashi University Journal* 20: 81–99.

Saito, Shizuki. 1973. Further considerations on the axiomatic formulation of accounting: A reply to Prof. R. Mattessich. *The Mushashi University Journal* 21: 95–107.

Sanders, Thomas Henry, Henry Rand Hatfield, and Underhill Moore. 1938. *A statement of accounting principles*. New York: American Institute of Accountants.

Schär, J. F. 1890. *Versuch einer wissenschaftlichen Behandlung der Buchhaltung*. Berlin.

Schär, J. F. 1911. *Allgemeine Handelsbetriebslehre*. Basel.

Schär, J. F. 1914. *Buchhaltung und Bilanz auf wirtschaftlicher, rechtlicher und mathematischer Grundlage*. Basel.

Schendge, Malati J. 1983. The use of seals and the invention of writing. *Journal of the Economic and Social History of the Orient* 26(2): 113–136.

Schmalenbach, E. 1919a. Grundlagen dynamischer Bilanzlehre. *Zeitschrift für handelswissenschaftliche Forschung* 13: 1–60, 65–101. Published in 1962 as *Dynamische Bilanz*. 13th ed. Köln & Opladen: Gabler Verlag.

Schmalenbach, E. 1919b. Selbstkostenrechnung. *Zeitschrift für handelswissenschaftliche Forschung* 13: 257–299, 321–356.

Schmandt-Besserat, Denise. 1977. An archaic recording system and the origin of writing. *Syro-Mesopotamian Studies* 1(2): 1–32.

Schmandt-Besserat, Denise. 1978. The earliest precursor of writing. *Scientific American* 238(6): 50–58.

Schmandt-Besserat, Denise. 1979. Reckoning before writing. *Archeology* 32(3): 23–31.

Schmandt-Besserat, Denise. 1980. The envelopes that bear the first writing. *Technology and Culture* 21(3): 357–385.

Schmandt-Besserat, Denise. 1983. Tokens and counting. *Biblical Archeologist* 46: 117–120.

Schmandt-Besserat, Denise. 1992a. *Before writing*. Vol. 1, *From counting to cuneiform*. Austin: University of Texas Press.

Schmandt-Besserat, Denise. 1992b. *Before writing*. Vol. 2, *A catalogue of near eastern tokens*. Austin: University of Texas Press.

Schmidt, Fritz. [1921] 1953. *Die organische Bilanz im Rahmen der Wirtschaft*. Leipzig: C. A. Gloeckner Verlagsbuchhandlung. Reprint. Wiesbaden: Betriebswirtschaftlicher Verlag Dr. Th. Gabler.

Schneeweiß, C. 1993. Kostenbegriffe aus entscheidungstheoretischer Sicht— Überlegungen zu einer Kostentheorie. *Zeitschrift für betriebswirtschaftliche Forschung* 45(December): 1025–1039.

Schreuder, Hein. 1984. Positively normative (accounting) theories. In *European contributions to accounting theory: The achievements of the last decade*, ed. Anthony G. Hopewood and Hein Schreuder, 213–231. Amsterdam: Free University Press.

Schumacher, E. F. 1974. *Small is beautiful: A study of economics as if people mattered.* Abacus edition. London: Sphere Books.

Schutz, A. 1962–1966. *Collected papers.* Vols. 1–3, ed. N. Nathanson. The Netherlands: Martinus Nijhoff.

Schutz, A. 1967. *The phenomenology of the social world.* Trans. G. Walsh and F. Lehnert. Evanston, Ill.: Northwestern University Press.

Schweitzer, Marcell. 1970. Axiomatik des Rechnungswesens. In *Handwörterbuch des Rechnungswesens*, ed. E. Kosiol, 83–90. Stuttgart: Poeschel Verlag.

Scott, William R. 1982. Discussion. In *Maintenance of capital: Financial versus physical capital*, ed. Robert R. Sterling and Kenneth W. Lemke, 259–266. Houston: Scholars Book Co.

Scott, William R. 1994. Research about accounting and research on how to account. In *Measurement research in financial accounting*, ed. Ernst & Young Foundation, 62–67. Workshop proceedings, September 30 to October 1, 1993. Waterloo, Ontario: Ernst & Young Foundation and Waterloo University, School of Accountancy.

Seicht, Gerhard. 1970. *Die kapitaltheoretische Bilanz und die Entwicklung der Bilanztheorien.* Berlin: Duncker & Humblot.

Sellien, S., and H. Sellien, eds. 1956. *Dr. Gabler's Wirtschaftslexikon.* 2 vols. Wiesbaden: Betriebswirtschaftlicher Verlag Dr. Th. Gabler.

Sharpe, William F. 1963. A simplified model for portfolio analysis. *Management Science* 10(January): 277–293.

Sharpe, William F. 1964. Capital asset prices: A theory of market equilibrium under conditions of risk. *The Journal of Finance* 19(September): 425–442.

Simon, H. A. 1951. A formal theory of employment relation. *Econometrica* 19: 293–305.

Simon, H. A. 1965. The logic of rational decision. *British Journal for the Philosophy of Science* 16: 169–186.

Simon, H. A. 1966. The logic of heuristic decision making. In *The logic of decision and action*, ed. Nicholas Rescher, 1–20. Pittsburgh: University of Pittsburgh.

Skinner, Ross M. 1982. The impact of changing prices: The Canadian position. In *Maintenance of capital: Financial versus physical capital*, ed. Robert R. Sterling and Kenneth W. Lemke, 117–169. Houston: Scholars Book Co.

Sneed, J. D. 1971. *The logical structure of mathematical physics.* Boston: D. Reidel.

Sneed, J. D. 1981. Conventionalism in kinetic theory. In *Proceedings: Second Annual International Symposium on Philosophy.* Mexico City: Autonomous University of Mexico.

Sneed, J. D. 1983. Structuralism and scientific realism. *Erkenntnis* 19: 345–370.

Solomons, David, ed. 1952. *Studies in costing.* London: Sweet & Maxwell.

Solomons, David. 1965. *Divisional performance: Measurement and control.* New York: Financial Executive Research Foundation.

Solomons, David. 1991a. Accounting and social change: A neutralist view. *Accounting, Organizations and Society* 16(3): 287–295.

Solomons, David. 1991b. A rejoinder. *Accounting, Organizations and Society* 16(3): 311–312.

Sombart, Werner. 1902. *Der moderne Kapitalismus.* Leipzig: Duncker & Humblot.

Spacek, Leonard. 1962. Comments. In *A tentative set of broad accounting principles for business enterprises*, ed. R. T. Sprouse and M. Moonitz, 77–79. New York: American Institute of Certified Public Accountants.

Spence, A. M., and J. R. Zeckhauser. 1971. Insurance, information and individual action. *American Economic Review* 61(May): 380–390.

Spengler, Oswald. 1928. *The decline of the west*. Vol. 2. New York: Alfred A. Knopf. Originally published in 1918 as *Der Untergang des Abendlandes—Welthistorische Perspektiven*. Munich: Beck'sche Verlagsbuchandlung.

Sprague, Charles E. 1907. *The philosophy of accounts* (in monthly installments). In *Journal of Accountancy* (January 1907 to January 1908).

Sprouse, R. T., and M. Moonitz, eds. 1962. *A tentative set of broad accounting principles for business enterprises*. New York: American Institute of Certified Public Accountants.

Sprowls, R. Clay. 1962. A role of computer simulation in accounting education. *The Accounting Review* 37(July): 515–520.

Stamp, Edward. 1980. *Corporate reporting: Its future evolution*. Toronto: Canadian Institute of Chartered Accountants.

Starr, Richard F. S. 1939. *Nuzi*, vol. 1. Cambridge: Harvard University Press.

Staubus, George J. 1961. *A theory of accounting to investors*. Berkeley: University of California Press.

Staubus, George J. 1987. The dark ages of cost accounting: The role of miscues in the literature. *The Accounting Historians Journal* 14(Fall): 1–18.

Stedry, A. C. 1960. *Budget control and cost behavior*. Englewood Cliffs, N.J.: Prentice-Hall.

Stegmüller, Wolfgang. 1975. *Hauptströmungen der Gegenwartsphilosophie*. Vol. 2. Stuttgart: Kroner.

Stegmüller, Wolfgang. 1976. *The structure and dynamics of theories*. New York: Springer-Verlag.

Stegmüller, Wolfgang. 1979. *The structuralist view of theories*. New York: Springer-Verlag.

Stegmüller, Wolfgang. 1983. *Erklärung, Begründung, Kausalität, Vol. 1, Part G—Studienausgabe*. 2nd rev. ed. Berlin: Springer-Verlag.

Stegmüller, Wolfgang. 1986. *Theorie und Erfahrung, Vol. 2, Part 3—Die Entwicklung des neuen Strukturalismus seit 1973*. Berlin: Springer-Verlag.

Stegmüller, W., W. Balzer, and W. Spohn, eds. 1982. *Philosophy of economics*. New York: Springer-Verlag.

Sterling, Robert R. 1970a. On theory construction and verification. *The Accounting Review* 45(July): 444–457.

Sterling, Robert R. 1970b. *Theory of the measurement of enterprise income*. Lawrence, Kans.: University Press of Kansas. Reprinted by Scholars Book Co.

Sterling, Robert R. 1972. Decision oriented financial accounting. *Accounting and Business Research* 2(Summer): 198–208.

Sterling, Robert R. 1988. Confessions of a failed empiricist. In *Advances in accounting*, vol. 6., ed. Bill N. Schwartz, 3–35. Greenwich, Conn.: JAI Press.

Sterling, Robert R. 1989. Teaching the correspondence concept. *Issues in Accounting Education* 4(Spring): 82–93.

Sterling, Robert R. 1990. Positive accounting: An assessment. *Abacus* 26(Fall): 97–135.

Sterling, Robert R., and Kenneth W. Lemke, eds. 1982. *Maintenance of capital: Financial versus physical capital*. Houston: Scholars Book Co.

Stevens, S. S. 1946. On the theory of scales of measurement. *Science* 103: 677–680.

Stigler, G. J. 1961. The economics of information. *Journal of Political Economy* 69(3): 213–285.

Stigler, G. J. 1962. Information in the labour market. *Journal of Political Economy* 70(5): 94–105.

Stigler, G. J. 1988. *Memoirs of an unregulated economist*. New York: Basic Books.

Strauss, Leo. 1959. *What is political philosophy?* New York: The Free Press.

Studenski, Paul. 1958. *The income of nations—Theory, measurement, and analysis: Past and present*. New York: New York University Press.

Study Group of the University of Illinois. 1964. *A statement of basic accounting postulates and principles*. Urbana: Center for International Education and Research in Accounting, University of Illinois.

Stützel, Wolfgang. 1967. Bemerkungen zur Bilanztheorie. *Zeitschrift für Betriebswirtschaft* 37: 314–340.

Subotnik, Dan. 1988. Wisdom or widgets: Whither the school of business? *Abacus* 24(Fall): 95–106.

Sunder, Shyam. 1973. Relationship between accounting changes and stock prices: Problems of measurement and some empirical evidence. *Journal of Accounting Research* 11(Supplement): 1–45.

Sunder, Shyam. 1975. Stock price and risk related to accounting changes in inventory valuation. *The Accounting Review* 50(April): 305–315.

Sunder, Shyam. 1976. Optimal choice between FIFO and LIFO. *Journal of Accounting Research* 14(Autumn): 277–300.

Suppe, Frederick, ed. 1974. *The structure of scientific theories*. Urbana: University of Illinois Press.

Swanson, G. A. 1984. The "roots" of accounting. *The Accounting Historians Journal* 11(Fall): 111–116.

Swanson, G. A. 1987. Accounting investigation can be used for scientific investigation. *Behavioral Science* 32(April): 81–91.

Sweeney, H. W. 1936. *Stabilized accounting*. New York: Harper & Brothers.

Swieringa, Robert. 1989. Accounting research and accounting standards. In *The state of accounting research as we enter the 1990's*, ed. T. J. Frecka, 181–195. Urbana: University of Illinois at Urbana–Champaign, Department of Accountancy.

Swieringa, R. J., and K. E. Weick. 1987. Management accounting and action. *Accounting, Organizations and Society* 12(3): 293–308.

Synge, J. L. 1970. *Talking about reality*. Amsterdam: North-Holland.

Thornton, Daniel B. 1985. [Review article of] *Modern accounting research: History, survey and guide* (ed. by R. Mattessich). *Contemporary Accounting Research* 2(Fall): 93–100.

Thornton, Daniel B. 1986. Current cost disclosers and nondisclosers: Theory and Canadian evidence. *Contemporary Accounting Research* 3(Fall): 1–34.

Thornton, Daniel B. 1988. Theory and metaphor in accounting. *Accounting Horizons* 2(December): 1–9.

Thornton, Daniel B. 1994. Accounting measurement. In *Measurement research in financial accounting*, ed. Ernst & Young Foundation, 73–79. Workshop proceedings, September 30 to October 1, 1993. Waterloo, Ontario: Ernst & Young Foundation and Waterloo University, School of Accountancy.

Thurow, Lester. 1993. *Head to head: The coming economic battle among Japan, Europe, and America*. Rev. ed. New York: Warner Books.

Tinker, Anthony M. 1984. Theories of the state and the state of accounting: Economic reductionism and political voluntarism in accounting regulation theory. *Journal of Accounting and Public Policy* 3(Spring): 55–74.

Tinker, Anthony M. 1991. The accountant as partisan. *Accounting, Organizations and Society* 16(3): 297–310.

Tinker, A. M., B. D. Merino, and M. D. Neimark. 1982. The normative origins of positive theories: Ideology and accounting thought. *Accounting, Organizations and Society* 7(2): 167–200.

Tinker, T. A. 1985. *Paper prophets: A social critique of accounting.* New York: Praeger Special Studies.

Tippett, Mark. 1978. The axioms of accounting measurement. *Accounting and Business Research* 8(Autumn): 266–278.

Tomkins, C., and R. Groves. 1983. The everyday accountant and researching his reality. *Accounting, Organization and Society* 8(4): 361–374.

Toulmin, S. 1953. *The philosophy of science.* London: Hutchinson.

Trueblood, R. M., and W. W. Cooper. 1955. Research and practice in statistical applications to accounting, auditing, and management control. *The Accounting Review* 30: 221–229.

Truesdell, C. 1984. *An idiot's fugitive essays on science.* New York: Springer-Verlag.

Tryon, Edwards P. 1973. Is the universe a vacuum fluctuation? *Nature* 246(December): 396–397.

Van Seventer, A. 1975. Replacement value theory in modern Dutch accounting. *The International Journal of Accounting Education and Research* 10(1): 67–94.

Vance, Lawrence L. 1950. *Scientific methods for auditing.* Berkeley: University of California Press.

Vance, Lawrence L., and John Neter. 1956. *Statistical sampling for auditors and accountants.* New York: John Wiley & Sons.

von Bertalanffy, Ludwig. 1968. *General systems.* New York: George Braziller.

von Helmholz, H. 1895. Zählen und Messen erkenntnistheoretisch betrachtet. In *Wissenschaftliche Abhandlungen.* Leipzig: Barth.

von Neumann, John, and Oskar Morgenstern. 1944. *Theory of games and economic behavior.* Princeton: Princeton University Press.

von Wright, G. H. 1968. *An essay in deontic logic and the general theory of action.* Amsterdam: North-Holland.

von Wright, G. H. 1983. *Practical reasoning—Philosophic papers.* Ithaca, N.Y.: Cornell University Press.

Wagenhofer, A. 1993. Kostenrechnung und agency theory. In *Zur Neuausrichtung der Kostenrechnung—Entwicklungsperspektiven in den 90er Jahren,* ed. J. Weber, 161–185. Stuttgart: Schäffer-Poeschel Verlag.

Walgenbach, P. H., N. E. Dittrich, and E. T. Hanson. 1980. *Principles of accounting.* 2nd ed. New York: Harcourt Brace Jovanovich.

Waller, W., and J. Jiambalvo. 1984. The use of normative models in human information processing research in accounting. *Journal of Accounting Literature* 3(Spring): 201–226.

Warburton, William. 1738. *Divine legation of Moses.* London.

Watts, Ross L. 1992. Corporate financial statements, A product of the market and political processes. In *The economics of accounting policy choice,* ed. Ray Ball and Clifford W. Smith, 7–29. New York: McGraw Hill. Originally published in *Australian Journal of Management* 2(1977): 53–75.

Watts, Ross L., and Jerold L. Zimmerman. 1978. Towards a positive theory of the determination of accounting standards. *The Accounting Review* 53(January): 112–134. Reprint. 1984. *Modern accounting research: History, survey and guide*, ed. Richard Mattessich, 81–102. Vancouver, B.C.: Canadian Certified General Accountants Research Foundation.

Watts, Ross L., and Jerold L. Zimmerman. 1979. The demand for and supply of accounting theories: The market for excuses. *The Accounting Review* 54(April): 273–305. Reprint. 1984. *Modern accounting research: History, survey and guide*, ed. Richard Mattessich, 103–129. Vancouver, B.C.: Canadian Certified General Accountants Research Foundation.

Watts, Ross L., and Jerold L. Zimmerman. 1986. *Positive accounting theory*. Englewood Cliffs, N.J.: Prentice-Hall.

Watts, Ross L., and Jerold L. Zimmerman. 1990. Positive accounting theory: A ten year perspective. *The Accounting Review* 65(January): 131–156.

Wells, M. C. 1976. A revolution in accounting thought? *The Accounting Review* 51(July): 471–482. Reprint. 1984. *Modern accounting research: History, survey and guide*, ed. Richard Mattessich, 47–57. Vancouver, B.C.: Canadian Certified General Accountants Research Foundation.

Welsch, G. A., D. G. Short, and G. R. Chesley. 1987. *Fundamentals of financial accounting*. Homewood, Ill.: Richard D. Irwin.

Whitley, R. 1988. The possibility and utility of positive accounting theory. *Accounting and Business Research* 13: 631–645.

Whittington, G. 1986. Financial accounting theory: An overview. *British Accounting Review* (Autumn): 4–41.

Whittington, G. 1987. Positive accounting theory: A review article. *Accounting and Business Research* 17(Autumn): 327–336.

Willett, Roger J. 1985. *Accounting measurement theory*. Ph.D. dissertation. Weatherby, Wyo.: University of Aberdeen/British Library Document Supply Centre.

Willett, Roger J. 1987. An axiomatic theory of accounting measurement—Part I. *Accounting and Business Research* 17(Spring): 155–171.

Willett, Roger J. 1988. An axiomatic theory of accounting measurement—Part II. *Accounting and Business Research* 19(Winter): 79–91.

Williams, Thomas H., and Charles H. Griffin. 1964. *The mathematical dimension of accounting*. Cincinnati: South-Western.

Williams, Thomas H., and Charles H. Griffin. 1969. On the nature of empirical verification in accounting. *Abacus* 5(December): 143–180.

Willmot, H. C. 1983. Paradigms for accounting research: Critical reflections on Tomkins and Groves' "Everyday accountant and researching his reality." *Accounting, Organizations and Society* 8(4): 389–405.

Winborne, Marilynn G. 1962. Application of sets and symbolic logic to selected accounting principles and practices. Ph.D. dissertation. Austin: University of Texas; Ann Arbor, Mich.: University Microfilms.

Wolk, H. I., J. I. Francis, and M. G. Tearney. 1992. *Accounting theory: A conceptual approach*. 3rd ed. Cincinnati: South-Western.

Yamey, Basil S. 1994. Benedetto Cotrugli on bookkeeping. *Accounting, Business and Financial History* 4(Spring): 43–50.

Zappa, Gino. 1927. *Tendenze nuove negli studi di ragioneria*. Milan: Istituto Éditorale Scientifico.

Zappa, Gino. 1937. *Il reddito di impresa, scritture doppie, conti e bilanci di aziende commerciali*. Milan: Editore Giuffrè.

Zappa, Gino. 1957. *Production in the economy of the enterprise*. Vol. 1. Milan: Giuffrè.

Zeff, Stephen A. 1982. *The accounting postulates and principles controversy of the 1960s*. New York: Garland.

Omission under References:

Schneider, Dieter. 1981. *Geschichte der betriebswirtschaftlichen Theorie*. München: R. Oldenburg Verlag.

Name Index

AAA. *See* American Accounting
  Association
Abdel-khalik, A. Rashad, 41, 145, 162,
  164, 185 n. 9
Abdel-Magid, Moustafa F., 170 n
Absalom, Karl, 38 n. 5
Accademia di Economia Aziendale
  (Italy), 185 n. 10
Ackoff, Russell, 75 n. 2
Ahmad, Yusuf J., 210 n. 6
AICPA. *See* American Institute of
  Certified Public Accountants
Aitken, Michael J., 75 n. 1
Ajinkya, Bipin B., 41
Akerlof, George A., 91, 148
Albach, Horst, 71, 151
Alchian, Armen A., 144
Alexander, Sydney S., 139
American Accounting Association
  (AAA), 9, 70, 73, 75, 88, 95, 126, 139,
  143, 151, 159, 178, 202, 216
American Institute of Certified Public
  Accountants (AICPA), 9, 78, 88, 108,
  109, 118, 155, 187, 196, 202, 208, 217
Amershi, Amin H., 185 n. 9
Amiet, Pierre, 20, 24
Andersen, Arthur, 50
Antle, Rick, 9

Archer, Simon, 7, 79, 191, 200, 209–210 n. 2
Argyris, Chris, 177
Aristarchus (of Samos), 9
Aristotle (of Stagira), 56, 200
Arnold, John A., 181
Arrow, Kenneth J., 90, 95, 210 n. 6
Arthur Anderson & Co., 6
Ashton, Robert H., 9, 180–181
Augustine, Saint. *See* Saint Augustine
Avilà, Hector E., 79

Backer, Morton, 154, 187, 208
Baiman, Stanley, 150, 157
Ball, Ray, 152–153, 159, 163, 219
Ballwieser, Wolfgang, 163, 169
Baltimore, David, 186 n. 16
Balzer, Wolfgang, 80, 94–95, 130, 136,
  137–138 n. 4, 156, 218
Barnea, Amir, 150
Bartusiak, Marcia, 76 n. 9
Baxter, William T., 181
Beaver, William H., 13 n. 2, 98, 123 n. 1,
  140, 152–153, 155, 159, 161, 166, 198,
  202, 219
Belkaoui, Ahmed, 8, 60, 126, 189, 196, 218
Bell, Philip W., 71, 102, 114, 118–119,
  139–141, 151, 166, 189, 222
Benston, George J., 152, 159

Subject Index

Capital markets: efficient, 160
Capital theory, 71; of Böhm-Bawerk and
 Irving Fisher, 151
Capitalism, 3; different types of, 13
Capitulare de Vilis (of Charlemagne), 36
CAPM. *See* Capital–asset pricing model
Case method, 164
Causal chain(s), link, or nexus, 74, 165,
 171
Causalities: presumed, 162
Cause and effect, 215; explanation, 188;
 positive theory, 201; relations, 4, 162
Chaos. *See* Theory: of chaos
Chart of accounts, 85
Check: arithmetical, 29; monetary, 28
Chemistry, 58, 166, 178, 191, 192, 221
Chicago School (of accounting), 166
Childhood years: of our discipline, 61
China, 36, 67; accounting in, 36
CICA. *See* Canadian Institute of Chartered
 Accountants
Claim asset: a social claim, 96
Claims, 66; debt and ownership, 212;
 debt or ownership, 17, 29, 84;
 ownership, 29; transferability of, 156;
 transferable, 157
Classification, 53, 83, 85, 156; methods,
 111; schemes, 82, 87
Clay: balls (hollow), 18; containers, 20;
 counters, 39; envelopes, 16, 39;
 objects, 16; seal, 27; symbols, 212;
 token(s), 15, 16, 18, 28, 204
Clean surplus: notion, 69; principle, 97
Cognitive science, 61
Coherence testing, 219
Command(s): 216; giving of a, 200
Commodities, 26, 38, 212; to be
 represented, 21; transfer of, 132
Commodity: account, 15, 26, 38;
 accounting, 21; aggregate, 26;
 transaction, 30; transfers, 62
Communication, 38; scheme, 89
Competition: among agents, 91; between
 specific scientific theories, 126;
 between theory elements within one
 theory, 216; between traditions, 126;
 nonparadigmatic, 146; perfect, 152
Comptroller General, 36

Computer: applications, 71; simulation, 59;
 simulation methods, 214; spreadsheet,
 71; technology, 70, 92
Computer science, 54, 60, 185
CoNAM (conditional–normative
 accounting methodology), 170, 189,
 191; maxims of, 194; practical tool,
 199; purpose of, 208; testing procedure
 of, 195. *See also* Conditional–
 normative: accounting methodology
Concepts: backed by reality, 132;
 empirically empty, 42; of higher
 generality, 76; of information content,
 153; interpreted and uninterpreted, 69;
 interpreted versus uninterpreted, 69; of
 lower generality, 76; mathematical and
 logical, 48; objective–formal, 69; pure,
 54, 132; purely theoretical, 133;
 reified, 56; scientific, 61; uninterpreted,
 69; versus reality, 43; versus social
 reality, 53; without any underlying
 reality, 213
Conceptual framework (structures), 60,
 78, 80, 88, 130, 133, 135–136, 204;
 FASB (Financial Accounting Standards
 Board), 79; project, 7
Conceptual representation, 27, 62–63; of
 economic transactions, 92; philosophic
 problems of, 38; positive, 82;
 pragmatic, 82
Conceptual thinking: figurative or
 pictorial to, 204
Conceptualization, 51, 81;
 Schmalenbach's disinterest in, 175
Conditional–normative: accounting
 methodology CoNAM), 162, 165, 187;
 approach, 80, 83, 120, 176; current
 state of, 189; framework, 209;
 methodology, 11, 13, 82, 168, 189,
 190, 208; synthesis, 183; system, 84;
 theory, 12–13, 164, 194, 183, 215. *See
 also* CoNAM
Confirmation(s), 86–87, 126; degree of,
 69
Conservation, 66, 79; of energy, 65;
 law(s) of, 65, 76; principles of, 65, 76
Consolidation, 85
Constellation(s), 48; stellar, 132

268   Subject Index

Management information: models, 60;
  systems, 9, 74, 80, 87, 176
Management science(s), 20, 80, 184;
  fundamental problems of, 75
Managerial accounting, 8, 128, 154, 160,
  181–182
Manager's activity: monitoring of, 146
Market(s), 42; complete, 198; conditions
  (imperfect and incomplete), 198;
  contingent, 91; efficiency, 166;
  imperfect and incomplete, 206;
  information, 90; portfolio, 42;
  predictions (valuation of), 152; strong-
  form, 42; system, 3; uncertainty, 91
Market value, 51, 67, 129, 210; approach,
  71; basis, 69
Marxian accounting, 181–182
Marxist "critical–radical perspective," 13,
  184. See also Critical perspective
Mass, 129; in Newtonian theory, 134; in
  relativistic mechanics, 134
Mass–energy, 76
Matching, 143; of costs against revenues,
  142
Materiality, 85. See also Relevance
Mathematical methods or models, 41, 70;
  structure, 131
Mathematics, 25, 37–38, 45, 60, 176;
  higher, 78; Indian, 35; training in, 6
Matrix, 27, 63: accounting, 72; algebra,
  71–72, 128; combined, 63; entry, 61;
  framework, 37; mode, 71–72
Matter–antimatter asymmetry, 76
Maximization: of profit or wealth, 173,
  201
Meaning postulates, 95
Means: inferring the proper, 221; test the
  efficiency of, 161
Means–end relations, 3–4, 13, 61, 82,
  123, 161–162, 168, 187–189, 201–202,
  212; are multi-ended, 207; empirical
  testing of, 201; epistemological
  exploration of, 124; exist in actual
  practice, 208; formalized, 11, 194;
  formulating, 206; implicit and explicit,
  207; multi-endedness of, 222; present
  confusion about, 184; testing, 207

Measure theory: of mathematics, 73
Measurement, 53; basic concepts, 73;
  concepts, 73; conceptualization of, 73;
  for decision making, 79; deficiency in,
  213; of divisional performance, 72; of
  effectiveness and efficiency, 195; of
  income, 46; indirect, 52; by means of
  discounted net cash flows, 142;
  methodological problem of, 213;
  paradigm-determined, 134; problem,
  43, 52, 101; of real properties, 51;
  reflections on, 174; in the social science,
  51; system, 74; theory, 11; of time, 51
Measuring: costs, 192; performance, 72;
  political costs, 163
Medicine, 5, 61, 92, 162, 166, 168, 171,
  183, 188, 191–192, 193; applied status
  of, 192
Mesopotamia, 17, 26, 33
Meta-language, 80
Metaphor, 42–43, 46, 54, 207; in our
  literature, 55; technological, 54
Methodological assumptions, 165;
  considerations, 218; disputes, 167, 219;
  dogmas: Kuhn's, 133; insights, 222;
  issues, 213; pluralism, 127
Methodology, 5, 8, 12, 59; absolute truth,
  8; for accounting, 167; appropriate for
  accounting, 219; appropriate for the
  specific purpose, 207; conditional–
  normative, 203, 208; conditional–
  normative accounting, 183;
  economic-based research, 166; of
  economics, 168; extreme, 163;
  Lakatos', 130; Lakatos' and
  Stegmüller's, 127; logic and scientific,
  7; natural science, 170; normative, 193;
  positive, 208; provides the guidelines,
  196; for selecting accounting rules,
  210; Sneed–Stegmüller, 155; of
  Sterling, 49; that forbids normative
  premises, 163; traditional scientific,
  177; truth in, 219; two-pronged, 9;
  Watts and Zimmerman, 163
Methods, 60; analytical–empirical, 60; in
  determining the means, 221. See also
  Accounting method

Phenomena, 43, 51; empirical, 10, 42; mental and quasi-mental, 44; physical, 43; real, 49

Philosophy, 38, 60, 125, 221; artificial, 135; of false idols, 3; post-Kuhnian, 196; of science, 135, 169

Physical capital maintenance, 112, 115, 118, 120–121, 124, 155, 206; logic, 119

Physicalist, 45, 51

Physics, 43–44, 66, 76, 92, 166–167, 178, 191–192, 221; Newtonian, 128

Pictographs, 25, 38

Placeholder(s): for the specific hypotheses, 81, 218

Planning, 72, 83

Policies: effectiveness of, 197; recommendations, 195; research, 209

Political: action, 164; costs, 145; forces, 7; interest, 182; phenomena, 145; process, 164; science, 187; trend, 6

Portfolio, 188; analysis (PA), 141, 158; diversification, 152; theory, 71, 160, 152, 217

Positive: approach, 83, 191; camp, 181; hypotheses, 162, 215; representation, 222; research, 145; science, 168, 206, 211; sciences, 6; theories, 162, 165–166, 192; trait, 51

Positive accounting theory (PAT), 1, 4, 56, 75, 145, 160–162, 183, 190, 192; the advent of, 88; American, 211; controversy, 161, 192; criticism of, 169; empirical results of, 163; hypotheses of, 12; limitations of, 12; methodology of, 165, 169

Positivism, 56, 125

Positivistic tradition, 216

Post-Kuhnian: era, 12; trend, 141

Postulates, 74; pragmatic, 154

Postulation, 78; approach, 78; attempt, 79, 138, 144; and axiomatic means, 11

Practical: action, 75; constraints, 197; inference, 203, 210; point of view, 190; reason, 201

Practitioners, 3, 5–6, 8, 53; find means to achieve their goals, 208; tools for, 183

Pragmatic hypotheses: formalized means–ends relations, 201

Pragmatic: process, 221; question, 154; representation, 7, 207, 222

Pragmatic–normative, 7, 12, 77, 186

Pragmatic–scientific approach, 194

Pre-paradigmatic, 140

Predicate logic, 78; first-order, 79

Predictions, 166, 167; overemphasis, 219; in the pure sciences, 72

Preference(s), 44, 48, 52, 55, 84; for actions in nontransferable claims models, 157; of agent, 157; based on specific goals, 128; different, 144; direct, 157; ideological and methodological, 169; of principal, 157; real, 216; structure, 157; structure of, 146; subjective, 51; subjective representations of, 213; user's, 165

Prehistoric: people, 204; record keeping, 29; times, 15–16, 212

Premise(s): epistemic and ontological, 182; normative, 56; two kinds of, 81

Prescription(s), 163–164, 195; in accounting, 221; from accounting theory, 166

Present value(s), 71, 119, 129, 151, 210; approach, 71; basis, 69, 119; model(s), 204, 217

Price: changes of specific assets, 98, 100, 111; dispersion, 91; indexes, 115; searches, 90

Price–earnings ratio(s), 48, 216; pure concepts, 132

Price-level: change, 100; disclosure, 162

Price-level adjustment(s), 6, 13, 59, 97–98, 108; changes, 85; disclosure of, 163; general, 101; models, 11, 97, 113; specific, 101; standards, 155, 202

Prices, 216; current year-end, 104; distribution of, 90–91; excess of increase in specific, 103; existing, 42; expected, 42; shifting, 155; specific, 119

Principal, 91, 144, 149, 157; risk averse, 147

Principal–agency relations, 144, 146

Principle(s), 166, 187; accounting symmetry, 67; basic 143–144; of change, 67; fundamental, 130; of

ABOUT THE AUTHOR

DR. RICHARD MATTESSICH is Professor emeritus of the University of British Columbia, where he held the distinguished Arthur Andersen & Co. Chair. He and his work have been profiled in many countries and several languages, for example, in *The Development of Accounting Theory: Significant Contributors to Accounting Thought in the 20th Century* (Gaffikin and Aitken 1982), discussing prominent scholars of the English accounting literature; in *History of Accounting at Berkeley* (Moonitz 1986); in *Twentieth Century Accounting Theorists* (Edwards 1994; Foreword by David Solomons), presenting a score of eminent accounting researchers of various language areas; and in two works, spanning centuries: *The Encyclopedia of Accounting and Accounting Thought* (Chatfield and Vangermeersch In press) as well as *Hundred Notable Accountants and their Historical Contributions* (Guo Dao Yang and Yang Shi Zhan In preparation; in Chinese). In addition to these, Mattessich's professional memoirs were published by Chuo University (in Japanese; see ed. and trans. Koguchi 1992–1993; and in English, 1995).

Mattessich was born on August 9, 1922 in Trieste (Italy), but grew up in Vienna (Austria) where he acquired degrees in engineering, business administration, and economics. He presently holds dual citizenship of Austria and Canada. His practical experience comprises several years as an engineer and accountant, as well as some activity in the actuarial and auditing department of the Prudential Assurance Co. Ltd. of England. He was a research fellow of the Austrian Institute of Economic Research and an instructor in St. Gallen (Switzerland). He held academic chairs in Austria, Canada, and Germany, a tenured Associate Professorship at the University of California at Berkeley, and visiting professorships in Berlin, Christchurch, Graz, Hong Kong, Parma, St. Gallen, Tokyo, and other places. His publications are numerous, and some of them were translated into French, German, Japanese, and Spanish. Among his books the best known are *Accounting and Analytical Methods* (1964a); *Simulation of the Firm through a Budget Computer Program* (1964b), which (together with a preceding paper of his) introduced computerized spreadsheets; *Instrumental Reasoning and Systems Methodology* (1978), an epistemology of the applied and social sciences; and two anthologies which he edited: *Modern Accounting Research: History, Survey and Guide* (1984) and *Accounting Research in the 1980s and Its Future Relevance.*

Mattessich received several literature awards. He is a Ford Foundation Fellow (USA), a distinguished Erskine Fellow (New Zealand), a Killam Senior Fellow (Canada), and a member of two national academies (Italy and Austria), as well as an honorary Life Member of the Academy of Accounting Historians (USA). He has served on the Board of Governors of the School of Chartered Accountancy of the Institute of Chartered Accountants of British Columbia and was for six years on the Board of Directors of the Canadian Certified General Accountants Research Foundation (now CGA-Canada Research Foundation). He has been on the editorial advisory boards of several journals, including the International Board of Advisors of the aforementioned research foundation and of Kluwer Academic Publishers.

ISBN 0-89930-863-5

HARDCOVER BAR CODE